James Joyce and Critical Theory:
An Introduction

JAMES JOYCE
AND CRITICAL THEORY:
AN INTRODUCTION

Alan Roughley

HARVESTER
WHEATSHEAF
New York London Toronto Sydney Tokyo Singapore

First published 1991 by
Harvester Wheatsheaf,
66 Wood Lane End, Hemel Hempstead,
Hertfordshire, HP2 4RG
A division of
Simon & Schuster International Group

Printed and bound in Great Britain by
BPCC Wheatons Ltd, Exeter

Typeset in 10/12pt Galliard by
Mathematical Composition Setters Ltd., Salisbury, UK

British Library Cataloguing in Publication Data

Roughley, Alan,
  James Joyce and critical theory: An introduction.
  I. Title
  823.9

  ISBN 0–7450–1018–0 ✓

1 2 3 4 5 95 94 93 92 91

Contents

Abbreviations

THE FOLLOWING ABBREVIATIONS are used in this book:

D   *Dubliners*, ed. Robert Scholes, London: Penguin, 1967

E   *Exiles*, New York: Penguin, 1973

FW   *Finnegans Wake*, London: Penguin, 1982

P   *A Portrait of the Artist as a Young Man*, ed. C. G. Anderson, London: Penguin, 1968

SH   *Stephen Hero*, ed. T. Spencer, J. J. Slocum, and H. Cahoon, London: Jonathan Cape, 1969

U   *Ulysses*, ed. H. W. Gabler *et. al.*, London: Penguin, 1986

L   *Letters of James Joyce*, Vol. I, ed. Stuart Gilbert. New York: Viking Press, 1957; re-issued with corrections 1966. Vols. II and III, ed. Richard Ellmann, New York: Viking Press, 1966.

SL   *Selected Letters of James Joyce*, ed. Richard Ellmann, New York: Viking Press, 1975

JJQ *The James Joyce Quarterly*

Page references to Joyce's texts are given in parentheses and incorporated into the text. Where citations of critical studies include references to Joyce's work, the reference may be to editions other than those listed above. Reference to *Finnegans Wake* provide page and line numbers, e.g. (38. 27) refers to line 27 on page 38. References to *Ulysses* are to the above edition. Following the publication of Gabler's revised edition of *Ulysses* the practice of providing references to episode and line numbers was introduced. xv, 4066, for example, refers to line number 4066 in 'Circes'. For articles and books following this practice the episode and line numbers are cited in this manner. All other references to *Ulysses* are to page numbers. Publication information is provided in parentheses for the first references to critical articles and books. Subsequent parenthetical references are to the page number and, where necessary, to the author's surname and year of publication. A full list of cited works is provided at the end of the book.

Preface

THIS BOOK IS offered not as a comprehensive survey of Joyce criticism but as an introduction and selective guide to some of the studies of Joyce which have analysed his writing from the vantage points afforded by a variety of critical theories. Of course all studies of literary texts use a theory, or theories, for their analysis of literary texts to some extent. In the case of the more traditional and conservative approaches to texts, however, the theoretical basis for the study of literature often operates in such a way that the theory is not immediately discernible to either the critic or the reader. In such traditional methods of literary analysis as rhetoric, prosody, historical criticism, paleography and manuscript studies, textual explication, genre studies, and biography, the theoretical basis of these methods is not always clear. Such methods are often held up as models for literary criticism which will enable students and teachers to approach literary meanings and structures in a way that is more immediate than that afforded by more obviously theoretical methods of engaging texts. In its most extreme form there is a mistaken notion behind such a claim. This is that the more traditional methods of literary studies are free of the theoretical encumbrances which come between the text and readers who use more obviously theoretical methods for reading. The idea that the study of literature can do very well without a theoretical hand servant is discernible in a number of guises. It can be detected in F. R. Leavis's refusal to place his critical methods under philosophical scrutiny;

in the conservative rejection of such critical approaches as structuralism, semiotics, psychoanalytic theory, etc.; and in the emergence of the neo-historicism with which some scholars and teachers are attempting to replace the complexities of poststructuralist theory.

The history of Joyce studies can in some ways be seen as a microcosm of the historical development of critical theory and its application to literary texts. Anyone who attends the International James Joyce Symposiums or one of the other numerous gatherings devoted to Joyce's work will quickly become aware that the debate between theorists and scholars who like to work from what they perceive as a less theoretical position is very much alive and well. In part Joyce's work is itself responsible for the division of Joyce scholars into theoretical and anti-theoretical camps. In *The Decentered Universe of Finnegans Wake: A Structuralist Analysis* (Baltimore: Johns Hopkins UP, 1974) Margot Norris offers a succinct history of this division and suggests that Joyce's readers and Joyce scholars can be divided into those who choose between 'a radical and a conservative interpretation' of Joyce's work. Norris is speaking specifically about *Finnegans Wake*, but her summary of the history of *Wake* criticism is also applicable to the history of Joyce studies in general, for sooner or later any reader who perseveres in his or her reading of Joyce will have to begin to try and come to terms with Joyce's most formidable work. Furthermore, what Norris says of a radical reading of the *Wake* can almost certainly be said of a radical reading of Joyce's last two texts: that Joyce's writing 'subverts not only the literary status quo but the most cherished intellectual preconceptions of Western culture as well' (1).

While readers interested in the radical nature of Joyce's writing insist upon the subversive nature of that writing, however, other Joyceans offer an equally persuasive argument that Joyce was essentially a conservative writer. There is much to support their claim:

> the conservative critics, who have dominated *Wake* criticism... possess a small but scholarly arsenal: the stylistic and thematic conservatism of the early manuscript drafts, the inclusion of traditional, even arcane, literary material in the work, Joyce's admission that the work's structural and philosophical models are derived from a sixteenth-century metaphysician and an eighteenth-century philosopher, and finally, Joyce's own decidedly reactionary tastes.
>
> (1–2)

Joyce's earlier works offer much evidence to support the argument that Joyce was a conservative writer. The poems of *Chamber Music* draw heavily on the tradition of the Elizabethan lyric; *A Portrait of the Artist as a Young Man* employs a very traditional symbolist method (as do many of the stories in *Dubliners*) and sets this to work within the form of a traditional *Bildungsroman*; and *Ulysses* draws upon the very origins of Western narrative in using the structure of Homer's Classical form and adhering to the Classical unities of time and place to depict the events which take place on Bloomsday. *Ulysses* is also, of course, the work which earned the praise of that most conservative of Modernists, T. S. Eliot, who admired Joyce because he thought that Joyce used myth in much the same way that Eliot used it himself in *The Wasteland*.

In part, the recognition of Joyce's work as a subversive practice of writing was limited by the lack of any theoretical framework with which the radical nature of Joyce's writing could be assessed. Early studies like some of the essays in *Our Exagmination Round His Factification For Incamination Of Work In Progress* (Beckett, Samuel, *et al.*, New York: New Direction Books, 1963) attempted to reveal the radical nature of the *Wake*, and Joyce's involvement in the production of those essays clearly indicates that they had Joyce's approval. However, as Norris points out, such attempts to explain the revolutionary qualities of Joyce's writing were stalled by the lack of any theory which might assist in the articulation of Joyce's radicalness, by the lack of what Norris terms the lack of 'scholarly pegs' on which the radical interpreters could 'hang their theories' (Norris: 1). Not until the advent of structuralism did any theory begin to emerge which could fruitfully contribute to the attempt to engage with the radical nature of Joyce's writing. Other methods which parallel structuralism's insistence on the importance of paying attention to the theoretical aspects of language and literature have also assisted in the understanding of the radical and subversive nature of Joyce's writing. Some, like feminist theory, predate the developments of structuralism, yet have been able to take advantage of some of the opportunities for textual analysis that structuralism affords. Others, like semiotics, emerged as a part of the growing theoretical interest in the structural operations and relationships of language and literature that contributed to the development of structuralist theory. Poststructural and psychoanalytic theories have developed beyond structuralism and offered further insights into the operations of language and literature. All of these theories have been used to investigate the radical nature of Joyce's writing. More importantly, Joyce's writing has often been used in varying degrees as a model for these theories. It is the relationships between these theories, their use of Joyce's writings, and the insights that they offer into these writings that is the subject of this book.

It would be impossible to cover all of the major critical studies of Joyce's work in one book, and it has been necessary to omit references to many major studies which are still of seminal importance to our understanding of Joyce. Many of the works that are covered in this book will appear somewhat marginal in a comparison with some of these studies. The latter are included while the former are not because this book is not about Joyce studies *per se*, but about the intriguing relationships which exist between Joyce's fiction and a variety of critical theories.

Acknowledgements

THIS BOOK IS in part a result of the work which I did on the relation between Joyce's *Finnegans Wake* and the critical theories of Jacques Derrida for my Ph.D. dissertation at the University of British Columbia. I wish to thank Graham Good and Elliott Gose Jr for their generosity in the time they gave in supervising that study and for their friendship. Professor Jacques Berthoud made it possible for me to work and teach at the University of York as an Honorary Fellow. I thank him for his warm hospitality and his encouragement. Dr W. A. Ward extended a very warm hand of friendship, and his unstinting generosity and stimulating conversation helped me to develop and clarify my ideas.

I thank Julian Croft and Catherine Waters, two of my colleagues in the Department of English at the University of New England, who have been generous enough to read drafts of the material and offer helpful comments. I thank Professor Alan Sandison and the Department of English at the University of New England for the time to allow me to complete the book, and I thank Nereda Christian for her help with proofreading and typing. Jackie Jones at Harvester Wheatsheaf commissioned this book, and she has more than fulfilled her obligations as an editor. I thank her for her generous support and particularly for her patience with my tardiness. To Megan Roughley I owe a particular debt of gratitude that cannot be fully expressed here.

Alan Roughley, University of New England, 1991

·1·

Structuralism and Structuralist Joyce

TO A CERTAIN EXTENT, most studies of Joyce have in one way or another concerned themselves with the structure of Joyce's work. Even Richard Ellmann's *James Joyce* (Oxford: OUP, 1982) could be said to cover the *structure* of Joyce's life. The number of studies that could be accurately described as *structuralist*, however, is not very large. Critics who concern themselves with textual explication, the analysis of character and plot, the poetic and rhetorical patterns of Joyce's prose and poetry, and even those critics who investigate the rich symbolism and polysemy of Joyce's writing – all of these critics deal with the structures of Joyce's work, but few of them offer structuralist analyses. Structuralism has now receded and been replaced by the various forms of poststructuralist theories which superseded it. The various critical debates that are now taking place suggest that poststructuralism, too, may be on the wane and losing ground to the various 'neohistoricists' who advocate a return to pre-structuralist, more 'historical', methods for literary studies. Structuralism may have all but disappeared, but the investigations into Joyce's work which it made possible still offer unique insights into that work. Before examining these, a brief summary of some of the historical developments that led to the development of structuralism may be helpful.

Structuralism developed for the most part from the theories of two very different disciplines: Linguistics and Anthropology. The work of the Swiss Linguist, Ferdinand de Saussure and the French Anthropologist, Claude

Lévi-Strauss, provided most of the theoretical groundwork upon which structuralism was based. Of particular interest to Joyce studies, however, is the work of an earlier writer, who, as Terence Hawkes (*Structuralism and Semiotics*, Berkeley: UCLA Press, 1977) points out, is a central figure in the history of structuralism. The Italian jurist and philosopher, Giambattista Vico, wrote *The New Science* (ed. T. Goddard Bergin and M. H. Fisch, Ithaca: Cornell UP, 1968), and it is from this work that Joyce took many of the philosophical and structural principles for *Finnegans Wake*. The 'new' science Vico developed was a method for analysing the structures of sociological groups and its goal was to 'perform for the "world of nations" what the renaissance scientists had achieved for the "world of nature"... in short... the construction of a "physics of man"' (Hawkes: 11–12).

Vico

At the centre of Vico's work is the idea that the history of sociological groups such as nations follows the same patterns as the history of the life of individuals. Both follow a three-stage pattern of development. The three stages of the individual's life are marked by the passage from birth through maturity and marriage to death. The history of mankind follows a similar pattern of development. Primitive peoples are analogous with infants, and the development of civic institutions parallels the life of the mature individual. In the case of nations and peoples, however, the decline that parallels the death of the individual is followed by a *ricorso* or recurrence which precedes the beginning of a new cycle. For Vico, the origins of civilization and matrimony can be found in the mythic story of God, the lawgiver, speaking through a thunder which scares humans and drives them into caves where they reproduce: 'The thunder surprised some of them... and frightened copulating pairs into nearby caves. This was the beginning of matrimony and of settled life' (Vico: xxvi). Joyce uses the three-stage pattern to structure the *Wake* in much the same way that he uses the three-letter groups HCE and ALP. He also uses the *ricorso*, and his one-hundred-letter words for thunder signify a thunder that is also derived from Vico.

In the human creation of myths and institutions Vico saw a process which is essentially the creation of *structures*. The establishment of laws and the creation of institutions is the creation of structures by which humankind civilises itself. The process is a poetic process in the radical, or root, sense of *poesis* as a making or a creating. This poetic process also helps humans to create themselves, for in making institutions and social structures humans also create themselves:

the first steps in the building of the 'world of nations' were taken by creatures who were still (or who had degenerated into) beasts... humanity itself was created by the very same processes by which institutions were created. Humanity is not a presupposition, but a consequence, an effect, a product of institution building.

(Bergin and Fisch: xliv)

Joyce sets this idea to work throughout the *Wake*, but combines it with the Freudian idea that all of society's creations result from a sublimation of the sexual drives. Artistic creation and the establishment of social institutions are always involved with a drive that is fundamentally sexual. When Bygmester Finnegan builds a 'waalworth of a skyerscraper' its shape is unmistakeable: 'his roundhead staple of other days rise[s] in undress maisonry upstanded' (4. 34–36). When Jarl van Hoother comes out of his castle to enter the prankquean's vagina, or 'her' 'port', their sexual union is an act of 'porthery' that creates alliterative poetry, or 'illiterative porthery' (23. 9–10).

Saussure

The *Cours de Linguistique Générale* (London: Fontana, 1974) is a record of the lectures which the Swiss linguist, Ferdinand de Saussure, gave between the years 1906 and 1911. In this work can be found the theory which formed the linguistic basis for structuralist thought. The major change which Saussure contributed to linguistics was that of moving from a theory of language which viewed it as a body of discrete words to one which viewed it as a system of *relationships*. The traditional view of language which Saussure inherited was based on a classical, scientific idea of taxonomy which saw the world as a body of 'independently existing objects, capable of precise objective observation and classification' (Hawkes: 19). Examined from the perspective afforded by this taxonomy, language is a set of individual words that somehow possess meanings which are attached to the words while remaining separate from them. The meaning of words develops historically, and semantics studies the historical development of meaning within a historical context which is diachronic. The historical examination of the development of meaning attempts to establish the 'observable and recordable laws of change' to which meaning is subject (Hawkes: 19).

Saussure recognised that the meaning of words is also determined by the relationships which words have with other words at any one particular time. Attention therefore should be given not only to the diachronic aspect of language and meaning but also to the *synchronic* dimension. Meaning is determined by both its historic, diachronic development and by the synchronic relationship between words and their meanings in terms of their 'current adequacy'. Saussure also insisted that language be studied not only in terms of the relationships between words and the objects which they signify, or 'mean', but also as a 'self-sufficient system', a 'universal field', or *Gestalteinheit* (Hawkes: 19–20). In this respect Saussure emphasises language's autonomy, an autonomy which was also important to philosophers like Nietzsche and to writers like the Symbolist poet Stephen Mallarmé. This autonomy of language was also to become important to Joyce. As Hugh Kenner points out in *Joyce's Voices* (Berkeley: UCLA Press, 1978), *Ulysses* is a text which continually draws our attention to the autonomy of language and its ability to function without necessarily engaging in a relationship with non-linguistic objects in the so-called 'real' world: 'All the book, the book [insists], is words arranged, rearranged' (49).

There are at least three other fundamental ideas in Saussure's structural theory of linguistics: that of distinguishing between the body of language as a whole and the individual's use of it; that of the arbitrary relationship between words and the objects that they signify; and that of the oppositional and differentiating relationship which exists between *phonemes* and allows the difference between similar words to be perceived. Saussure considers language as divisible into the two basic parts of *langue* and *parole*. *Langue* consists of all the elements of the linguistic universe, including all of the relationships between letters and words and the rules which govern the ways in which these relationships operate. *Parole* consists of the actual manifestations of *langue* in the speech of the individuals who use a language. Saussure compared *langue* to the abstract 'rules and conventions' which comprise the game of chess and *parole* to the games of chess which are played by people in the 'real' world. Terence Hawkes suggests that for speakers of English the distinction can be made between 'language, and the concrete everyday situations which we call speech' (Hawkes: 20).

In ideogrammatic and pictoral languages the symbols or characters which are used to depict objects in the world often demonstrate a visual similarity to the shape of the object which they signify. In phonetic languages this is not the case. For Saussure the relationship between signifiers (words) and their signifieds (the objects which they 'mean') is an arbitrary relationship, and this arbitrariness gives language a conservative stability:

> There is literally no reason to prefer any other word from any other source, *arbre, baum, arbor* or even an invented word, *fnurd*, to 'tree'. None is more adequate or 'reasonable' than another. The word 'tree' means the physical leafy object growing in the earth because the *structure of the language* makes it mean that, and only validates it when it does so. It follows that language acts as a great *conservative* force in human apprehension of the world.
>
> (Hawkes: 26)

For Saussure language is a 'self-defining', 'relational structure whose constituent parts have no significance unless and until they are integrated within its bounds' (Hawkes: 26).

In terms of language's *phonemes*, or the minimal units of sound which are required to determine meaning, Saussure described a system of relationships which are a fundamental part of a basic linguistic structuring process. In distinguishing between words such as *kin* and *bin*, for example, we distinguish a difference in meaning on the basis of a difference in the initial 'k' and 'b' sounds of the words. The difference in meaning is thus determined by a linguistic difference which is essentially a *structural* difference in the relationship between words which are also in some ways similar. As Hawkes points out, the relationship between such similar-sounding words which can be distinguished through the difference of the phonemes 'k' and 'b' allows us to observe a 'fundamental structural concept': 'The notion of a complex pattern of paired functional differences' ('kin' and 'bin' can be paired because of the 'in' sound which they share) is an example of binary opposition which is fundamental in both structuralist and poststructuralist theory (Hawkes: 24). Joyce's writing, and particularly the *Wake*, exhibits an awareness of the importance of paying close attention to the operations of language at the phonemic level and suggests that 'every word, letter, penstroke, and paperspace is a perfect signature of its own' (115. 7–8).

Lévi-Strauss

Claude Lévi-Strauss developed a view of the relationship between language and society that is in some ways similar to Vico's. Like Vico, Lévi-Strauss saw the myths of primitive human cultures as an example of a poetic way of responding to the world. Lévi-Strauss also shared Vico's interest in language as a 'major aspect of the "science of man"' and his 'ultimate aim' was, like Vico's, 'to produce a "general science of man"' (Hawkes: 32–3). In the same way that Vico saw human thought as both determining, and, in turn, determined by, cultural institutions, Lévi-Strauss's work is concerned with 'the extent to which the structures of myths prove actually formative as well as reflective of men's minds: the degree to which they dissolve the distinction between nature and culture' (41). The sources of much of Lévi-Strauss's importance for the development of a literary structuralist theory are the discoveries he made in studying social structures as a system of kinships and his investigation of myth as a language.

Lévi-Strauss investigated social structures as a system structured by units of kinship, in particular in terms of the *avunculate* kinship structure and its relationship to a larger kinship structure which Lévi-Strauss termed a 'global structure which [like Saussure's *langue*] must be treated like a whole'. Lévi-Strauss based much of his investigation upon the earlier work of Radcliffe-Brown. Radcliffe-Brown had identified the mother, father, maternal uncle and son as the basic units of the avunculate structure in primitive societies. In *Structural Anthropology* (London: Penguin, 1972) Lévi-Strauss shows how this system also operates according to a binary opposition between the relationships father/son and maternal uncle/son:

> In groups where familiarity characterizes the relationship between father and son, the relationship between maternal uncle and nephew is one of respect; and where the father stands as the austere representative of family authority, it is the uncle who is treated with familiarity.
>
> (41)

For Lévi-Strauss, Radcliffe-Brown's study of the relationship between father/son and maternal uncle/sister's son was 'not enough': 'This correlation is only one aspect of a global system containing four types of relationships which are organically linked, namely: *brother/sister, husband/ wife, father/son, and mother's brother/sister's son*' (42). Lévi-Strauss uses this wider system as the basis for defining a principle which operates on the basis of a binary opposition:

> the relation between maternal uncle and nephew is to the relation between brother and sister as the relation between father and son is to that between husband and wife. Thus if we know one pair of relations, it is always possible to infer the other.
>
> (42)

In order to comprehend the avunculate system it is necessary to view it within the context of the larger social system and to consider the larger system 'as a whole in order to grasp [the avunculate's] structure'. The avunculate is in the last resort 'the most elementary form of kinship that can exist. It is, properly speaking, *the unit of kinship*' (46).

In his investigation of myth Lévi-Strauss turns his attention on language as 'the semantic system *par excellence*: it cannot but signify, and exists only through signification' (48). One of his ultimate goals is the determination of the structural units of myth, the extent to which myths can be 'reduced to a small number of simple types if we abstract from among the diversity of characters a few elementary functions' (204). Myth is intrinsically grounded in linguistic structures. It is a 'language, functioning on an especially high level where meaning succeeds practically at "taking off" from the linguistic ground on which it keeps rolling' (210). Like Saussure's categories of *langue* and *parole*, myth is divided into two parts: 'meaning' and 'content'. The *langue* of myth is its unconscious 'meaning', and a part of this meaning is articulated as the content or plot in any specific articulation of the myth. Lévi-Strauss offers the two following propositions about myth:

> 1. The 'meaning' of mythology cannot reside in the isolated elements which constitute the myth, but must inhere in the way in which those elements are combined, and must take account of the potential for transformation that such a combination involves.
> 2. Language in myth exhibits specific properties, above the ordinary linguistic level.
>
> (210)

Like Saussure's *langue*, which comprises all of a language, myth consists of 'all of its versions' (Lévi-Strauss: 217). Each telling of a myth, each of its individual articulations, is to myth what Saussure's *parole* is to *langue*.

As Hawkes points out, the similar dual aspects of language and myth which are identified by Saussure and Lévi-Strauss are also in accord with the discoveries made by another important contributor to the development of structuralism, Roman Jakobson. Jakobson sees language as structured by polarities which are similar to those uncovered by Saussure. Indeed, Jakobson's polarities are in part derived from 'Saussure's insights concerning the syntagmatic [linear and horizontal] and associative [vertical] planes of linguistic performance' (Hawkes: 76). Jakobson's contribution to structuralism lies in his further developments of Saussure's theory and in his application of these theoretical developments in an analysis of both poetic and non-poetic language. He sees 'metaphor and metonymy as the characteristic modes of binarily opposed polarities which between them underpin the two-fold process of *selection* and *combination* by which linguistic signs are formed' (Hawkes: 77):

> the given utterance (message) is a *combination* of constituent parts (sentences, words, phonemes, etc.) *selected* from the repository of all possible constituent parts (the code).
>
> (Jakobson and Halle: 75)

The final combination selected corresponds to Saussure's *parole* and the 'code' or 'repository' to Saussure's *langue*.

Jakobson also refines the ways in which the words of each articulation are chosen and operate. Each word has a relationship which can be described as a horizontal, linear relationship with its neighbours in the syntagmatic sequence of individual articulations. This is what Jakobson terms the metonymic aspect of language. It corresponds with Saussure's diachronic dimension and is characterised by the combining process which creates the syntagmatic sequences of each utterance or articulation. The metonymic is binarily opposed to the metaphoric aspect of language.

The latter corresponds with Saussure's synchronic dimension and is characterised by selection and association in terms of the ways in which individual words are chosen from the repository of *langue*. Each word in a particular utterance must first be selected from a particular associative group which exists synchronically and then combined with other words in order to produce the diachronic sequence of the syntagmatic order. As Hawkes suggests, Jakobson's distinction makes it possible to propose that:

> human language in fact does exist in terms of the two fundamental dimensions suggested by Saussure and, moreover, that these dimensions crystallize into the rhetorical devices on which poetry characteristically and preeminently draws.
>
> (Hawkes: 78)

There are, of course, other theorists who made significant contributions to the development of structuralism. The above brief examination of some of the insights of Vico, Saussure, Lévi-Strauss and Jakobson is offered by way of an introduction to some of the fundamental principles that are used in structuralist analyses of Joyce's writing. As we shall see, the contributions made by other theorists (V. I. Propp, for example) appear in some of the structuralist examinations of Joyce's work which we will examine in the rest of this chapter. We have noted that Joyce incorporated some of the principles developed by Vico into his writing of the *Wake*. Because of this, his last work has been treated as a sort of proto-typical example of a text that was consciously modelled on what we now term structuralist principles. As several critics have suggested, this makes structuralism a particularly appropriate method for investigating Joyce's last work. Joyce's earlier writings, however, have also been used as models for structuralist theory.

Pre-structuralism Structuralists

Clive Hart

Clive Hart's *Structure and Motif in Finnegans Wake* (London: Faber and Faber, 1962) represents the first major attempt at investigating Joyce's work in terms of its structural principles. Earlier works like Campbell and Robinson's *A Skeleton Key to Finnegans Wake* (London: Faber and Faber, 1947) had made what Hart calls a 'very brave attempt... to reveal the general architectural design' of the *Wake*, but Hart's book is probably the first to deal with Joyce's work by investigating it in terms that could be called structuralist. Surprisingly, Hart's work predates the emergence of structuralism as a method of literary analysis and, lacking structuralism's technical vocabulary and methods of analysis, Hart had to rely upon his ingenuity and invent his own. He discusses this problem in the *Preface* to his book: 'An initial difficulty was the lack of an agreed system of terminology. Throughout this work I adhere consistently to an *ad hoc* terminological convention which it would be as well to summarise here' (20).

Hart uses the term *leitmotiv*, or '*motif*', to deal with small semantic units which he describes as 'short verbal construct[s], characterised by certain easily recognisable patterns of rhythm, sound, form and, sometimes, sense'. The traditional term, theme, is one which Hart applies to 'major narrative and allegorical elements of the book'. Hart uses this term to cover myth material that structuralists like Lévi-Strauss term 'mythemes', small definable units within the larger structures of myth: 'Eating the God' and 'ritual murder'. Finally, Hart deals with recurring narrative signifiers which frequently exist in a structural relationship with the themes and motifs. Joyce's work is full of such elements. One thinks, for example, of terms like 'light' and 'dark' in 'The Sisters', the symbol of the rose in *A Portrait*, or the 'potted meat' in *Ulysses*. Hart uses 'tea, the tree, [and] the rainbow' from the *Wake*. He considers the term *leitmotivistische symbol* but settles on the simple term 'symbol' (20).

One of the insights with which Hart begins his investigation of the structures of the *Wake* is that in choosing the material for his work, Joyce worked very much like the so-called 'primitive' *bricoleur* whom Lévi-Strauss discusses in *Le cru et le cuit* (Paris: Plon, 1964). The *bricoleur* gathers diverse materials and 'carefully and precisely orders, classifies and arranges' them into 'improvised' or 'made-up' structures 'by means of a logic which is not our own' (Hawkes: 51). Jacques Derrida's *Of Grammatology* (Chicago: Chicago UP, 1974) defines *bricolage* as the use of 'tools such as "means" "collected or retained on the principle that they may always come in handy"' (104). Hart clearly recognises the importance of this in Joyce's method of composition and comments on Joyce's 'filling his later book with literary rubbish – Catch phrases, clichés, journalese, popular songs, and the worst kind of gush from girls' weeklies'. He agrees that Joyce found 'considerable' and 'not always critical' 'delight in such trash', but also recognises that Joyce succeeded 'by his devious methods, in making functional necessity and uncritical delight go hand in hand'. The so-called 'trash' material that Joyce collected was often set to work in the puns that are the basic structural unit of the *Wake*. The importance of paronomasia in Joyce's book was well known before Hart's study, but Hart recognises the *structural* importance of Joyce's puns:

A pun is effective only when its first term is vividly prepared for by the context. By using a vocabulary and style packed with well-worn units Joyce is able to play on what the psychologists call the reader's 'readiness'.... If Joyce builds [the motifs] up from familiar phrases... he is immediately able to make the widest punning excursions while remaining sure of his reader's powers of recognition....

The essential value of the pun... in *Finnegans Wake* lies not in its elusive and suggestive qualities but in its ability to compress much meaning into little space. Too... little [has been written] about the power of Joyce's polyhedral vocabulary to accumulate denotation. ...[T]he more one reads *Finnegans Wake* and learns how to recognise how all the bricks fit into the finished structure, the less suggestive the book seems.

(Hart: 32)

As we will see in the chapter on Joyce and Semiotics, Hart's insight into the importance of context and the preparation of the reader in the operations of the pun are like the kernels of Umberto Eco's later analysis of the *Wake*'s paronomasia.

Hart identifies two major patterns of organisation in the structure of the *Wake*. The first of these is a three-plus-one pattern which Joyce took from the Viconian pattern of three ages and a *ricorso*. The second pattern consists of 'Lesser Cycles' which 'make up a four-plus-one quasi-Indian' pattern (62). These sustain the *Wake*'s over-all double, cyclic structure. In addition to Vico's 'The New Science', Hart suggests three main sources of interest for Joyce's use of the model of the circle: 'the world-ages of Indian philosophy', which Joyce took from the 'turgid outpourings of H. P. Blavatsky', the 'opposed gyres of Yeats' *A Vision*, and Blake's *The Mental Traveller*'. Hart sees the four Books of the *Wake* following the Viconian pattern. Within each of the 'three Viconian Ages of Books I, II, and III, Joyce allows four four-chapter cycles to develop'. Each of these lesser cycles also sustains an 'implicit identification' with one of the four 'classical elements' of earth, water, fire, and air:

Major Viconian Cycle	Lesser Cycle
Book I (Birth)	1. I. 1–4: Male cycle; HCE *earth*
	2. I. 5–8: Female cycle; ALP; *water*
Book II (Marriage)	3. II – Male and female battles; *fire*
Book III (Death)	4. III – Male cycle; Shaun as Earwicker's spirit; *air*

(62)

Hart uses the traditional terms of plot and character to discuss the ways in which Joyce uses the Viconian pattern, and he demonstrates how Joyce puts 'cyclic ideas to work in organising an individual chapter' by analysing

Book III.1. The structure of this chapter is 'mainly Viconian' and is 'the prototype for many other chapters', Hart sees the starting paragraphs of this section as a prelude which 'recalls the four-paragraph overture at the beginning of *Finnegans Wake*'. This is followed by three cycles which take place in pages 403–414; 414–424 and 424–427 respectively. Hart's method of analysis can be understood from his following analysis of the first cycle:

Cycle I

Age i (403. 18–405. 03):	Description of Shaun as a 'picture primitive'; he does not speak (first Viconian Age).
Age ii (405. 04–407. 09):	Shaun has become a Hero – 'Bel of Beaus Walk'; there is an allusion to the heroic slaying of the Jabberwock and an entertaining Rabelaisian description of Shaun's heroic eating habits.
Age iii (407. 10–414. 14):	Introduced by 'Overture and beginners'; this is the beginning of the Human Age, in which the gods can appear only in dramatic representation on a stage; Shaun has become a popular representative – 'vote of the Irish'; the word 'Amen' brings to an end the group of three Ages forming the main part of this first Viconian cycle.
Age iv (414. 14–414. 18):	A short *ricorso* brings us back to the theocratic Age with the introduction to the Fable.

Thunder (414. 19)

(58)

Hart analyses the following sections of the Book along these lines and demonstrates how Cycle IV brings III.i 'to a conclusion with a prayer... to Shaun the god-figure, who is to be resurrected in the next chapter' (57–60).

He suggests that the overall structure of the *Wake*, which is sustained by the three-plus-one pattern and its four-plus-one, contrapuntal counterpart, can also be understood in terms of the symbol ⊕. This cross within a circle is the symbol which in the MSS of the *Wake* Joyce gave to the 'highly important ninth question in I. 6.' This is the question that asks, among other things, 'if a human being duly fatigued... having plenxty off time on his gouty hands... were... accorded... with an ear-sighted view of old hopeinhaven. ... then *what* would that fargazer seem to seemself to seem seeming of, dimm it all?' (143. 4–27, *passim*). The answer to the question is 'A collideorscope' (143. 28), one of the many terms with which the *Wake* describes itself, and both the question and answer concern the structure of Joyce's work. Hart suggests that Joyce's use of the ⊕ symbol to 'designate a passage dealing with the structure of *Finnegans Wake* suggests that in one structural sense, the whole of the book forms a *mandala*' that the ⊕ symbol represents. He schematises this mandalic structure as follows:

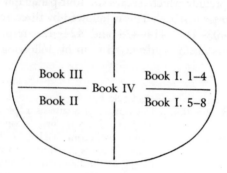

The four quadrants of the circle constitute 'the Wheel of Fortune, while Book IV lies at the "hub"' (77).

Although his book focuses primarily on the *Wake*, Hart also sees Joyce employing the structural device of the *leitmotiv* in his earlier works: 'there are unmistakeable signs at least as early as "The Dead" of the deliberate use of verbal motifs for structural and tonal effects, while in *A Portrait* and *Ulysses*, of course, they are employed with brilliant assurance and, some will say, perhaps even a little facilely and pretentiously at times' (Hart: 163).

Roland McHugh

Roland McHugh is known to all students of the *Wake* for his *Annotations to Finnegans Wake* (Baltimore: Johns Hopkins UP, 1980), a work which clearly demonstrates McHugh's extensive knowledge of the sources for much of Joyce's work. Also of significant importance for *Wake* readers is McHugh's earlier study, *The Sigla of Finnegans Wake* (London: Edward Arnold, 1976), a study of the ways in which Joyce used symbols such as △, X, ∧, T, and □ to represent the characters of the *Wake*, or, in the case of the square, the text itself. *The Sigla* also emphasises what later became an important insight for both structuralist and poststructuralist studies of Joyce: that the sigla represent not only 'personages' but also 'fluid composites which also signify "nonhuman elements"' (McHugh, 1976: 10). Like Hart, McHugh does not seem to have been familiar with structuralist theory, but he, too, grasped the idea that an important part of the meaning of Joyce's work could only be understood through an analysis of the work's structure. 'A Structural Theory of *Finnegans Wake*' (*A Wake Newslitter*, **V**, 6, 1968) formulates nine basic propositions and their implications for the basic structure of the *Wake*. The first of these is that the text is divided into two parts by the 'endless circular sentence' contained within parentheses and occupying pages 287–292 of the work. McHugh sees this sentence as a microcosm of the work as a whole, a representation of 'the whole work in miniature' (83).

Like Hart, McHugh concentrates for the most part upon the traditional notion of character for his analysis, yet he also realises the structural importance of the relationship between textual components as a determiner of meaning. In examining what he terms the 'continuous personality, usually male, [who] is present throughout the text', McHugh emphasises that this character, or 'personality' is subject to a continual change which is essentially different from the process of change that is most often understood by such traditional notions as 'character development'. He sees the 'continuous personality' as 'subject to variation' depending upon its relationship with what he labels 'ultimate character[s]' like Shem and Shaun. The 'ultimate character[s]' exist in a relationship with each other that is quite similar to the relationships Lévi-Strauss describes in his examination of the avunculate structure. Lévi-Strauss described the inverse nature of the relationship between the binary units of father/son and uncle (maternal brother)/son within the familial structure, and McHugh describes a similar inverse relationship between the 'continuous personality' and the 'ultimate character' dependent on 'whether the level of... Shem or Shaun is higher in it' (83).

McHugh does not use the structuralist term 'binary opposition', but it is quite clear that this is the concept with which he is dealing. He details the two relationships between 'continuous personality'/Shem and 'continuous personality'/Shaun, and explains that the nature of the 'continuous personality' is structurally determined. When the relationship between one ultimate character and the continuous character becomes dominant:

i) 'a person, dynasty or civilization has been replaced by another more strongly biased in this direction, and ii) an individual consciousness has become more subject to one motive than its antithesis... implying both the genetic and environmental influences on the composition of personalities.
(83)

The nature of the continuous personality is clearly the result of *structural* relationships, and the Shem/continuous personality Shaun/continuous personality exist in an inverse relationship in such a way that the dominance of one of the relationships produces an opposing response from the other: 'When the level of one force is high an external opposing personality appears by necessity, with an equally high level of the other force and an equal potential for expressing it' (83).

Robert Scholes

Robert Scholes is both a Joyce scholar and a theorist who has written on the history of narrative, structuralism and semiotics. He was one of the first critics to realise that Joyce's work, particularly the final chapters of the *Wake* and *Ulysses*, is not only suitable for structuralist analysis but was itself a very important part of the structuralist revolution. Scholes' structuralist perspective on Joyce is developed in his larger study, *Structuralism in Literature: An Introduction* (New Haven: Yale UP, 1974) and offers, essentially, the material which first appeared in '*Ulysses*: A Structuralist Perspective' (*JJQ*, **10**, 1, 1972). Scholes addresses the question, 'What have we learned in fifty years that enables us to see *Ulysses* more clearly than it could have been seen by those who were contemporary with it in mere chronology?' His answer is structuralism. Scholes also sees the resistance to Joyce's work as part of a larger resistance to structuralism: 'the reluctance of many critics to accept the later Joyce... is an aspect of this larger reluctance to accept the structuralist revolution'. This reluctance is a result of the anxieties that some people experience in witnessing the structuralist assault upon the traditional idea of the self as a unified, individual subject: 'some of us do not *want* to become Joyce's contemporaries, and we find the collapse of individuated characterization in the later Joyce as threatening as the loss of our own identities in some dystopian nightmare of the future' (Scholes, 1972: 161).

Although Scholes sees the *Wake* and the final chapters of *Ulysses* as the places where Joyce is most clearly a participant in the structuralist revolution, he also offers a closing passage from an early draft of *A Portrait* as a 'wonderful combination of Marx, Nietzsche, and D'Annunzio' which depicts 'a kind of global village' whose inhabitants are 'cybernetically related' through the 'wires of the world':

> Already the messages of the citizens were flashed along the wires of the world, already the generous ideas had emerged from a thirty years' war in Germany and were directing the councils of the Latins. To those multitudes, not yet in the wombs of humanity but surely engenderable there, he would give the word: Man and Woman, out of you comes the nation that is to come, the lightning of your masses in travail; the competitive order is employed against itself, the aristocracies are supplanted; and amid the general paralysis of an insane society, the confederate will issues in action.
>
> (Cited, Scholes: 161–2)

Scholes uses Joyce's assertion that he 'would give the word' to those yet to be born to support his idea that Joyce was a revolutionary in his own eyes and not 'merely from [Scholes' own] perspective'. 'Though we have been learning to read' Joyce, Scholes argues, 'he may speak more clearly and more powerfully to our children. And the good news that he brings, in his final work, is the good news of a structuralist revolution' (162).

Scholes defines the structuralist revolution as a 'revolution in the larger sense – as we might say that the American... and the French revolution [s] were instances of some larger meta-revolution called "liberalism" or "democracy"'. The structuralist revolution 'begins... with a turning-over of our ways of thinking'. Scholes cites Gregory Bateson's argument that the 'arrogant scientific philosophy' of the Industrial Revolution has become 'obsolete', and 'in its place there is the discovery that man is only a part of larger systems and that the part can never control the whole' (162–3). The revolution has 'put something like God back in the universe... a God who truly "is not mocked" because It *is* the plan of the universe, the master system which sets the pattern for all others' (Scholes: 163). Scholes' structural view of the universe 'resembles the theology of Dante' as Scholes admits. He defends this similarity on the grounds that '[i]t would be a strange comment on the ecology of ideas if Catholicism could persist for two millenia without a grain of truth in its theology... Freed from the letter, the spirit of Catholic theology is quite capable of accommodating all the truth of science.' His main point is that:

> Dublin's Dante could work himself into a structuralist position more easily by taking medieval theology as a starting point of departure than could someone handicapped by conversion to a more 'reasonable' world view. Thus I submit that Joyce, taking a few ideas well learned from Catholic theology, and adding notions from Vico and others, worked himself into an intellectual position which has much in common with that of Lévi-Strauss, or Piaget, or Bateson.
>
> (163)

In discussing Joyce's attack upon the concept of the ego, Scholes employs Bateson's idea of the bioenergetic as a way of thinking about individuals (and living objects) in terms of 'units bounded at the cell membrane, or at the skin'. In *Steps to an Ecology of Mind* (New York: Ballantine Books, 1972) Bateson describes bioenergetics as viewing these units as 'boundaries', as the frontiers at which measurements can be made to determine the additive–subtractive budget of energy for a given unit' (Bateson: 461; cited Scholes: 164). Scholes traces the development of the ideas of character in Joyce's work as a movement from a bioenergetic concept of characters 'bounded by their own skins, and of actions which take place in one location in space-time', to a cybernetic concept of character in which the notion of ego begins to be dispersed:

> Joyce attacked the ego itself beginning with his own.... Nothing could be sharper than the division between self and others as we find it in his early Epiphanies, with their focus upon the verbal or gestural 'vulgarity' of others and the 'memorable' phases of his own mental life. This same bioenergetic separation persists through *Stephen Hero*, *Dubliners*, and *A Portrait*. Though there are hints of it in this latter work, it is only in *Ulysses* that we really find

the ego breaking down... Stephen Dedalus is Joyce's bioenergetic self-portrait, while Leopold Bloom is his cybernetic self-portrait.

(164)

Ulysses is a 'transitional work *par excellence*'. It was transitional for Joyce and remains transitional for his readers: 'In reading it we learn how to read it;... We are led gradually to a method of narration and to a view of man (the two are inseparable) different from those... in previous fiction.' These 'inseparable' components (view and method) are structuralist, and 'Joyce's later work can not only be seen more clearly from a structuralist perspective but... is structuralist in its outlook and methodology' (166).

The structuralist Jean Piaget offered one of the most fruitful definitions of structure in *Structuralism* (London: Routledge and Keegan Paul, 1971). He defined structure as an organisation of entities which embodies the basic ideas of wholeness, transformation, and self-regulation (5–16). Scholes adopts this triad and explains its terms in relationship to *Ulysses*. Piaget's notion of wholeness as an arrangement of elements 'according to laws of combination' is obviously applicable to all recognised literary texts, so *Ulysses* really requires no special discussion in this context. The fact that it is based, in part, on Homer's *Odyssey* and observes a unity of time and place, at least in the mode of its mimetic narration, offers sufficient evidence for its wholeness. As Scholes notes, Piaget defines transformation in terms of the 'ability of parts of a structure to be interchanged or modified according to certain rules, and he specifically cites transformational linguistics as an illustration of such processes'. In *Ulysses*, Scholes suggests, the 'metempsychotic way in which Bloom and Odysseus are related' is a 'notable principle' of such transformation. Piaget's idea of self-regulation covers the 'interplay of anticipation and correction' and the 'rhythmic mechanisms such as pervade biology and human life at every level'. Scholes applies this idea to his notion of the cybernetic and suggests *Ulysses'* 'Homeric parallels function as a kind of feed-back loop, operating to correct imbalance and brake any tendency for the work to run away in the direction of merely random recitations from Bloom's day'. Such self-regulating 'feed-back loops' operate in each of *Ulysses'* chapters. They are 'designed to run down when certain schematic systems are complete and when a certain temporal segment of the Dublin day has been discovered. Whereupon the next Homeric parallel is activated to provide a diachronic scheme for the following chapter' (Scholes, 1974: 166–7).

The 'Oxen of the Sun' chapter of *Ulysses* 'exhibits all of the structural properties' that Scholes has discussed and serves 'to illustrate their working in some detail'. Scholes summarises the chapter as 'basically a simple narrative segment of the day' in which Stephen and Bloom come to the hospital where Mrs Purefoy is in labour and gives birth before 'Stephen and some medical students, accompanied by Bloom, go off to a pub for some superfluous drinking'. This 'base narrative is transformed according to a complex set of rules':

1. The events must be narrated by a sequence of voices that illustrate the chronological movement of English prose from the Middle Ages to contemporary times.
2. Each voice must narrate an appropriate segment of the events taking place. ...a Pepysian voice must deal with Pepysian details and a Carlylean voice with a Carlylean celebration...
3. The voices must be pastiches or parodies of clearly recognizable stylists or stylistic schools.

(167)

Scholes finds 'roughly six sets of narrative materials' arranged by the above rules. These narrative materials cover 'Bloom's [and Stephen's] present words and deeds... [their] thoughts of the past... the... actions of the medical students, Haines, and so on, along with... the birth itself' (167). As the subsequent analysis reveals, much of the meaning of the chapter is generated from the relationships between these narrative materials as their play is regulated by the operations of the structuralist rules.

Scholes investigates the 'Cyclops' episode by using Saussure's distinction between the synchronic and diachronic aspects of language and the 'further distinction' between the *syntagmatic* and *paradigmatic* axes of sentences derived from it. This second distinction is one which we have already seen: that between the vertical, selective/associative, synchronic dimension of the metaphorical axis and the combinative/syntagmatic, diachronic dimension of the metonymic axis. Scholes explains the distinction between: a) 'the meaning of a single word [in a sentence as] determined partly by its position in the sentence and its relation to the other words and grammatical units of that sentence'; and b) 'the meaning of the word in a sentence [as]... determined by its relation to some groups of words *not* in the actual sentence but present in a paradigmatic (or "vertical") relationship to the actual word'. He also discusses the distinction which structuralism makes between fiction, which emphasises the 'syntagmatic or linear (horizontal) dimension of language' (characters 'are nouns; their situations or attributes are adjectives; and their actions are verbs') and poetry, which is 'more inclined to play with paradigmatic possibilities'. This distinction helps us to understand why Joyce's fiction, particularly in passages like the 'Cyclops' chapter, can be considered as a strongly *poetic* fiction:

Joyce, in *Ulysses*, is often very reluctant to speed along the syntagmatic trail like an Agatha Christie. Often it is as if he cannot bear to part with many of the paradigmatic possibilities that have occurred to him. He will stop and climb up the paradigmatic chain on all sorts of occasions, such as the various lists in 'Cyclops'... in which displaced possibilities are allowed to sport themselves and form syntagmatic chains of their own.

(169)

In order to illustrate Joyce's play along the paradigmatic axis of meaning, Scholes cites the passage describing the ladies who attend 'the wedding of the... grand high chief ranger of the Irish National Foresters with Miss Fir Conifer of Pine Valley. Lady Sylvester Elmshade, Mrs Barbara Lovebirch', etc. (*U*: 268). The names of these characters are of course chosen from the paradigmatic group of words composed of the names of various trees. Joyce is not content in playing with this one group, however, and as Scholes demonstrates, he enriches the pattern of an already heavily paradigmatic sentence by opening up further paradigmatic relationships which 'complicate its syntagmatic relationships'. The name 'Mrs Barbara Lovebirch' 'introduces into this green world the whole motif of sado-masochistic perversion which will culminate in the "Circes" chapter... [O]nce directed this way the reader may well see sexual connotations lurking beneath every bush'. Scholes' discussion opens up the problem of reading Joyce's text and points to the necessity of structuralism for an appreciation of how that text operates: 'A book as long as *Ulysses* which was really paradigmatic in its emphasis would be virtually impossible to read – as *Ulysses* is for those who do not see its structure' (169). Structuralism is a valuable way of helping the reader to perceive that structure.

Structuralism and the Reader–Text Relationship

Following the appearance of the initial structuralist analyses of Joyce that we have considered, a number of Joyceans started to investigate structuralism as a tool for understanding Joyce. A representative selection of their findings was published in the 1978–79 issue of the *James Joyce Quarterly*. Two studies in particular deal with the text–reader relationship which is a central concern of some structuralist theories. One of these studies draws on the theories of Saussure and Gérard Genette in order to investigate the reader's relationship with *Ulysses*; the other focuses upon the 'nodality' and 'infra-structure' of the *Wake* in order to investigate some of the ways in which the text makes itself accessible to its readers. Both studies deal with the relationship between the text and the 'ideal' reader as an essentially structuralist relationship.

Joseph Kestner

In 'Virtual Text/Virtual Reader: The Structural Signature Within, Behind, Beyond, and Above' (*JJQ*, **16**, 1–2, 1978–79) Joseph Kestner suggests that Joyce conceived 'the act of reading as a structural system of exchange between the text and its reader'. He finds 'the precise form of structuralist activity relevant to Joyce' in Genette's *Figures 1* (Paris: Seuil, 1966):

> The Structuralist method exists as such at the precise moment when one discovers the message in the code, released by an analysis of immanent structures, and not from the outside by preexistent ideologies.
>
> (Genette: 150; Cited, Kestner: 27)

The structuralist nature of finding the 'message in the code' supports the idea that 'the act of critical interpretation is also structuralist':

> literary criticism... uses the same material (writing) as the works which concern it... [it] speaks the language of its object: it is meta-language, 'discourse on a discourse'; it can thus be meta-literature, that is to say, 'literature of which literature itself is the imposed object'.
>
> (Genette: 145–6; Cited, Kestner: 26–7)

To this, Kestner adds Tzvetan Todorov's description of Genette's notion of structure as one which is 'purely spatial'. From these ideas he develops the fundamental concept that he applies to Joyce: that of a 'spatial' 'palimpsest'. He refines this concept with Genette's four aspects of spatial structure: its linguistic nature; its 'employment of a written text'; the 'semantic space created between the apparent *signifié* and the real *signifié*; and 'literature *in toto*, a... production atemporal and anonymous' with an 'effect and convergence and... retroaction which makes of literature a vast simultaneous domain' (Kestner: 28–9).

Kestner considers Joyce's texts not as discrete works which were written in a chronological sequence, each 'new' piece of writing supplanting its predecessor, but as parts of a structural, spatial palimpsest in which 'one text [is] superimposed on and interfusing another'. Furthermore, Joyce's texts are part of the larger body of literature defined by Genette. They operate as texts which transform, and are transformed by, the texts upon which they are imposed. Kestner believes that Joyce indicated this himself by using a passage from Ovid's *Metamorphoses* as the epigraph for *A Portrait*: '*Et ignotas animum dimittit in artes*'. He sees the 'second text' (in this case *A Portrait*) as engaged in an active relationship with the first and argues that this is the case 'even when the "next" text has not been written'. Offering the case of *A Portrait*'s relation to *Ulysses* as an example, he cites a 1906 comment by Joyce as evidence:

> The character of Ulysses has fascinated me ever since boyhood. I started writing a short story for *Dubliners* fifteen years ago but gave it up. For seven years I have been working at this book – blast it. It is also a kind of encyclopaedia.
>
> (*SL*: 271; Cited, Kestner: 31)

Kestner illustrates Joyce's spatial and structural palimpsest by looking at the relationships between the essay, 'Portrait', *Stephen Hero, A Portrait of the Artist*, and sections from *Ulysses*. He represents the layers of what he terms 'sur-signification', or the signification within the 'meta-discourse' of the palimpsest, and the 'sur-spacialization' as '"Portrait": *Stephen Hero::Stephen Hero: A Portrait::A Portrait:* "Proteus".' These texts and their relations to each other constitute a 'sequence of virtual texts, in Genette's terms, converging and reacting' (31).

In a well-known passage from *A Portrait* Stephen compares the artist with God: 'The artist, like the God of the creation, remains within or behind or beyond or above his handiwork, invisible, refined out of existence, indifferent, paring his fingernails' (P: 215). Kestner compares Stephen's view of the God-like artist with Joyce's position in relation to his palimpsest:

> Joyce, like God, is literally within, beyond, above a text, through a complex of sur-significations as the text is a sur-text, text, then ur-text, written over and interwoven with another text. The previous text becomes a sign as *signifiant*, which has the next text as its *signifié*. The artist is thus like the God in *Ulysses*, who 'sitteth on the right hand of His Own Self but yet shall come'. Genette... shows the nature of this God, even echoing Stephen's ideas.
>
> (31)

The relation Kestner adopts from Genette is that of the 'signification' which joins the *signifiant* to the *signifié*. In turn this signification constitutes a 'figure' that designates a 'poetical state of discourse' and opens up a secondary plane of signification on which the 'figure' becomes 'a *signifiant* of a new *signifié*' (Genette, 1966: 192). These shifting signifying relations are applied to the ways in which Ovid's text operates not only as the epigraph to *A Portrait* but also within the sequence of significations described by Genette: 'Since the Stephen Daedalus of *Stephen Hero* and the Stephen Daedalus of *A Portrait* derive from Ovid's Daedalus, it is no coincidence that Daedalus is mentioned in *Ulysses* during "Scylla and Charybdis", since that myth deals with the relation of "between", the structured layer of the palimpsest' (Kestner: 32). The result of using Genette's structural view of the signifying chain is a clearer view of the relationships that constitute Joyce's palimpsest: '"A Portrait" is the *signifiant* to the *signifié Stephen Hero*, then to *Portrait*, then to "Proteus"' (Kestner: 32).

To 'prove' that the structure operates, Kestner analyses the 'palimpsest virtual text "A Portrait"/*Hero*/*A Portrait*/"Proteus"'. The 'ur-text' of this virtual palimpsest is the essay 'A Portrait of the Artist', written on 7 January 1904. In this essay-as-ur-text Kestner sees 'in embryo' both the artist figure that is later developed in *A Portrait* and the important concept of the *epiphany* first developed in *Stephen Hero*. 'His heaven was suddenly illuminated by a horde of stars' (*P*: 261), for example, is the ur-text for *Stephen Hero*'s 'By an epiphany he meant a sudden spiritual manifestion' and 'The soul of the commonest object... seems to us so radiant' (*SH*: 216 and 218). This 'epiphany' operates as a 'form of structuring' and 'also of a structure, of "the signature of nature", of the base-text' (Kestner: 32). The process of artistic refining is first described in 'A Portrait's' metaphorical linking of the artist and the alchemist: 'Like an alchemist he bent upon his handiwork, bringing together the mysterious elements, separating the subtle from the gross' (*P*: 261) This, too, signifies a way of structuring and a form of structure: 'The artistic purpose is one of "separating" the elements of the palimpsest, suppressing some, refining others, the text, as Joyce declares in "A Portrait", "imprinting thine indelible mark" [*P*: 264]: "the fountain of being (it seemed) had been interfused".' (Kestner: 33)

As a 'virtual text', the end of 'A Portrait' offers a statement of the text's 'virtual reader'. This is the passage in which, as we have already seen, Joyce writes of 'those multitudes not as yet in the wombs of humanity but surely engenderable there, [to whom] he would give the word' (*P*: 265). From the perspective which he develops through Genette's structuralist theory, Kestner is able to analyse this passage in terms of the relation between the palimpsest as a virtual text and the virtual reader who, in Genette's terms, 'discovers the message in the code... by an analysis of immanent structures, and not from the outside by preexistent ideologies'. The 'virtual reader' whom the 'virtual text must find' is, in Joyce's term, 'engenderable' in, and by, the text. From this point of view Kestner sees 'Oxen of the Sun' as dealing with forms of style and occuring 'in a maternity hospital' because 'its subject is a genetic, literary code, the virtual text, the virtual reader' (33).

Like Scholes, Kestner draws on Piaget's idea that wholeness, transformation, and self-regulation constitute structure. In attempting to uncover the virtual palimpsest of Joyce's writings, he suggests that we can find these three components of structure already at work in the famous triad from Aquinas with which Stephen describes the process of apprehension:

> Joyce's theory and his text reveal the palimpsest structure: *integritas* (wholeness/ur-text), *claritas* (self-regulation/text of 'next' text) and, compelling the reaction of these, *consonantia* (transformation/sur-text), as happens to 'A Portrait'/*Stephen Hero* when its future increases as a result of *A Portrait*.
>
> (36)

In *A Portrait* Stephen desires and anticipates the future in a passage which is a transformation of the ur-text's desire to 'give the word' to those future, 'engenderable' readers: 'He wanted to meet in the real world the

unsubstantial image which his soul so constantly beheld... in that
moment of supreme tenderness he would be transfigured' (*P*: 65).
Kestner follows the process of the transformation of this transfiguration
as it 'continually transform[s] structure':

> To live, to err, to fall, to triumph, to recreate life out of life! ...On and on
> and on and on!
>
> (*P*: 172)

> O life! I go to encounter for the millionth time the reality of experience and
> to forge in the smithy of my soul the uncreated conscience of my race.
>
> (*P*: 252–3)

The 'On and on' signifies the 'virtual text', and the 'millionth time' and
'the reality of experience' 'indicate the previous strata of texts'. The
'engenderable' of the essay, 'A Portrait', is transformed into the 'un-
created'. Kestner follows this transformation to *Ulysses* where Stephen
declares 'Our national epic has yet to be written' (*U*: 192). 'Stephen's reference to his "race" indicates the previous self which will be written over
in a new form: the "net" has become an ur-text grid' (Kestner: 36).

The relationship between the virtual reader and the text is not the same
as that between the actual reader and the text. Todorov indicates the
difference:

> literary points of view do not concern the actual perception of the reader,
> which remains always variable and dependent on factors external to the
> work, but a perception inherent in the work, attributed to a virtual receiver,
> presented at the interior of the work.
>
> (Cited, Kestner: 37)

Joyce 'begins to create his "virtual reader" as Stephen reads [in his diary]
of his own self in the super-text "A Portrait"/*Stephen Hero*/*A Portrait*'. As
a virtual reader Stephen is concerned not with 'actual' but with 'possible'
literature, with 'engenderable texts and potential readings'. Kestner finds
Stephen's role as the virtual reader or 'destined receiver' of the palimpsest
articulated in 'Scylla and Charybdis':

> As we, or mother Dana, weave and unweave our bodies, Stephen said, from
> day to day... so does the artist weave and unweave his image. ... In the
> intense instant of imagination, when the mind, Shelley says, is a fading coal,
> that which I was is that which I am and that which in possibility I may come
> to be. So in the future, the sister of the past, I may see myself as I sit here
> now but by reflection from that which then I shall be.
>
> (*U*: 194; Cited: 38)

In so far as the actual reader can fictionalise himself, or herself, and
occupy the position of the virtual reader engendered by the text, then he

or she undergoes a similar process of transformation to that which operates within the text and is able to perceive the literary points of view and
operations of the text. This is similar to the importance for the reader of
apprehending the text's structural operations which we saw articulated by
Scholes: for readers 'who do not see its structure' Joyce's writing is 'impossible to read' (Scholes: 169). For Kestner the creation of the 'virtual
reader of the virtual text' represents Joyce's 'consummate achievement':
'the "receiver" of the "message" has become "part of its enunciation"'
(Kestner: 39).

David Hayman

David Hayman's 'Nodality and the Infra-Structure of *Finnegans Wake*'
(*JJQ*, 16, 1–2, 178–9) first appeared in *Poétique* (26, Spring 1976). Its
reappearance in English some three years later suggests something of the
developing interest in structuralism for English-speaking readers of Joyce.
Like Kestner, Hayman is interested in the incorporation of Genette's
narrataire, or 'ideal reader', and he distinguishes between texts 'which
incorporate the figure Genette has called the... "ideal reader"... implicitly', and the ways in which *Finnegans Wake* 'manipulates and teases in
the reader's name and virtually in his person' (135). In order for the *Wake*
to do this, it 'must give the appearance of randomness when in fact it is
organized down to its least unit'. Hayman is interested in the test's
micro-structures, in what he terms its 'infra-structure', but he begins his
article by using the 'macro-structure' of Vico's three-plus-one pattern
in order to show how the *Wake's* Book I 'divides into four male chapters
and four female which can be doubled over to make [the following]
equivalence':

$$\begin{array}{cccc}
\underline{1\text{-}2\text{-}3\text{-}4} & & & 45 \\
8\text{-}7\text{-}6\text{-}5 & \text{or} & 3 & 6 \\
& & 2 & \quad 7 \\
& & 1 & \quad 8
\end{array}$$

$$(135)$$

Along with this Viconian pattern, Hayman offers Hart's structural patterns of the 'circles, crosses [and] counterpoint' as examples of how such
patterns can be 'impos[ed]... upon the larger matrix of the *Wake* without
distortion' (135). He admits that Hart's concept of the 'Leitmotif' 'over-
laps and foreshadows' his own idea of 'nodalization', but points out that
the two function 'in very different ways'. Hart's leitmotif is involved with
allusions and motifs which are built up into larger groups of two kinds.
The first is a group of 'disparate motifs', and the second, a 'true interacting *leitmotif*-complex, of which the [*Wake's* model of] the letter is the

most outstanding example' (Hart: 180). Hayman contends that Hart's latter group (the 'interacting... complex') is 'more handily viewed as a primal node, that it is used in *Finnegans Wake* far less "sparingly" than Hart claims, and that it should be seen as generating as well as bringing together motifs' (Hayman: 149).

Hayman's 'prime node' is the 'apex of the nodal system'. Like Hart, Hayman treats Joyce's texts in quite conventional terms. He approaches the nodal system through passages where 'some act, activity, personal trait, allusion, theme, etc. surfaces for its clearest statement in the text, is made manifest... and in the process brings together and crystallizes an otherwise scattered body of related material' (136). The evolution of the nodes is dealt with in the traditional terms of the historical development from manuscript to text: 'Joyce's manuscripts and letters provide us with clues to the history and function of... his nodal systems.' Hayman's nodes can be the draft sketches which Joyce described to Harriet Shaw Weaver: 'these are not fragments but active elements and when they are more and a little older they will begin to fuse themselves' (*L* I: 205, cited in Hayman: 136). They can also be 'vignettes' which, 'like *Ulysses*, *Dubliners*, and the epiphanies... convey pauses in the action, stills, anti-climaxes [and] bring into focus the moment as a transparency through which significance may shine' (137–8).

Hayman divides the nodes into eight basic categories, thereby providing an overview of the text's infrastructure. These categories are:

1. The early sketches plus the letter.
2. Passages devoted to character exposition: the profiles and Monologues.
3. Symmetrical passages like the three brother-confrontations [of Shem and Shaun in their various guises] and the fables.
4. Expositions of major themes: the fall, the flood, the crime, historical decay, sexual deviation, writing, etc.
5. Developments of aspects of the landscape: river, mountain, ocean, tree, stone, city, park, etc.
6. Allusive parallels drawn from history, religion and literature: Oscar Wilde, Shakespeare, Ezra Pound, Humphry Clinker, Christ, Buddha, etc.
7. Key rhythms or rhythmic clusters: the tonality of the river, the legalistic 'tion' passages of the twelve patrons/judges, the Quinet passage, HCE's stutter, the thunder words, song tags, etc.
8. Foreign language clusters.

(147–8).

Hayman sees this basic structure of nodes as an infra-structure, which is 'the *Wake* experienced most directly by the reader'. They also help the reader to orientate himself, or herself, by functioning as 'strategically placed reference points for those who feel themselves "lost in the bush" (*FW*: 112.03)'. Finally, they function as 'what might be called a primary structure to which everything else is at least secondary in terms of accessibility and/or strategic placement' (Hayman: 138).

Structuralist Patterns in Joyce's Narrative

The structuralist study of narrative proved to be fertile ground for literary applications of structuralist theory. Much of the structuralist work on literary narrative shows some influence from Vladimir Propp's seminal study, *Morphology of the Folktale* (Bloomington: Indiana Research Centre in Anthropology, 1958). Propp worked on some one hundred folk tales and discovered thirty-one basic functions. In *Structuralist Poetics* (London: Routledge & Kegan Paul, 1975) Jonathan Culler states that these functions 'form an ordered set ... whose presence or absence in particular tales may serve as the basis of a classification of plot'. Propp describes 'four classes [which] are immediately formed': 'development through struggle and victory, development through the accomplishment of a difficult task, development through both and development through neither' (Culler: 208). Propp's analysis 'leads [him] to the conclusion that all fairy tales are structurally homogenous, and embody the following basic principles':

1. Functions of characters serve as stable, constant elements in a tale, independently of how and by whom they are fulfilled. They constitute the fundamental components of a tale.
2. The number of functions known to the fairy tale is limited [as noted above, Propp identifies thirty-one].
3. The sequence of functions is always identical.
4. All fairy tales are of one type in regard to their structure.

(Hawkes: 68–9)

As Hawkes explains, Propp's thirty-one functions are distributed among seven 'spheres of action' corresponding to their 'respective performers' as follows:

1	the villain	5	the dispatcher
2	the donor (provider)	6	the hero
3	the helper	7	the false hero
4	the princess (a sought-for person) and her father		

(Hawkes: 69)

While not all critics agree with the usefulness and validity of Propp's categories, most structural analyses of narrative do deal with character as a narrative structural unit which serves particular narrative functions and breaks down plots into small, definable narrative patterns which are suitable for categorising into groups sharing similar features.

Doris T. Wight

Doris T. Wight's 'Vladimir Propp and *Dubliners*' (*JJQ*, **23**, 4, 1986) is one of the best examples of a Proppian, structuralist analysis of Joyce's work. Wight begins by separating 'The Dead' from the rest of the stories, explaining that '[a]t one point fourteen tales, not fifteen, were to have comprised the fictional biography of Dublin's people'. She sees the final story, 'The Dead', as essentially different from the stories that precede it:

> What is different about 'The Dead'... is that for the first time in that story, not merely human institutions but external nature, the power of the universe expressed through the symbols of death and snow – this new kind of 'villainy' for humans – is perceived. The difference in viewpoint is momentous. Using Propp's seven characters-as-functions, one finds one set for the first fourteen tales, a changed set for the crowning fifteenth tale.
>
> (416–17)

Wight qualifies these assertions somewhat, admitting that they cannot be 'proved'. A Proppian analysis, however, can contribute to an understanding of Joyce's work, enabling the reader to 'arrive at a deepened understanding of the text... and use it to supplement other discoveries and revelations about the book called "the foundation of Joyce's art"' (417).

Wight omits 'The Dead' and divides the remaining *Dubliners* stories into the usual four groups of childhood, adolescence, and mature and public life. In each of the four sets, 'heroes (or anti-heroes) are those, as Propp says, whose intentions create the axis of the narrative':

> Their support has created and continues to create the Church, although individuals – even official representatives of that Church like Father Flynn – may have had their chalices broken. Their political weakness issues from neo-partisan's committee rooms not as the report of bullets but of stout bottle corks. The institution of marriage brutalizes men who in turn brutalize their wives and children. The institution of celibacy leaves one outcast from life's feast.
>
> (417)

Because Wight sees similar structural patterns repeated in different stories she analyses only five from the group of fourteen – 'The Sisters', 'Two Gallants', 'Counterparts', 'Clay' and 'Grace' – plus the final story, 'The Dead', which she sees as separate from the earlier stories.

The analysis of 'The Sisters' begins with the first of Propp's thirty-one functions: 'Some member of a family absents himself from home.' Wight argues that because of his close relationship with the priest, the boy in the story is a member of the family, albeit a 'less obvious' member than the sisters, Eliza and Nannie. The death of the priest is the Proppian *dispatcher* which sends the boy as *hero* 'on his search to understand Father Flynn's secret' (418). Propp's categories are applied to the story as follows:

Hero: the boy who leaves his (symbolic) home.
Dispatcher: death provides the reason/opportunity for the boy to leave.
Donor: the 'priest has been giving the boy learning'.
Magical agent or helper: the knowledge the boy receives from the priest.
Villain: the 'doubt... with which the priest and protégé must fight'.
Punishment: the madness visited upon Father Flynn after his own failure to defeat the villain, or doubt.

Obviously the priest serves at least a double function. He is a donor who helps the boy, but he also occupies the role of hero in the set of actions which comprise his own struggle with doubt. Wight recognises that the nature of the priest's own 'struggle is unclear'. It 'is involved with a broken chalice, hence some flaw in the symbol of religious faith... yet there is another dimension... one... that the boy recognizes... unconsciously'. This latter dimension is the possible 'sexual perversion' which is hinted at by some of the story's symbolism (417–19).

Wight analyses more stories, but a summary of her analysis of 'Clay', the story she probes most deeply, will suffice as an example of her use of Propp. In the 'Notes' to her article, Wight gives all thirty-one of Propp's functional categories, but her identification of the twenty or so categories that she finds in 'Clay' will enable us to appreciate her adaptation of Propp's functions as well as her structuralist understanding of Joyce's story. These functions and Wight's shorthand for them (given in parentheses) are as follows:

Initial situation: The members of a family (group) are enumerated, or the future hero is introduced by mention of his name or status (α), Hero's departure on a search (C↑), reactions to demands of donor (E)

1) A member of a family absents himself from home (abstention β)
6) Villain tries to deceive his victim (η)
7) Victim, deceived, unwittingly aids his enemy (complicity θ)
8a) A family member lacks or desires something (lack a)
9) Misfortune or lack is made known... (mediation, the connective... B)
10) The seeker decides to counter (beginning, counteraction, C)
11) Hero leaves home (↑)
12) Hero is tested... the way for... receiving either a magical agent or a helper (first function of Donor, D)

13) Hero reacts to actions of the future donor (hero's reaction, E)
14) Hero acquires use of a magical agent (receipt of magical agent, F)
15) Hero is moved to location of an object of search (spatial transference between two kingdoms, guidance, G)
16) Hero and villain join in direct combat (struggle, H)
17) Hero is branded (branded, marking, J)
18) Villain is defeated (victory, I)
19) The initial misfortune or lack is liquidated (misfortune liquidated, K)
25) A difficult task is proposed to hero (difficult task, M)
26) Task is resolved (solution, N)
27) Hero is recognised (recognition, Q)
28) False hero or villain is exposed (exposure, Ex)
29) Hero given a new appearance (T)
31) Hero is married and ascends the throne (wedding, W)

(432–3, n.8)

Using these functions, Wight breaks the narrative down into the following units:

Preparatory section

Maria introduced (α) → looks forward to evening out (β) → Maria's lack (a) of a husband is revealed → Maria unwittingly helps her opponent (the women who tease her about getting the ring) by laughing (θ)

Main section

Maria's lack (a') → Maria changes (T) → Matron's permission to leave the laundry (Hero dispatched; connective incident) (B) → Maria leaves (C↑).

This is followed by a section constituted by narrative groups of three functions. Wight emphasises the importance of this trebling in Propp's fairy tales:

> In the first set in her search for *magical agents* to make herself loved [Maria] first buys cakes for the children, then buys plumcake after so much hesitation the clerk accuses her of wanting a wedding cake (which is precisely what she does want of course). In the third test, her search for a seat on the tram, a symbolic seat, a place, the wonderful occurrence happens. The *donor* mustached gentleman gives Maria a *sought-for-object*, a seat, and he talks to her so sweetly that we have implicitly a *wedding* (W∗) with the prince and a new home. We also have *transfiguration* in the description of Maria's walking along happily in the rain....
>
> (426)

The second set consists of Maria: giving the children the cakes and receiving thanks; becoming aware of the lost plumcake and being consoled by Joe; and being given nuts 'by the neighbour girl but no nut-

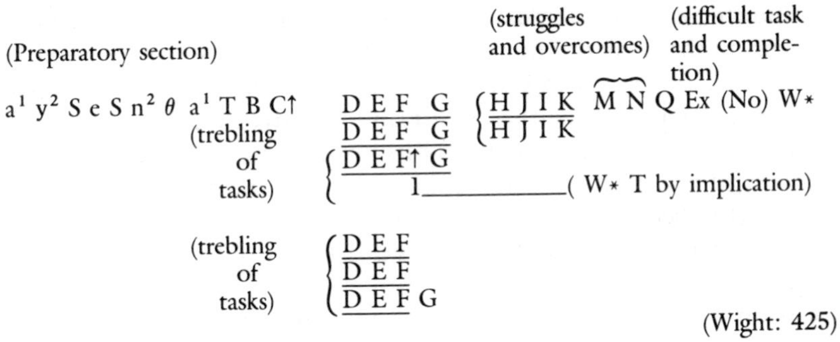

		(struggles and overcomes)	(difficult task and comple- tion)
(Preparatory section)			

$$\text{a}^1 \text{ y}^2 \text{ S e S n}^2 \, \theta \text{ a}^1 \text{ T B C}\!\uparrow$$

(trebling of tasks)	$\underline{\text{D E F G}}$ $\underline{\text{D E F G}}$ $\overline{\text{D E F}\!\uparrow\,\text{G}}$	$\begin{cases} \text{H J I K} & \widetilde{\text{M N}} \text{ Q Ex (No) W}* \\ \text{H J I K} & \end{cases}$

$$\left\{ \underline{1} \,(\text{ W}* \text{ T by implication}) \right.$$

(trebling of tasks)	$\begin{cases} \underline{\text{D E F}} \\ \underline{\text{D E F}} \\ \overline{\text{D E F G}} \end{cases}$

(Wight: 425)

Figure 1

cracker' and being rescued by Joe who gives 'her a seat by the fire, a drink, and pleasant talk'. A third set of treble actions consists of 'struggles and outcomes':

> In the first, Maria puts in a good word for Alphy, which angers Joe. Maria is wounded, hurt (*branded* in her *struggle* with *villain*, Joe's anger), but Joe overcomes his bad temper. In the second, and chief, struggle, Maria gets the clay (negative *magical agent*) as well as *brand*, wound) in her struggle with the two neighbor girls representing both bad *donors* and, chiefly, *villain*; but she ultimately wins the struggle (ironically) by being given a face-saving prayerbook (good *magical agent*) and by adopting her pose of ignorance towards life's cruelties. The high point of the tale... is (K), *lack is liquidated*, when after the clay incident Joe is nicer to Maria than he has ever been in his life.
>
> (427)

The third, and final 'struggle and outcome' identified by Wight is found in Maria's singing of 'I Dreamt that I Dwelt'. This is a Proppian *difficult task* and *completion*, and *recognition* of her true value and *exposure* of her loneliness cause Joe and his wife to be much moved...'. Propp's functions of marriage and return home exist 'only in the negative – Joyce's message about the lot of the female celibate' (427). Wight draws this analysis of 'Clay' together and depicts it in diagrammatical form (see Fig. 1.).

Seymour Chatman

Seymour Chatman is primarily recognised as a theorist rather than a Joyce scholar, and his *Story and Discourse: Narrative Structure in Fiction and Film* (Ithaca: Cornell UP, 1978) offers a remarkable synthesis of the work of a number of narratologists. Chatman's theory owes a considerable amount to the work of Propp, but it also incorporates the modifications and further developments in narrative theory made by writers like Genette, Todorov and Barthes. Chatman's narrative theory is of particular interest to Joyce's readers because of its frequent use of Joyce's writing as a model of narrative structure. Unlike the many theorists who focus on Joyce's later fiction, and particularly on the *Wake*, Chatman focuses primarily on earlier works like *Dubliners* and *A Portrait of the Artist as a Young Man*.

Chatman's primary interest is in the form of narrative rather than its substance, and the beginning of *Story and Discourse* offers a graphic illustration of Chatman's theory of narrative structure. As he uses Joyce's fiction to illustrate several important features of his theoretical categories it will be helpful to keep Chatman's structure in mind as we look at his use of Joyce's work (Fig. 2).

As this structure reveals, Chatman's first distinction is between a narrative's story, or plot, and its discourse. The story provides narrative content; the discourse provides its expression in the form of 'a set of narrative statements' (146).

Chatman first discusses Joyce when illustrating his distinction between narrator's time and character's time. This distinction parallels that between 'story-time and discourse-time' (81). Chatman is interested in the structural relation between narrative time and 'purely linguistic phenomena such as tense and aspect', and he distinguishes between, on the one hand, time as a 'matter of narrative, of story and discourse', and, on the other, tense as a matter 'of the grammars of language' (81). This

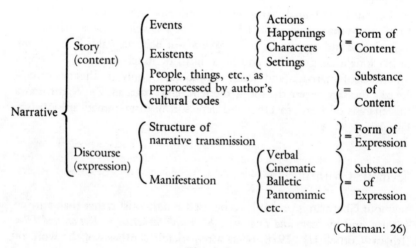

(Chatman: 26)

Figure 2

is a part of the graphed distinction between the 'structure of the narrative transmission' (grammar, tense) and the time framework for the characters. This distinction is important in the structure of Joyce's 'An Encounter'. The grammatical aspect of the narrative involves 'the simple preterite [which] marks practically every temporal contingency', yet a change in the story's context is sufficient to distinguish a temporal shift from the period when the narrator and characters occupy the time frame and the period when the narrator reports 'events taking place much later': 'It was Joe Dillon who introduced the Wild West to us. He had a little library ... we met in his back garden' marks the shared time frame. 'Everyone was incredulous when it was reported that he had a vocation for the priesthood' establishes a contextual difference (between playing 'Wild West' games and 'vocation for the priesthood') which makes a shift in grammatical tense unnecessary. The 'context is sufficient' (82).

Chatman sees a fundamental structure of fictional narrative created between the 'existents' of character and setting. Unlike the traditional focus upon the relationship between character and plot which considers setting as subordinate to this relationship, Chatman's theory considers the binary opposition between character and setting as a powerful and fundamental part of narrative structure. This is a useful theory for stories like 'Eveline' where Joyce creates a powerful narrative depiction of emotional turmoil and sustains his arch-theme of paralysis with a minimal use of action. One view of setting confines it to the role of contributing 'to the mood of the narrative', but Chatman's theory allows us to perceive Joyce's use of setting as something that is much more important. Chatman identifies 'multiple functions' for the setting of 'Eveline', beginning with the use of 'scenic props' for the creation of three distinct spheres:

1. 'In her home everything is grimy and poverty-ridden. Cretone curtains and broken harmonium, "her entire wages – seven shillings", her black leather purse (she would not permit herself a more cheerful color)... the "close dark room"... in which her mother died, and so on.'
2. 'But in her internal, mental setting we find... pleasant homey elements: before the fire, the picnic on the Hill of Howth, her mother's bonnet that her father playfully dons.'
3. 'Outside her home everything is exotic, frightening, and finally unacceptable. Chief is the night-boat itself (not a *day*-boat), whose dark mass and illuminated portholes lurk beyond the wide doors of the sheds. The boat is suitably shrouded in mist. The soldiers with their brown baggage invoke far-away and hence meaningless violence and threat.'

(142)

These three complexes are combined by 'the street organ's rich evocation', and Chatman's analysis demonstrates how Joyce could make a relatively minor object like the street organ serve an important structural purpose by using it to unite the three 'complexes of settings – poverty, homey comforts, and the exotic':

> The street-organ is commoner in poorer parts of the city than in rich, where policemen keep the streets free of beggars. ... Eveline associates it with the painful memory of her mother's death. But there is... comfort in a street-organ tune to one who has heard it all her life. ... And finally, the organ is exotic: it is operated by an Italian and plays Italian airs.
>
> (142)

Chatman concludes his investigation into the structural importance of setting in Joyce's narrative by considering the 'remarkable ... way' in which Joyce elevates setting 'to a symbolic dimension in the finale' of 'Eveline'. At the climactic point in Joyce's story the 'normally effaced narrator' is foregrounded in the narrative structure as he becomes the source for a group of 'clustered metaphors' articulating Eveline's 'greatest anguish' and emphasising the 'extremity of her situation': 'A bell clanged upon her heart ... All the seas of the world tumbled about her heart. He was drawing her into them: he would drown her ... Amid the seas she sent a cry of anguish.' What Chatman terms the 'existents' of the setting, the 'real bell sound[ing] the boat's departure and the real sea... beyond the harbour', are combined into the 'metaphors [which] inhere in the juxtapositions'. These metaphors are made more powerful by the 'way in which they fuse character and setting [and] subject and character to the onslaught of setting, making setting almost a character' (143).

Like Kestner and Hayman, Chatman is also interested in the role of the virtual reader (as opposed to the actual reader) as that reader is created by, and functions within, the narrative structure. Focusing upon the second major aspect of his narrative structure (the narrative as discourse and expression rather than story and content) he depicts the the structure of the narrative texts as:

Narrative Text

Real	Implied			Implied	Real
--→					--→
author	author	→ (Narrator)→	(Narratee)→		reader
				reader	

This diagram shows how Chatman's theory considers only the 'implied author and implied reader' as 'immanent to a narrative'. The 'narrator and narratee are optional (parentheses). The real author and real reader are outside the narrative transaction as such' (151). There emerges a 'crucial difference between "point of view" and narrative voice', and only narrative voice need be created by the narrator as he, or she, functions within the narrative text as it is depicted by Chatman's diagram. It is through the narrative voice, as 'speech or other overt means' that 'events and existents are communicated to the audience' (153).

Expression is the 'province of narrative voice' while '[p]erception, conception, and interest points of view are quite independent of the manner in which they are expressed'. Chatman finds this distinction confirmed at several places in Joyce's narrative structures and uses Joyce's text to demonstrate how 'point of view is *in* the story (when it is a character's) but voice is always outside'. In an episode from *A Portrait* when Stephen appears on stage, his perceptual point of view is expressed not by Stephen himself but by Joyce's narrator: 'A few moments after he found himself on the stage amid the garish gas and the dim scenery' (*P*: 154). 'Characters' perceptions need not be articulated [by the characters themselves]': 'Stephen is not saying to himself the *words* "garish gas and dim scenery"; the words are the narrator's' (154). A more complex example is provided by a passage from *Ulysses*' 'Hades' episode when Leopold Bloom observes the horse-drawn hearse carrying Paddy Dignam's coffin: 'Coffin now. Got here before us, dead as he is. Horse looking round at it with his plume skewways [sic.]. Dull eye: collar tight on his neck, pressing on a blood-vessel or something. Do they know what they cart out here everyday?' (*U*: 83; Cited: 154). The point of view here is clearly Bloom's. It constitutes what Chatman terms as a 'perceptual point of view'. The words, too, are Bloom's but 'he is no narrator [because] [h]e is not telling a narratee anything. Indeed, he is not speaking even to himself: the convention argues that he is directly perceiving the coffin and the nag's dull eye, and nothing more. There *is* no narrator' (155).

Chatman concludes *Story and Discourse* with an examination of the differences between the two fundamental types of narrators which he terms the 'covert' and 'overt' narrators. Both operate within the central area marked out in Chatman's diagram of the narrative text, and within the larger structure of narrative which we examined earlier: they function at the structural level of 'narrative transmission' where they constitute an integral part of the 'form of expression'. The covert narrator functions upon the 'middle ground between "nonnarration" and conspicuously audible narration' (197). From this middle ground we hear the covert narrator as a 'voice speaking of events, characters, and setting, but [the identity of the covert narrator] remains hidden in the discursive shadows' (197). Chatman sees one of Joyce's major narrative achievements in his creation of a diversity of covert narrative styles. He would thus seem to agree with the assessment of Joyce's narrative style offered (in largely non-structuralist terms) by Hugh Kenner's *Joyce's Voices*. Chatman disagrees with the 'impropriety of assigning the term "narrator" to the... mental voice' of Joyce's characters, and he corrects this view with his analysis of several of Joyce's covert narrators, beginning with the narrative voice of 'The Two Gallants':

> In his imagination he beheld the pair of lovers walking along some dark road; he heard Corley's voice in deep energetic gallantries and saw again the leer of the young woman's mouth. This vision made him feel keenly his own poverty of purse and spirit. He was tired of knocking about, of pulling the devil by the tail, of shifts and intrigues.
>
> (*D*: 57, cited 198)

Chatman believes that Lenehan's speculations and reminiscences do not 'tell[ ] a story to anybody, not even himself'. Like those of Bloom in 'Hades', Lenehan's words are not directed to a narratee. Unlike Bloom, however, Lenehan does not have a vocabulary which includes all of the words of his speculations. Chatman's view is that in the above passage, it 'is an outside speaker who is reporting ("internally analyzing") [Lenehan's] thoughts', because 'Lenehan's vocabulary does not include "deep energetic gallantries", "his own poverty of purse and spirit", [or] "shifts and intrigues".' Since these are not Lenehan's words, Chatman says, 'he cannot be the narrator of the story which they recount. The narrator is *imputing* the feeling of "poverty of purse and spirit" to Lenehan, but it is only an imputation, an internal analysis or report by a covert narrator.' There are words and phrases in this passage that Lenehan could know, but Chatman sees such phrases as 'tired of knocking about' and 'pulling the devil by the tail' as 'quotation in indirect free form' (198).

Chatman concludes his study of passages from Joyce by returning to 'Eveline' in order to illustrate the subclasses of 'free indirect' narrative style. These subclasses consist of 'narrated monologue' and 'narrative report (internal analysis)'. Chatman borrows the term 'narrated monologue' from Dorrit Cohn's 'Narrated Monologue: Definition of a Fictional Style' (*Comparative Literature*, **18** (1966): 102) and uses it to describe language that is clearly the character's: '"Narrated" accounts for the indirect features – third person and prior tense – while "monologue" conveys the sense of hearing the very words of the character' (203). In contrast to this 'monologue' subclass, 'narrative report (internal analysis)' is the narrative form that we have seen operating in Lenehan's discourse in 'Two Gallants'. It is the form 'where the character's thinking or speech is communicated in words that are recognizably the narrator's' (201). The opening sentence of 'Eveline' is: 'She sat at the window watching the evening invade the avenue.' Even this opening sentence reveals the complex structures of Joyce's narrative. Chatman contends that we are 'at first... uncertain that there is a narrator' because the 'discourse may be only an enactment, the narrative equivalent of an actress sitting on-stage by a window painted on the backdrop'. The act of '"sitting at the window" could clearly pass as "nonnarrative", but "watching" is ambiguous', as a character could be 'described as watching something from an external vantage, hence no narrator'. On the other hand the 'verb may verbalize [Eveline's] perception, hence a covert narrator' (204).

As in his analysis of 'Two Gallants', Chatman finds words and phrases in this story which he believes could not belong to the character. The phrase 'evening invade the avenue', for example, offers a metaphor which 'presupposes a mind capable of its invention; if it is not Eveline who does so, the speaker can only be the narrator'. Chatman finds this hypothesis validated in the last of five examples which he uses to illustrate the 'logic by which ... we decide whose voice it is that we hear in indirect discourse'. After examining the opening sentence (his first example), Chatman selects and comments on four more passages in the following manner:

> 2) 'Her head was leaned against the window curtains and in her nostrils was the odor of dusty cretonne.' The first part of this sentence again might seem to present a simple enactment. But in the jelling context it seems more like a covert narrator's pronouncement, a free indirect perception.
> 3) 'She was tired.' This is ambiguous: either 'She felt [that she was] tired', or 'My [the narrator's] report is that she was tired', whatever she thought. (Or *both*: the ambiguity of free indirect forms.)
> 4) 'Few people passed.' Ditto: 'She saw few people pass' or 'On my [the narrator's] authority few people passed.' Or both.
> 5) 'The man out of the last house passed on his way home.' Here clearly we distinguish two vocalic styles. 'Out of' is a class dialect form of 'from.' The voice that speaks of the evening 'invading' the avenue is clearly not the one that speaks of a man 'out of' the last house; clearly the former belongs to an 'author'-narrator and the latter to the character. The basic form of the sentence is indirect free perception but the phrase 'out of the last house' is a direct quotation, hence narrated monologue.
>
> (204–5)

This analysis attempts to assess the complexity and rich ambiguities of Joyce's early narrative style from a structuralist view, yet it also takes into account the changes which Joyce made in 'Eveline' between its first publication in the *Irish Homestead* (10 September 1904) and its appearance in *Dubliners*. In looking at the ways in which Joyce attempted to make Eveline's 'mental voice more prominent', Chatman illustrates that structural analysis can also draw on more conventional forms of literary investigation to support and assist a primarily structuralist endeavour. The primary source for the distinction between Eveline's 'simple colloquial voice' and the covert narrator's more literary voice, however, is Chatman's structuralist theory. As we have seen, this theory enables the reader to start with the conventional view of the differences between literary form and content and a move onto a more technical, structuralist analysis which allows for a better understanding of Joyce's narrative achievements. As Chatman admits his method of analysis is both 'laborious and unnatural'. It is 'not what the reader actually does, but only a suggestion of what his [or her] logic of decision must be' (206). 'Laborious and unnatural' it may be, but it is also a necessary reading strategy for understanding how Joyce's (and other) texts programme the reading strategies for their virtual, or ideal, readers within themselves.

Margot Norris

Margot Norris's *The Decentered Universe of Finnegans Wake: A Structuralist Analysis* occupies an important and pivotal position among theoretical studies of Joyce. It can be seen as a major (if not *the* major), in-depth structuralist analysis of Joyce's most difficult work, and it is also one of the first Anglo-American assessments of the *Wake* from a poststructuralist perspective. This pivotal position is confirmed by the title of the work. While it clearly offers itself as 'A Structuralist Analysis', Norris's study also deals with the *Wake* as a 'decentered' text. On the one hand, it draws together an impressive amount of research into structuralist theory and earlier structuralist studies of Joyce (Norris clearly acknowledges the importance of Hart's work to her own study); on the other hand, it attempts to show how Joyce's last work functions deconstructively by refusing the reader any stable, central position for a reading of the text. Norris sees what she terms the 'literary heterodoxy of *Finnegans Wake*' as 'the result of Joyce's attack on the traditional concept of structure itself'. This attack 'was not isolated, but belonged to an "event" or "rupture" in the history of the concept of structure... which... took place in the history of thought sometime in the late nineteenth and early twentieth centuries' (121). The 'event' to which Norris refers was important for the development of poststructuralism, particularly Deconstruction, and in the concluding chapter of her book, Norris considers how the work of Jacques Derrida provides an important context for appreciating the radical and subversive nature of Joyce's writing. We will examine this in more detail in the chapter on poststructuralism and Joyce. First let us look at some of Norris's structuralist insights into *Finnegans Wake*.

Norris derives much of her theoretical material from Vico, Freud, Lévi-Strauss and Lacan. The fundamental premise which she adopts in her approach to the *Wake* is that approaching the text as a novel will not get the reader anywhere because expecting it 'to "make sense" in the way *Portrait*, *Ulysses*, or traditional novels "make sense" implies a conceptual framework and epistemology that Joyce strongly intimated he wanted to undermine'. Norris's investigation into Joyce's use of Freud is very detailed, and it is worth noting here that Norris sees the *structures* of

Freud's model of the dream both as an integral component of the *Wake*'s structure and as a key to understanding the puzzling nature of Joyce's text: '*Finnegans Wake* is a puzzle because dreams are puzzles – elaborate, brilliant, purposeful puzzles, which constitute a universe quite unlike any we know or experience in waking life' (5). While Norris makes considerable use of Hart's study, she strongly disagrees with the view of the *Wake*'s dream structure which Hart shares with Edmund Wilson. In *Structure and Motif*, Hart claims that 'Joyce hated psychoanalysis and "used only so much of its techniques and *Weltanschauung* as he found useful"' (Hart: 82; Norris: 146, n. 6). Few, if any, scholars would be likely to agree with Hart today, but Norris's book was one of the first to recognise and detail the *Wake*'s extensive use of Freud.

In *Axel's Castle* (New York: Charles Scribner & Sons, 1969) Edmund Wilson complains that 'as soon as we are aware of Joyce... systematically embroidering on his text, deliberately inventing puzzles, the illusion of the dream is lost' (235). Noting that Hart's view echoes that of Wilson, Norris contends that both earlier critics 'misrepresent two crucial aspects of the nature of the dream'. The first misrepresentation concerns the 'status of knowledge, particularly self-knowledge, in the dream'. Both Wilson and Hart saw Joyce depicting the consciousness of an omniscient dreamer, but, as Norris points out, in a dream, the 'dreamer is not unitary, or conscious, or omniscient', and 'the vantage point of the dream is not an area of consciousness, but... a place where the unconscious... tries to communicate with the... conscious self'. The second misrepresentation in the theory which Hart shares with Wilson concerns the form of dreams. Norris sees their concept of the form as 'essentially incompatible with the complicated, deviant language' of Joyce's writing. Unlike the model to which Wilson and Hart adhere, the Freudian model Norris finds in the *Wake* is a model of the dream as a *structural* process wherein 'the unconscious manifests itself through certain structural operations'. These operations include 'the ordering and organization of materials, preferential selections, and substitutions – the processes Freud called distortion, displacement, and condensation' (Norris: 99).

An important clue to Norris' insights into the *Wake* is found in her re-examination of both Joyce's source material and his method of incorporating this material into his book. In much the same way that she re-examines Joyce's use of Freud, she also reconsiders his use of Vico's *The New Science*. Vico's work has been one of '[t]wo predominant models [which] have governed attempts to define the *Wake*'s structure' (the other model is the 'familiar plan of *Ulysses*' which Stuart Gilbert's *James Joyce's Ulysses* presented). Norris agrees with the importance of Vico in the *Wake*, but she disagrees with critics like Campbell and Robinson, or Hart, who see the structures of Joyce's book maintaining and sustaining the historical, linear and progressive patterns of its source models. Vico's model is 'historical in its foundation on the linear progress of events through time'. Its 'movement is both cyclical and evolutional: events, though repeated at the end of the cycle, unfold in a logical and necessary sequence'. In Norris' view Joyce's writing becomes more synchronic and less diachronic during the course of his career as his 'literary evolution traces a gradual abandonment of diachronic structures'. Joyce makes extensive use of Vico, but the 'evolutional progress' of his model is 'difficult to discern in the *Wake*'. This is because Joyce incorporated Vico's 'emphasis on recurrent social states' into the *Wake* but relies much less on Vico's 'belief in ineluctable evolution' (25).

In support of this argument Norris considers several key scenes and events from the *Wake*'s narrative. She contends that the 'recurrent events... though "presenting varied faces in different lightings and movements", do not represent historical cross-sections that are static – a series of frozen tableaus or movie stills, to use Lévi-Strauss's image'. The basic nature of each narrative 'reenactment of a scene, whatever its imaginative "reality", is *dynamic*' (25, my emphasis). Putting it another way, Norris sees 'the repeated events' as 'constitut[ing] temporal narratives':

> the washerwomen (I. 7) do the laundry, chat about Anna, bicker, pick up the drying clothes at dusk, and go home. Later in the book the event is repeated: the boys in the nursery (II. 2) do their homework (family history is found in school texts as well as in dirty linen), gossip about their mother, fight, close their lesson with a night letter, and presumably go to bed.
>
> (25)

For Norris the sort of repetition illustrated by the comparison of these episodes 'does not appear to be merely predetermined like Vico's events'. Instead of following the 'logical progression of evolutionary change bring[ing] each cycle to a close in precisely the same condition as it began', the *Wake*'s narrative follows a 'compulsive' pattern of repetition. This repetition is 'produced by irrational rather than logical necessity, and therefore actively induced – the result of human impulse rather than time' (15–16). As we will see in the chapter on psychoanalysis, Joyce's use of 'compulsive', 'human impulse' as a source for the *Wake*'s narrative repetition is a part of his structural use of the Freudian model of the dream and his attempt to depict the operations of human desire within that dream structure.

Norris finds that the *Wake* is structured by a group of interrelated themes which maintain a close connection with their mythic origins. Each articulation of a particular theme operates like one of the 'mythemes' which Lévi-Strauss identifies as an important structural unit of the *parole* wherein a particular mythic pattern from the larger *langue* of the myth is made manifest. Like the Viconian cyclic pattern these themes operate according to a 'compulsive' and 'irrational' pattern of repetition as they are used to structure different episodes and scenes. Norris illustrates this by analysing an opening passage which combines the themes of 'family and society', 'law' and the myth of Oedipus: 'Amid the catalogue of themes in the second paragraph of *Finnegans Wake*, the distinct oedipal elements of law and family conflict are presented in neat juxtaposition.' The passage is 'nor avoice from afire bellowsed mishe mishe to tauftauf thuartpeatrick: not yet, though venisoon after, had a kidscad buttended a bland old isacc: not yet, though all's fair in vanessy, were sosie sesthers wroth with twone nathandjoe' (3.9–12). Norris identifies the following 'mythemes' in the passage:

> The unbegotten Yahweh announces His name to Moses from the burning bush – *mishe* is Gaelic for "I am"

> [t]*auf*, the German word for baptize and christen, is followed by a reference to "Thou art Peter,..." Christ's simultaneous conferral of a new name and the temporal authority over the Church on Simon.

> Next is a reference to Jacob's deception of his blind father, Isaac, by which he stole the birthright from his twin brother, the goatherd Esau.

> [T]his segment also includes a reference to an Irish Isaac: Isaac Butt, who was replaced as head of the Irish Party by the younger Charles Parnell.

> Finally, there is reference to a divided and reversed Jonathan Swift, "nathandjoe," whose amours with two girls, Esther Johnson (Stella) and Esther Vanhomrigh (Vanessa), form one of the basic configurations for a recurrent father–daughter incest motif throughout the work.
>
> (41–2)

These passages represent events from different periods of history but are combined with no apparent regard for the historical gaps separating the events. They are combined synchronically with no attention given to the 'reality' of historical diachronicity.

Norris continues her analysis of the structural themes and their appearance in the *Wake*'s combinations of mythemic units. In so doing she identifies several fundamental themes which are used in the book's repeated structural patterns. In addition to 'family and society', Norris uncovers the themes: 'The Primal Scene', 'Triangular Desire', 'In The Name Of The Father', 'Redemption: The Failure of The Son' and 'Redemption: Maternal Salvage' (44–72). These themes are used to structure the *Wake*'s dreamscape, a dreamscape in which the shifting, fluid characters experience various ontological conditions like guilt, inauthenticity (which Norris links with Heidegger's notion of *Gerede*, or 'idle talk'), the quest for the nature of truth, and the contemplation and experience of death. The way in which Joyce treats these ontological issues in his final work provides both a sense of continuity and a point of contrast between the *Wake* and his earlier fiction. Discussing Joyce's use of guilt as a source of alienation, Norris suggests that:

> Joyce's fictional characters are always alienated from their worlds. In the paralyzed citizens of *Dubliners* and in Stephen's agitated defense against societal institutions in *Portrait*, the assault on the self is from without, and therefore defensible with silence, cunning, and exile, as Stephen concludes at the end of *Portrait*. Yet in Joyce's later works, the self becomes increasingly imperiled from within, as Stephen is gnawed by 'agenbite of inwit', and Bloom tormented by sexual guilts in *Ulysses*. ...Bloom's alienation is simultaneously sexual and racial; as the wandering Jew, subject to forbidden fantasies, he reflects an exiled Odysseus, driven and delayed by sexual desire. But Bloom most perfectly fuses the psychological and social functions of guilt in the mythic analogue of Christ, the divine masochist.
>
> (73)

In contrast to this individual experience of guilt, *Finnegans Wake* 'makes the status of guilt extremely problematic' because the fluid characters are continually changing their identities and exchanging their qualities with those of other characters. Thus, the 'theme of guilt... and the interchangeability of characters are related in important ways' (74–5). The distinction between 'self' and 'other' ceases to be clear as the *Wake*'s characters are subject to the important structural process of change and mutability. Norris sees the question of guilt as ultimately 'insoluble' 'because of [the *Wake*'s] circularity' (76). Trying to deal with this question of guilt 'necessitates defining the reality or level of reality, in the work'. Early critics who treated 'Wakean figures as as though they were characters in a nineteenth century novel', did not need to concern themselves with this question, because they treated the *Wake*'s characters like any of the 'characters in fiction who mirror characters in life'. Norris's recognition of the inadequacy of this approach enables her to recognise and define one of the essential problems that Joyce's last work poses for the reader:

> But if we assume that *Finnegans Wake* represents a dream, then Wakean figures become the creature of the dreamer, figures that may represent persons in an offscreen waking reality, or the dreamer himself, or composites of several figures... . The great problem, of course, is that the reader is trapped inside the dream in *Finnegans Wake*. A dream can't be analyzed from the inside, because the dream is precisely the place where self-knowledge breaks down. The dreamer confronts a disguised message from his own unconscious. He is unable to know his unconscious directly, and yet it is utterly and truly himself.
>
> (78)

Norris uses a rigorous structuralist analysis to demonstrate this fundamental problem which Joyce's final work offers to its readers. She then formulates the problem in terms which reveal its relevance for poststructuralist investigations into the language of Literature and Philosophy: 'By writing *Finnegans Wake* as he did, Joyce confirmed the impossibility of metalangue, that is, the impossibility of making a critique in language of the epistemology embedded in language' (140). One of the problems which Jacques Derrida's deconstruction of Western metaphysics elaborates is that which arises in using terms from the metaphysical tradition to deconstruct that tradition. That Joyce elaborates and confirms this problem in his final work may explain why Derrida has maintained an interest in Joyce since the publication of his first work on Edmund Husserl. Any speculation, on this question, however, must wait until we examine Joyce's relation to poststructuralist theory.

•2• JOYCE'S SIGNS:

Joyce and Semiotics

> A Science that studies the life of signs… would be a part of social psychology and consequently of general psychology; I shall call it *semiology* (from the Greek *sēmeíon* 'sign'). Semiology would show what constitutes signs, what laws govern them. …Linguistics is only a part of the general science of semiology; the laws discovered by semiology will be applicable to linguistics, and the latter will circumscribe a well-defined area within the mass of anthropological facts.
>
> (Saussure; Cited, Hawkes: 123)

SEMIOLOGY AND *SEMIOTICS* refer to the same 'science' that Saussure describes: the study of linguistic units and other symbols as *signs*. The development of modern semiotics can be traced back to the work of two men, Saussure and the American, C. S. Peirce. The idea of a 'science of signs' was 'conceived independently' by these two men as they worked 'at about the same time… on opposite sides of the Atlantic' (Hawkes: 124). While the idea of a modern science for investigating signs originates in their work, however, the interest in words and objects as signs is much older. The idea that objects in the natural world can function as signs lies behind the medieval philosophy that viewed the world as a book of signs which could be interpreted to reveal the divine nature of creation. Joyce was familiar with this idea through his extensive knowledge of medieval thought, and, as several commentators have noted, Stephen Dedalus's idea of the visible world as 'Signatures of all things I am here to read' (*U*:

31) incorporates a reference to the work of Jacob Boehme (1575–1624). Joyce owned a copy of Boehme's *The Signature of All Things*, a work which was based on this medieval philosophy.

Terence Hawkes argues that semiotics' boundaries are 'coterminous with those of structuralism', and 'the interests of the two spheres are not fundamentally different'. Both disciplines concern themselves with the nature of the structural relationships between words, and according to Hawkes 'both ought properly to be included' within the discipline of communication studies (Hawkes: 124). The close relationship between semiotics and structuralism is explained by the common origins which they share in linguistic theory. Saussure and Jakobson created much of the theoretical ground for both structuralism and semiotics. With the possible exception of Pierce (whose philosophical work focused on words as signs and symbols), the concerns of many early semioticians were also structuralist concerns. This may not be the case today, and Hawkes' argument may no longer apply. As the work of semioticians like Julia Kristeva demonstrates, semiotics survived when structuralism gave way to the transition from structuralist to poststructuralist theory. Semiotics was able to incorporate the '"stretching" [of] our concept of language' as it came to "include[ ] non-verbal areas' (Hawkes: 125). Kristeva sees this as an important feature of semiotic theory: 'What semiotics has discovered... is that the *law* governing, or if one prefers, the *major constraint* affecting any social practice lies in the fact that it signifies; i.e. that it is articulated *like* a language' (Kristeva, 1973; Cited, Hawkes: 125). This 'stretching' of language to include non-verbal phenomena has an analogue in the shift from the structuralist interest in texts to the poststructuralist concern with the 'intertext'. As we will see in the chapter on Joyce and poststructuralism, Jacques Derrida's idea that there is no outside to the text, that 'the outside [of the text] is the inside' articulates a similar view (Derrida, 1974: 44).

When semiotics focuses on the operations of language it concerns itself with the ways in which words and letters operate as *signs* which are the unity of a *signifier* and a *signified*. In his *Selected Writings* (4 vols., The Hague: Mouton, 1962) Jakobson explains that 'every message is made of signs; correspondingly, the science of signs termed *semiotic* deals with those general principles which underlie the structure of all signs'. He calls upon the classical view of the sign as consisting of 'an immediately perceptible *signans* and an inferable *signatum*' (vol. II: 698–9). As Hawkes points out, this is essentially the same 'distinction between signifier and signified recorded by Saussure: both elements function as aspects of the "indissoluble unity" of the sign, and the various relationships possible between them form the basis of semiotic structures' (Hawkes: 126). In his theoretical application of Saussure's theory to contemporary *Mythologies* (London: Cape, 1972) Roland Barthes describes the relationship between the signifier and signified as one of 'equivalence', rather than 'equality'. Hawkes explains that what 'we grasp in the relationship is not the sequential ordering whereby one term *leads to* the other, but the correlation which *unites* them. ...[T]his "structural relationship" between sound-image (signifier) and concept (signified) constitutes what Saussure calls the *linguistic* sign.' For Barthes, the relationship also exists in non-linguistic structures where the 'associative total' of the signifier and the signified is simply a 'sign' (Hawkes: 130–1).

Barthes demonstrates how the same object can function semiotically in different ways. In its relationship with the word 'rose' the flower known by that name functions as a signified of the linguistic signifier, 'rose'. When roses are given as a gift to a lover, the 'bunch of roses is the *signifier*' and the emotion (Barthes uses 'passion') expressed by the flowers is the *signified*. As Hawkes explains, the 'relation between the two (the "associative total") produces the *third* term, the bunch of roses as a sign. And, *as a sign*, it is important to understand that the bunch of roses is quite a different thing from the bunch of roses as a signifier: that is, as a horticultural entity.' The distinction between the flowers as a sign and as a signifier is a functional distinction between *emptiness* and *fullness*: as horticultural object which signifies, the 'bunch of roses is empty'. As a sign it is filled with signification by a 'combination of [the sender's] intent and the nature of society's conventional modes and channels'. These modes and channels 'offer a range of vehicles' for the expression of the message which the giver of the flowers wishes to send (Hawkes: 131). There is a wide range of vehicles, but these are subject to a system of social (and other) conventions which place a limit on the ways in which the vehicles can be used. Nevertheless the system for signifying is complex:

> I can make [a black pebble] signify in several ways, it is a mere signifier; but if I weigh it with a definite signified (a death sentence, for instance, in an anonymous vote), it will become a sign.
>
> (Barthes: 113)

In the last chapter we looked at how myth operates on the two levels of *langue* and *parole*. The complete version of a myth (and all of its variations) functions like the complete body of a language, and each articulation of the myth in a specific story can be compared with *parole*, or individual speech utterance. Barthes also distinguishes between two levels of signification, but in his semiotic analysis, myth is a *second-order* of signification which results from the *sign* in one signifying process becoming the signifier of a *second-order* of signification:

> Everything happens as if myth shifted the formal system of the first signification sideways. As this lateral shift is essential for the analysis of myth, I shall represent it in the following way, it being understood, of course, that the

spatialization of the pattern here is only a metaphor:

(Barthes: 115)

In Barthes' analysis myth constitutes an order of signification which is greater than verbal language (it can, for example, appear in pictures, rituals, and other signifying systems). It functions by turning a *full* sign into a new, *empty* signifier and initiating a new signifying relationship which allows the sign-become-signifier to exist in a new signifying relationship with another signified in order to create a full, mythic sign.

Hawkes refers to one of Barthes' 'best known' examples of this process which illustrates the movement from the first-order of signification to the second-order myth. Barthes analyses a picture from the cover of *Paris-Match* in which 'a young Negro in a French uniform is saluting, with his eyes uplifted, probably fixed on a fold of the tricolour'. This initial description of the picture includes recognisable signs such as 'negro', 'soldier', 'French', 'uniform', 'tricolour' (flag), salute, etc., and together these function on the first order of signification and produce what Barthes terms 'the *meaning* of the picture'. The second order of signification comes into play when these signs are read as signifiers of a particular ideology:

> France is a great Empire, that all her sons [it is worth noting the mother–son mythic pattern which Barthes does not discuss] without any colour discrimination, faithfully serve under her flag, and that there is no better answer to the detractors of an alleged colonialism than the zeal shown by this Negro in serving his so-called oppressors. I am therefore again faced with a greater semiological system: there is a signifier, itself already formed with a previous system (*a black soldier is giving the French salute*); there is a signified (it is here a purposeful mixture of Frenchness and militariness); finally, there is a presence of the signified through the signifier.
> (Barthes: 116)

At the level of the myth Barthes calls the third term (the *sign* on the first-order level) the *signification*, and he turns to the conventional terms of *form* and *concept* for the first (signifier) and second (signified) terms respectively. This would produce modifications in Barthes' diagram of the first- and second-level (myth) planes of signification (Fig. **3**).

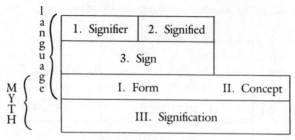

Figure 3

As Hawkes points out, the usefulness of this change in terminology becomes apparent when Barthes 'applies it to the process of signification which we traditionally term "denotation" and "connotation"'. The realm of connotative meaning is 'characteristic of the "literary" or "aesthetic" use of language' (Hawkes: 133). In *Elements of Semiology* (New York: Hill and Wang, 1980) Barthes explains how the shift from denotation to connotation entails the same sort of shift as that from the first-order signifying process to the level of myth:

> the first system is then the plane of *denotation* and the second system... the plane of *connotation*. We shall therefore say that a *connoted system is a system whose plan of expression... is itself constituted by a signifying system*: the common cases of connotation will of course consist of complex systems of which language forms the first system (this is, for instance, the case with literature).
>
> (89–90)

The reversal of the movement from the denotative system to the connotative system constitutes a *Metalanguage*. Barthes draws on Hjelmslev's *Essais Linguistiques* (Copenhagen: Nordisk Sprog-og Kulturforlag, 1959) in order to make the 'notion of metalanguage explicit': 'an *operation* is a *description* founded on the empirical principle, that is to say non-contradictory (coherent), exhaustive and simple, scientific semiotics, or metalanguage, is an operation, whereas connotative semiotics is not' (92). There are numerous signifying, or semiotic systems, and Barthes shows how such things as the fashion industry, cooking, and the design of automobiles operate as semiotic systems. Language, however, is 'the most "pure" organic semiotic system', because 'every aspect of it signifies' and 'it is produced solely by means of the body' (as opposed to systems which manufacture signs with the aid of technology). Semiotic systems which rely on technology use it as an "extension" of the body', and this extension, or '*medium*', can cause 'one organic factor to become dominant over the others (the telephone has this effect on the voice[;] silent film... on bodily gesture)'. The result of such domination has an impact upon the discourse, and the 'medium will begin to effect the message'. When the medium has an extreme impact upon the message the result is 'an *autonomous* semiotic system, with a 'life' – that is, with messages – of its own' (Hawkes: 135).

The question of how the theory of semiotics can assist in the study of writers like Joyce is one which Hawkes raises, and he suggests that the 'peculiar structural properties of writing' are a 'crucial' part of the answer because 'they form, semiotically, a large part of what any writing communicates':

> Writing... combines two kinds of sign. Language, which is normally *auditory* in mode, is made *visual* when... written down or... printed. ...To the auditory sign's commitment to *time* as its structuring agent is... added... the visual sign's commitment to *space*. ... [A] uditory 'temporal' signs tend to be ...*symbolic* [arbitrary] in character, where visual 'spatial' signs tend to be iconic [the signifier and signified are in some way similar]. It follows that, in writing both kinds of sign will be present.
>
> (136)

Using this distinction, Hawkes examines the 'two distinctive *genres* of language in its written form, poetry and prose' and suggests that both 'emit *iconic* messages about their nature through the visual means of typography over and above... the *symbolic* messages of their content'. The obvious example of this is poetry, which is '"set out" in a different form from that of a passage of prose: a novel "looks like" a novel, not like a text book' (136). Of course writers can choose to alter the nature of the iconic message transmitted by their writing, and Hawkes uses *Ulysses* to illustrate Joyce's choice in this matter.

Writers of prose who are primarily concerned with the content of their work will usually pay little or no attention to the iconic aspect of their work: 'the writer, say, of a detective novel, is normally concerned with content, and would find any iconic message... an interference'. In contrast to this, writers like Joyce might 'raise the iconic level of the total message so as to generate tension, irony, social comment etc.' This is illustrated by the following passage from *Ulysses*:

> Oyster eyes. Never mind. Be sorry after perhaps when it dawns on him. Get the pull over him that way.
> Thank you. How grand we are this morning.
>
> ### IN THE HEART OF THE HIBERNIAN METROPOLIS
>
> BEFORE NELSON'S PILLAR TRAMS SLOWED, SHUNTED, CHANGED trolley, started for Blackrock, Kingstown, and Dalkey, Clonskea, Rathgar and Terenure...

THE WEARER OF THE CROWN

Under the porch of the general post office shoeblacks called and polished
(*U*: 115–16; Cited, Hawkes: 137)

The first paragraph in this passage concludes the 'Hades' episode from the early edition of *Ulysses*. The subsequent lines are from the following episode, 'Aeolus'. Hawkes reads the iconic message of the first paragraph as 'this is a novel' and that of the 'Aeolus' section as 'this is a newspaper'. The iconic shift is thus appropriate to the shift in setting from the graveyard to the newspaper office.

A further iconic message could be read in the shift from the emboldened capitals of the 'headlines' to the regular type. The first of the two 'Aeolus' passages offers the movement of the trams as they leave the capital city of Dublin, moving from Nelson's pillar on the journey to suburban destinations. As the centre of economic and political power, Dublin (the '**HIBERNIAN METROPOLIS**') is signified by the iconic message 'this is the capital city'. The political power signified by 'NELSON'S PILLAR' (which is, itself, an *iconic sign* of England's colonial power and a geographical sign of the centre, or '**HEART**' of the city) is conveyed in the iconic capitals beneath the 'headline'. The pillar is a less powerful signifier than the city but still deserving of capitals as it is at the centre of the city and its transport system. A third iconic message is conveyed by the shift from the smaller capitals of 'NELSON'S PILLAR' to the regular type announcing the destinations of the trams. The shift occurs between the words which describe the trams' trolleys being moved from one electric wire to another: 'TRAMS changed trolley'. The iconic message here is 'this is a change from more powerful to less'. Presumably, the trolley is changed from the electric wire used for the journey into the city to that used on the outward trip. The *content* message of the trolley being moved from one electric wire to another supports (and is supported by) the *iconic* message transmitted by the change from capital to regular letters: 'the movement from the city to the suburbs is a movement from greater to lesser power'. A similar iconic message is given in the shift from '**THE WEARER OF THE CROWN**' to 'under the porch of the general post office shoeblacks called...'. This iconic message is simply 'a monarch' (**THE WEARER OF THE CROWN**) has greater power than a 'shoeblack'.

In drawing attention to its own *iconic* messages *Ulysses* functions in an 'auto-referential' mode, and semiotics is particularly useful for engaging with this aspect of Joyce's writing. Contemporary criticism in general, and semiotics and poststructuralism in particular, links literature's aesthetic qualities with its auto-referentiality. Jakobson notes this link: 'introversive semiosis, a message which signifies itself, is indissolubly linked with the aesthetic function of sign systems' (Cited, Hawkes: 140). In transmitting a message while simultaneously signifying itself, an aesthetic sign system (any of the 'arts') creates a plurality, or ambiguity. Hawkes thus sees 'Art... as a way of connecting "messages" together, in order to produce "texts" in which the "rule-breaking" roles of ambiguity and self-reference are fostered and "organized".' In *A Theory of Semiotics* (Bloomington: Indiana UP, 1979), Umberto Eco uses Jakobson's six subdividing categories for the function of language to clarify the 'ambiguous and self-focusing text':

> a message can possess either one or a combination of the following func-
> tions: a) referential; b) emotive; c) imperative; d) phatic; e) metalinguistic;
> f) poetic. The message assumes a poetic function (though in this context
> it is preferable to call it an 'aesthetic' one, granted that we are dealing with
> every kind of art) when it is *ambiguous* and *self-focusing*.
>
> (262)

Ambiguity and auto-referentiality are thus characterising features of art and literature. As we will see in looking at semiotic investigations of Joyce, his writing becomes increasingly more ambiguous and self-referential as it develops from his earlier to later work. Because of this, semioticians like Eco and Julia Kristeva have used Joyce's last two texts as models of the semiotic process.

Robert Scholes

Robert Scholes has used semiotic theory as well as structuralism to investigate Joyce's work. He has drawn on the theories of several major contributors to semiotics in order to produce an in-depth study of 'Eveline', which offers considerable insights into the short story and the value of semiotic theory. The study first appeared as 'Semiotic Approaches to a Fictional Text: Joyce's "Eveline"' (*JJQ*, 16, 1–2, 1978–79) and was later reprinted as a part of Scholes' *Semiotics and Interpretation* (New Haven: Yale UP, 1982) (the edition referred to below). Scholes combines the approaches of Todorov, Genette and Barthes into 'a single methodology', or 'meta-method'. His thesis is that:

> all three... methods... have wider applications, that they complement one
> another in addressing the fictional text from different angles, and further,
> that they even suggest a sequence of use, each of them presenting itself
> as a segment in a meta-method in which they function as units of a
> syntagmatic process, units whose order should always be the same.
>
> (87)

Scholes starts his investigations with the two main features of Todorov's 'grammar', a method of analysis based 'on the hundred tales of Boccaccio's *Decameron*'. The two features are a reduction of the fictional text 'to plot structures that can be represented by simple symbolic logic' and an encoding of the 'semantic features of [Todorov's] symbolic notation so that they reveal the principal thematic concerns of the action in any story'. Before attempting to show the value of this method, Scholes warns that it has 'two large faults': first, the summary must be intuitive, governed by no explicit system; and second, the resulting notation has a spurious exactitude, based upon its resemblance to the summary rather than to the fiction itself. He thus suggests using Todorov's method only as an 'heuristic tool' for establishing the groundwork of his meta-method (88).

Using Todorov, Scholes defines a story as a 'certain kind of sequence of propositions'. These propositions 'are of two kinds: attributions and actions', and the 'most fundamental fictional sequence is attribution, action, attribution', or the traditional pattern of beginning, middle and end. Using grammatical characters and equating characters with nouns, attributes with adjectives, and actions with verbs, Scholes offers the following summary of a simple story:

$$X - A + (XA) \ optX \rightarrow Xa \rightarrow XA$$

where
$X = Boy$
$A = love$, to be loved by someone
$a = to$ seek love, to woo
$optX = Boy \ (X)$ wishes (opt)
$- = negation$ of attribute: $-A$ is to lack love, to be unloved.

(88)

The story depicted is 'Boy lacks love plus Boy wants to be loved which yields Boy seeks love which yields Boy is loved.' Scholes emphasises the importance of transformation of the propositions: 'we know this is a story because it is a sequence of propositions involving the same subject, in which the last proposition is a transformation of the first. ...Stories are about the successful or unsuccessful transformations of attributes' (89).

A further limitation of this reductive method is that the 'chain of symbols' represent 'just one aspect' of a story's grammar and do not include the lexical or semantic aspect. The 'complex of qualities associated with the characters (what Barthes calls the connotative code)' must be reduced 'to a few summary features that are activated by the story itself'. Nevertheless, Scholes offers the following version of 'Eveline':

$$
\begin{array}{ccccc}
1 & 2 & 3 & 4 & 5 \\
\end{array}
$$
$$XA + XB \rightarrow X - C + YaX + (X - A + X - B \rightarrow XC) \ predX \rightarrow$$
$$
\begin{array}{cccc}
\quad 6 & 7 & 8 & 9 \\
\end{array}
$$
$$(XbY)predX + XA! \rightarrow XnotbY \rightarrow (XB = X - C) \ ! \ imp$$

X	Eveline
Y	Frank
A	a Dubliner
B	celibate
C	Happy – respected, secure
a	to offer elopement
b	to accept elopement
–	negative of attribute
not	negative of verb
pred	predicts or expects
imp	is implied by discourse

(90)

Scholes offers a prose summary in which he reads the annotation before isolating the 'three attributive propositions which constitute the "situation" of "Eveline".' He sees these propositions repeated 'with emphasis at or near the close' of the story. This repetition is 'more a matter of implication than of statement': the 'attributes remain unchanged' and an 'essentially unhappy situation finally persists, even intensifies'. From this Scholes extracts what he terms a 'rule of *Dubliners*': 'the grammar of these stories tends towards the persistence of unpleasant conditions – from bad to worse'. A small number of the *Dubliners* stories 'show a change from better to worse', but only 'Two Gallants' 'shows any improvement of an opening situation' as the 'impecunious Lenehan is... likely to benefit by sponging off his friend Corley'. Even in this story, however, the 'happy ending' covers a 'portrait of Lenehan as an aging sponger... trapped in his Dublinesque existence' (91).

Scholes proceeds from this use of Todorov's grammar to his adaptation of the method for narrative analysis developed by Gérard Genette in *Narrative Discourse* (Ithaca: Cornell UP, 1980). Like that of Todorov, Genette's method is more structuralist than semiotic. Scholes uses both methods to establish the basic groundwork of his study before completing his semiotic approach with methods of analysis developed by Roland Barthes. Genette's approach can be seen as a more complex version of the sort of grammar developed by Todorov, and it analyses fictional narrative with terminology 'from the traditional grammar of the verb': narrative structure is seen in terms of its 'tense, mood, and voice'. Genette's method begins by dividing narrative into the following three fundamental aspects which allow us to 'recognise' the texts as 'fictional':

1) 'Every fictional text' is conveyed in a '*récit* or narrative discourse' which presents the 'fictional events that can be distinguished from the text itself'.

2) Each text conveys a 'story... which exists in a different spatio-temporal situation from the text itself, and from its own production or our reading of it'.

3) '[E]very narrative text also conveys explicitly or implicitly some circumstances of narrating, some explanation for its own existence as a text, both in relation to the events narrated and to some *narratee* or audience' (this aspect of the text concerns the 'auto-referential' signification which semiotics identifies as a characteristic feature of literature).

(Cited, Scholes: 92)

In addition to these three categories, Genette establishes 'three major areas' in the temporal organisation of fictional texts: 'order, duration, and frequency'. Order concerns the 'arrangement of events expressed as a relationship between story and text' and distinguishes between 'the chronology of the story' and the ways in which 'the discourse arranges this chronology' and conveys it to the reader. Duration concerns the ratio between the time of the story (the 'hours, days, and years of story time') and the space (the 'words and pages of the printed text') used in conveying the story. It is the 'relationship between the temporal extension of events in the story and the attention devoted to them by the discourse'. Frequency, or the 'third temporal aspect', 'involves the ways in which events may be repeated either in the story itself' as the repetition of a fictional event, or 'in the discourse', when the same event is 'described more than once' (Scholes: 93).

Using these categories, Scholes concentrates on 'fairly large and readily distinguishable blocks of time' in 'Eveline' and delineates the following 'temporal movement' by 'numbering [the] time blocks from 1 to 6':

A. Base time (beginning, into second paragraph) 5
B. Childhood (mid second par.) 1
C. Base time (end second par. and beginning of third) 5
D. (A complex section to scrutinize more closely later on)
E. Recent past (Miss Gavan and the Stores) 4
F. Future ('her new home'...) 6
G. Recent past (Saturday night, etc.) 4
H. Future ('She was about'...) 6
I. Recent past (Eveline's relationship with Frank) 4
J. Earlier past (Frank's history) 2
K. Base time (... the 'evening deepened') 5
L. Earlier time (Eveline's mother's illness and death) 3
M. Base time mixed with the future (end of first section) 5/6
N. Ellipsis in base time 5
O. Base time (whole second section, with only a hint of future) 5

(93–4)

These 'fifteen distinct sections' cover 'six separate periods' in Eveline's life, but Joyce's writing contains both the sections and periods in the 'base time of... two scenes'. All of them 'are... presented... as aspects of Eveline's thoughts in a base time which is very close to "present" tense even though narrated in a conventional past'. Scholes delays his discussion of the fourth (D.) temporal unit listed above because of its complicated nature. In order to follow the complex temporal movement in the passage, he cites it in its entirety:

> She looked [base time] round the room, reviewing [base time] all its familiar objects, which she had dusted [past, iterative] once a week for so many years, wondering [past, iterative] where on earth all the dust came from. Perhaps she would never see again [future, conditional, negative] those familiar objects from which she had never dreamed [past, negative, subordinated within future] of being divided [future, within past negative, within future].
>
> (94)

From his analysis Scholes concludes that this section of 'Eveline' is structured around a 'rapid oscillation between the past seen as iterative... and a future dimly perceived as the absence of... familiar surroundings'. Eveline is 'trying to "weigh each side of the question".' As a result, her thoughts shift back and forth from a frightening 'future as absence ("never see again")' to an equally frightening past that includes her poor health (her 'palpitations'), her mother's illness and death, and her father's threats. Eveline's thoughts of the future 'inevitably lead[ ] her back' to this past, and she remains trapped, and ultimately paralysed, within this cycle (94–5).

In moving on to Genette's theory of textual duration (as opposed to the text's temporal order), Scholes adopts Genette's 'four basic speeds of narration'. These are

1. The ellipsis – infinitely rapid
2. The summary – relatively rapid
3. The scene – relatively slow
4. The descriptive pause – zero degree of progress

(96)

Joyce's story offers all of these 'varieties of duration':

> an ellipsis between the two sections of the narrative; a summary of Eveline's and Frank's past lives; the dramatic scene at the Quay; and... some description, though so little as to make virtually no pause in the story.
>
> (96)

Scholes analyses Joyce's use of these techniques in some detail:

> [H]e manages things so that all description and summarizing are presented as aspects of Eveline's thought... function[ing] as drama or scene. The narrative segments set in base time... constitute a scene of extended duration, in which a relatively short time in the story occupies a long part of the text. ...[T]he first scene... gives us a sense of the base time passing very slowly.

Then the second scene, after the ellipsis, by stretching time out even more, emphasizes the passing of seconds, as the inexorable process of the ship's departure... brings the future and the present to a point of congruity, whereupon Eveline, no longer able to weigh past against future, is driven out of human time altogether into the frozen past of animal existence.

(96)

For the third and final part of his 'meta-method' Scholes turns to Roland Barthes' *S/Z* (New York: Hill and Wang, 1974). He considers this to be the 'fullest, richest, and most successful application of semiotic methods to the analysis of a single fictional text that we have' (Scholes: 153). In *S/Z* Barthes analyses Balzac's 'Sarrasine' and identifies five distinct codes by which small narrative units like phrases and sentences (Barthes terms them 'lexias') signify. These codes and some of their characteristics are listed below along with some of the ways in which Scholes sees them operating in 'Eveline':

1. The Proairetic Code

The 'code of actions'. Barthes calls this the 'main armature of the readerly text'. He 'sees all actions as codable, from the most trivial... to a romantic adventure. ...We recognize actions because we are able to name them. ...[W]e expect actions begun to be completed; thus the principal action becomes the main armature of... a text' (Scholes: 99–100). In 'Eveline' the proairetic code functions within all of the actions from the 'relatively trivial "She sat", completed four pages later by "She stood up", to the more consequential action of her leaving Dublin for good, which of course never occurs' (101).

2. The Hermeneutic Code

This code of 'enigmas', or 'puzzles' involves the 'reader's desire for "truth", for the answers to questions raised by the text'. This code and the proairetic are both a 'principal structuring agent of traditional narrative'. The hermeneutic code creates a 'narrative suspense' that involves the 'reader's desire to complete, to finish the text'. This is a very complex code and Barthes identifies 'ten phases of hermeneutic coding', and 'eight different ways' of maintaining a riddle once it has been established' (100). Scholes does not think that Joyce uses this code very much in 'Eveline'. Although there are engimatic elements like the cause of the mother's death and Frank's character and background, the greatest puzzle, the 'reason for Eveline's refusal, forces us back out of the text... to the other *Dubliners* stories to find solutions that will never have the assurance of discursive "truth"' (101–2).

3. Cultural Codes

These codes are numerous and 'constitute the text's references to things already "known" and codified by a culture' (100). In 'Eveline', cultural coding is 'more in the minds of the characters' than in any 'narrative voice' or the 'discourse itself'. Scholes illustrates this with the contrasting ways in which Eveline and her father codify Frank: Eveline 'sees him as codified by romantic fiction', as 'very kind, manly, open-hearted'; her father views him 'under a code of cynical parental wisdom' which leads him to claim to "know these sailor chaps"'. The discourse of the story 'ratifies neither view' and 'avoids the cultural codes of Dublin which so dominate the characters' lives'. The 'powerful... code of Irish Catholicism... would classify Eveline's action as sin' (102).

4. Connotative Codes

There are many of these codes. The reader recognises 'clusters' constituting a '"common nucleus" of connotations' which enable him or her to locate particular themes and 'thematize' the text (102). In Joyce's story (and the rest of *Dubliners*) the 'dominant connotative code is paralysis'. This is connoted by things like 'Eveline's motionless-ness. ... the dreary, monotonous sentence structure – subject, verb, predicate, over and over again. ... [a]nd... such details as the promise made to Blessed Margaret Mary Alacoque, who was paralyzed until she vowed to dedicate herself to a religious life'. An ironic 'level of connotation' is produced by Alacoque's life as a commentary on Eveline's life: 'Through its ironic combination of signs, the discourse paraleptically leads us to a view of Eveline's situation beyond her own perception of it'. Although Eveline might see herself as 'weighing evidence. ... the discourse ironically indicates that she has no choice. She is already inscribed as a Dubliner in Joyce's code, and a Dubliner never decides, never escapes' (102).

5. Symbolic Code

This is the 'aspect of fictional coding that is most specifically... post-structuralist... in Barthes's presentation'. The code relies on a system of opposition like that delineated by the structuralist critics whose work was examined in the first chapter. The opposition can work on several levels: 'at the level of sounds becoming phonemes in the production of speech;... at the level of psychosexual opposition...; or at the level of primitive cultural separation of the world into opposing forces or values that may be coded mythologically' (100–1). Scholes sees the primary opposition of *Dubliners* not as 'male versus female but [as] sexed versus unsexed'. Moreover, in 'Eveline' 'Frank is set in opposition to the father as a rival for Eveline, who is filling her mother's role in the household'. Scholes outlines a complex symbolic system of opposition in which the following opposed symbols and values are assigned to Eveline and Frank,

Eveline:	dust	enslaved	the known	the past	fruitless
Frank:	water	freedom	the unknown	the future	potency

In the binary oppositional relationship with her father, Eveline is 'sterile, impotent, celibate, a kind of nun, [and] a Dubliner'. Scholes sees this symbolic opposition emerging 'most powerfully in [the] single sentence' 'when Eveline sees "the black mass of the boat, lying in beside the quay"'. The phrase 'black mass' is an 'innocent descriptive phrase which also connotes the sacrilegious power of the act Eveline is contemplating':

> To board that boat, leave the land and enter upon the sea, would be to leave what is known, safe, already coded. It would be above all to flout the teach-ings of the church, to sin. The virgin, the nun, a celibate safely within the cultural codification of ritual is opposed to the defiled woman upon whose belly the black mass is blasphemously consummated. ...In that other harmless descriptive phrase, "lying in" another terror is connoted. To "lie in" is to be delivered of child, to be fruitful. ...It is to accept life – and the danger of death.
>
> (102–3)

Scholes concludes his semiotic analysis of 'Eveline' by looking at Joyce's last depiction of his character as one in which she is a 'creature in a state of symbolic deprivation'. In the scene besides the quay, Eveline has been transformed into a 'creature who has lost' the 'fundamental processes of cognition and articulation', 'not only at the level of speech and language but even the more fundamental semiotic functions of gesture and facial signals'. We see Eveline 'set her white face to [Frank], passive, like a helpless animal. Her eyes gave him no sign of love or farewell or recogni-tion' (*D*: 41). For Scholes, Eveline has lost a basic human ability which is also a semiotic ability: she is 'capable of giving "no sign"' (103–4).

Umberto Eco

Umberto Eco is something of a polymath. He is a medieval scholar, a semiotician, and a popular novelist. Joyce seems to have had an impact in all areas of Eco's work. Eco explains his interest in Joyce in *The Aesthetics of Chaosmos: The Middle Ages of James Joyce* (Tulsa: Tulsa UP, 1982) where he reminds us that Joyce was 'also an Italian author'. Eco began his 'scholarly career studying medieval aesthetics'. 'Immediately after... [he] studied the language of contemporary avant-gardes' and 'the study of Joyce was first published as part of [his] book *Opera Aperta*'

(Milano: Bompiani, 1962). The first chapter of this book, which offers a condensed model of Eco's semiotic theory, appears as the *Introduction* to *The Role of the Reader* (Bloomington: Indiana UP, 1979), the book in which Eco's semiotic study of *Finnegans Wake* also appears. Eco is interested in the 'permanence of a medieval model' (Eco, 1982: vii) in both Joyce's early and later work, and he sees the *Wake*, in particular, offering itself as a model of language, as 'an excellent model of a Global Semantic System' (Eco, 1979: 68). Even Eco's fiction attests to his interest in Joyce. In *Foucualt's Pendulum* (London: Secker and Warburg, 1989), the character Belbo writes a fictional account of his life as the author of Shakespeare's works. He is incarcerated in the Tower of London along with a character called Soapes who writes the 'incomprehensible message: "riverrun, past Eve and Adam's..."' (Eco, 1989: 416).

Eco's *A Theory of Semiotics* is one of the major textbooks on semiotic theory, offering what Hawkes terms a 'rather daunting survey' of the development of semiotic theory as well as Eco's own contributions to it (Hawkes: 124). It is in *The Role of the Reader*, however, that Eco offers his major contribution to the semiotic study of Joyce's work. *The Aesthetics of Chaosmos* offers an important look into Joyce's use of medieval thought, but in terms of semiotics it is really only a starting point which, to use Ellen Esrock's words, 'foreshadowed issues that would be more fully developed within the framework of contemporary semiotics' (Eco, 1982: v).

In the *Introduction* to *The Role of the Reader*, Eco concentrates on the role that readers play in interpreting texts which can be 'cooperatively generated by the *addressee*'. The sort of text Eco has in mind is an 'open' text, but this text cannot be 'described as a communicative strategy' if the 'role of its addressee... has not been envisaged at the moment of its generation *qua* text'. For the text to operate, the reader's responses to it must be generated by the text itself: the interpretation of the text must be '*foreseen*' as a 'part of [the text's] generative process'. The fundamental categories indispensable to an understanding of the communication process between the 'open' text and its reader (fundamental, in fact, to 'the understanding of every act of communication') are those used by Jakobson: 'sender, addressee and context'. Eco's postulation of the reader's cooperation in the interpretive process 'does not mean [the pollution of] the structural analysis with extratextual elements' but the reader's role as an 'active principal of interpretation is a part of the picture of the generative process of the text' (3–4).

In *A Theory of Semiotics* the 'standard communication model proposed by information theorists (Sender, Message, Addressee – in which the message is decoded on the basis of a Code shared by both the virtual poles of the chain) does not describe the actual functioning of communicative intercourses'. Pointing out that a 'message' is also 'usually a *text*', or a 'network of different messages depending on different codes and working at different levels of signification', Eco suggests that the 'usual communi-cation model should be rewritten', albeit 'to a still extremely simplified extent' (Fig. 4).

While this model is 'extremely simplified', it nevertheless allows for the message's function as encoded text, 'channel' (means of communication, medium), 'expression', and 'content' to be recognised. It also indicates the important role of codes and subcodes in both the sender's, or writer's, encoding, and the receiver's, or reader's, decoding, of the message, and of the functions of context and circumstance in the communications process. It is also worth noting that the domain of the more traditional approaches to interpretation such as historical and biographical criticism belong to the parallel 'philological reconstruction' and are not an essential part of the interpretive/communicative process as that process is analysed from a semiotic perspective.

In creating the text, the author must make the same assumptions made by anyone who wishes to communicate a message: 'that the ensemble of codes he relies upon is the same shared by the possible reader'. The writer must 'foresee a model of the possible reader' or 'model reader' who has much in common with the 'ideal' reader described by the structuralist writers considered in Chapter One. This reader should 'supposedly [be] able to deal interpretively with the expressions in the same way as the author deals generatively with them'. The model reader is different for closed and open texts, and Eco distinguishes between authors and their texts on the basis of a consideration of the codes that the reader might use in intepreting the text: 'In the process of communication, a text is fre-quently interpreted against the background of codes different from those intended by the author.' Authors who 'do not take into account such a possibility', 'have in mind an average addressee referred to a given social context'. Authors who produce texts 'that obsessively aim at arousing a precise response' from a 'more or less precise empirical reader' paradoxi-

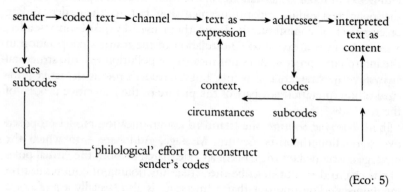

(Eco: 5)

Figure 4

cally produce a 'closed' text. Eco offers examples of 'precise empirical reader[s]': 'children, soap-opera addicts, doctors, law-abiding citizens, swingers, Presbyterians, farmers, middle-class women, scuba divers, effete snobs, or any other imaginable sociopyschological category'. The writer striving to hold his text open to such a precise audience of empirical readers will produce a text 'open to any "aberrant" decoding'. Eco labels such 'immoderately "open" texts' as '*closed* text[s]' (7–8).

Unlike their closed counterparts, open texts cannot 'be read in various ways' according to the codes and interpretive skills of their readers. Open texts 'work at their peak revolutions per minute only when each interpretation is reechoed by the other and vice versa'. Eco's model for the author of open texts is Joyce, and he asks us to consider the 'interplay of possible interpretations foreseen by Joyce apropos of the trial of Shaun'. Open texts generate 'productively ambiguous messages' which 'leave' the reader 'free to reconsider the whole of [his or her] semantic universe', but simultaneously bind the reader 'to the indecomposable unity of... alternative interpretations'. In *Finnegans Wake* Joyce describes the perfect reader of his text as 'that ideal reader suffering from an ideal insomnia' (120. 13–14), and Eco cites this as an example of the author 'foresee[ing]' the model reader as one who is 'able to master different codes and eager to deal with the text as with a maze of many issues'. The reader cannot use the text as he or she desires, however, 'only as the text wants [the reader] to use it'. What finally matters is 'not the various issues [raised by the text] in themselves, but the maze-like structure of the text' (9).

Eco also uses *Ulysses* to illustrate his distinction between the reader of closed texts and the model reader for open texts. 'When reading a Fleming novel or a Superman comic strip', he says, 'one can at most guess what kind of reader their authors had in mind, not which requirements a "good" reader should meet.' In reading Joyce's text, however, 'one can extrapolate the profile of a "good *Ulysses* reader" from the text itself, because the pragmatic process of interpretation is not an empirical accident independent of the text *qua* text, but... a structural element of its generative process' (9). Eco next proceeds to outline the various strategies, textual levels and discursive structures which the reader must take into consideration during the reading process. As there is insufficient space to summarise all of this material, some of the major points from Eco's concluding summary will have to suffice:

1. Eco emphasises the importance of the aesthetic function of a text in determining its semiotic status as a closed or open text. There is an 'aesthetic dialectic[ ] between [the] openness and closedness of texts', and this 'depends on the basic structure of the process of text interpretation in general'.
2. The structure of the process for textual interpretation depends on

codes and subcodes which 'constitut[e] the world of the encyclopedia'. Although there is a *structure* to the process, the process is not *structural* but *semiotic*. It is 'ruled by a constitutive mechanism of unlimited semiosis'; it is 'contradictory in its very format'; and the 'semantic space [created in, and by, the structure of the process] can be reduced only through the cooperative activity performed by the reader in actualizing a given text'.

3. Interpretive freedom is found for the reader '(i) in deciding how to activate one or another of the textual levels and (ii) in choosing which codes to apply'.

4. In much the same way that writers like Jakobson find a relationship between the aesthetic and auto-referential texts, Eco finds a link between aesthetic and open texts: 'certain aesthetic texts... give the impression of being particularly open'. He would seem to find openness as a direct correlative of aesthetics: 'in a "well-made" literary work... there is no openness at a given level which is not sustained and improved by analogous operations at all other levels'.

5. What Roland Barthes terms '*jouissance*' in *The Pleasure of the Text* (New York: Hill and Wang, 1975) is integral to Eco's definition of the open text. Barthes uses the term to signify the play of the text which provides 'bliss' and 'pleasure', but as Richard Howard points out, the term also connotes sexual climax, or 'coming' (Barthes: v–vi). Eco says that those texts which 'are able to produce the "jouissance" of the unexhausted virtuality of their expressive plane succeed in this effect just because they have been planned to invite their Model Readers to reproduce their own processes of deconstruction by a plurality of free interpretive choices'.

6. The function of semiotic theory is to 'offer[ ] the proper categories to explain' the sort of experience defined in 5.

'The Semantics of Metaphor'

'The Semantics of Metaphor' is the second chapter of *The Role of the Reader*. Eco's semiotic analysis has a purpose which is at least twofold: i) to show how the puns in *Finnegans Wake* depend on a greater cultural code which enabled Joyce to produce the puns which dominate so much of the text and, ii) to demonstrate a semiotic process which the reader can follow in order to decode Joyce's puns and participate in the role of a model reader in the *Wake*'s textually generative process. A fundamental proposition about the nature of codes governs much of the direction for Eco's analysis: 'If a code allowed us only to generate semiotic judgments, all linguistic systems would serve to enunciate exclusively that which has already been determined by the system's conventions.' However, a code enables us to do much more than 'generate semiotic judgments'. It also 'allows us to enunciate events that the code did not anticipate as well as *metasemiotic* judgments that call into question the legitimacy of the code itself'. This raises a serious question: How can a code 'which in principle ought to have structured the speaking subject's entire cultural system... generate both factual messages which refer to original experiences and... messages which place in doubt the very structure of the code itself?' The answer to this lies, in part, in the 'arbitrary' 'nature of the code'. In enabling its user to refer to 'predictable cultural entities' the code, because of its arbitrary nature 'also allows [its user] to assign new semiotic marks' to these cultural entities (Eco: 67–8). This is not the complete answer to the question, however, and Eco's analysis of the *Wake* provides more information to answer the question by dealing with 'problems of interaction between metaphoric mechanisms and metonymic mechanisms' (68).

As we have already seen, Eco finds Joyce's text of value in its presentation of itself as, among other things, 'an excellent model of a Global Semantic System'. This is because it 'posits itself, quite explicitly, as the Ersatz of the historical universe of language'. Furthermore, it is of particular interest in a semiotic investigation of semantics because it stages a 'methodological exigency of the sort found in a study of general semantics proposing to illuminate the ways in which language can generate metaphors' (68). Eco's primary interest is in the 'semantic aspect of metaphor'; not only in 'poetic metaphor but... metaphor in general' (69). Through its relations with metonymy, metaphor would appear to possess the same ambivalent powers as the code which enables the reader either to refer back to cultural entities or to 'assign new semiotic marks to them':

> the mechanism of metaphor, reduced to that of metonymy, relies on the existence... of partial semantic fields that permit two types of metonymic relation: (i) the *codified* metonymic relation, inferable from the very structure of the semantic field; (ii) the *codifying* metonymic relation, born when the structure of a semantic field is culturally experienced as deficient and reorganizes itself in order to produce another structure. Relations of type (i) imply *semiotic* judgments, whereas relations of type (ii) imply *factual judgments*.
>
> (68)

Finnegans Wake is also of value because of the metaphors which it produces: 'as a literary work it produces sufficiently violent metaphors without interruption or reservation... in proposing itself as a model of language... it focuses our attention specifically on semantic values' (69–70).

Eco looks at a name which occurs in 111.3 of the *Wake*. In this section 'Shaun, in the form of Yawn, undergoes the trial in... which the Four old Men bombard him with questions.' The passage which interests Eco is

'Now, fix on the little fellow in my eye, Minucius Mandrake, and follow my little psychosinology, poor armer in slingslang' (486. 12–14). Eco hypothesises that the 'Mandrake' in the passage is Mandrake the Magician, the 'famous character of Lee Falk and Phil Davis'. He summarises Mandrake's abilities as an illusionist and magician, referring to him as a 'master of diabolic tricks... in short... a "devil's advocate"'. This allows Eco to link the character with the historical 'advocate', Minucius Felix, the 'apologist father, whose historic function was to convince the Gentiles of the truth of the Christian faith'. 'From this point on', Eco says, 'the relation between the two characters, in the interior of the Joycean context, becomes crystal clear' (70).

In the passage where this name occurs, there is a central struggle between the 'ancient Irish church and the Catholic church'. Using the form of a pun the old men ask Shaun if he is Catholic, or a 'roman cawthrick' (486. 02). Eco points out that 'caw' is a crow's cry, and that Joyce could have learned of 'crow' (*cornacchia*), as the Italian nickname for a priest, in Trieste. The phoneme 'thrick' is a deformation ('in order to echo one of the phonemes of "catholic"') of 'trick'. This establishes a semantic link between Minucius Mandrake and Shaun. That 'Mandrake (alias Shaun) is a *trickster* is repeated several times in the context; for example, we find /Mr. Trickpat/' (71). Eco offers the following analysis of Shaun as a '*trickster*':

> When he is called /Minucius Mandrake/... he... must submit to a typical Dantean *contrapasso*. As an advocate he must undergo a trial; as a hypnotist he is asked to fix his eyes on his interrogator ['Now, fix on the little fellow in my eye']. In this manner his art is neutralized and turned back against itself. The magical gesticulation... too, is turned against itself, and the following gesticulation is ascribed to him: 'Again I am deliciated by the picaresqueness of your irmages' – where the root /arm/ (the arm that makes the gesture) is inserted in the key word /image/, which is found at the base of all illusion.
>
> (71)

Eco believes it 'reasonable to consider' this character, 'whether Minucius or Mandrake, as a metaphoric substitution in the place of something else ... the series of attributes and faults proper to Shain'.

In order to 'verify the credibility' of his interpretation and 'the mechanism of [the] substitution', Eco analyses how the idea of linking Mandrake with Minucius might have come about. 'Mandrake' does not occur in the first draft of this passage, which 'dates from 1924'. The reason for this is 'simple enough', Eco says, as 'the comic strip character' did not appear until 1934, and Joyce revised his passage 'between 1936 and 1939'. Joyce's use of Mandrake as a 'metaphoric "vehicle"' is therefore 'plausible'. The 'key' which allows Eco to find the answer for the linking of Mandrake and Minucius, thereby 'reinforc[ing]' his 'original hypothesis' is another cartoon character, Pat Sullivan's cat, Felix. The metonymic 'mechanism subjacent to the metaphoric substitution' of Mandrake and Minucius is as follows:

> Minucius refers by contiguity to Felix, Felix refers by contiguity (belonging to the same universe of comic strips) to Mandrake. Once the middle term has fallen, there remains a coupling that does not seem justified by any contiguity and thus appears to be metaphoric.
>
> (72)

What this analysis reveals is only 'how the metaphor came about' and 'not why it functions'. It is possible for the reader to comprehend the link between the two terms without knowing of the 'existence of a third term'. 'However', Eco states, 'it could be said that [the reader] depends upon an extremely long series of third terms that exist in the general context of the book.' These 'third terms' include '*trickster*, arm, image, and so on'. Each of the metaphors that Joyce's text produces should be 'comprehensible because the entire book, read in different directions, actually furnishes the metonymic chains that justify it'. In order to 'test this hypothesis' on what he calls the 'atomic element' of the text, Eco investigates several examples of the pun as a 'particular form of metaphor founded on subjacent chains of metonymies' (72).

Joyce's use of the pun 'constitutes a forced contiguity between two or more words'. Eco points to the example of 'Sanglorians' (4. 07). The terms forced into contiguity are *sang*, *glorians* and *riant*. The contiguity is one 'of reciprocal elisions' which results in 'an ambiguous deformation', 'free[ing] a series of possible readings' and 'interpretations'. The term operates as a 'metaphorical vehicle of different tenors', and the words, or 'lexemes (or lexematic fragments)... acquire a kind of natural kinship and often become mutually substitutable'. In the case of the pun, however, 'the metaphoric substitution assumes a particular type of status' in which 'vehicles coexist with tenors'. Eco's example is 'Jungfraud Messonge' [*sic*], which appears as part of Joyce's 'Jungfraud's Messongebook' (460. 20–21). He 'reads' the lexemes as '"Jung" plus "Freud" plus "young" plus "fraud" plus "Jungfrau"; message plus *songe* plus *mensonge*'. Each of the lexematic terms is 'at the same time vehicle and tenor, while the entire pun is a multiple metaphor'. Eco proposes a distinction between 'two types of puns' based on the nature of their contiguity:

> *contiguity by resemblance of signifiers*: for example, 'nightiness' contains 'mightiness' by phonetic analogy ('m/n'); 'slipping' contains, for the same reasons, 'sleep' and 'slip';
> *contiguity by resemblance of signifieds*: 'scherzarade', for the playful analogies between '*scherzo*' and 'charade' (sememes in which 'game' would be the

archisememe); but it is also true that the origin could lie in the simple phonetic similarity between /cha/ and /za/. One could then ask if the allusion
to 'Scheerazade' is born first from the phonetic similarity or from the
semantic similarity (the tale of Scheherazade as game and enigma and so on).

(73)

Puns achieve their force and the 'inventive metaphor' is successful
because of their seeming originality: 'prior to it no one had grasped the
resemblance'. Eco suggests that before Joyce produced the pun 'Jungfraud', there was 'no reason to suspect a relationship between Freud,
pyschoanalysis, fraud, lie, and lapsus (*linguae or calami*)'. Once the
'contiguity is realized', however, the 'resemblance becomes necessary'.
Finnegans Wake is the 'proof' that it is 'enough to find the means of rendering two terms phonetically contiguous for the resemblance to impose
itself'. Eco sees his investigation of the *Wake* as both 'useful and derisive'.
A reading of Joyce's text can show us better than anything else that 'even
when semantic kinship seems to precede the coercion to exist in the
pun... a network of subjacent contiguities makes necessary the resemblance which was presumed to be spontaneous'. Exploring the *Wake* as
a 'contracted model of the global semantic field' is derisive because 'everything being given in the text already, it is difficult to discover the "before"
and the "after"' (74). In other words, Joyce makes it very difficult for us
to decide if he created a particular pun or metaphor because he perceived
an already existing relationship between its terms or if his creation produced a new relationship which looked as if it should have previously
existed.

Having traced two terms found inside the *Wake* back to their origins,
Eco then takes the lexeme '/Neanderthal/', which appears in the text only
in a modified form, and attempts to discover why Joyce modified it. This
is a sort of reverse process to the one he followed with 'Minucius Mandrake' and 'Jungfraud messonge'. The fact that we 'can conceive of two
possible courses', Eco says, 'indicates that the two moments coincide: it
was possible to invent the pun because it is possible to read it; language,
as a cultural base, should be able to allow both operations'. Using Peirce's
theory of language as 'the place of unlimited semiosis... where each term
is explained by other terms', Eco explains that the 'other terms' constitute an 'infinite chain of interpretants' and that any one particular term
is 'potentially explainable by all the others'. This also implies the notion
of an arbitrary code, which, as we have already seen, produces the signs
with which the operations of the code can be explained. Eco's experiment
with /Neanderthal/ has 'two senses: first, to see if, from a point outside
Joyce's linguistic universe, we can enter into the universe; then departing
from a point internal to that universe, to see whether or not we can con-
nect, through multiple and continuous pathways, as in a garden where
the paths fork, all the other points' (74).

Eco starts with /Neanderthal/ and looks at how Joyce uses it to generate, 'through phonetic association', the three lexemes, '/meander/, /tal/ (in German, 'valley'), and /tale/'. Forced into a contiguous sequence they produce the pun '/meandertale/' (18. 22). From the associative chain between all four terms 'intermediate modes create themselves from terms that are all present' in Joyce's text. The associative relations 'can be either a phonetic or a semantic type'. Eco's purpose here is to demonstrate how Joyce's reader is 'controlled by the text' and 'led into a game of associations that were previously suggested to him by the co-text'. This means that 'every text, however "open" it is, is constituted, not as the place of all possibilities, but rather as the field of oriented possibilities' (76). In order to illustrate the interconnections and the associations with which the *Wake* controls its readers, Eco offers a diagram (Fig. 5). As he states, such a 'bidimensional graph cannot reproduce the game of interconnections produced when lexemes are brought into contact with their respective sememes' (76).

The diagram does, however, have an 'orientative' value and allows us to see some of the possible paths which can be followed in a 'reading' of the *Wake*. Moving from the diagram to the text itself, 'we are able to see how... the [semantic and phonetic] associations have been developed'. Eco outlines how the associations actually 'produce the puns which define the book':

The book is a /slipping beauty/ (and thus a beautiful sleeper who, in sleeping, generates lapsus by semantic slippages, in remembering a flaw, and

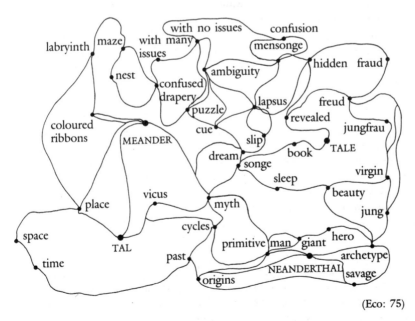

(Eco: 75)

Figure 5

so on), a /jungfraud's messongebook/ (where, to the previously cited associations, is added that of a 'message'), a labyrinth in which is found /a word
as cunningly hidden in its maze of confused drapery as a fieldmouse in a nest
of coloured ribbons/, and thus at last a /Meandertale/.

(76)

Another possible limitation of the diagram is that its 'associative
sequences' are based primarily upon semantic similarity ('except for the
first quadripartition'). Even though a 'componential investigation...
can... prove [ ]... all the associated sememes have in common a series of
semes', an explanation of the 'association by... partial [semantic] identity... means once again to explain it by similitude'. This means that the
diagram would seem to support the idea that 'at the roots of the pun's
forced contiguity, previous resemblances are found' (77).

To solve this problem Eco turns to semantic theory in order to show
that rereading the 'associative sequences' allows us to see how each
sequence 'could be constructed in retracing itself to a [cultural] "field of
notions"'. The lexeme /Tal/: 'space' and 'place' generates a sequence of
'archisemes codified by the dictionary itself', but time exists in a relationship which is not always codified in this way, but which belongs to a 'no-
tional' realm. Together with 'time', 'space' operates to produce a 'typical
antonymic relation by complementarity, which one imagines to be already
acquired by a culture in the form of a semantic axis'. 'Place' and 'time'
constitute a relationship 'also acquired in the interior of a very obvious
field of notions. ...Vico's past-cycles relationship is born out of a type of
classbook-like contiguity'. Distinguishing between the sort of semantic
association made possible by the semantic codification of lexicons based
on a prior cultural association, Eco concludes that 'all associations... are
grasped as contiguity internal to semantic fields and axes or to a componential spectrum of the lexeme that considers even the most peripheral
connotations'. This sort of contiguity provides a code for associations
which is in operation 'before' the associations are 'grasped as identity or
similarity of meaning'.

What Eco's semiotic investigation is able to demonstrate is that all
associative connections 'were already codified before the artist could recognize them by pretending to institute or discover them'. In terms of
Joyce's achievement in writing *Finnegans Wake*, Eco provides an appreciation, not only of Joyce's puns, which are based on pre-codified relationships that Joyce recognised, but of his creativity in making the 'short
circuit, the so-called metaphoric one':

> Because... between /mensonge/ and /songe/, except for the phonetic
> similarity, there is no contiguity; in order to unite them, a leap was first
> necessary from one to another of the diagram's discontinuous points. But
> if the points are discontinuous, it is because the diagram is incomplete. ...

This means that, under the apparent metaphoric short circuit (for here the similarity between two senses seems to click for the first time), there is an uninterrupted web of culturalized contiguity that [can be traversed] through a sequence of binary choices.

(77–8)

Eco's semiotic analysis also offers an understanding of the ways in which Joyce's puns, the fundamental figures of the *Wake*, provide a method for following the associative, metonymic paths that support the metaphors and puns. In traversing the text by following these paths, the actual reader is led to a gradual understanding of the reading process that the *Wake* generates for its 'ideal', or 'model', reader to undertake.

Julia Kristeva

Like Eco, Julia Kristeva is a semiotician who is also known for major contributions to other areas of critical theory. Kristeva has made significant contributions to feminism and the cultural studies of women, the visual arts, psychoanalytic theory and psychoanalytic interpretations of literature. While she has not written any major studies devoted exclusively to Joyce, her work reveals a significant understanding of *Ulysses* and *Finnegans Wake*. She makes frequent references to these texts and reveals their importance as exemplary models for her semiotic and psychoanalytic theories. In *Desire and Language: A Semiotic Approach to Literature and Art* (New York: Columbia UP, 1980) Kristeva draws on the work of writers like Saussure and Greimas in order to develop a semiotic theory which also incorporates Mikhail Bakhtin's distinction between monologic and dialogic discourse. Her aim is to produce a theory for better understanding writing which serves a subversive social purpose, and she shares some of the conclusions of critics like Margot Norris who see Joyce as part of a radical and subversive tradition of writing.

Desire and Language also illustrates Kristeva's role as a participant in the development of poststructuralist theory. Instead of looking at works of literature as discrete, self-contained texts, Kristeva considers their functions as *intertexts*. As Leon S. Roudiez explains, the French word *intertextalité* 'was originally introduced by Kristeva', and while it 'has... been much used and abused', it 'met with immediate success' (Kristeva: 15). We will consider Joyce's texts as 'intertexts' in more detail in the final chapter on poststructuralism, but as the concept of the intertext is an integral part of Kristeva's semiotic theory a brief explanation is appropriate here. Traditional criticism deals with the relationships between different authors and texts with terms such as 'allusion', 'reference', 'quotation' and 'borrowing'. In *A Portrait*, for example, Joyce 'borrows' '*Et ignotas animum dimittit in artes*' from Ovid's *Metamorphoses*, VIII, 188, and 'quotes' Ovid's passage as the epigraph for his book. Similarly, in 'The Boarding House', Joyce can be seen 'alluding' to the biblical account of the crucifixion and 'borrowing' certain details from it in order to add to the symbolism of his story (the name of the servant, 'Mary', who collects the 'pieces of broken bread'; Bob Doran's 'three day's... beard', and his longing 'to ascend', etc.).

Intertextuality, however, has nothing to do with such borrowing, alluding, or quoting. As Roudiez explains:

> It has nothing to do with matters of influence by one writer upon another, or with the sources of a literary work; it does, on the other hand, involve the components of a *textual system* such as the novel... It is defined... as the transposition of one or more *systems* of signs into another.
>
> (Kristeva: 15)

This transposition is analogous to the semiotic shifts we saw defined by Barthes and Eco: Barthes describes the shift as the sign that one system becomes the signifier of another; Eco sees semiotic codes generating signs (different from those of the code) that can still signify the code and its operations. For Kristeva, the transposition operates as the production of a new system of signs which generates an accompanying 'new articulation of the enunciative and denotative position'. Any semiotic network or 'signifying practice' is a 'field', or a semiotic 'space traversed by lines of force... in which various signifying systems undergo such a transposition' (Kristeva: 15).

Kristeva is particularly interested in the *polyphonic* novel as a form which incorporates 'carnivalesque structures'. She begins defining this form by distinguishing between 'three dimensions of textual space': 'writing subject, addressee, and exterior space'. Like those structuralists who distinguish between the horizontal (diachronic) and vertical (synchronic) axes of language, Kristeva defines the 'status' of 'the word', of language, in terms of two similar axes:

> The word's status is thus defined *horizontally* (the word in the text belongs to both writing subject and addressee) as well as *vertically* (the word in the text is oriented toward an anterior or synchronic literary corpus).
>
> (66)

As Eco's theory of the 'model' reader (Joyce's 'ideal reader suffering from an ideal insomnia') situates that reader within the text and defines him or her as a product of the text, so Kristeva's theory sees the reader as an 'addressee' (the 'receiver' of Jakobson's 'message') who 'is included within a book's discursive universe only as discourse itself' (66). Where traditional criticism considers the triad of author, book and reader as three discrete 'subjects' with separate identities, Kristeva sees the identity of the reader bound up with a position within the language of the text and continually altered by the operations which language performs and which affect the psychological structure of the reader. In Chapter One we considered Norris's view of the problematic nature of identity that is created by the *Wake*'s use of a similar psychological theory of the relationship between identity (of 'character') and language; this problem constitutes an important element of pyschoanalytic interpretations of Joyce's work.

For Kristeva the individual words of any text constitute a 'minimal textual unit', and 'each word (text)' functions as the intersection point for the vertical '(text-content)' and horizontal '(subject-addressee)' axes. This creates the dialogical structure defined by Bakhtin:

> each word (text) is an intersection of words (texts) where at least one other word (text) can be read. In Bakhtin's work, these two axes,... he calls *dialogue* and *ambivalence*. ... [A]n insight first introduced into literary theory by Bakhtin [is]: any text is constructed as a mosaic of quotations; any text is the absorption and transformation of another. The notion of *intertextuality* replaces that of intersubjectivity, and poetic language is read as at least a *double*.
>
> (Kristeva: 66)

The importance of *Finnegans Wake* as a model of such a theoretical perspective can be glimpsed in that text's identification of itself as the work of Shem the Penman. He dwells in his own text and his writing is a mosaic of 'once current puns' and 'quashed quotatoes' (183. 22), or 'quotations'. Shem's (and Joyce's) writing is in part constituted by an endless list of deformed quotations which are put together to produce the 'piously forged palimpsests' which come from a 'pelagiarist' (and plagiarist's) 'pen' (182. 2–3). Joyce's text also operates as a model for the notion of the poetic text as a double, and one can use Eco's model of associative chains (a model derived from the *Wake*) in order to follow a continually bifurcating chain of signifiers generated from the signifier 'Dublin': 'duble', 'doob', 'doubloons', 'doubleyous', 'doublin', etc. One could follow these chains in order to experience Joyce's text as a chain of signifiers which, like 'Laurens County's gorgios' (doubled by 'Laurens County, Georgia') are 'doublin their mumper [and "doubling their number"] all the time' (3. 8–9).

Central to Kristeva's theory of the novel is the distinction between what she terms '0–1' and '0–2' logic. Discussing the traditional concept of the sign as a unity of signifier and signified, or the 'notion of *sign* (Sr–Sd)', Kristeva argues that this notion 'is a product of scientific abstraction (identity–substance–cause–goal as structure of the Indo-European sentence), designating a vertically and hierarchically linear division'. This 'scientific abstraction' is responsible for 0–1 logic:

> Scientific procedures are indeed based upon a logical approach... founded
> on the Greek (Indo-European) sentence. Such a sentence begins as sub-
> ject–predicate and grows by identification, determination and causality.
> Modern logic ... evolves out of a 0–1 sequence: George Boole, who begins
> with set theory, produces formulae that are more isomorphic with language
> – all of these are ineffective within the realm of poetic language, where 1
> is not a limit.
>
> (69–70)

This is the logic which Bakhtin calls 'monological', the 0–1 logic. For
Kristeva 'literary semiotics must be developed on the basis of a *poetic logic*
where the concept of the *power of the continuum* would embody the 0–2
interval, a continuity where 0 denotes and 1 is implicitly transgressed'
(70).

Bakhtin distinguishes between dialogic and monologic structures. He
'assimilates narrative discourse into epic discourse, [and] narrative is a
prohibition, a *monologism*, a subordination of the code to 1, to God'.
Because of this, the 'epic is religious and theological; all "realist" narrative
obeying 0–1 logic is dogmatic.' Literature which operates on the principles of 'realism' 'tends to operate within this [0–1] space.' From
Bakhtin's perspective the realist novel is monological: 'Realist description,
definition of "personality", "character" creation, and "subject" development – all are descriptive narrative elements belonging to the 0–1 interval
and are thus *monological*' (Kristeva: 70). One of the reasons why Kristeva
refers to Joyce's texts as examples of a writing which escapes the limitations of 0–1 logic can be found in Joyce's creation of a form which can
incorporate realism within itself yet not be constrained by so-called realist
principles. Nothing could be more realist in aim than the attempt to
reproduce as many events as possible from one day in the life of Dublin
and her citizens on 16th June 1904, but while Joyce could be said to have
been almost obsessed with his attention to realistic details, he also
combines Leopold Bloom's actions with those of Odysseus. By the use of
this parallel he doubles Bloom's actions, and the realistic portrait of an
advertising salesman as a middle-aged man is contained within a form that
fuses Dublin's citizen with Homer's hero.

For both Bakhtin and Kristeva, the 'only discourse integrally to achieve
the 0–2 poetic logic is that of the carnival'. Kristeva cites Joyce along with
Proust and Kafka as creators of a '*polyphonic*', '"modern" novel' 'incorporating carnivalesque structures' (71). The reason for the inclusion of
Joyce is quite clear. The *Wake*, of course, offers itself as a dream (many
critics discuss the text as such), and Kristeva defines carnival as discourse
which '[b]y adopting a *dream* logic... transgresses rules of linguistic code
and social morality as well' (70, emphasis added). The transgression of the

carnivalesque discourse succeeds because it operates according to the poetic 0–2 logic: 'In fact, this "transgression" of linguistic, logical and social codes within the carnivalesque only exists and succeeds... because it accepts *another law*' (71).

Kristeva aims to produce a 'radical' 'typology of discourses'. She distinguishes between:

1. '*monological discourse*, including, first, the representative mode of description and narration (the epic); secondly, historical discourse; and thirdly, scientific discourse. In all three, the subject both assumes and submits to the rule of 1 (God).'
2. '*dialogical discourse* [which] includes carnivalesque and Menippean discourses as well as the polyphonic novel. In its structures, writing reads another writing, reads itself and constructs itself through a process of destructive genesis.' (76–7)

As a writing which 'reads itself' the dialogical discourse entails the notion of auto-reflection which other semioticians whose work we have examined consider characteristic of aesthetic systems in general and of literary or poetic texts in particular.

While these distinctions suggest that the polyphonic novel is separate from monological discourses, Kristeva draws on Bakhtin's concepts of the 'status of the word, dialogue, and ambivalence' in order to show how a 'reading of Bakhtin... leads to an understanding' of the polyphonic novel's ability to incorporate the various forms of monological discourse within itself. This is illustrated in Fig. 6.

The carnivalesque element of dialogical discourse is part of a tradition that 'was absorbed into Menippean discourse and put into practice by the polyphonic novel' (79). Joyce's last two texts are examples of the 'most

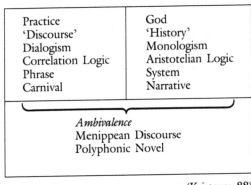

(Kristeva: 88)

Figure 6

important polyphonic novels [which] are inheritors of the Menippean, carnivalesque structure: those of Rabelais, Cervantes, Swift, Sade, Balzac, Lautréamont, Dostoievski, Joyce, and Kafka' (71). Joyce's well-documented, secularising, artistic use of Catholic rituals and symbols confirms his participation in the carnivalesque and Mennipean tradition, for its history 'is the history of the struggle against Christianity and its representation; this means an exploration of language (of sexuality and death), a consecration of ambivalence and of "vice"' (80).

After situating Joyce's novels as polyphonic novels in the tradition of Mennipean satire and the carnivalesque, Kristeva draws on Barthes in order to reconsider the distinction between linguistics and semiotics. Her aim is to uncover what lies beneath the 'phenomenological idealities' that linguistics discovers in language. These idealities include such phenomena as the 'substansified, opaque linguistic categories' that constitute linguistics' taxonomic approach to language (102). Kristeva wishes to distinguish between what she sees as linguistics' limited approach to writing (limited because it operates on the monologic, scientific model) and semiotics' more flexible and (for her) more useful method for engaging with the fundamental ambiguity of writing's 0–2, poetic logic. To do this she uses Barthes' notion that signifying systems 'both *do and do not* pertain to linguistics' (101). '"Linguistics is not a part of the general science of signs, even a privileged part," says Barthes, "it is semiology which is a part of linguistics" (*Elements of Semiology*, p. 11).' For Kristeva, the operations of the sign-systems which are investigated by semiotics exceed the analytic capabilities of linguistics:

> signifying systems are *trans-linguistic*. They are articulated as large units that run across phonetic, syntactic order, and even stylistic order, to organize an *other* combinative system with the help of these same linguistic categories operating to the second power [of the poetic, 0–2, "*other*" order] in that system impelled by another subject.
>
> (101)

The importance of Barthes' semiotic methods, as opposed to linguistic analysis, is that it facilitates 'research into the dialectical laws of the signifying process'. Behind the 'categories and structures' that linguistics discovers in writing, 'there functions a scene where the subject, defined by the topos of its communication with an other, begins by *denying* this communication in order to formulate another device'. This 'device' is formulated as part of the 'auto-reflective' operations which, as we have already seen, characterises poetic, or aesthetic, writing. Kristeva sees linguistics as capable of dealing with the function of language as communication, as what she terms '"natural" language', but limited by its incapability of dealing with language which denies communication and functions in an auto-referential mode. In this mode 'language is no longer communicative', but what Kristeva terms '*transformative*, or even *mortal*, for the "I" as well as for the other'. According to Kristeva, linguistic analysis is incapable of dealing with Joyce's writing because that writing is a model example of this 'transformative language' and functions 'in borderline experiences, [as] an antilanguage', a 'double' (0–2) writing, 'indicating in other respects but simultaneously a disrupted social structure' (102).

At this point, Kristeva has almost completed the semiotic analysis which she uses as the grounds for her investigations of writing from a psychoanalytic and feminist perspective. Joyce's texts are important in these later investigations and we will return to Kristeva in the chapter on French feminist studies of Joyce. Before leaving Kristeva, however, it is important to note that she sees Joyce's writing as radical not only in a literary context but also within the much wider social and political contexts of all Western discourse. Indeed, *Finnegans Wake* would seem to provide a semiotic model (in functioning as a transformative sign-system) of the only language that is today still capable of producing a subversive and poetic discourse:

> As capitalist society is being economically and politically choked to death, discourse is wearing thin and heading for collapse at a more rapid rate than ever before. Philosophical finds, various modes of 'teaching', scientific or aesthetic formalisms follow one upon another, compete, and disappear without leaving either a convinced audience or noteworthy disciples. Didacticism, rhetoric, dogmatism of any kind, in any 'field' whatsoever, no longer command attention. They have survived, and perhaps will continue to survive in modified forms, throughout Academia. Only one language grows more and more contemporary: the equivalent, beyond a span of thirty years, of the language of *Finnegans Wake*.
>
> (92)

•3• IS IT A 'GRAMMA'S GRAMMAR'? (I)

Joyce and Anglo-American Feminism

FINNEGANS WAKE DESCRIBES a female character who:

> From gramma's grammar she has it that if there is a third person, mascarine, phelinine or nuder, being spoken abad it moods prosodes from a person speaking to her second which is the direct object that has been spoken to, with and at.
>
> (268. 16–22)

While the complex grammatical relations raised by this passage are numerous, the reference to a 'gramma's grammar' as a system of rules from which the female has learned ('she has it') points to the possibility of a female 'grammar' originating from a 'gramma' or 'grandmother'. This 'grammar', passed on from grandmother to granddaughter, suggests a female language. To what extent could Joyce as a male writer understand such a language enough to recreate it in his own writing?

The 1980s saw the emergence of a major debate in Joyce studies about Joyce's attitudes towards females and the nature of his portrayal of girls and women in his writing. This debate had been developing for some time before this period, but it is probably safe to say that it did not become a central issue in Joyce studies until the last decade. At the centre of the debate are two questions that continue to attract serious critical attention and which have yet to be fully answered: were Joyce's attitudes to women sexist, and, if so, to what extent? Are the females in Joyce's writings the product of a writer who could be sensitive to the lives of females or are they stereotyped characters created by a male author incapable of understanding or sympathising with females? Put in these crude terms, the questions would not seem to be difficult questions to answer. Surely one could look at the attitudes which Joyce expressed about women during his life in order to answer the first question. This answer, combined with a detailed study of Joyce's female characters, would probably provide a fairly accurate answer to the second. As is often the case with Joyce, however, questions such as these are not so simple and cannot be satisfactorily answered in such terms.

Joyce is supposed to have told Mary Colum that he hated 'intellectual women' and said to Frank Budgen that he would never hear of a woman 'who was the author of a complete philosophical system' (Ellmann, 1982: 529 and 634). This would seem to suggest that Joyce disliked some women and believed all women incapable of the same philosophical achievements as men. Even with such apparently clear-cut statements, however, certain difficulties arise. The most obvious point to be considered is whether or not Joyce was serious when he made these statements. If Joyce did 'hate intellectual women' what are we to make of his friendship with 'intellectual women' like Adrienne Monnier, Sylvia Beach or Djuna Barnes? A cynical answer might be that he found them useful. This could certainly be said of the first two people, for in addition to all of the help which Beach gave Joyce in the publication of his work, she and Monnier also acted as what Ellmann calls Joyce's 'main sources of information about French literature of the nineteen twenties' (Ellmann, 1982: 489). In the case of Barnes, however, this does not hold true, and there is little to suggest that Joyce availed himself of her help in the way that he did with Beach and Monnier; nor is there any evidence that Joyce used Barnes in the way he used Beckett and others in a secretary-cum-editor capacity. Bonnie Kime Scott offers a detailed account of Barnes' knowledge of Joyce in *Joyce and Feminism* (Brighton: The Harvester Press, 1984). Unfortunately, little information has come to light about Joyce's attitude to Barnes, and Scott offers only the back-handed compliment that 'Joyce treated [Barnes] a little more like the young male writers who surrounded him than is usually the case in his relationship with women' (108).

Joyce and Feminism, which is one of the major Anglo-American studies of Joyce from a feminist perspective, demonstrates the problems that can arise in assessing Joyce's attitudes towards women on the basis of biographical accounts of Joyce's comments. Scott gives the example of another remark which Joyce made to Colum: 'I hate women who know anything'. As Scott points out, 'scholars often quote this remark', but they do not always acknowledge the context in which it was made. The context was recalled by Colum herself in 'The Confessions of James

Joyce', and it reveals that Joyce's attitude was quite different from the one immediately suggested by the statement alone, 'I hate women who know anything':

> It has a significantly fuller context. ...Joyce's habit of pulling people's legs – in one case an American instructor whom he had fed tales of his indebtedness to Dujardin. Mary Colum challenged him to acknowledge his debts to the 'great originators', Freud and Jung. Joyce was 'evidently angry, and moved irritatedly in his chair,' he said, 'I hate women who know anything'. But the exchange did not end there. Colum responded, '"No, Joyce, you don't. ...You like them". After a few seconds of silent annoyance, a whimsical smile came over his face, and the rest of the afternoon was pleasant for all three of us'.
>
> (117)

In providing this account Scott demonstrates two problems facing anyone who wishes to make sense of Joyce's attitude towards the females whom he knew. On the one hand, in providing the context for Joyce's line, she allows the reader to understand Colum's belief that the 'smile seems to offer the half-grudging admission that Colum had found him out, that he did like spirited women' (117). On the other hand, she fails to quote the poem which Joyce recited to Colum on the subject of his female acquaintance shortly after their disagreement:

> As I was going to Joyce Saint James'
> I met with seven extravagant dames;
> Every dame had a bee in her bonnet,
> With bats from the belfry roosting upon it.
> And Ah, I said, poor Joyce Saint James,
> What can he do with these terrible dames?
> Poor Saint James Joyce.
>
> (Ellmann, 1982: 634–5)

In failing to mention this poem, Scott's study perpetuates the same sort of misunderstanding created by scholars who only quote the one line. Ellmann, who does quote the poem, suggests that it 'was scarcely corroborative evidence' for Colum's belief (634).

Accepting Ellmann's account as the final story, however, also creates problems. Joyce was very capable of spending time writing poems against those whom he perceived as his enemies, as 'Gas from a Burner' clearly demonstrates, but the tone of 'As I was going to Joyce Saint James' hardly reproduces the 'wholly personal invective' which Ellmann finds in the earlier poem (335). The later poem is much more playful in tone. It does present a gross parody of women with opinions, but parody can be a form of admiration. This is a possibility which Ellmann does not consider when he uses the poem as evidence of Joyce's misogyny. To be fair, Ellmann does cite Joyce's comment to Carola Giedion-Welcker,

'Throughout my life women have been my most active helpers', but he also seems to want confirmation of Joyce's dislike of women. In his note to the episode of Joyce and Colum he prefaces Joyce's comment about women and philosophy with his own summary of Joyce's attitude: 'Joyce objected to Budgen that the female was attempting to usurp all the functions of the male except that which is biologically preempted, and even on that ... she was casting jealous eyes' (634). It seems highly unlikely that Joyce's comment about women never authoring a 'complete philosophical system' expresses the same paranoia about women which is detectable in Ellmann's account of Joyce's opinions.

If the attempt at determining Joyce's attitudes towards the females whom he knew seems problematic, then the attempt at deciding if Joyce's female characters are unfavourable stereotypes or sympathetic portrayals is much more so, at least on the basis of feminist studies of Joyce's characters. Of course, not all of the studies of Joyce's female characters are feminist studies. Some of the best interpreters of Joyce's work have been women who do not emphasise a particularly feminist point of view. Margaret C. Solomon's *Eternal Geomater: The Sexual Universe of Finnegans Wake* (Carbondale: Southern Illinois UP, 1969), for example, provides a profound insight into the *Wake's* Anna Livia Plurabelle and her central position as the maternal matrix and genetrix of the text's sexual domain. Solomon's study sees ALP as a sympathetically-drawn female character, and there is little in *Eternal Geomater* to suggest that Joyce was either a misogynist or chauvinist in his depiction of female characters. It is largely from feminist studies that condemnations of Joyce as a misogynist or chauvinist have issued. Of course not all feminists see Joyce in this light, but writers like Sandra Gilbert and Susan Gubar take the point of view that Joyce's female characters are evidence that he could not have been anything but a misogynist. Their work has provided one of the main sources of criticism of Joyce in the feminist debate.

There is of course no single, central theory to which all feminist critics of Joyce adhere. As we shall see, feminist studies of Joyce use all of the theories that we are considering in this book. More often than not they combine various strands from different theories in order to explore Joyce's writing from a variety of different angles. This is the case with writers like Norris, who does not write from a particularly feminist perspective but does explore Joyce's depiction of females. As we saw in Chapter One, Norris draws on structuralism, Freudian psychology, and deconstructive theory in order to explore the *Wake*. In contrast to Norris, Kristeva combines feminism with semiotics and psychoanalysis and uses Joyce's writing as a model which addresses important aspects of what she calls the female semiotic.

In the rest of this chapter we will look at feminist studies of Joyce which have been written by members of what can be called the Anglo-American feminist movement. In the next chapter we will look at studies of Joyce by continental Europeans. To a certain extent the division of Joycean feminists into these two groups is quite arbitrary and adopted as a matter of convenience. There is, however, some justification for the division to be found in the theoretical orientation of the writers we will examine. As a general rule of thumb (but one, admittedly, with many exceptions) European feminists tend to develop their own theories by combining such European theories as semiotics, the psychoanalytic theories of Freud and Lacan, and the deconstructive theories of Derrida. While Anglo-American critics use these theories, they also rely more on historical and biblio-graphical approaches to literature than do their European counterparts. The recognition of these general trends in criticism has been recognised by Stephen Heath. In a 'translator's note' to Philippe Sollers' 'Joyce & Co.' (in *The Wake of the Wake* [Madison: Wisconsin UP, 1978]), Heath distinguishes between Sollers' very French theoretical approach to Joyce and the approaches taken by English and American critics. He sees the theoretical differences producing different Joyces. Sollers' text:

> goes against both the English and American Joyces, the outcast from a moralizing criticism bent on protecting its tradition. ...It is useless to add that the 'structuralism' currently, and usually ignorantly, being bandied about by the literary intellectuals in England and America is a new version of the old refusal of Joyce...
>
> (Sollers: 121, n. 9).

Women in Joyce

Women in Joyce (Brighton: The Harvester Press, 1982) is a collection of essays which looks at Joyce's female characters from a variety of perspec-tives and includes several feminist assessments of Joyce's treatment of females. In the 'Introduction' Suzette Henke and Elaine Unkeless quote Jung's admiration for Joyce's 'remarkable insight into the female psyche'. After reading the 'Penelope' episode of *Ulysses*, Jung described it as 'psychological peaches' and said 'I suppose the devil's grandmother knows so much about the real psychology of a woman'. Of course such a view supports only one side of the debate about Joyce's depiction of women, and Henke and Unkeless balance this male psychologist's opinion of Joyce's achievement with Nora Barnacle's protest that her husband 'knew nothing at all about women' (xi). After contextualising the debate about Joyce and women in these terms, the editors explain their own decision to participate in the argument:

> Although a new understanding of women's role in literature has recently begun to emerge, few critics have sought to provide fresh descriptions of

Joyce's female characters. We have collected the following essays for precisely this purpose: to offer a contemporary perspective on the women that Joyce created and to present analyses that do not restrict the female personality to preconceived literary or social categories.

(xi)

Indeed, one of the major problems about which the opponents in this debate seem to agree is that early studies of Joyce tended to deal with Joyce's female characters in precisely the terms which *Women in Joyce* seeks to avoid. The introduction provides a useful overview of earlier studies and the ways in which Joyce's 'women characters were assigned almost exclusively to archetypal or symbolic roles':

> Figures like Gretta Conroy of 'The Dead', Bertha Rowan of *Exiles*, Molly Bloom of *Ulysses* were seen as prototypes representing a pure sexual abstraction. Stuart Gilbert set the stage for a mythic interpretation of Molly when he described her as 'Gaea-Tellus, the Great Mother Cybele' [Gilbert: 339]. William York Tindall observed that Bertha Brown and Gretta Conroy 'are studies for Mrs. Bloom, whose image is the earth. The relationship between proud Richard and earthy Bertha, anticipating that between Stephen and Mrs. Bloom, is that between intellect and reality' [Tindall: 121]. Hugh Kenner, reading *Ulysses* in the Flaubertian tradition, saw Molly not only as an 'earth-goddess' but as a sensuous embodiment of material inertia, a deity that presides over an 'animal kingdom of the dead' [Kenner, 1978: 262]. And S. L. Goldberg synthesized these archetypal perspectives when he declared in *The Classical Temper* that 'Joyce's women are never really women'. Molly ... 'is meant as a simple, shrewd, elemental figure, a spokesman and a symbol of the processes of Nature.... Molly is less a woman than Woman, a portrait decked with individual details... . She is the Jungian Anima, the mystery of animate Flesh, the Earth, Nature' [Goldberg: 293–5].

(xii)

The tendency to view Joyce's women in terms of symbolic and archetypal clichés received considerable biographical support from Ellmann. As Henke and Unkeless state, Joyce's critics 'have generally accepted Richard Ellmann's assertion that women in Joyce's fiction consistently reflect the virgin/whore dichotomy dominant in Western cultures'. Ellmann believed that Joyce was limited by this stereotype as it was manifest in Catholic culture, that he 'never transcended the Catholic urge to stereotype women as untouched virgins or defiled prostitutes' (Henke and Unkeless: xii–xiii). Henke and Unkeless admit that Ellmann could recognise 'both the naturalistic and the symbolic dimensions of Joyce's female characters' but argue that 'even when he analyzes them as realistic rather than archetypal figures, he sees them as representative of all women'. In support of this thesis, they cite Ellmann's biographical interpretation of 'Molly's monologue' as illustrating 'Joyce's theory of [Nora Barnacle's] mind (and of the female mind in general) as a flow...' (Ellmann, 1982:

387; Cited, Henke and Unkeless: xiii). This view is sustained by the 'traditional critics [who] frequently praise Joyce for creating women who are at once symbolic and realistic' (Henke and Unkeless: xiii).

The stereotypical view of women in these terms is one to which several feminist critics have objected, because 'feminist readers often find Joyce's archetypal representations unconvincing'. Among these objectors Henke and Unkeless (xiii–xiv) list:

1. Kate Millet, who 'in *Sexual Politics* questions Joyce's assumptions concerning female passivity. She objects to his fondness for "presenting woman as 'nature'," "unspoiled primeval understanding," and the "eternal feminine" [Millet: 285].'
2. Florence Howe, who 'in "Feminism and Literature", asserts that Joyce's view of women... is tinged with a specifically male bias. ...[T]he women in *A Portrait of the Artist* are "land bound. The artist can fly and create, even in motion. We women are of the earth... we are the earth-mother" [Howe: 263–4].' Henke and Unkeless cite Howe's corrective to Joyce's depiction of male-female relations: 'the "male artist, whether he is Stephen or Joyce or someone else, must conceive his power, or his difference from women, must take his measure against them, must finally define the two sexes as different species, active and passive, master and servant" [Howe: 263–4].'
3. Marilyn French, who in *The Book as World*, 'contends... that Molly Bloom is a... distorted "surrealistic" version of woman: "Molly is the mythic, the archetypal other. Not only for Bloom but for the rest of Dublin, she is the woman as the object of desire" [French: 259].'
4. Marcia Holly, who objects to Molly on similar grounds to French: 'Joyce's Penelope [is] "sensually inadequate because her sensuality exists not for herself but for the men to whom she reacts... Because Molly represents only male fantasy of sensuality and not what a truly sensual woman is or might be, it is an error to define her as a realistic portrayal" [Holly: 41].'

Although these are strong, negative criticisms of Joyce's depiction of Molly Bloom, not all feminists condemn Joyce for his depiction of females. As Henke and Unkeless point out, the context of the historical period in which Joyce wrote must be taken into consideration: 'It is possible... for Molly to be male-identified but nonetheless realistic. It might, in fact, be historically accurate to assume that a woman of Molly's era would probably interpret her sexuality in terms of male attraction.' Historical accuracy and 'social authenticity' are 'crucial to feminist evaluation' (xiv). Together they are a part of the context which the essays of *Women in Joyce* use in order to explore Joyce's female characters: 'Although their approaches varied, all the contributors, whether or not they employed a feminist mode of analysis, attempted to place Joyce's writing within a "contextual" framework.' This critical practice contrasts with that of critics who 'advocate' the importance of 'stylistic formalism'. The contextual studies from *Women in Joyce* 'refuse[ ] to abstract the work of art from its psychological, cultural, and economic environment'. They 'try to situate the aesthetic object within a larger frame of politics and history'. The feminist essays from this collection which we will now examine demonstrate an even 'more specialized form of contextual interpretation': they 'examine the ways in which a work of literature reflects, verifies, or criticizes prevalent beliefs about women, about gender identity and sex-role stereotyping, and about the relationships between the sexes... ' (xi).

Florence L. Walzl: *Dubliners*

'*Dubliners*: Women in Irish Society' reveals the importance of the historical and social dimensions of the contextual criticism which Henke and Unkeless emphasise. The thesis of this essay is that 'Joyce's treatment of women in *Dubliners*' should be understood within the larger context of Joyce's short stories as an 'anatomy of Irish society' which is 'scrupulously realistic' (32). Walzl treats the stories as a 'set of social casebooks' and argues that 'the role of women is quintessential in Joyce's exploration of the relations of human beings'. Joyce's depiction of females, his 'treatment of women... needs examination as a social document, since historically women have been particularly vunerable to societal pressures'. The most important questions for Walzl concern 'Joyce's accuracy in [the] depiction of the social milieu of his women characters and... the realism of his portraits of women as social entities' (32–3).

For Walzl Joyce's fictional depiction of the Irish social situations of the time neither 'glosses over' nor 'sentimentalizes' any of the real historical conditions, and Walzl argues (34–5) that the stories depict the 'harshness of family life' which was created by three important historical conditions:

1. 'For a full century after 1845, the year of the great Famine, economic deprivation drove millions abroad. For those who remained, poverty was widespread, jobs few and precarious, salaries meagre, and opportunities of advancement rare.' These harsh personal and social conditions which this created for men are treated in 'The Two Gallants', and 'The Boarding House'. But the 'effects of such conditions upon women' were equally 'severe', and should be considered in an assessment of Joyce's creation of 'Eveline' and Maria from 'Clay'.
2. For 'over a century following 1841, Ireland had the lowest marriage and birth rates in the civilized world', a condition 'radically affecting women's lives'. As a 'natural concomitant, it also had the highest rate

of unmarried men and women in the world'. Walzl says that '*Dubliners* throughout reflects these adverse conditions in the few marriages depicted and in the number of unmarried characters. ...[I]n the four stories devoted to youth, only one has marriage as its outcome. ...Of the four tales of "maturity", two depict the lives of lonely celibates.'

3. Also important for *Dubliners* is a 'third set of statistics involving the late ages of marriages for both sexes [which] is characteristic of Ireland during the century following the Famine'. After the famine 'marriage was delayed [for men] until the period between [the ages of] thirty-five and forty-five years'. Women 'began marrying in significant numbers... after thirty; men after thirty-five, frequently not before forty'. The result of such delays often meant that marriage became a 'deliberate, unromantic business involving acquisition of money and property on the bridegroom's part in exchange for presumed security on the bride's'.

According to Walzl, an understanding of these conditions is essential for an appreciation of the 'authenticity of Joyce's picture of courtship and marriage' in *Dubliners*. The stories have 'many wary bachelors' whose wariness can only fully be appreciated within the context of the social conditions described above, and Walzl also sees these conditions as important for a fuller understanding of Mrs Kearney in 'A Mother'. She is a sort of 'deliberate wooer' whose attitudes towards courtship are largely determined by these conditions:

> as a well-educated young woman and an accomplished pianist, [she] had at the 'age of marriage' been 'sent out to many houses where her playing and ivory manners were much admired'. 'Pale and unbending', she had long sat 'amid the chilly circle of her accomplishments', waiting for a proper 'suitor to brave it'. But the young men were 'ordinary', and when she drew 'near the limit' of age and her friends had begun to talk, she had 'silenced them' by marrying an elderly bootmaker. She well 'knew the small number of his talents', but she respected him 'as she respected the General Post Office as something large, secure and fixed'. After the first year of married life, she 'perceived such a man would wear better than a romantic person'.
>
> (*D*: 136–7, 141; Cited, Walzl: 35)

The distinction Mrs Kearney makes between a practical choice like her husband and a 'romantic person' reflects the preference for a marriage of security and convenience that the historical conditions produced. Indeed, as Walzl notes, 'romantic love' was 'denounced as "lustful infatuation,"' an 'approach to love' 'described ... in *Stephen Hero* as moral "simony"' (*SH*: 202)' (35).

For the most part, the women depicted by Joyce in his stories are from a middle-class background. The few exceptions are Lily, the maid servant of 'The Dead', the slavey of 'Two Gallants', and the 'magdalen-inmates of the Dublin by Lamplight Laundry', who 'are all lower class' (40). Walzl finds it significant that Joyce paid close attention to the sort of occupations that his largely middle-class characters would have been likely to hold in Dublin at that time: '*Dubliners* includes woman shopkeepers, and shop assistants, office clerks and typists, the operator of a lodging house and the housekeeper of an institution, schoolteachers, and especially musicians – pianists, vocalists, and music teachers.' She notes that the sort of occupations Joyce provides for his characters are typical of those which the 1904 *Thom's Directory* lists in its 'Trade's Directory' section as occupations held by women. She suggests that Joyce may have drawn on the occupations listed in the *Directory* in order to provide his female characters with typical jobs: 'Since one of Joyce's principal goals in *Dubliners* was the presentation of social types, he may have aimed at typicality of occupations for women also' (40).

In addition to providing information on the sort of occupations in which women worked, the *Directory* provides an abundance of information on what percentage of particular positions were held by women. There is so much information provided that, as Walzl points out, Joyce 'could not deal with the scope of such material', '[w]ithin the compact limits of the brief tales'. As an example of how 'tellingly he used selective details' like those provided by *Thom's Directory*, Walzl cites 'The Boarding House', and, specifically the 'career of the redoubtable Mrs. Mooney'. She follows a typical 'familial and occupational pattern' for women of the time. After marrying an employee of her father's, she opens a shop of her own in her father's trade of butchery. When the business fails because of her husband's drinking and bad business practices ('By fighting his wife in the presence of customers and buying bad meat he ruined his business.'), they separate, and Mrs Mooney starts running her boarding house, another typical occupation for women at the time: the boarding houses listed by the *Directory* were all operated by women (41).

Walzl also considers Mrs Mooney in the context of typical 'Mother and daughter' relationships of the period. She compares Mrs Mooney's relationship with Polly and that which Eveline would have shared with her mother. As girls of the same generation and approximately the same age, Polly and Eveline are both subject to the sort of social pressures created by the conditions we have already examined. Walzl suggests that both young women follow a pattern which was common in Dublin as they succumb to social pressures and begin a life which will, in all likelihood, repeat the pattern of their mother's lives. Eveline has a chance to break away from these social pressures, but they prove much too strong:

Eveline, conditioned by her mother's sense of duty, exhausted by her own hard work in the stores [another typical occupation for women of the time] and at home, and haunted by a deathbed promise to her mother to take care of the younger children and 'keep the home together', chooses a death-in-life, rejection of the man who loves her and can offer her a new life.

(48)

Walzl believes that 'Joyce makes the point explicit' in the passage: 'As she mused the pitiful version of her mother's life laid its spell on the very quick of her being – that life of commonplace sacrifices closing in final craziness' (*D*: 40). 'The life she returns to', Walzl states, 'is a repetition of her mother's life of commonplace sacrifices and confusion. ...Eveline's spinsterhood represents in *Dubliners* the fate of the large portion of Irish women who will never marry' (48).

In contrast to Eveline, Polly Mooney does marry, but this is largely because of Mrs Mooney's efforts on her behalf: 'Mrs Mooney, by social pressures and economic threats, brings the unwilling Mr. Doran to the altar.' As Walzl points out, the future of the new Mrs Doran is 'only hinted at in *Dubliners*, but the story of her marriage... is continued in *Ulysses*'. On Bloomsday, 'Bob Doran is on his great "annual bend" of boozing and women, driven to this excess by his demanding "little concubine of a wife", who with her mother, the "old prostitute", makes him "toe the line" the rest of the year.' Polly may have married, but like Eveline, her life is doomed to follow the course of her mother's, as the 'family pattern of the dominant wife and the inebriate husband is repeated'. In addition to this, Polly's life with Doran typifies another situation common in Ireland at the time: 'Polly's "managed" marriage to a man older than herself reflects an Irish social pattern in which marriages are late and carefully calculated' (48).

Walzl examines other stories in which Joyce makes the mother–child relationship an important part of the narrative, but instead of focusing primarily on the 'mothers in relationship to their daughter's romance' these stories deal in more general terms with the mother's influence upon the children's lives. 'A Mother' deals with 'maternal influence upon a girl's career'. As Walzl has already established, it also depicts 'two intrinsically Irish situations affecting women: for the mother, a marriage to an older commonplace man, entered into out of desperation at the prospect of spinsterhood; and for the daughter, a chance at one of the few professional careers open to women at this period: music'. Walzl has already examined the frustrated Mrs Kearney who marries a bootmaker, giving up on her youthful hope for a 'brilliant life'. She returns to the story in order to discuss how Mrs Kearney's 'disappointment in her own marriage finds outlet in her maneuvering her daughter toward a concert career' (48).

The daughter, Kathleen, is educated in the same fashion as her mother. Mrs Kearney had 'learned French and music' (*D*: 136) in her youth, and she 'sends Kathleen to the Academy to learn "French and music", in preparation for a career as pianist and popular vocalist' (48). Mrs Kearney's actions on Kathleen's behalf eventually have an effect opposite to that which Mrs Kearney had intended. On the evening of an important concert Mrs Kearney makes a fuss about the fee her daughter is supposed to receive and 'orders the girl out of the theater rather than risk her not being paid for [the] concert' (49). Walzl sees this in terms of a repetition of the events of the mother's life: 'in the end, the mercenariness and unwillingness to take chances which Mrs Kearney had exhibited in her own life choice overcome her ambition for her daughter'. When Mrs Kearney stormed out of the concert rooms, 'Kathleen followed her mother meekly' (*D*: 149). Walzl sees the fates of Eveline, Polly and Kathleen ironically echoing the cliché 'like father, like son'. She describes it as a case of ' [a]s mothers so daughters' and explains that '... in these stories... the situation of the first generation becomes the condition of the second. ...[M]others tend to transform their daughters into replicas of themselves' (49).

A similar situation exists in mother–son relationships. Walzl asserts that this type of relationship is 'equally destructive because of the matriarchal system in Ireland. In support of her argument she quotes an article from the *Journal of the Irish Medical Association*. The article discusses a family which J. B. Lyons, in *James Joyce and Medicine* (Dublin: Dolmen Press, 1973), describes as 'characteristic of Irish culture':

> The male, doted on by his mother, reared in a monosexual atmosphere in school, who has never learned to form a friendship with the opposite sex of his own age – then marries and takes a 'housekeeper' into his home – while he continues his friendship with his male friends – 'the lads'. She goes on to become the mother of his children, invests her life in these and so carries on the pattern into the next generation.
>
> (Lyons: 93; Cited, Walzl: 49)

Walzl finds this pattern illustrated in 'A Little Cloud', when Little Chandler... discovers he is a 'little man' who has been trapped by marriage in a little life in a 'little house' by a 'little wife': Chandler's 'wife, rejecting her ineffective husband, turns to their infant son, whom she fondles as "My little man! My little Mannie!"' (49). The child's life, Walzl suggests, will repeat the pattern of Little Chandler's:

> The child's future as the coddled son who will replace [the wife's] husband in her affections and for whom every sacrifice will be made is thus forecast. He will grow up an incomplete human being, unable to sustain a mean-ingful relationship with anyone other than his mother.
>
> (49)

Walzl believes that her study 'provides one reason for *Dubliners*' renown': Joyce's depiction of 'Dublin social life', and particularly its depiction of the lives of female Dubliners, is 'solidly based on historical reality' (53). The accuracy of Joyce's picture of the lives of his female characters is supported by historical records of the time: 'the lives and careers of [his] different women of different ages and types can be authenticated in full, verifiable detail from a variety of sociological sources'. Walzl sees the male and female characters living equally bleak lives, both sexes being subject to the 'drastic economic and social pressures [which] actually forced Dubliners into such situations of frustration, deprivation, and hostility'. She does not believe, however, that Joyce was fair in his treatment of males and females. While Joyce 'spares neither sex... and sympathizes with both', he is more sympathetic to the male than to the female characters.

Walzl finds what she calls a 'male signature' on the stories of *Dubliners*: while Joyce 'felt sympathy for women caught in restrictive social conditions', his sympathy 'is... often tempered by [an] ironic dissection of feminine weakness or hypocrisy or sometimes biased by male ambivalence or even hostility to the smothering role of women in the various developing phases of their lives' (53). Walzl clearly believes in the value of *Dubliners* as an 'extraordinary combination of factual social reality and artful techniques', but she thinks Joyce's sympathetic bias toward his male characters sufficient to justify a slight modification of Joyce's idea of the indifferent artist's god-like qualities:

> In these stories of women, the complexities of motivation, shifts in point of view, and uncertainty of interpretation, especially of conclusions, all reveal in Joyce a subtle, elusive artist standing ambivalently behind his characters – like a man, not a god – alternatively biting and paring his fingernails.
>
> (53–4)

Suzette Henke: *A Portrait of the Artist as a Young Man*

In keeping with the chronological order in which the essays of *Women in Joyce* investigate Joyce's work, the next essay is Henke's investigation of *A Portrait* as 'As a Portrait of the Artist as a Young Misogynist'. Drawing on Freud's theory of the Oedipus complex and de Beauvoir's ideas on the mother–son relationship, Henke examines Stephen Dedalus' relations with the females in his life and the thoughts and emotions which he expresses about them. Henke's aim is to determine the extent to which Joyce's depiction of his young artist's attitudes to females is a result of his ironic satirising of Dedalus' 'logocentric paradigm' (101). The thesis of her study is that females 'are present everywhere and nowhere' in the novel; they 'pervade' it, 'yet remain elusive'. But because the females are 'portrayed almost exclusively from Stephen's point of view ... they often appear as one-dimensional projections' of Stephen's 'narcissistic imagination' and 'emerge as the psychological "other", forceful antagonists in the novel's dialectical structure ... [and] emblems of the flesh, – frightening reminders of sex, generation, and death' (82).

Henke finds Stephen's misogyny taking root in his infantile experience of the distinction between males and females: 'At the dawn of infantile consciousness, Stephen perceives the external world in terms of complementary pairs.' These constitute a series of opposing binary pairs like those which we saw as central to structuralist theory. The terms opposing each other in a complementary form for the baby Stephen are: 'male and female, father and mother, politics and religion, Davitt and Parnell'. Henke believes that these pairs organise 'Baby Tuckoo's cosmos' and 'set the stage for a dialectic of personal development' that ultimately structures much of the novel. The figures of the mother and father, when viewed 'from a psychological perspective', offer contrasting powers to the child. His 'mother seems to be in touch with the overwhelming chaos of nature'; his father 'offers a model of logocentric control' in which actions and emotions are governed and controlled by central logical principles. Mr Dedalus is seen as 'masculine and aloof, visually separated by a glass monocle and a hairy face'. He is the 'bearer of the word' and tells a story that appeals to the child's imagination and awakens him to a sense of individual 'identity'. In contrast to this, Mrs Dedalus 'relates to the boy primarily as caretaker; she satisfies her son's physical desires and encourages his artistic expression by playing the piano' (82).

Stephen grows and his social circle expands, and Henke sees the mother and the character of Dante assuming the role of inhibitors in 'a reality principle that begins ... to take precedence over the gratifications of infantile narcissism ... [and demands] the repression of libidinous tendencies and a conquest of the id in favour of a developing social ego' (83). Henke cites the passage where Mrs Dedalus and Dante join forces in demanding that Stephen 'apologise' as an example of the 'first of many imperatives that thwart the boy's ego':

> He hid under the table. His mother said:
> – O, Stephen will apologise.
> Dante said:
> – O, if not, the eagles will come and pull out his eyes.
> (*P*: 8; Cited, 83)

In *Stephen Hero*, Stephen proposes what Henke sees as a 'misogynist' 'theory of dualism which would symbolize the twin eternities of spirit and nature in the twin eternities of male and female (*SH*: 21)' (84). Henke draws on Freud and de Beauvoir in order to create a context in which she can examine these 'twin eternities' as they structure Stephen's early life in *A Portrait*. From Freud she adopts the idea that:

the primordial conflict between male and female takes root in the infant's early discovery of a world alien to his sensibilities and antagonistic to the demands of his omnipotent will. ...[T]he child begins to distinguish between ego and environment, between self and other... become[ing] aware of a dangerous threat to his own struggle for individuation. ...[H]e symbolically equates the mother... with the enemy that frustrates his desires and threatens to engulf his newly-acquired sense of self.

(83)

One result of this process is that the female takes on 'extraordinary and mysterious powers. A goddess in her authority, she is unconsciously identified with the hated flesh that eludes the infant's control' (83). From Simone de Beauvoir's *The Second Sex*, Henke takes the theory that:

The uncleanness of birth is reflected upon the mother.... And if the little boy remains in early childhood sensually attached to the maternal flesh, when he grows older, becomes socialized, and takes note of his individual existence, this same flesh frightens him... calls him back to those realms of immanence whence he would fly.

(Beauvoir: 136; Cited, 84)

Drawing upon these theories, Henke attempts to fathom Stephen's growing alienation from his mother and his simultaneous retreat to the maternal realm as a haven of safety from the unpleasant reality of life at Clongowes: 'He disdains his mother's feminine vulnerability and thinks that she is "not nice"' when she cries, but '[c]aught in a stampede of "flashing eyes and muddy boots", he is horrified by the bestial fury of the crowd ... [and] mentally takes refuge in artistic evocations of the family hearth' (84). At school he steels himself to 'adopt an ethic of male stoicism because "his father had told him... whatever he did, never to peach on a fellow" (*P*: 9).' But when he remembers Wells pushing him into the ditch, 'Stephen projects himself... to an apparently dissociated reverie... recall[ing] his mother sitting by the fire in hot "jewelly slippers" that exude a "lovely warm smell" (*P*: 10)' (84).

Tracing Stephen's development as he matures, Henke sees him as a character 'compelled to cast off allegiance to maternal figures'. Dante, his 'childhood educator', 'a clever woman and a wellread women' is replaced by Father Arnall 'who knew more than Dante because he was a Priest' (85). Stephen respects the priests who 'invite [him] to ponder the mysteries of religion, death, canker, and cancer'. The priests confirm Stephen's rejection of the female as they 'introduce him to a system of male authority and discipline, to a pedagogical regimen that will ensure his "correct training" and proper socialization'. Henke emphasises the impersonal and militaristic nature of this education:

Through examinations that pit red rose against white, Yorks against Lancastrians, they make education an aggressive game of simulated warfare. The students, like soldiers, are depersonalized through institutional surveillance.

(85)

In the famous Christmas dinner scene where Dante and Mr Casey argue about the political responsibility of the Catholic clergy, Henke sees Stephen 'assimilat[ing] the knowledge that rabid women like Dante support ecclesiastical authority in the name of moral righteousness'. In the battle between the sexes, she suggests, 'Mother Church emerges as a bastion of sexual repression defended by hysterical women', and 'Dante's... credibility is negated by spinsterhood and [the] involuntary celibacy' of which Stephen becomes aware when his father describes Dante as a "spoiled nun"' (85–6).

From Henke's feminist perspective, Stephen's education teaches him 'to survive in a society that protects bullies like Wells and sadists like Father Dolan, that condones brutality, and that takes advantage of the weak and the helpless'. She finds this process accurately described in Philip Slater's *The Glory of Hera* as a 'young boy's socializ[ation] into... a culture of male narcissism' (Slater: 416, cited 86). Using Slater's description as a context for Stephen's education she states that:

> single-sex education and the separation of male children from the emotional refuge of the family promotes misogyny, narcissism, and a terror of the female. ...Once the child is deprived of maternal affection, he 'seeks compensation through self-aggrandizement – renouncing love for admiration – and in this he is encouraged by the achievement pressures placed upon him, and presumably by the myriad narcissistic role models he finds around him. He becomes vain, hypersensitive, invidious, ambitious,... boastful, and exhibitionistic.'
>
> (Slater: 439; Cited, 86–7)

This is the process that Henke sees at work as Stephen appeals to Father Conmee after the pandying by Father Dolan. She believes that Stephen is 'motivated not only by optimistic faith in a male-controlled world, but by personal vanity and a tendency toward exhibitionism'. This faith is misplaced, however, and Joyce satirises his young character's attempt to seek justice. While Stephen 'naively believes that he will be exonerated', the eventual outcome of the episode is that 'Dolan and Conmee, in smug condescension, "had a famous laugh over it" (*P*: 72).' (87)

Henke divides many of *A Portrait*'s female characters into basic stereotypes: the 'virgin and the whore', the 'Catholic Virgin', and the 'birdgirl' or 'aesthetic muse'. Stephen replies to Cranly's question, 'Tell me, for example, would you deflower a virgin?' 'Excuse me,... is that not the ambition of most young gentlemen?' (*P*: 246). Henke examines the unconscious link between the females in Stephen's life and the Virgin Mary. These females include both the imaginary characters like Mercedes and the 'real' characters like EC and the prostitute. 'Figuratively', Henke explains, 'it is Stephen's ambition throughout the novel to "deflower" the Blessed Virgin of Catholicism. He wants to supplant the Catholic Madonna with a profane surrogate, an aesthetic muse rooted in sensuous reality' (87). Stephen cannot, of course, meet the shadowy Mercedes of his imagination, and he is 'no longer the Count of Monte Cristo' when he experiences his 'holy encounter' with the prostitute. Even after this 'real' experience, however, his idea of females stays the same, his 'vision of the female... has remained essentially unchanged':

> The traditional dichotomy between virgin and whore, madonna and temptress, breaks down. ...For him, all women encompass both roles. As a child, he feared the sexual implications of his mother's kiss. He... spurns... Mercedes and finds temporary salvation in the arms of a prostitute, who exacts the kiss earlier withheld from Emma. All the women in Stephen's life are both nurturant and demanding. They are sporadically aloof, solicitous, and sexually receptive.
>
> (91)

In short, they all embody some aspect of the traditional, male, stereotypical cliché of the whore with the heart of gold, the whore who is 'an ambivalent figure of masculine aggression and feminine protection. She demands erotic surrender, yet shelters her adolescent charge in a tender, maternal care' (91).

Emma Clery is the character whom Henke finds linked most closely with the Catholic Virgin in Stephen's mind. Hence his shame at 'making her the object of his masturbatory fantasies':

> The image of Emma appeared before him and, under her eyes, the flood of shame rushed forth anew from his heart. If she knew to what his mind had subjected her or how his brutelike lust had torn and trampled upon her innocence! Was that boyish love? Was that chivalry? Was that poetry?
>
> (*P*: 115; Cited: 91)

The link between Emma and the Catholic Virgin is reinforced when Stephen repents. After feeling 'that he has violated both Emma's honour and his own code of chivalry – not to mention the rigorous ethic of purity enforced by Catholicism... Emma, he decides, shall serve as his envoy to the Blessed Mother'. For Stephen, Emma does not exist as a person in her own right; only as a vehicle to help him 'recoup his spiritual losses'. Without the help of the 'innocent and virginal Emma', Henke argues, 'Stephen is as "helpless and hopeless" as the souls of the damned (*P*: 138)' (92). Stephen returns to the church, determined to 'repress the emergence of adolescent sexuality and to repent of the one sin that mortifies him even more than murder'. In so doing he must 'turn back to the woman emblematic of Catholic worship' (93).

Henke concludes her investigation of Stephen's attitudes towards the female characters in the novel with a consideration of how Stephen distances himself from any real involvement with the novel's females. In part his narcissism is to blame: in 'his return to ritualistic devotion, Stephen has actually become involved in an aesthetic love affair with his own soul. The anima, the feminine aspect of his psyche, has won his passion and holds him enthralled' (93). Stephen never learns how to overcome his fear of females in *A Portrait*, and even in the epiphanic vision on the beach, he perceives the bird-like girl not as a fellow human being, but as an idealised form of the female: the inspiring muse. Joyce, however, depicts Stephen's fear of the female with a 'pervasive irony' that Henke sees operating in Stephen's religious duties, his aesthetic theories, and his attitudes towards females:

> The pervasive irony that tinges the hero's scrupulous devotions, and gives his aesthetic theories that 'true scholastic stink' surely informs his relations with women – from his mother and Dante Riordan to Emma and the unnamed bird-girl he idealizes on the beach.
>
> (102)

Henke believes that Joyce wanted to make it clear to his readers that 'Stephen's fear of women and contempt for sensuous life are among the many inhibitions that stifle his creativity'. While Stephen is not aware that he must overcome his fear of women in order to create, his creator most certainly was. With *Ulysses* 'a new model begin[s] to emerge – one that recognizes the need for the intellectual artist to "make his peace" with woman and to incorporate into his work the vital, semiotic flow of female life' (102).

Ruth Bauerle: *Exiles*

Ruth Bauerle's study, 'Bertha's role in *Exiles*' does not offer itself as a particularly strong feminist reading of Joyce, but it does concentrate on the leading female character in order to show that she is the strongest character in the play. Bauerle relies primarily on traditional character analysis to show that although Bertha 'is an object,... [a] sexual... one [also] representing artistic achievement or political victory' for the male characters, she is the character who ultimately triumphs by the end of the play (116). Bauerle describes Bertha as a 'natural, untutored being, with little formal education, a Joycean women not concerned with a career, but able and willing to follow Rowan's desires even if they should direct her to Hand's bed' (111). She finds Bertha's lack of a surname a significant indication of her strength. 'Only Bertha stands alone, without surname or profession: to join Rowan in exile she has given up "religion,

family, my own peace" (*E*: 100).' Bertha's name is examined in the
context of the 'enlightening' 'folklore surrounding her single name':

> Twelfth Night was called in the Eastern church both *Epiphania*... and
> *Theophania* (meaning a showing forth of God). Joyce, of course, associated
> this sense of showing forth with the term 'epiphany'. In Old German this
> feast of Theophania, the showing-forth, became translated as '*Giperahta
> Naht*, the brightened night', or 'Bertha's night'.
>
> (111)

Bauerle draws on Charlotte M. Yonge's *History of Christian Names* in
order to trace the etymology of 'Bertha':

> By the analogy of saints' days, Perahta, or Bertha, was erected into an indi-
> vidual character, called... the mild Berchte; in whose honour all the young
> farming men in the Salzburg mountains go dancing. ...Sometimes she is a
> gentle white lady, who steals softly to neglected cradles, and rocks them...
> Herrings and oat-bread are put outside the door for her on her festival –
> a token of its Christian origin; but there is something of heathenism
> connected with her... .
>   That Frau Bertha is an impersonation of the Epiphany there seems little
> doubt, but it appears that there was an original mythical Bertha, who
> absorbed the brightened night.
>
> (Yonge: 213–14; Cited: 112)

Tracing the name's Teutonic links with the 'earth goddess Hertha' and
its association with the 'earth goddess Perchta', Bauerle argues that 'a
number of correspondences between... details of the myths and... Joyce's
drama serve to deepen our understanding of the play'. She admits that
Joyce 'nowhere... state[s] directly that he had the Perchta myths in mind
when he wrote the play', but argues that the number of correspondences
between the myth and the play 'make his use of the Perchta material
probable' (113).

Bauerle cites a number of passages in which Robert and Richard treat
Bertha as an object:

> 'While you have a thing it can be taken from you... But when you give it,
> you have given it. No robber can take it from you... It is yours then for
> ever when you have given it. It will be yours always. That is to give.'
>
> (*E*: 46–7)
>
> 'Steal you could not in my house because the doors were open: nor take
> by violence if there were no resistance.'
>
> (*E*: 62)
>
> 'I thought he [Robert] was a common robber, prepared to use even
> violence against you. I had to protect you from that.'
>
> (*E*: 73)

She argues that Robert 'follows Richard's concepts of possession',
expressing the 'same sense that a man may own any women, including

Bertha' (116–17). 'In most of these exchanges' she explains, 'Rowan and Hand might be discussing a ship or a horse rather than a woman they profess to love.' On Bertha's initial refusal 'to contest this view', Bauerle says that the character's passivity 'makes her an object-victim for the male characters' (117). She sees this passivity as deriving 'in part from Joyce's conception of [Bertha] as a Christ figure' and cites Joyce's 'Notes' to the play:

> Bertha's state when abandoned spiritually by Richard must be expressed by the actress by a suggestion of hypnosis. Her state is like that of Jesus in the garden of olives. It is the soul of woman left naked and alone that it may come to an understanding of its own nature. She must appear also to *be carried forward* to the last point consistent with her immunity *by the current of the action.*
>
> ('Notes' 115, Bauerle's emphasis; Cited: 117)

Bauerle sees the ambivalence created by Bertha's associations with Christ and the earth goddess as an important part of her character. She believes that Joyce would have found 'no inconsistency in a heroine who is at once Perchta... and Christ'. '... both are mild and gentle. Christian myth adds, as Perchta's myth does not, the Joycean elements of wounding and betrayal' (118).

Bauerle sees Bertha's character in terms of 'elemental traits'. These include the passivity which she links with Bertha's Christ-like quality; the passionate rage which Bertha displays at the end of the first act and which Bauerle attributes to Bertha's 'suspicion that Rowan grants Bertha freedom only to free himself to pursue Beatrice'; and an 'unaffected naturalness which links her to Perchta, the earth goddess'. This last quality of naturalness is revealed for Bauerle by Bertha's 'praise of Archie (who "had too much nature" not to love her)' and by her 'criticism of Richard (who was unnatural in hating his own mother) [*E*: 52]'. Bertha's naturalness 'also leads [her] to easy action'. While Richard's exile is 'self-conscious[ ]', an 'act of defiance against his race and homeland', and Robert wants to 'enjoy a *reputation* as a free spirit', 'Bertha simply acts' (118). Bauerle finds this naturalness manifest in diverse forms: it allows Bertha to accept things 'in quietude' and it is 'evident in her attitude towards language'. This attitude is a 'major contrast between her and Robert'. Bertha is capable of saying 'openly... words that Hand fears to utter', and she 'disdains the inflated, unnatural language he so often uses'. Bertha's naturalness is also linked with her honesty: 'She is the only character', Bauerle says, 'who... never lies on her own initiative' (119).

Bertha's honesty leads her to speak frankly, and Bauerle contrasts this honesty and frankness both with the cowardice that Robert shows in refusing to speak truthfully with Richard, and with Robert's tendency to speak and act with what Bauerle describes as 'hyperbole... and a sense of

shame ("craftily, secretly, meanly, in the dark, in the night" [*E*: 69]).'
Bertha's honesty also 'distinguishes her from... Beatrice Justice', a
character whom Bauerle compares with 'the educated, literate women of
Joyce's own class in Dublin – women like Mary Sheehy, whom he
admired in his student days, or like the fictional Miss Ivors of 'The Dead'
and Emma Clery of *Stephen Hero* and *A Portrait*' (120–1). Bauerle concludes her examination of Bertha with a consideration of the common
critical view of Bertha as a 'forerunner of Molly Bloom'. 'She is more',
Bauerle contends. 'She is herself the precursor of Joyce's new hero, the
humane and lovable Leopold Bloom':

> As the Odyssean Bloom will do in 'Scylla and Charybdis', she has... steered
> her difficult passage between arrogant intellect and coarse sensuality. Like
> Bloom, she has nurtured the young... faced an antagonistic world with
> courage, and moved forward even when assailed by doubt. ...[S]he has
> shone like the moon, revealing to Hand courage and honor; to Beatrice,
> friendship; and to Rowan, compassion and the knowledge that he cannot,
> finally, know. Having once made Rowan a man, she now makes him
> human. It has been Bertha's night.
>
> (128)

Elaine Unkeless: *Ulysses*

Unkeless's 'The Conventional Molly Bloom' offers itself as an analysis of
Molly's character as a realistic figure. While examining Molly from this
perspective, it also offers a useful critique of previous critical views of
Molly, correcting what Unkeless sees as inaccurate assessments of Joyce's
Penelope. The thesis of the essay is that although 'many readers' have
'found [Molly] to be' an 'elusive and multifaceted character', the 'traits
with which [Joyce] endows her stem from conventional notions of the
way a woman acts and thinks' (150). Joyce's view of women, according
to Unkeless, is conventional and incorporates the stereotypical male view
of the woman-as-whore figure. Molly is preoccupied with sex: 'most of
[her] actions are associated directly or indirectly with sex, and non-sexual
activities are scarcely mentioned'. Unkeless believes that Joyce wanted the
reader to see Molly as a 'middle-class housewife who would like to be a
queen', that he 'emphasizes [her] laziness and suggests that she has spent
much of the day beautifying herself'. In support of her argument that
Joyce saw 'Molly's lethargy' as 'typically female', Unkeless cites his
comment to Valery Larbaud: 'Autour de cette parole ["yes"] et de trois
autres également femelles l'episode tourne lourdement sur son axe'.
Because the 'episode turns ponderously around four "female" words
("because", "bottom", "woman", "yes", [*Letters* 1, 169, 170]),'
Unkeless finds its 'heaviness becoming too female by implication' (150).

The first critical views of Molly which Unkeless considers are put forward by Stanley Sultan and Darcy O'Brien who condemn 'Molly for begrudging what "little housework" she has to do' and imply that 'she is not fulfilling her feminine role'. Unkeless thinks such views stem from the practice of allowing Bloom's role as representative of 'the feminine warmth of the hearth' to overshadow consideration of Molly as the character who actually 'performs most of the drudgery'. 'Critics delight in pointing out... that Mr. Bloom buys his own breakfast, cooks the kidney, and serves his wife tea' she states, but 'few readers note that Molly does most of the shopping, prepares dinner, and... is responsible for maintaining order'. Joyce's own assumption that 'the responsibility of executing household chores rests on the female' is partially responsible for the confusion: 'the one sphere in which she regularly acts is hardly touched upon. ...That Bloom's fewer and more palatable tasks are described extensively by Joyce does not preclude Molly's conventional female tasks' (150–1).

In 'The Theme of *Ulysses*' (*Kenyon Review*, **18**: 31, 1956) William Empson states that music 'is one of the few serious positive arts' in the novel (Cited: 151). Unkeless argues that while Molly's singing is 'stressed', 'Joyce also disparages it'. She cites Ruth von Phul's 'Joyce and the Strabismal Apologia' (*A James Joyce Miscellany*, Carbondale: Southern Illinois UP, 1959): 'one of the reasons that Joyce rejected a musical career... is that to him, "the interpreter of another man's music has a role inferior to the creative role Joyce... elected".' For Joyce, Unkeless contends, songs can be 'merely airs – the flatulence of Simon Dedalus or the "winds" of Molly Bloom':

> yes Ill sing Winds that blow from the south... give us room even to let a fart God or do the least thing better yes hold them like a bit on my side piano quietly sweeeee theres that train far away pianissimo eeeeeee one more song
> that was a relief wherever you be let your wind go free
> (*U*: 628; Cited, 153–4)

Unkeless sees Joyce using music to confirm Molly's primary interest in sex, because 'throughout *Ulysses*, music is frequently linked with sex:'

> The warbling sirens lure with song and body, ...Stephen talks about the theory of music and plays the piano in Bella Cohen's 'music room'. Molly's singing is almost always connected with her sexuality – in the way she envisions herself on stage... and in its association with men. Invariably, when Molly sings with someone, flirtation accompanies the performance.
> (152)

Boylan is arranging Molly's singing tour, and 'to Molly... singing with Boylan means making love with him'. For Molly, Unkeless argues, 'singing is a talent which helps to create her identity not as a singer or as an independent person but as a lover' (153).

On Bloomsday, Unkeless argues, 'Molly Bloom's one significant act is to have an affair with Blazes Boylan'. Her creator is '[d]elineating [her] mainly as a sexual being', which 'confines her character to a conventional role'. This stereotypical view of Molly is not confined to her sexual behaviour but also extends to her lack of action, to 'the fact that she does so little'. That Molly remains in the house, and primarily in bed, limits her perspective. Unkeless draws on Mary Ellmann's *Thinking About Women* (New York: Harcourt Brace Jovanovich, 1968) to show how Molly's bed contributes to Joyce's stereotyping of her: 'Beds, as the most amorphous articles of furniture in the house, are favoured in the stereotype' (Ellmann: 76; Cited: 154). Molly occupies the conventional role of the woman '[i]n bed, [who] waiting alone for her husband-lover to return... daydreams about her pleasures and anxieties'. The 'consequences' of woman's 'passive... inaction' are analysed by de Beauvoir:

> In the world of men, her... thought, not flowing into any project, since she *does* nothing, is indistinguishable from daydreaming. She has no sense of factual truth...; she never comes to grips with anything but words and mental pictures, and that is why the most contradictory assertions give her no uneasiness... She is content, for her purposes, with extremely vague conceptions, confusing parties, opinions, places, people, events; her head is filled with a strange jumble.
>
> (de Beauvoir: 564; Cited, 154)

Unkeless finds this analysis applicable to Molly, adding that Molly's 'outpouring of words' is a 'manifestation of her frustration at not participating in the world outside of 7 Eccles Street' (154).

Unkeless does not agree with T. S. Eliot's view that 'discussion of plot and characterization are more suitable for nineteenth-century novels than for modern works like Joyce's'. Although Joyce uses '*monologue intérieur* to examine the conscious mind and the unconscious', Unkeless believes that he also uses the 'nineteenth-century... emphasis on characters' feelings, their subtle moral decisions, and the resulting rational or irrational behaviour'. The character's actions constitute the behaviour which 'forms the plot of *Ulysses*', but 'more importantly' this behaviour 'helps to reveal the attributes of a character'. Molly's activity with Boyland is 'one of the foundations of the novel's plot', and one of the important ways in which Joyce reveals this 'one major action' is through Molly's interior monologue (154). Unkeless believes his depiction of Molly as 'a lethargic and passive woman... indicates Joyce's assumption about one of his major female creations': Molly is revealed not through a 'chronicling [of] her interaction with others... but, almost exclusively, by revealing her fantasy world and her emotions' (155).

Unkeless examines the world of Molly's fantasies in order to 'discover Molly's characteristics and... opinions'. She sees Molly as a 'comic figure whose unravelling thoughts, composed of illogical juxtapositions and conclusions, reveal her naiveté'. In 'The Empirical Molly' David Hayman argues that Molly's contradictions 'make her... intriguing: her bold earthiness and curious reticence; her tendency to be by turns masterful and submissive, unsentimentally frank and lyrically sentimental...' (*Approaches to 'Ulysses': Ten Essays* [Pittsburgh: Pittsburgh UP, 1970]: 120). Unkeless agrees with Hayman's 'general' assessment of Molly's character, but finds James Van Dyck Card's more specific analyses of Molly's contradictory statements a little more helpful. In '"Contradicting": The Word for Penelope' (*JJQ*, 10 [Summer, 1973]: 439–1), Card says that 'Molly can have it both ways because she's mindless'. Unkeless finds this an accurate description of Molly's character, but also sees Joyce's view of the mindlessness of his character as very important: 'one must question whether "Joyce is laughing with her as well as at her" since Molly, unaware of the incongruities, does not laugh at herself'. Unkeless seems somewhat ambivalent in her thoughts on Joyce's own attitude to Molly. While his 'derision of Molly is not predominantly bitter', 'his comedy is based on a supposition that a woman's method of thinking is irrational and disconnected'. This ambivalence, however, may be a result of Unkeless's recognition of an ambiguity which she believes Joyce intended:

> Even if Molly's sentences can be punctuated, even if each statement follows the one before it 'realistically' within the stream of consciousness technique, and even if scholars can find patterns in Molly's thoughts, Joyce intends the sentences to be flowing and elusive, and the statements to be illogical.
>
> (Unkeless: 155)

Molly's attitude towards language enables Unkeless to distinguish between Joyce's own powerful language and his use of it to depict a stereotypical female who is both uneducated and stupid. Unkeless disagrees with Sultan's belief that 'what is taken to be [Molly's] stupidity is a lack of education in a rather perceptive mind' (Sultan: 426; Cited, 163). While Joyce has created 'Penelope' as a 'chapter... which consists only of thoughts, Molly belittles the importance of words' (162). Molly makes 'poor use of language', and has a 'lack of intellect'. Together, these limitations contribute to making her a 'stereotype of the simpleminded woman'. Even while he uses his linguistic skills to create a powerfully evocative, poetic language, Joyce does not let the reader forget that Molly 'is being ridiculed' (162). Unkeless does not accept the critical view that 'Molly's anti-intellectuality is... a positive attribute'; nor that in 'giving Molly the "last word", Joyce is humbling himself'. She believes that 'Molly herself thinks words are unimportant because she lacks comprehension of them, not because she adopts the critical attitude that words can never fully express human experience'. Molly is 'not ironic, only negative'. While she accepts that Molly can be seen as a 'symbol' with which Joyce 'shows deference to the natural', she contends that as an individual character, Molly's 'lack of knowledge limits her to the stereotyped role of the ignorant female':

> Thinking of Molly's anti-intellectuality as praiseworthy for her sake, as some critics do, saying that she is the wisest character in *Ulysses* and that she represents a world superior to Joyce's is at best fallacious.
>
> (164)

Shari Benstock: *Finnegans Wake*

There are two essays on *Finnegans Wake* in *Women in Joyce*: Benstock's 'The Genuine Christine: Psychodynamics of Issy' and Margot Norris's 'Anna Livia Plurabelle: The Dream Woman'. Norris studies the female ALP within the context of the *Wake*'s 'transformations of the female's form and functions in the work as symptoms of the dreamer's disturbances concerning psychological issues that are generated within family life: erotic desires, aggressive impulses, conflicts over authority, and dependence, repression, and rebellion'. Because we have considered Norris's work, it is Benstock's essay that we will consider here as a representative study of the *Wake* in *Women in Joyce*.

Benstock's essay provides an example of the diversity of theoretical perspectives used in feminist approaches to Joyce. Indeed, her essay is less a strictly feminist essay than one which draws on manuscript analysis, traditional textual explication, structuralism and psychoanalytic theory in order to examine the role of the *Wake*'s Issy while at the same time remaining sensitive to the feminist implications of Joyce's depiction of the daughter–father relation between Issy and HCE. The essay begins with Clive Hart's assertion that 'duality of being is perhaps the most important of all the basic structural concepts in *Finnegans Wake*'. Benstock uses Hart's principle as the basis of her own approach: 'whatever other more complex numerological systems Joyce experiments with in the *Wake*, the most fundamental and pervasive structure is rooted in the concept of duality'. This concept shapes her fundamental view of 'Issy, daughter of HCE and ALP, the young nubile who is both the saccharine sweet "nuvoletta in her lightdress, spunn of sixteen shimmers" (157. 8), and the sexually precocious writer of obscene footnotes to the children's lessons in II, 2'. Issy's dual roles are 'contrasting aspects' of her personality. They 'predominate in any discussion of her role... and she is often referred to as the "lookingglass girl", a reference to the mirror image with which she is narcissistically involved' (169).

Benstock investigates Issy in several different contexts. In the section 'Dr. Prince's Patient' she draws on Adaline Glasheen's '*Finnegans Wake* and the Girls from Boston, Mass' (*Hudson Review*, 7 [Spring, 1954]), a study which investigates Joyce's use of material from Dr Morton Prince's *The Dissociation of a Personality: A Biographical Study in Abnormal Psychology* (New York: Greenwood Press, 1969). Glasheen's study finds similarities between Issy and Christine L. Beauchamp, a patient of Prince's who possessed a multiple personality and exhibited an alter ego named Sally. Glasheen looks at Issy as 'one of those girls with a multiple personality' (Glasheen: 90; Cited, 169). As Benstock notes, Glasheen found an abundance of references to '"Beauchamp"... and to "Sally"... in the Issy section of *Finnegans Wake*', and 'sees similarities between the two women':

> the Christine/Sally split is reflected most obviously in Issy's uneasy amalgam of the sacred and profane, one side of the split ego characterized by the virginal Nuvoletta, the other by the sexually provocative and enticing temptress.... Glasheen suggests that the 'Maggies', Earwicker's temptresses in Phoenix Park, are another extension of Issy and 'her grateful sister reflection in a mirror' (220. 9) and that the famous letter from Boston, Mass., is written from one Maggy 'selfpenned' to her 'other'. (489. 33–4)
>
> (169–70)

The implications of Glasheen's argument, as Benstock states, are that 'Issy-as-temptress is her father's downfall, but Issy-as-letterwriter is her father's salvation, the letter itself constituting the defenses which can resurrect him' (170). Benstock agrees with this in part, but finds that Issy's complex nature requires a more sophisticated theory. The theory which Glasheen uses is similar to that which we saw in Unkeless's 'realistic' analysis of Molly Bloom, and it 'rests on the assumption that character delineation in *Finnegans Wake* functions much as it does in more traditional frameworks – i.e., that we can talk about Issy's psychological motivations in the same terms that we might use in discussing a character like Gerty MacDowell'. While such a theory might be relevant to *Ulysses*, however, 'Issy's complexities elude such straightforward answers: there is simply not enough evidence to justify any single theory of Issy's personality structure'. For this reason, Benstock establishes a number of contexts for investigating Issy.

A second context in which Benstock examines Issy is that provided by 'Earwicker's Vision', and in this context Benstock considers the infamous event in the park as a central episode of the entire book: 'The "sin" in the park, involving Earwicker and the two young mistresses, becomes the central mystery of the novel'. While she sees 'all possible combinations of motive and method' for the hidden action 'left open' 'in good Joycean fashion', Benstock nevertheless manages to reduce the 'basic variations' of the episode to two groups of possibilities which reflect the stereotype of the female as an ambiguous virgin/whore figure:

> either the two girls in the park are harmlessly urinating while Earwicker accidentally and innocently watches (34. 12–29, 178. 26–30, 348. 21–25); or the two girls are temptresses willingly titillating their aging observer, who in turn is either a casual bystander or a participant responding by urinating, defecating, or possibly masturbating (52. 1–3, 107. 1–7, 366. 22–25).
>
> (176–7)

Benstock points out that while the text offers 'numerous versions of the basic incident' (these include an elevation of the 'micturation-voyeurism theme to the level of incest coupled with heterosexual or homosexual perversion'), there is one constant: 'whatever the two maidens are doing (...incidental urination or deliberate exposure), they are doing it *together*' (177). She rejects the possibility that one of the females could be innocent while the other is guilty. The difference between the two alternatives depends on the context created by Earwicker's vision: 'the alternations in behaviour occur over time as Earwicker's dream exposes his ambivalence towards his wife, daughter and mother' (177).

A third context for her investigation of Issy's personality is provided in the section Benstock entitles 'The Real Missisliffi'. This part of 'The Genuine Christine' summarises a considerable amount of material outlining Joyce's incorporation of elements from a variety of sources into the story of Issy. These sources include Morton's study of Christine Beauchamp; *Alice in Wonderland* and biographical information about Charles Dodgson (Lewis Carroll) and his relationship with the model for Alice, Alice Liddell; and Jonathan Swift's *Journal to Stella* and his relation to Stella and Vanessa. Ultimately, however, it is in one of Joyce's letters to Harriet Shaw Weaver that Benstock finds a model for Issy. She quotes a letter of 7th March 1924, in which Joyce explains that 'Izzy will later be Isolde' of the King Mark–Tristan–Isolde triangle. 'In this version of the story', Benstock explains, 'the emphasis is upon Isolde of Ireland (a lady with a divided nature, "eyesolt of the binnoculises" [394. 30]) and her two lovers, Tristram and Mark.' 'If we can single out a primary model for young Miss Issy,' she declares, 'this "Isobel" seems to be it' (183).

Benstock draws on Joyce's *Letters*, David Hayman's *First Draft Version of 'Finnegans Wake'* (Austin: Texas UP, 1963) and the *Wake* manuscripts in order to establish the order in which Joyce gradually incorporated the material from his sources into the account of Earwicker's meeting with the two females. Joyce's goal was to discover 'analogue[s] for the old lover/young girl theme', and the Swift material is of particular importance. Benstock shows that this material provided Joyce with a 'comprehensive collation' which enabled him to draw together 'elements found in the other models for Earwicker and Issy':

> Swift is a tutor (as Joyce portrayed Dante) to young girls (Pepette, Beatrice, or Alice) on whom he has sexual designs... and his relationship with these women is recorded in letters... More interested in the private persona, Joyce cast Swift as another Lewis Carroll/Charles Dodgson (and Earwicker/ Porter), a man with ambivalent attitudes toward pubescent females. That a divided nature, possibly an aspect of Swift's madness, should take its form in writing love letters to himself... fits the last chink in this Joycean puzzle: less interested in the ingénue... than the 'doubled' male lead, Joyce directs his light into the dark corners of the male consciousness, questioning the motives of Swift, Dante, Dodgson, and Morton Prince – another male who may have been a 'tompip' under the guise of a medical practitioner.
>
> (183–4)

Finnegans Wake describes itself as a letter found in a midden heap, and fragments of letters abound throughout the text. These letters constitute a fourth context for Benstock's investigation of Issy. Referring back to her idea that Issy's ambiguity is a result of Earwicker's ambivalent attitude to his daughter, Benstock offers the hypothesis that ' [i] f the solution to the puzzle of Issy's personality lies in her father's ambivalence toward her, as the guilty dream seems to suggest, then the letters which record various versions of the park incident and Earwicker's culpability offer other important evidence about this "relationship"' (184). She begins by identifying 'two basic letters': 'one dug up on the midden heap by Biddy the hen, the letter from Boston, Mass., and one being written by ALP, dictated to Shem, to be "posted" by Shaun and addressed to the "Reverend" (615. 12)'. These letters become 'fused' in the dream, and, 'like the Swift letters... seem to be written in some kind of "secret" language, which, if decoded, Earwicker fears will provide damaging evidence of his guilt in the park incident' (184).

The letter from the midden heap is 'most often associated with Issy because it mentions a girl named "Maggy"'. Benstock sees the attempt at gaining evidence against Earwicker from this letter as an 'attempt to make something out of nothing', but after Biddy the hen turns 'the letter into literature', she produces a 'second version' which 'contains incriminating evidence against both Earwicker and Issy'. Biddy's version of the letter, which Benstock compares with a 'good critic['s]' 'reading' of a text, is:

> He had to see life foully the plak and the smut, (schwrites). There were three men in him (schwrites). Dancings (schwrites) was his only ttoo feebles. With apple harlottes. And a little mollvogels. Spissially (schwrites) when they peaches. Honeys wore camelia paints. Yours very truthful. Add dapple inn.
>
> (113. 13–18) (185–6)

While this document contains what might be 'incriminating evidence', Benstock sees it as 'fictions that Biddy weaves from the "facts" she has exhumed'. These fictions are a 'part of Earwicker's own guilt and his fear that a local gossip like Biddy will make his secret desires public – which she does'. The phrase 'his only ttoo feebles' offers an 'image' of Issy as 'double' (186).

Another variation of the Boston letter 'comes from Issy herself'. Benstock describes Issy in this context as 'a young student at her lessons', practising writing, who is 'learning all about domesticity... from her mother' in preparation for her 'impending marriage'. The letter is 'intended' for Maggy, the Boston relative, and records 'the entire writing process... including comments on Issy's mannerisms as she composes the missive':

> Dear (name of desired subject, A.N.), well, and I go on to. Schlickser. I and we (tender condolences for happy funeral, one if) so sorry to (mention person suppressed for the moment, F.M.). Well (enquiries after all-healths) how are you (question maggy). A lovely (introduce to domestic circles) pershan of cates. Shrubsher. Those pothooks mostly she hawks from Poppa Vere Foster but these curly mequeues are of Mippa's moulding. Shrubsheruthr. (Wave gently in the ere turning ptover.) Well, mabby (consolation of shopes) to soon air. With best from cinder Christinette if prints chumming, can be when desires Soldi, for asamples, backfronted or, if all, peethrolio or Get my Prize, using her flower or perfume or, if veryveryvery chumming, in otherwards, who she supposed adeal, kissists my exits. Shlicksheruthr. From Auburn chenlemagne.
>
> (280. 8–28) (186)

In terms of Issy's relation with her father, Benstock finds the 'intrusion of the father' into this letter 'an important signal of her role in the novel'. While the letter seems 'perfectly innocent and domestic', she says, 'Earwicker's guilt leads him to suspect otherwise'. On the pages before the letter's, Issy's footnote suggests that she may 'have designs on [Earwicker]: "He gives me pulpititions with his Castlecowards never in these twowsers and even in those twawsers and then babeteasing us out of our hoydenname" [276. n. 28–29]' (187). Benstock suggests that while words and phrases like 'Shlicksher', 'Shrubsher', and 'kissists my exits' 'take on double meanings' in the light of the footnote: 'Issy's letter with its erotic *double entendres*,' is, again, 'perhaps a product of Earwicker's own guilt' (187).

Benstock examines two other letters which 'seem to bear [Issy's] stamp'. These are the letters written to [Issy's] 'pepette' lover like the one which operates as answer to question 10 in I. 6: 'I know, peppette, of course, dear, but listen, precious!' (143. 31). They are marked by what Benstock calls 'Issy's gushy-gooey style' and show a 'preponderance of the diminutive form ("you perfect little pigaleen" [143. 35]) coupled with babytalk and the lisping "s"... ' (187). Benstock's analysis leads her to the conclusion that 'Issy is no mindless female, however much she babbles'. Issy is sexually aware and HCE's 'guilt over the park incident and his fear that Issy may have knowledge of his sin are directly linked' to this awareness. A part of Issy's sexual awareness, Benstock suggests, is a result of the episode in which she sees her parents as 'they prepared to engage in lovemaking': 'The dame dowager's duffgerent to present wappon, blade drawn to the full and about wheel without to be seen of them. The infant Isabella from her coign to do obeisance toward the duffgerent, as first furtherer with drawn brand' (566. 21–24). Benstock uses this episode and the nature of Issy's sexual awareness further to discount the argument that Issy was directly modelled upon Christine Beauchamp: 'A similar sight of sexual prowess probably caused Miss Beauchamp to disintegrate and fragment, producing multiple personalities, but Issy's early knowledge results in her early sexual precocity and engenders the lingering fear in her father that she knows – or perhaps remembers – too much' (190).

'Anna Livia's Version' of the future events that will transpire concerning Issy provides the final context for Benstock's investigation of 'The Genuine Christine': 'It is left to Anna Livia, who has the final "word" in the novel, to confirm the future for her daughter'. Part of Anna's last speech concerns Issy:

> Yes, you're changing, sonhusband, and you're turning, I can feel you, for a daughterwife from the hills again. Imlamaya. And she is coming. Swimming in my hindmoist. Diveltaking on me tail. Just a whisk brisk sly spry spink spank sprint of a thing theresomere, saultering. Saltarella come to her own. I pity your oldself I was used to. Now a younger's there.
> (627. 1–6) (190–1)

Benstock sees Issy replacing Anne 'in the cosmic (and at the human) level' in this passage. She sees the relation between the two as a case of like mother, like daughter and provides several examples of the similarities between the two from chapter 8:

> the gossips... washing the Earwickers' dirty linen in public, have confirmed that Anna Livia too was a 'gadabout in her day, so she must, more than most (202. 4–5), and that she too was a young temptress who led Earwicker to his first sexual fall. As a young girl she was busy 'making mush mullet's eyes at her boys dobelon' and spent hours gazing at her mirror image ('I recknitz wharfore the darling murrayed her mirror' [208. 32–33, 35]). The description of her as a 'young thin pale soft shy slim slip of a thing then' (202. 7) echoes her description of her daughter, whose present 'spankiness' counters the mother's earlier shyness.
> (191)

'In many ways', Benstock asserts, 'the mother and daughter are mirror images of each other'. Issy herself seems to have realised this when she 'told the four elders': 'Narcississies are as the coaters of inversion. Secilas through their laughing classes becoming poolermates in laker life' (526. 35–36). Benstock believes that although 'Issy is currently the inversion of her mother', Anna Livia's 'hints' allow us to see that the 'diverse and flighty Issy' will eventually develop into 'the calm and unified mother/wife that Anna Livia now is: "For she'll be sweet for you as I was sweet when I came down out of me mother... And let her rain now if she likes. Gently or strongly as she likes. Anyway let her rain for my time is come" (627. 7–9, 11–13)' (191).

In depicting Issy's personality, Joyce would seem to have succeeded in creating a female character who transcends the limitations which Unkeless finds in Molly Bloom. Benstock shows that the duality of Issy's personality 'may be seen as another extension of the virgin/whore complex... familiar to readers of Joyce as it dominates descriptions of females from *Chamber Music* through *Ulysses*', but her analysis reveals that the personality of Issy may be far too complex to be summarised simply as another case of such stereotyping (175). 'At the level of cosmic correspondence', Benstock states, 'Issy's role as her mother's past and future provides a correlative to her familial role' (173). Together with the similarities which Benstock shows existing between ALP and Issy, Issy's complex personality suggests that she, too, may be able to achieve what her mother has and transcend the 'human level to assume status as woman' (171). Benstock believes that the 'surface reality that confines Molly Bloom to 7 Eccles Street does not contain ALP', and her analysis of Issy strongly suggests that Issy also escapes this confinement. To the question of whether Joyce could create a 'gramma's grammar' and create a complex female character not limited to Western stereotypes, 'The Genuine Christine' would seem to reply in the affirmative.

Bonnie Kime Scott

Scott is a leading Anglo-American feminist writer on Joyce, and she has written two books examining Joyce from a feminist perspective. In *Joyce and Feminism* (Bloomington: Indiana UP and Brighton: The Harvester Press, 1984) she establishes a set of feminist frameworks for studying Joyce and examines the 'mythical, historical and cultural contexts' for an investigation of the women in Ireland before moving on to consider the women in Joyce's life and his three female characters of Emma Clery, Molly Bloom, and Issy. In her second book, *James Joyce* (Brighton: The Harvester Press, 1987) Scott summarises her earlier study and its approach to these characters. Explaining that she views her own work as 'connected and ongoing', Scott states that:

In *Stephen Hero*... Emma Clery plays opposite Stephen Dedalus, whose perceptions of her include muse and goddess. But Emma has a set of aspirations that had been neglected in previous criticism. I have examined her educational and nationalist interests as aspects of female culture in Joyce's background. Molly Bloom... emerged in my study with several roles. As a realistic character she takes on the values and limitations of identities such as Jew, child of the Gibraltar garrison, and Dubliner – in the aspects of married woman, mother and female artiste. More forcefully, she also plays an iconoclast whose complaints coincide with much of the feminist consciousness-raising of her own era and of the late 1960s. Finally, I questioned the ideologies behind usual critical interpretations of her as earth mother and offered new goddess associations, particularly from the Celtic world... The third female character... was Issy, the daughter figure of *Finnegans Wake*, and like Emma Clery, a young woman with intellectual potential. Issy uses wit, sarcasm and linguistic invention to comment upon patriarchal culture and to respond to the artist figure of the *Wake*. She also has mythical dimensions – including identification with the Egyptian goddess, Isis, and Deirdre, a fugitive from patriarchal plot in Irish myth.

(xiii–xiv)

In the context of the ongoing nature of her work, Scott sees these earlier studies as the beginning of a project which she continues in her second book: they 'only began [her] feminist character analysis in Joyce' (xiv). As Scott has contributed much more to the feminist studies of Joyce's work than any other Anglo-American critic, and as she herself views her work as connected and ongoing, it is on her second study that we will concentrate our attention.

While *Joyce and Feminism* relies primarily on the critical approaches traditionally favoured by Anglo-American feminists, *James Joyce* takes a much more eclectic critical approach. In the 'Introduction' to *James Joyce*, Scott explains how she has modified her theoretical approach to include French feminist theory:

> The feminist side of my designation began... with an Anglo-American tendency... My first interests were to recover the real women around Joyce, and to investigate the role of women Joyce selected to depict as characters... I subsequently found the Continent a valuable wandering ground... this has meant an attraction to French feminist theory... Keeping up with Joyce studies in the last decade has required acquaintance with French psychoanalytic and linguistic approaches to Joyce. Joycean feminists... have tended to be more comfortable with and interested in Continental theory than most American feminists, and have done their own adapting of it to feminist concerns.
>
> (xiv)

The underlying rationale behind Scott's expanding theoretical interest in Joyce is his importance for feminists. She believes that his writing 'merits feminist attention' because of the 'considerable dimension and variety' which it gives 'to the investigation of gender in language and life'. The theoretical approach informed by French feminist theory also provides a greater insight into Joyce's status as a modernist writer: 'we gain a new sense of Joyce and modernism', Scott argues, 'by taking up the issues' dealt with in *James Joyce* (xvi).

In her 'Introduction', Scott also suggests that an 'American feminist' who is a Joycean 'may be able to provide a valuable overview of current feminist practices, while setting them to work on Joyce' (xvi), and her first chapter, 'Plurabilities: Joyce in a Matrix of Feminist Theory' provides such an overview in the form of a survey of the various feminist theoretical approaches to Joyce that have developed in recent years. Scott is aware that some feminists object to the study of Joyce: 'Feminist separatists might ask, "Why take up a male author when there are so many neglected women writers?".' She also recognises that the difficult nature of Joyce's work and 'the remote critical discourses that have responded to it are off-putting to advocates of an accessible, egalitarian feminism' (1–2). This view operates as one end of an axis in Scott's model of Joyce's writing 'in a matrix of feminist theory'. As we will later see, it is the view taken by the feminist critics, Sandra Gilbert and Susan Gubar, who have devoted considerable energy in the attempt to show that Joyce was extremely chauvinistic in both his life and his writing. At the other end of the axis is what Scott terms 'Overlapped feminist–male theory and writing' (4). Scott's own feminist perspective on Joyce could be situated at this end as she believes that it is 'not necessary or sufficient that the [feminist] critic be female, that s/he write about female characters or about women writers, or that s/he adopt a feminist identification'. At the same time Scott is very aware of the political aspects of sexual power in Joyce studies and points out that the 'Joycean critical canon has been superintended by men, and male critics have emerged as its stars and privileged theor-eticians, though women began to occupy more visible positions in the late 1970s' (2).

The degree to which feminist critics align themselves with separatist views constitutes the horizontal axis of Scott's model; the vertical axis is constituted by what Scott terms 'conceptual orientation', or the psycho-logical area in which a feminist and/or writer is interested. At one end of this axis is the imaginative realm; at the other, the realm of the repres-entational. In between these two poles lie varying degrees of con-sciousness. Scott aligns each of Joyce's works along this axis. She offers a graph of her matrix (Fig. 7). This graph of Scott's matrix situates 'overlapped male + feminist territory (left) and separate female territory (right)'. It also indicates a problem that Scott believes 'feminists working with Joyce should be aware of': 'male critics, including the fashionable deconstructionists, have not recognized their debts to new feminist work in their overlapped fields; this seems a liability of the politics of the feminist overlap' (4–5).

In order to 'fulfill its goal of comprehending Joyce', Scott's study

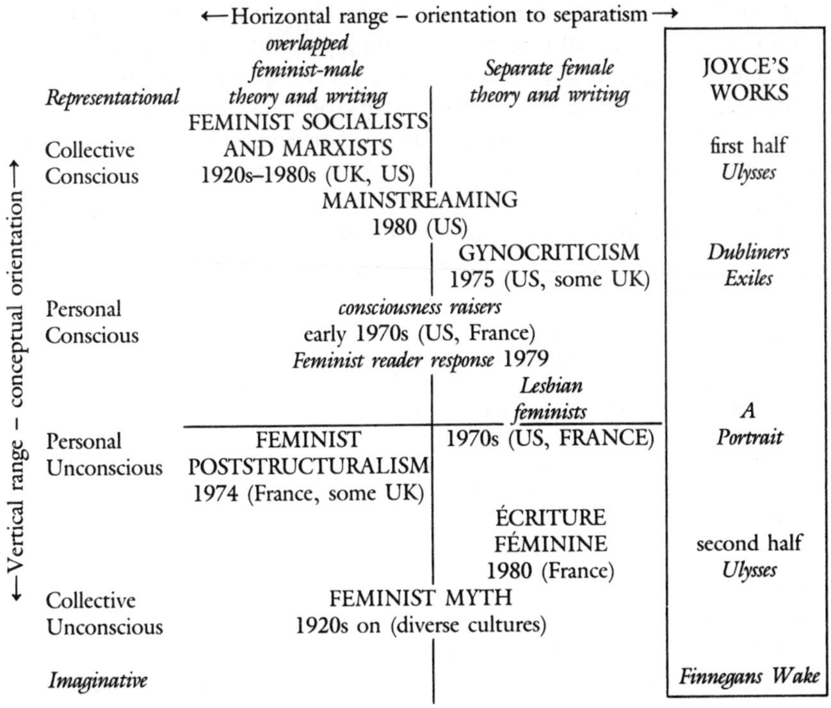

←Horizontal range – orientation to separatism→

	overlapped feminist-male	*Separate female*	JOYCE'S
Representational	*theory and writing*	*theory and writing*	WORKS
	FEMINIST SOCIALISTS		
Collective	AND MARXISTS		first half
Conscious	1920s–1980s (UK, US)		*Ulysses*
	MAINSTREAMING		
	1980 (US)		
		GYNOCRITICISM	*Dubliners*
		1975 (US, some UK)	*Exiles*
Personal	*consciousness raisers*		
Conscious	early 1970s (US, France)		
	Feminist reader response 1979		
		Lesbian	
		feminists	*A*
Personal	FEMINIST	1970s (US, FRANCE)	*Portrait*
Unconscious	POSTSTRUCTURALISM		
	1974 (France, some UK)		
		ÉCRITURE	
		FÉMININE	second half
		1980 (France)	*Ulysses*
Collective	FEMINIST MYTH		
Unconscious	1920s on (diverse cultures)		
Imaginative			*Finnegans Wake*

←Vertical range – conceptual orientation→

(Scott, 1987: 4)

Figure 7

'selects feminist approaches that are widely distributed in the matrix', including 'feminist socialism and Marxism (upper left), mainstreaming (upper centre), gynocriticism (upper right), post-structuralist feminism (lower left), feminist myth (lower centre) and *écriture féminine* (lower right)' (6–7). Scott finds 'mainstreaming' an approach that is 'quite relevant to Joyce'. Also known as 'rebalancing the curriculum', this approach is a result of the efforts in American educational institutions to 'bring[ ] the lessons of separate women's studies and the research on other muted or marginal groups like blacks and colonials to bear on the canon'. Its aim is 'to change what is read and taught, how it is conceptualized and... communicated, rejecting many received notions of cultural and academic authority'. Scott finds this relevant to the study of Joyce because it reflects Joyce's own development: he 'entered a new curriculum of modern literature in his own day, having encountered a classical canon in his early Jesuit education. His work refers to an older canon, but reacts, challenges, and replaces it as well.' 'Mainstreaming' may well have very serious implications for more traditional ways of approaching Joyce. Whatever their theoretical orientation, these approaches have worked towards defining Joyce's literary and critical canon. Scott points out that mainstreaming puts the very idea of 'Joyce's canonical status... at stake', and even raises the question of whether or not 'we wish' 'canonization... to survive' (6).

In her second chapter, 'The Canon: Challenges to Male-centered Literature and History', Scott returns to the idea of Joyce's canon in order to demonstrate the challenges to it which feminism creates. She begins by outlining what the process of canonisation entails and pointing out the sexual and political implications of the process:

> James Joyce is one of the 'great writers'. He appears in anthologies and on course lists; he is known to educated people in the west and beyond. He has come to represent the experimental prose of the modernist period of literary history. In other words, Joyce is 'canonized'. The canon we have today is largely the product of industries and institutions dominated by men; it was composed by male writers, centered upon men's experiences and views of history, and was more readily available to men than to women. It leaves out a great deal that women have written and largely writes and conceptualizes them out of history.
>
> (15)

The rest of the chapter investigates passages from Joyce's texts in the context of popular literature and draws on the 'realist range of critical theories' which are represented in the 'upper, or conscious' area of Scott's critical matrix (15).

For much of his life Joyce received support and assistance from women. Scott suggests that, in part, these women found affinities with Joyce's work: 'Joyce's nurturing by females was not just a fortunate fall into female altruism. He was selected from other modernists because the women involved found revolutionary affinities in Joyce' (16). Scott sees Joyce's early development as one which drew increasing attacks from the 'male patronage' under which he began his career:

> Joyce began under male patronage – his father's.... Next... *The Fortnightly Review* published his review on Ibsen (1900). With the exception of the relatively conventional... *Chamber Music* (1907), Joyce's increasingly experimental and iconoclastic works met with rejections. *St. Stephens's*, his college newspaper, censored his attack on the Irish literary revival, 'The Day of the Rabblement', and Joyce published it privately with an equally marginal essay on women's education by Irish feminist and friend, Francis Skeffington.
>
> (16)

The Irish Homestead published only three *Dubliners* stories because of readers' objections, and 'prospects for *A Portrait* seemed gloomy until Ezra Pound put [Joyce] in touch with the daring women editors of *The Egoist*. Dora Marsden and Harriet Shaw Weaver were willing to deal with printers' fears of litigation, to defy the norms of established literature and economics of the marketplace, as were other female editors of small, individualistic magazines' (16).

From the perspective of gynocriticism, female culture is 'muted' by the larger, male-dominated, mainstream culture. Scott sees the 'concept of a muted female culture' as being applicable to the 'operations of women editors and publishers of Joyce' like Marsden, Weaver, 'Rebecca West, H.D., and Bryher (Winnifred Ellermann)'. She describes Joyce's residence in Paris from 1920 as his entrance into a 'rare time and place for women' which was 'focused for him during the critical early years by [Sylvia Beach's] "Shakespeare and Company"'. When the attempt to get *Ulysses* published in England failed, Shakespeare and Co. 'became the outlet and office of a publishing house, and even an agency for typists, many of them female'. Scott sees Joyce as coming to the mainstream literary canon 'with substantial though marginal and unconventional forms of female assistance' (18).

For most of Chapter Two, Scott details the male education that Joyce received and examines how this education is fictionalised in Joyce's texts. She looks at how his 'early realistic works' function as a 'male *bildung*' which allows the reader to understand Joyce's Jesuitic education and 'draw inferences about the nature of the canon experienced by his young male characters' (19). She believes that although 'Joyce learned these [conventional and Jesuitic] modes of thought and performance well... in his writing, he could distance himself by placing a persona... in the position of the learner'. One of the achievements that makes Joyce valuable to feminists is his use of his personae in an exploration of 'alternatives to the rational tradition of canonized great men'. Scott examines some of the ways in which the alternatives Joyce explored 'drew upon female subculture... which posed serious challenges to the classical curriculum' and made use of popular forms of writing. In particular, she traces Stephen Dedalus's growing disenchantment with the classical canon in which he was educated and examines how this reflects Joyce's own gradual development towards the models of writing which he used in *Finnegans Wake*. She shows that Joyce's attitudes towards women writers were frequently dismissive and that although *Ulysses* 'allude[s] repeatedly' to women writers, these writers could 'fall victim to Joyce's attitudes toward the movements with which they [were] associated' (40). Nevertheless, Scott's overall view of Joyce's development is one of a gradual movement from traditional, canonized forms to experimental forms with which feminists can identify. In *Finnegans Wake*'s approach to history, Scott argues, the 'paradigm is no longer the classical text, but comes much closer to the "litters" of obscure, collective, working-class and even non-human origin, recovered and even written by the hen and her sisters' (45).

In the third chapter of *James Joyce*, Scott moves away from Joyce's relations to the traditional literary canon in order to consider 'Gender, Discourse, and Culture' as a feminist context for Joyce's work. She looks at the traditional roles which Joyce's female characters occupy, particularly in *A Portrait*, *Ulysses*, and *Exiles*. The thesis of this chapter is that 'if we apply the anthropological feminist model of overlapping circles of male and female sub-cultures, we find in Joyce a particularly rich recording of the discourse and experience of all-male culture' (46). Where Chapter Two examined 'issues of canonical history and literature... chart[ing] Stephen Dedalus's acquisition of academic male discourse from the classical and theological [Jesuit] education', Chapter Three focuses upon a 'second male discourse': the 'bourgeois Irish nationalist discourse' which is 'taught to Stephen by his father, Simon', and 'prepares [his] way with the men of Dublin' (47). Scott looks at the 'Baby Tuckoo' tale which opens *A Portrait* as Stephen's first rhetorical model. Drawing on the association which Lacanian theory makes between the 'paternal phallus and the *logos*... as well as the laws by which society operates', she emphasises the importance of this tale for Stephen's developing sense of identity; 'By making "Baby Tuckoo" or Stephen the subject or centre of his narrative, Simon encourages the self-centred, egotistical, solipsistic narrative so obvious throughout Stephen's artistic development' (48). As he grows Stephen continues to learn from his father's 'performance[s]' of 'personal or political discourse', and is 'moved to sort out his own personal history and eventually his artistic course'. In contrast to this paternal dominance, maternal discourse is muted: 'Mrs Dedalus... has ...most of her performances edited out' of the novel and 'complies generally with the stereotypical feminine roles of accompanist and observer, displaying muted and inhibited discourse or providing a mouthpiece for the words of the father or the patriarchal church' (48).

Scott traces the patriarchal discourse through Joyce's texts, marking its appearance at the Christmas dinner, in the moral code of Simon's advice 'never... peach on a fellow' (*P*: 9), in the 'speech of Joe Hynes in "Ivy Day in the Committee Room"' and in *Ulysses*. Although we do not hear or see Simon Dedalus very often on Bloomsday, 'he moves about the male preserves of the city, and everywhere he is or has been, we find recollections and repetitions of his discourse' (48). Scott sees the 'rhetorical tropes of the headlines... in "Aeolus"... related to his discourse' and although she sees it 'culminat[ing] in the "Cyclops" chapter of *Ulysses*', she suggests that 'echoes' of it resonate in the *Wake*, particularly in the 'speeches of the four chroniclers and Shaun as "Jaun the Boast" [469. 29] with his "barrel of leaking rhetoric" [429. 8]' and '"stone of law" [430. 6]' (49). Scott also uses the *Wake*'s humorous parody of the discourse as the epigraph to her chapter:

Did you note that worrid expressionism on his megalogue? A full octavium

below me! And did you hear his browrings rattlemaking when he was
preaching to himself? And, whoa! do you twig the schamlooking leaf
greeping ghastly down his blousyfrock? Our national umbloom! Areesh!

(467. 7–11; Cited, 46)

The rhetoric of the Irish patriarchal discourse dominates much of Joyce's
work until the *Wake*. It is always marked by male gender; it is egocentric;
and it frequently incorporates a politically chauvinistic rhetoric of Irish
history and Nationalism. Scott looks at how it operates in *Dubliners*, *A
Portrait*, and *Ulysses*, following various strands of it as they are woven
through the texts:

> Simon's final tearful utterances on Parnell [during *A Portrait*'s Christmas
> dinner scene] are familiar to readers of 'Ivy Day in the Committee Room',
> where Joe Hynes shares both the subject and the discourse, as he will again
> on the all-male occasion of the funeral in the 'Hades' chapter of *Ulysses*.
> Stephen's memories of Paris in the 'Proteus' episode ... are haunted by a
> fallen Fenian father, Kevin Egan. ...
> Comparable display of historical recall is evident also in the 'Aeolus'
> episode of *Ulysses*, where the great journalist, Ignatius Gallaher, is lionized
> for his communication of details of the Phoenix Park murders, and where
> the great Irish orators are memorialized. Readers can experience bravado
> more directly from Gallaher in the central pub scene of the *Dubliners* story,
> 'A Little Cloud' or from Buck Mulligan in the opening episode of *Ulysses*.
> Additional examples of Irish national discourse are provided by the keeper
> of the cab shelter, the sailor, and Leopold Bloom in the 'Eumaeus' episode
> of *Ulysses*, and, on the unionist side, by Mr Deasy in 'Nestor'. The
> preaching of HCE in *Finnegans Wake* receives more open mockery from his
> sons than Stephen's implied disappointment in Simon. As Joyce's final male
> rhetorician, HCE develops a stammer that matches his daughter's lisp.
> (*FW*: 197. 6, 467. 9)

(53–4)

In contrast to his extensive depiction of this discourse in all-male
environments, Joyce's depiction of women in the works before *Finnegans
Wake* is very limited, and '[e]xclusively female domains are rarely
observed' (59). In the thoughts of Bloom and Stephen, however, Joyce
depicts an interest in such domains, and Scott remarks that Stephen 'is as
curious about them as Bloom': 'He imagines the rooms to which Emma
Clery and her fellow female students retreat, and their "quiet rosary of
hours"' (59). Scott believes that when Joyce depicts women at work, he
does so with a 'peripheral vision', his 'scrupulous re-creation of turn-of-
the-century Dublin provid[ing] glimpses, sounds and sharp clear
memories of working-class women – a fishmonger in *Exiles*, a flower-seller
proclaiming herself Stephen's "own girl" in *A Portrait*, the servant girl
beating a rug under Bloom's gaze in *Ulysses*, and typists, one with spare
time to correspond to Bloom, others clearly doing better than Farrington
in "Counterparts"' (60). Joyce gives more attention to 'middle-class

women seen, not in work outside the home, but in domestic roles: in marriages, as mothers, or as single women visiting or entertaining a group composed at least partly of family members'. His depiction of 'female domesticity represents middle-class Catholic–Irish–Victorian norms' (60). Ultimately, Scott finds Joyce's realism failing when it comes to a depiction of female characters in the daily routines of living, and she suggests that this failure might be linked to Joyce's symbolic and mythical views of women: 'Joyce's realism wears away particularly early with women, perhaps because they had always functioned for him as symbols and in myth.' Even female characters whom Scott finds 'very believable', like Brigid, the 'old servant in *Exiles*', or the woman who delivers milk in 'Telemachus', are given a symbolic or mythical dimension: the former 'has the name of an Irish goddess and saint to go along with her practical female wisdom'; the latter 'Stephen... mystifies and mythologizes... into a political, female embodiment of Ireland' (61–2).

Scott concludes her third chapter with a comparative examination of *Ulysses*' Gerty MacDowell and *Exiles*' Bertha Rowan. Gerty is not, for Scott, a very realistic female character. She 'shares the cultural situation of earlier, more realistic Dublin characters', but her language is 'not realistic female speech' (62, 63). As Scott notes, Joyce's depiction of Gerty has drawn the wrath of feminist critics like Gilbert and Gubar, who in 'Sexual linguistics: gender, language, sexuality' (*New Literary History*, 16. 3 [1985]) attack what they describe as Joyce's use of 'the commercial crap of Gertie's [*sic*] genteel Victorian diction [which] symbolises a larger historical phenomenon – namely the reaction–formation of intensified misogyny with which male writers greeted the entrance of women into the literary marketplace' (63). Scott disagrees with this criticism because she believes that 'Joyce came too late to be part of this phenomenon', but she does think it 'worthwhile... to consider how Joyce makes use of the discourse of the popular romance, in the light of recent feminist research on women's reading and writing of the genre'. She examines the narrative intervention into Gerty's stream of thoughts and sees it assuming 'the manner of magazines and novels written for women living in a patriarchal society'.

Joyce clearly draws on the genre of such popular romances, but Scott finds one very significant difference between the genre and Joyce's use of it: where the romantic story of popular literature 'commodifies women... and directs them toward male-centering... and a romantic quest', Joyce satirises the genre with a 'refusal of its ending'. Scott believes that this refusal allows Joyce to be considered along with female modernist writers whose 'efforts... to write beyond the usual romance ending' provide a 'counterpart' to Joyce's 'refusal of [such an] ending in "Nausicaa", *Exiles* and *Dubliners*' (63). Gerty invents a story in which she and Bloom 'would be just good friends... in spite of the conventions of Society with a big ess', and declares that 'Come what may she would be wild, untrammelled, free' (Cited: 66). Scott finds that this 'text of freedom is undermined by [Gerty']s limping', but concludes that the 'romance remains open-ended, even in Bloom's writing of it' (67). 'Gerty's declaration of freedom from Society with its capital ess' also balances Joyce's concerns with male quests, 'and her quest for an ideal male corresponds rather well with Stephen's female quest and his societal mission ...' (66).

Exiles 'sets up a series of encounters between mature men and women'. In comparison with Joyce's other works (with the exception of *Finnegans Wake*), it depicts a 'domestic setting where freedom from patriarchal Irish marital norms has at least been attempted' (67). Like Unkeless, Scott sees Joyce's depiction of Bertha Rowan as a major achievement in his creation of female characters: 'Unlike the married women of *Dubliners*, or Mrs Dedalus or Gerty MacDowell, Bertha Rowan has a variety of positive interactions with characters of both genders' (67–68). Scott sees the concern for the 'public's sense of their own lives' which Joyce expresses in the play's notes 'match[ing] the gynocritic's responses to women's interests in realistic rendering of experience', although she also thinks that 'Joyce's obsession with the "cuckold"... suggests a double standard.' 'Nevertheless', she continues, 'the movement to "husband or cuckold" defines the male character by his relationship to a woman – an identification that would never have been taken up by [Joyce's earlier] characters' (68). Scott devotes considerable attention to a very close character analysis of Bertha and Richard which it would be supererogatory to reproduce here. It is worth noting, however, that Scott sees the play as a major transitional point in Joyce's writing. While she admits that it is a 'confusing play because of its efforts to sort out themes of freedom and the creations of character where men and women are co-involved', and disappointing in its 'conservative reassertion of heterosexual monogamy', she argues that it also creates a 'principle of incertitude' with which Joyce was able to move beyond the limitations of a restrictive gender-biased realism: 'The principle of incertitude replacing authority moves Joyce toward new territory, narrative patterns and language that are more dependent upon the female and the unconscious...' (76).

In examining Joyce's use of 'Myths of Female Origins', Scott's fourth chapter covers a vast amount of feminist and psychological theory in order to try and determine the extent to which Joyce's 'mythical method' might have enabled him to create fiction with 'affinities in modernist women's writing' (106). She points out at the outset that the mythic 'order sustained by these male modernists [Eliot, Joyce and Yeats] is masculine' to 'many feminist critics' (77). Scott agrees with the assessment to a certain extent but believes tht Joyce moved beyond the limitations that a masculine order implies: 'While the classical, heroic Greek myths of Daedalus, Ulysses, and Oedipus seem privileged in Joyce his mythic archive is far richer' (78). The closing words of *A Portrait* – 'Old father, old artificer, stand me now and ever in good stead' – remind us of a 'mythical method' that 'poses a number of problems for contemporary feminist theorists', but Scott attempts to show how these problems can in part be solved by a consideration of the diversity of Joyce's mythic material.

Much of Chapter Four details Joyce's use of myths ranging from the classical and biblical to those which can be considered as a part of Joyce's extensive use of Gnosticism. Scott points out that Joyce's archive of myth:

> extends to Gnosticism, which supplies the goddess Sophia, to Dante and his Beatrice, to Mohammed, Buddha, and the Hindu Goddess Shakti, and to the Egyptian figures of Thoth, Isis, and Osiris... One of his most elaborate systems of mythical doubles is Irish – the god Manaan, the goddess Dana, and the semi-divine heroes and heroines of Irish mythological cycles, all reaching back to Celtic rather than Greek sources.
>
> (79)

Joyce used 'fables, legends and tales' which 'border on the mythological archive' and 'mixe[d] them in without giving the classics hierarchical prominence'. Furthermore, while Joyce used traditional tales with a 'paternal focus' which were 'provided by his father' (Scott cites the examples of the '*Wake Tales*', 'Buckley Shot the Russian General' and 'The Norwegian Captain'), his work also 're-creates love triangles featuring a bypassed older male – Mark with Tristan and Iseult, Finn with Diarmid and Grania' (79–80). 'Perhaps of greater interest to feminists,' Scott suggests, 'is his mythologizing of local legends that border on lost history and popular culture – Grainne O'Malley (a woman pirate, as prankquean), Biddy Moriarty (a famed Dublin scold, as letter writer), Jack the Ripper and psychoanalytic case histories... [like] Christine Beauchamp.' Joyce gives such popular figures as much attention as he does to the figures of the highly hierarchical classical myths. 'Thus to charge Joyce with limitation to a narrow selection of western classical mythology is not accurate', Scott insists, 'though [the charge] persists, especially in comparative feminist work where the critic is unfamiliar with *Finnegans Wake*' (80).

The question of familiarity with Joyce's final work is important. Gilbert and Gubar, for example, rarely mention *Finnegans Wake*, and their charges against Joyce stem largely from their readings of *Ulysses* and earlier works. As Scott points out, Gilbert and Gubar are two of the 'many feminists' for whom Joyce's 'Greek connection weighs heavily' (80). They 'charge that *Ulysses* transformed "a comment on Homer's epic into a charm that inaugurated a new patrilinguistic epoch"' (80). It is of course impossible to say what such critics might think of Joyce's use of myth in the *Wake*, but Scott's investigation strongly suggests that the 'charge' laid against Joyce on the grounds of 'patrilinguistic' 'inaugurat[ion]' might have to be dropped.

Before its concluding consideration of Joyce's use of mythic female figures, 'Myths of Female Origins' examines the feminist theories which could be used in such an analysis. Scott contends that 'critics better schooled in women writers now hold up female standards in judging Joyce's creative achievements in the area of myth' (80). These women writers include Joyce's contemporaries, Djuna Barnes and H.D. and more recent writers like Hélène Cixous. The 'mythical patterns detected in women's writing by critics Estelle Lauter, Susan Friedman and Rachel Blau DuPlessis' can also 'pose a new and compelling challenge to the vision of Joyce' (80). Scott sees the work of such writers creating 'mythical patterns' which 'go beyond those previously detected by such master theorists as psychoanalysts Sigmund Freud and Carl Jung, and anthropologists Claude Lévi-Strauss and James Frazer' (80–1). The new mythic patterns produced from feminist reworkings include Cixous' and Irigaray's revisions of male versions of myth in order to 'deconstruct Freudian concepts of the subject and of family romance' (81). The images of '[w]oman as "temptress" and "muse" [variations of the virgin–whore figure we have seen explored by other feminists] are familiar archetypes in the criticism of male Joyceans,' Scott states, 'but insufficient [as tools in the analysis of] female modernist texts, and perhaps to Joyce as well'.

There has been such a 'considerable' and 'varied', '[f]eminist critical interest' in myth that Scott says she found it 'was difficult to situate' it on her 'feminist matrix'. Nevertheless, she outlines its position in relation to other feminist theories:

> The feminist mythic method has been most attractive to those working in the 'imaginary' paradigmatic ground of feminism, especially those concerned with concepts of the unconscious, hence its situation toward the bottom of the matrix. Marxist feminists tend to be firmly attached to history and revolutionary change, and determined not to romanticize pastoral paradises or non-human archetypes. Gynocritical emphasis upon cultural experience and literary tradition rather than upon psychoanalytic paradigms presents another important tension. Still, DuPlessis combines Marxist considerations of family economies and colonial narratives with myth; Anglo-American feminist critiques have used mythical characters within discussions of cultural images of women... Julia Kristeva studies the elaboration of the Virgin Mother in Christian discourse. She finds modern disruption of this allows her to move into her own writing of the experience of motherhood.
>
> (82–3)

Scott suggests that Kristeva's writing on the Virgin may provide an important analogue for Stephen Dedalus's experience: 'The decay of the Virgin, literally portrayed in *A Portrait* may have functioned similarly from Stephen (*P*: 162)' (83).

Scott concludes her Chapter Four by focusing on Joyce's own use of feminine myths. She considers how 'Joyce's mythical explorations of the psychological subject greatly favour the male subject' and points out that Stephen's 'mode of rejecting his mother and other women' 'seems... controversial in feminist terms' (86). After tracing Stephen's encounters with various females, including several that are clearly versions of the stereotypical virgin or whore figure, Scott concentrates on the 'Circe' episode of *Ulysses*. Her purpose is to show how Joyce's use of the Homeric Circe makes 'slightly different statements on power and gender' than those suggested by critics like Stuart Gilbert. Scott carefully examines the view of 'Circe' offered in Gilbert's *James Joyce's Ulysses*, showing that 'Gilbert's Circe is a worker of evil with whom men must deal forcefully' (92). She finds the following variations in Joyce's reworking of the tale:

> Stephen's possible poisoning... is by his male companions, not Circe's maids... Bloom's moly (identified as his potato) is provided by his mother, not Hermes....
> Circe in her most bellicose phase toward Odysseus as Bloom is masculinized from Bella to Bello.... While Homer's Odysseus is spared the humiliation of Circe's magic, the less heroic Bloom gives up his moly, and is made swinelike, and simultaneously a 'she'.... Homer's Odysseus clearly followed Circe to her bed... Joyce's Bloom is sufficiently egalitarian to think of male adultery as an issue. Zoe is more benevolent than Bella, protecting the feminine Bloom from Bello by hiding him behind her skirts and... returning his potato. While she is hardly the 'fair-tressed goddess' described by Homer, Zoe comes closer to this aspect of Circe than Bella.
>
> (92–3)

Drawing on Daniel Ferrer's 'Circe, regret and regression' (*Poststructuralist Joyce: Essays from the French* [Cambridge: Cambridge University Press, 1984]), Scott argues that Stephen's rejection of his mother is not simply a male dismissal of the female parent. Ferrer describes the spectral mother as an 'intruder in the father and son relationship'. Scott admits that 'standing alone, this interpretation would sustain the typical emphasis upon the search for a father figure in *Ulysses*', but points out how Ferrer 'works carefully with gender... noting how forms of domination are masculinized in Bello as Circe and in the phallic looming of the mother's ghost'. Stephen's spectral mother is not simply the female parent, but 'a combined parent figure older than the Oedipus complex'. Ferrer finds support for this view in 'the combined gender of the omnivorous sea, first used in juxtaposition with the mother in the "Telemachus" episode'. Joyce uses the 'Circe' episode 'to purge his heroes', Scott concludes, 'while simultaneously making important points about the effect of masculine power on the feminine'. The 'transformational aspect of female myths and the sisterhood with nature suggested by Lauter are persistent throughout' (94).

The final chapter of *James Joyce* begins with an epigraph from *Finnegans Wake* about ALP:

> In the name of Annah, the Allmaziful, the Everliving, the Bringer of Plurabilities, haloed be her eve, her singtime sung, her rill be run, unhemmed as it is uneven!
>
> (*FW*: 104. 1–3) (107)

'Gender, Language and Writing' begins with the mock declaration 'The word was with Joyce in the beginning and especially at the end with *Finnegans Wake*', and Scott begins her concluding chapter with a survey of some of the criticisms of Joyce's last two texts as 'another example of male mastery and power of performance, an excess of author-ity' (107). She begins with Gilbert and Gubar's use of Joyce as 'their primary example of "*avant-garde* fantasists of language" who transform a common mother tongue into father speech, thus soothing the modernist "male linguistic wound" and, in *Ulysses*, "inaugurating a new patrilinguistic epoch"' (107–8). Such a view, however, is not the only feminist view of Joyce, and Scott contrasts the criticism that 'discredits' 'Joyce's composition by accretion' as a 'materialist economy of acquisitiveness and retention' with Hélène Cixous' view of Joyce's '"giving, dispersing" feminine economy' (108). Scott believes that 'Joyce offers much more than the male symbolic order, the word of the father, and the virtuoso author' (108), and she is disturbed by Gilbert and Gubar's unwillingness even to consider the possibility that Joyce might have been capable of creating in the 'same joyous spirit' exhibited by the women writers whom they favour:

> Gilbert and Gubar are prepared to celebrate the fact that 'for H.D., a word is... a sort of mystic egg that can "hatch" multiple-meanings' that 'she punningly revises words to turn "ruins", say, into "runes"', that 'all words, as she meditates on them, become palimpsests'. They are not prepared to see Joyce's puns and word images (he even hatches word/eggs...) in the same joyous spirit.
>
> (108)

Her argument is that while '[c]ontemporary feminists' plays on words... are usually easier to read than Joyce's lengthy portmanteau words... Still it is comparable deconstructive play' (108).

Joyce's words are 'more dense and elaborate', Scott contends, but his 'project with words bears many analogies to Virginia Woolf's'. Like 'Miss la Trobe of *Between the Acts*', who appreciates and uses '[w]ords without meaning – wonderful words', '[w]omen in late Joyce react to language and write their own, though it is hidden away, written over and tediously deciphered by the male authorities'. Scott offers the following passage from the *Wake* as an example of how the text 'analyses its own intentions with language... emphasi[zing] diversity and multiplicity of [its] sign, language and focus':

> It is told in sounds in utter that, in signs so adds to, in universal, in polyglutteral, and in each auxiliary neutral idiom, sordomutics, florilingua, sheltafocal, flayflutter, a con's cubane, a pro's tutute, strassarab, ereperse and anythongue athall. Since nozzy Nanette tripped palmyways with Highho Harry there's a spurtfire turf a 'kind o'kindling when oft as the souff-souff blows her peaties up and a claypot wet for thee, my Sitys, and talkatalka tell Tibbs as eve:
>
> (117. 12–19)

Analysing this passage, Scott finds that ' [l]anguage production takes place at the hearth, not in the academy, and it emerges from interactions of "nozzy Nanette" and "Highho Harry", from gossip, "talkatalka", tea and peat'. Using Margaret Solomon's identification of tea and urine in *Eternal Geomater*, Scott argues that the 'tea as urine and the peat as a woman's panties suggest a telling tale of the female body, a return to Eve' (109).

Scott believes that the female characters of ALP and Issy 'have remarkable relations to language'. ALP operates as a 'semiotic resource, the provider of an alternative language to the developing subject'. The language of Issy and 'that of her twenty-eight rainbow girls mixes norms and forms and attempts a corrective vision' (110). The males in the *Wake* 'scorn... the female production of language', and Scott sees this language 'bearing a perverse resemblance to the traditionalist Eliot: "those gloompourers who grouse that letters have never been quite their old selves since that weird weekday in bleak Janiveer... when... Biddy Doran looked at literature" (112. 24–27).' While the *Wake*'s 'female production of language is filtered through the dream of the patriarch, HCE', Scott thinks that it still 'retains powerful suggestions of another order of expression, distinct from both male language and dream language as did the "Penelope" episode of *Ulysses*'.

Scott approaches the question of language and gender in Joyce's writing by drawing on a variety of French theories and by using gender in a 'non-deterministic sense, as in Lacan's psychoanalysis, Derridean deconstruction, or Kristeva's feminist semiotics'. She also draws 'comparisons between Joyce and the qualities attributed to *l'écriture féminine* by Hélène Cixous and Luce Irigaray' (111). Her use of Irigaray's 'This sex which is not one' (*New French Feminisms*, New York: Schocken Books, 1981), produces a radical reading of Stephen's childhood relation to his mother. 'Stephen takes note of his father's stories', as Scott has already noted in her discussion of Simon's discourse, but he also uses 'a variety of his senses', to 'carefully notice[ ] his mother's emissions':

> She has a nice smell; she plays music and encourages his dance, an art form

usually associated with women in Joyce. At... College, he remembers 'her feet on the fender and her jewelly slippers were so hot and they had such a lovely warm smell (*P*: 7, 10). She has an erotic relation to language. Her image serves his definition of the word kiss: 'His mother put her lips on his cheek; her lips were soft and they wetted his cheek: and they made a tiny little noise: kiss (15). This begins Stephen's focus on maternal lips.

(112)

Scott sees the description of Mrs Dedalus's lips as 'soft and wet' suggesting 'not just her lips, but her vulva, and both are "they" or two'. Using Irigaray, Scott explains that the 'two lips of the vulva are only one aspect of the multiple sites and surges of female libidinal energy, as opposed to the singular identity and orgasm of the male penis and corresponding phallocentric language'. The importance of Stephen's focus on his mother's lips is that they 'produce minimal sound, and no word', but because this sound [of the "kiss"] which is not a word is onomatopoeic' it 'becomes the partial source of the word for Stephen' (112).

Scott traces how Stephen 'continues to read the semiotics of the maternal body in the girls and women he meets, and to note occurrences of silence and suggestions of alternative language'. In the passage where Stephen observes water 'falling softly in a brimming bowl' (59) 'at the culmination of chapter 1 of *A Portrait*', she sees an example of 'his... imagery re-creat[ing] female pulsions and genital forms'. She cites Stephen's remembrance of the 'dark eyes [which] had invited him and unnerved him' (*P*: 82), as an instance of his reading, 'almost as a language, the look in the eyes of [the] girl'. Even the touch of the girl's hand is read as a language: 'her non-verbal expressions have a fluid, soothing effect that reaches to his brain and body... setting a pattern for future reception of female semiotics' (113). Scott considers Stephen's loss of verbal control in the company of the prostitute in terms of 'communication by gesture and pressure' rather than 'actual language' (113). Joyce describes Stephen as close to 'hysterical weeping' (*P*: 100), and Scott considers this in Freudian and feminist contexts:

'Hysterical', derived from 'hyster', the Greek word for womb, is a negative symptom attributed to women by Freud; it has been rehabilitated in some feminist theory as an expressive and useful form for organizing language. Stephen ceases his gaze [on the prostitute] and opens his brain to an alternative experience which is articulated in terms of the female body's warmth, the rise and fall of her breasts, the pressure of her soft parted lips, experiences darker and softer than the intellectual, moral or sensuous experiences he has known in the world but reminiscent of his mother's early kiss.

(114)

Apart from the one poem which he composes in the novel, Stephen's development as an artist is depicted through a growing interest in language. Scott analyses the passage in which Stephen meditates on the phrase 'A day of dappled seaborne clouds' (*P*: 166). She is aware that Stephen's interests are 'not comprehensive of Joyce's', but points out how his linguistic interests 'bear elements of what has been identified as male as well as female literary form':

> His direction toward an 'inner world' diverts him from the masculine realm. His multiple interests, his fascination with rhythm, his willingness to watch colours in the process of changing, and his 'supple period prose' suggest multiplicity, fluidity and recycling, aspects attached to the female body and female writing. But the 'periodic' also suggests what Virgina Woolf called the exact and culminating phrase, a control of language and desire for representation... that has been identified with male language.
>
> (116)

Stephen's sensitivity to the female semiotic continues in *Ulysses* where Scott uncovers a 'full panoply of ambivalences over male and female sources of the word in Stephen's musings in the "Monologue (male)" of "Proteus". Scott believes that Joyce is able to escape, albeit briefly, the 'stereotypical [female] churchly role of receptacle, servant and lady' (117). She examines the 'inspiring woman' who, in Stephen's mind, 'trudges, schlepps, trains, drags, trascines her load. A tide westering, moondrawn, in her wake' (*U*: 40). Scott sees her as the 'many forms of woman': the 'tides represent the female body; they are also internal, menstrual, periodic; she is flow. She is "other" to the male, "blood not mine"' (117).

Scott again considers the strong criticism against Joyce made by Gilbert and Gubar. They 'resist Joyce's "fluently fluid women, ALP and Molly Bloom", and see their "scatologos" as a product of misogyny, a "Swiftian language that issues from the many obscene mouths of the female body"' (Gilbert and Gubar, 1985: 532–3; Cited, 117). Scott contends that 'their point would be stronger if "scatalogos", secretions, emissions, and excretions were negatively viewed, or practised and aspired to only by female characters in Joyce and not by Stephen, Bloom and HCE as well'. 'Most interesting', Scott suggests in this context, is 'the play with language that escapes the word of the world, a rite that immediately precedes Stephen's scribbling words'. Considering the kiss which Stephen 'lips and mouths to his departed mother' – 'mouth to her moomb. Oomb, alwombing tomb' (*U*: 40) – Scott finds the 'soft alliterative sounds and repetitive rhythms suggest[ing] semiotic pre-speech associated by Kristeva with the mother' (117).

James Joyce concludes with a consideration of language and gender in *Finnegans Wake*. Scott finds that the 'female identities' in the text 'write themselves in several ways' which is 'somewhat surprising in the case of the mother' because she is 'seen written but not writing in early Joyce'

(120). Scott cites Susan Rubin Suleiman's 'Writing and motherhood' (*The (M)other Tongue: Essays in Feminist Psychoanalytic Interpretation* [Ithaca: Cornell UP, 1985]), an essay which suggests that 'female as well as male writers offer a written, but not a writing mother' (120). The 'most obvious woman's writing' in the *Wake* is 'probably' the letter of Biddy Doran, the hen, says Scott, 'although there is constantly the issue of forgery by Shem or Issy, or even T. S. Eliot, where the language of "The Wasteland" seems evident'. Scott describes Biddy's text as 'written, written over and analysed... a collective expression of both genders, a palimpsest, an anastomotic text'. In 'Nightletters: woman's writing in the *Wake*' (*Critical Essays on Joyce* [Boston: G. K. Hall & Co., 1985]) Shari Benstock offers the 'Derridean suggestion that the... letter is a writing on the hymen' because the 'document has been buried in a womb-like midden heap' (120). Scott considers this interpretation but finds it 'unlikely': 'Though this satisfies a Derridean paradigm of dissemination on the hymen, I find the hymen unlikely stationery for the sexually-experienced ALP' (140, n. 31). She thinks that the 'hen's "scribbling scrawled on eggs" would seem to be writing on her children more than her own body' (121).

Within the various layers of Joyce's writing, Scott isolates a 'palimpsest' which designates clothing, and this clothing becomes, in turn, a sort of text: 'ALP... writes on clothing [which provides] the texts the washer-women read. "Porpor patches! And brahming to him down the feed-chute, with her femtyfyx kinds of fondling endings, the poother rambling off her nose: *Vuggybarney, Wickeymandy! Hello, ducky, pleast don't die!*" (200. 2–7)' (122). While she admits that such texts are 'hardly feminist', Scott thinks it worthwhile to follow Susan Gubar's suggestion and 'look at the language of clothes, at blank bedsheets, and at cross-dressing mod-ernist writers'. She points out that bedsheets are noted as 'texts of sexual coupling' by both Molly Bloom and the *Wake*'s washerwomen. This is probably because 'Joyce was extremely interested in female clothes' and even 'made distinctly misogynistic statements... to the effect that women's clothes interested him more than the women themselves' (122). Scott is particularly interested in a version of a cross-dressed ALP, whom she describes as 'dressed to kill, more or less, HCE's attackers' (122). Scott analyses the passage in which ALP appears in male clothes (208. 6–26) and points out that although '[n]o real person could wear so many garments simultaneously' the variety of the clothing has implica-tions for ALP's own gender: 'She is by turns the sort of fashionplate that Gerty aspires to, and the labouring male' (123).

The *Wake* continually draws the reader's attention to its own letters, punning on the relations between letter as epistle, letter as alphabetic character, and the depiction of human characters in words composed of alphabetic characters. Scott contends that the women in the text are 'connected repeatedly with other alphabets than that of modern English, suggesting that they possess a more ancient, lost language' (125). The midden-heap letter is stained with 'tea, or urine', and Scott links these liquids with a 'female writing from her own body'. ALP uses "cunniform letters", and Scott describes them as 'cunning in form as well as cuneiform'. These letters also link ALP with a Sumerian goddess:

> Cuneiform writing originated in the Sumerian culture that worshipped the goddess of earth and sky, Inanna... Their wedge shape duplicates the triangle or delta, the silted languages of the rivers of Babylon and the world that flow through the chapter. The geometric delta represents ALP to her sons and is a fairly universal representation of female pubic structure.
> (125)

Whatever the alphabetic form of the women's language in the *Wake*, it is adaptable and 'makes do with available surfaces, an egg or a rock' (128).

Scott believes that Joyce does offer us a 'female modernism' (128). While 'he may raise a "meandering male fist" of control', she says, 'the action is sure to be mocked by his own female writer' (128–9). ALP's feminine language 'provide[s] the umbilicus' of the text, the '"vicus" of recirculation and offers a new politics of relationship and authorship'. Scott is aware that not all feminists share her views. Her view of 'Anna's route cannot fully satisfy the woman writer or gynocritic who has a shaping vision, a self-defining ambition and tradition, along with her physical female form, to equate with language.' In contrast to gynocritical theory, however, 'French feminist paradigms of writing the feminine enrich our reading of Joyce, taking us beyond Freud and beyond structuralism.' Scott sees the problems in 'Joyce's writing of women still serv[ing] a male author's ego [by] proving he can move into "other" forms', but her answer to the question of whether or not Joyce could write a 'gramma's grammar' is clearly in the affirmative: 'we should wish for more male writers who will follow in Anna's wake' (129).

Sandra Gilbert and Susan Gubar

Gilbert and Gubar established themselves as major feminist critics with *The Madwoman in the Attic: The Woman Writer and the Nineteenth-Century Literary Imagination* (New Haven: Yale UP, 1979). As we saw in *James Joyce*, Gilbert and Gubar share strong views on Joyce's writing, and they have spent considerable time in making their views known. One of their first attacks on Joyce appeared in 'Sexual linguistics: gender, language, sexuality' where they look at Leopold Bloom's sexual transformation in the 'Circe' episode of *Ulysses* in terms of transvestite humiliation and what they see as Joyce's misogyny. Their criticisms of Joyce would seem to be a part of the larger criticism of all male writers that is offered in *The Madwoman in the Attic*: 'because *he* is an *author*, a "*man* of letters" is simultaneously, like his divine counterpart, a father, a master or ruler, and an owner' (7). *No Man's Land: The Place of the Woman Writer in the Twentieth Century* (New Haven: Yale UP, Vol. 1, 1988, Vol. 2, 1989) offers the same sort of perspective on Joyce as 'Sexual linguistics' and continues the criticism of Joyce that Gilbert and Gubar offer in the earlier essay, so it is on this work that we will focus.

Gilbert and Gubar have a narrower critical perspective than some of the other feminists that we have considered, and they rely for the most part on traditional historical and biographical scholarship. In the first volume of *No Man's Land: The War of the Words*, they begin their criticism of Joyce by describing Leopold Bloom as a cuckold and one of the 'maimed, unmanned, victimized characters created by early twentieth-century literary man' (36). They believe that along with Eliot, Lawrence, Hemingway and West, Joyce experienced a 'social and metaphysical cris[is] in masculine confidence', and that Bloom is one of the 'male-authored no-men' that each of these writers produced as a result of this crisis (89). They also cite Joyce among the writers 'driven – not just by general cultural disillusionment but also perhaps by specifically sexual anxiety – to dramatize… ferocious misogyny and racism' who 'may have been as disturbed by their economic dependence on women as they were troubled by women's usurpation of the market place' (147). The 'Nausicaa' episode of *Ulysses* expresses Joyce's 'highbrow male modernist… disgust with the [female] lowbrow scribbler'. While Joyce produces 'often adulatory stylistic tributes to his literary patrilineage' in 'Oxen of the Sun', 'Nausicaa' is a 'parody [which] indicts the banality and bathos inculcated in young girls by the pulpy fiction of literary women'. Joyce 'satirizes' the very language that he has created, 'Gerty MacDowell's school language', and this language 'both revolts him and titillates him' (146).

Gilbert and Gubar consider Joyce in the context of his contemporaries. They see him as one of a 'number of twentieth-century men of letters' who defended themselves 'against the emergent frailties of literature's patrilineage' by 'surround[ing] literary women with a wall of resistance and rage' (223). *Ulysses*, which they see as a brick in this wall, is a part of what they describe as Joyce's project in 'taking upon himself the Holy Office of pronouncing that woman, both linguistically and biologically, is wholly orifice' (232). They view Molly Bloom as a woman who 'dribbles and drivels as she dreams of male jinglings' and describe her pronunciation of 'metempsychosis' ('Met him pike hoses') as 'babble' exemplifying what they see as the 'parrot-like blankness with which Joyce's women respond to abstract concepts'. They look at 'Gertie [*sic*] McDowell [*sic*]' as a 'poignant example of Joyce's women having an 'inability to name, and thus claim, even the functions of their own bodies'. What they term the 'omission of intellect' in Joyce's women is 'best summarized by Bloom's musicological meditations in "Sirens"'. Bloom is of course no musician, but as Gilbert and Gubar point out, the 'notion that female singers "can't manage men's intervals" and have a *"Gap* in their voices too"' (Gilbert and Gubar's emphasis) does flit through his mind. This notion, along with Bloom's thoughts 'on the "chamber music" of his wife's "tinkling"'; his idea that a female's '"Blank face"... needs to be written on like a "page"'; and his comparison of 'the female body [with] a "flute alive" on which men must "Blow gentle" or "Loud" because "Three holes all women"' constitutes Gilbert and Gubar's evidence that Joyce viewed 'woman' as 'wholly orifice': 'Clearly', they state, 'in endowing Bloom with such speculations, Joyce is taking upon himself the Holy Office of pronouncing that woman ...' (232).

Gilbert and Gubar draw on the biographical information provided by Joyce's private letters to Nora in order to prove that Joyce's primary interest in women's language was in what they term 'a scatalogos, a Swiftian language that issues from the many obscene mouths of the female body'. While they do not examine the language of the 'Penelope' episode, they contend that '[w]hen [woman] speaks as Molly in Joyce's passage, she passes blood and water'. Gilbert and Gubar cite Joyce's letter to Nora written in 1909 as an example of Joyce 'implor[ing] woman-as-Nora to write. Joyce asks Nora to write a letter including 'dirty words' written 'big' and 'underline[d]'. He also requests Nora to 'kiss' the words and to perform a variety of acts which Freudian theorists would consider examples of anal eroticism. Gilbert and Gubar, however, are primarily interested in scatological implications, and although there are no direct references to faeces in the letter they use it to support their view that Joyce 'begged' woman-as-Nora 'to express a calligraphy of shit' (232). Using a conservative, traditional theory of authorial intention to argue that 'when, like Joyce's Gertie [sic], a woman attempts to etherealize herself, the author wants his readers to realize that she can only ascend to sentimentality' (232–3). Returning to their scatological concerns, they argue that 'while Gertie's [sic] bloomers titillate Bloom as Nora's did Joyce, the commercial crap of her genteel Victorian diction is at least in part associated with the reaction-formation of intensified misogyny with which male writers greeted the entrance of women into the literary marketplace' (233).

Gilbert and Gubar believe that Joyce is one of the male writers who was 'reacting against or seeking to appropriate the primal verbal fertility of the mother'. They cite Walter Ong's *Fighting for Life* (Ithaca: Cornell UP, 1981), a work which considers the phrase 'mother tongue' and speculates that a first language 'perhaps in all languages is designated by direct or indirect reference to mother'. Ong suggests that the lack of 'father tongues' may be a 'truth that calls for deeper reflection than it commonly commands' (Ong: 36; Cited, 263). Gilbert and Gubar state that '[c]learly, it is this "deeper reflection" that is reflected in the incongruent fantasies of male and female writers' (263). Male writings are 'vindications of what Lacan terms the "Name of the Father"' and 'seem ultimately to be vilifications of the Gnosis of the Mother' (263).

The first volume of *No Man's Land* contends that Tennyson's *The Idylls of the King* gave a clear message to "male readers": 'even if the (male) magician no longer knows "the language that has long since gone", he must at all costs retain the charm that resides in the comment on the sacred power of the text'. Gilbert and Gubar note that the language to which Merlin refers is from a 'paradigmatic book of patriarchal authority' (257), but they use it to refer to what they call 'the *materna lingua*'. The goal of male writers is a 'definitive cure of the male linguistic wound' which is seemingly offered by 'the transformation of the *materna lingua* into a new *patrius sermo*' (258). In this context they consider Joyce as 'the man who definitively converted the comment into the charm'. Their criticism of Joyce is twofold. On the one hand, his writing 'transforms what Hélène Cixous calls "the old single-grooved mother tongue" into what we are calling a *patrius sermo*'. On the other hand, as a 'densest condensation, hard', his writing would seem to require considerable work because it 'can only be comprehended by those who... can translate what has been "scribbled, crost and cramm'd" on the margins of literature into a spell of power' (259). Gilbert and Gubar believe that Joyce devoted himself to his writing as a 'feat of legerdemain' in order to create 'a spell of power... by deriding or disintegrating what Jolas' revolutionaries of the word called the "primal matter" of the mother tongue' (260). They offer a brief analysis of four or five phrases from a page of the 'Oxen of the Sun' episode from *Ulysses* and consider '[p]rovisionally, tentatively' that a 'similar maneuver' to Joyce's 'may be at the heart of what Geoffrey Hartman calls Derridadaism'. They conclude that the phrase 'Hoopsa Boyaboy Hoopsa' from 'Oxen of the Sun' is 'motto', a 'charm' that 'male modernists and postmodernists' 'consistently find in the commentary they ceaselessly study' (261).

In *Sexchanges*, the second volume of *No Man's Land*, Gilbert and Gubar describe Joyce as a 'regionalist' (90) and comment on *Dubliners* and *Ulysses* as examples of an 'artful combination of surface and symbol' (98). They consider how the 'environment that fostered the achievements of such modernists as... Joyce', was shaped in part by 'the lesbian expatriates about whom [Radclyffe] Hall was writing' (221). The chapter 'Cross-Dressing and Re-Dressing: Transvestism as Metaphor' examines the trans-formation of Bloom and Bella in the 'Circe' episode of *Ulysses* as '[o]ne of the most dramatic transvestite episodes in modern literature'. Noting

Joyce's parody of Leopold Von Sacher-Masoch's *Venus in Furs*, Gilbert and Gubar suggest that Joyce 'is also satirizing a distinctively nineteenth-century pornographic genre' which depicted transvestism and bondage (332). They consider the possibility that Joyce's parody may 'suggest a serious if covert acceptance of the original pornography' and think it 'mistaken' to take what they see as Joyce's 'grotesque androgyny' as 'hint-[ing] at the possibility of a nobler and more vital androgyny' (333). 'Joyce's parodic narrative', they state, 'implies that to become a female or to be like a female is not only figuratively but literally to be degraded... Joyce is also hinting that to be a woman is inevitably to be degraded, to be "a thing under the yoke" (523)' (333).

Paradoxically, Gilbert and Gubar equate the degradation which Bloom experiences in becoming a woman with a renewal of his power; his 'dramatic recovery of power', they note, 'is... curiously associated not only with his repudiation of the feminine and the female costume but also with his wearing of that costume' (334). Unlike Scott, who sees Bloom's potato as his version of the 'ritual magic plant *Moly* [which] saved Homer's Ulysses from the degradation threatened by Circe', Gilbert and Gubar believe that 'Bloom saves himself from the degradations of Bella/Bello Cohen by not only having but pretending to *be* his own Molly' (336). While this ignores the fact that Bloom is not pretending to be transformed and might also seem to undermine their view of Joyce's women as lacking in all power, Gilbert and Gubar see Bloom becoming a 'covertly phallic version of the recumbent "Ewig-Weibliche", a "new womanly man" whose secret manliness may ultimately seduce and subdue insubordinate New Woman' (336). Clearly, they believe that Joyce was not only incapable of writing a 'gramma's grammar', but also that he so loathed and feared woman that he would not have wanted to.

•4• Is It a 'Gramma's Grammar'? (II)

Joyce and French Feminism

FRENCH FEMINIST EXAMINATIONS of Joyce's work tend to be much more theoretically sophisticated than their Anglo-American counterparts. There are of course many exceptions to this, and as we have already seen, the work of Anglo-American critics like Scott, Benstock and Norris, to name but three, make considerable use of similar theoretical perspectives to those of the French feminists who we shall examine in this chapter. Scott incorporates into her own work some of the complex ideas developed by French writers like Kristeva and Irigaray. Benstock has made considerable use of Derridean theory, and Norris has investigated *Finnegans Wake* in the context of structuralism, Freudian psychology and from the perspective of Derrida's ideas on the radical changes which philosophy underwent in the nineteenth century. Nevertheless, French feminists, and indeed French theorists in general, offer views of Joyce that are very different from those provided in the work of Anglo-American critics.

The reasons for the differences are difficult to pin down, but it seems quite likely that the traditional English resistance to Continental philosophy in general and the more specific resistance to French critical theory encountered in some English departments are in part responsible. As we saw in the chapter on structuralist investigations of Joyce, Stephen Heath has offered some suggestions to account for the differences. In a 'Translator's note' to Philippe Sollers' 'Joyce & Co.' (*In The Wake of the Wake*), Heath comments on the problems of translating Sollers' French view of

Joyce into English. These problems involve more than the difficulties encountered in the translation from one language into another:

> the difficulty of translation here lies in the fact that this text goes against both the English and the American Joyces, the outcast from a moralizing criticism bent on protecting its tradition from what it calls 'the revolution of the word' and the puzzle to be solved at all costs by a massive 'recovery' of 'facts' (the reconstitution of a hated object, a hatred often present in the Symposium). Is it useless to add that the 'structuralism' currently being bandied about by the literary intellectuals in England and America is a new version of the old refusal of Joyce... and Freud?
>
> (121)

It is highly unlikely that the situation is still as bad as that which Heath describes because American and English critics did gradually move to a serious consideration of French theories. Resistance does remain, however, as the current widespread desire to move from the complexities of poststructuralism to a more simple neohistoricism would seem to suggest.

As the title of *New French Feminisms* indicates, there is no one French feminist theory but a multitude of different feminisms. If there is a notion shared by these feminisms it is probably the impossibility and undesirability of defining a central ideological structure to which one could appeal in the name of feminism. How can one define the feminine? In her contribution to *New French Feminisms*, Cixous writes: 'It is impossible to *define* a feminine practice of writing, and this is an impossibility that will remain, for this practice can never be theorized, enclosed, coded – which doesn't mean that it doesn't exist' (253). As we saw in examining Scott's work, there is a very wide range of theories with which some feminists align themselves. What these feminists would seem to have in common is the idea that phallogocentrism, the traditional form of male-dominated thought and male-defined logic, is inappropriate and indeed incapable of allowing many women to write as they desire to. Much feminist writing strives for a practice that 'will always surpass the discourse that regulates the phallocentric system; it does and will take place in areas other than those subordinated to philosophico-theoretical domination' (253). Of course, not all feminists feel the need to break away from traditional forms of discourse, 'to break' what Cixous calls the 'arid millenial ground' (245). Gilbert and Gubar, for example, seem quite content to launch their attacks upon male writers in the traditional genre of historical and biographical criticism and in a traditional form of scholarly writing. As we will see, the French feminists whose work on Joyce we will examine do not find it desirable to work on this ground.

While it is not possible to summarise all of the reasons why French feminists are attracted to Joyce's writing, there are several areas in which his writing would seem to operate in modes which are important to French feminist theorists like Cixous and Kristeva. Cixous sees Joyce's writing not as a writing about something, but as a writing which articulates a process of becoming and which attempts to provide an experience of the unconscious rather than a discussion about it in a representational mode. Scott thinks that 'Cixous' description of the feminine text as endless, wandering, circulating from body to body, immediately suggests the functions of Joyce's Anna Livia Plurabelle' (Scott, 1987: 10). In Cixous' sense of the terms Joyce's is not *novelistic* but *poetic*. Cixous seems to see Joyce as one of the 'failures... in that enormous machine that has been operating and turning out its "truth" for centuries', as one of the 'poets who would go to any lengths to slip something by at odds with tradition'. It might even be possible that *Finnegans Wake*'s ALP could be seen as a creation resulting from Joyce 'imagining the woman who would hold out against oppression and constitute herself as a superb, equal, hence "impossible" subject, untenable in a real social framework' (Cixous, 1981: 249). And it certainly seems that the *Wake* allows us to consider Joyce as one of those 'poets – not the novelists, allies of representationalism... [whose] poetry involves gaining strength through the unconscious and because the unconscious, that other limitless country, is the place where the repressed manage to survive: women, or as Hoffmann would say, fairies' (250). It is worth noting at this point that Gilbert and Gubar's view of Joyce's women as the result of a misogynistic male's fears and hatreds is a view which in all cases rests on theories of realism and representationalism.

We have already considered some of Kristeva's interests in Joyce's writing in the chapter on semiotics. She is particularly interested in Joyce's writing as an example of modernist, avant-garde writing which owes much to the genre of subversive menippean satire and which also participates in the carnivalesque. She is primarily concerned with Joyce's last two texts, and she sees his writing as operating according to the 0–2 logic which we looked at earlier. Kristeva also considers Joyce from a psychoanalytic perspective developed from her adaptation of the theories of Jacques Lacan, and she looks at his writing as an example of the 'polylogue', a type of writing also practised by Philippe Sollers. Considering Kristeva as a feminist theorist creates some problems. As Scott notes in *James Joyce*, Kristeva has 'allied herself... with male theory' much more than many other feminists. 'Her position', Scott says, 'is to accept the existence of a male-centered "symbolic" order, and to work to deconstruct it from the inside'. Scott believes that Kristeva 'sees the deconstructive work as a far more advanced stage of feminism than the liberal pursuit of equality seen in the 1920s and still detectable in much Anglo-American feminism; she also resists the radical rejection of the male symbolic order which she equates with *écriture féminine*' (Scott, 1987: 12).

In addition to Kristeva's and Cixous' visions of Joyce we will also consider Christine van Boheemen's work on Joyce in *The Novel as Family*

Romance: Language, Gender and Authority From Fielding to Joyce (Ithaca: Cornell UP, 1987). Boheemen is a Dutch Joycean, but her thinking owes much more to French than to Anglo-American thought even though she writes in English, so it is here rather than in the previous chapter that we will consider her work. Boheemen draws on the theories of Descartes, Lévi-Strauss, Foucault, Derrida and, more importantly, Lacan. Her study of Joyce is primarily a semiotic, psychological study, but Boheemen also addresses the 'question of the feminist method of [her] study' (9) and points out that her 'readings demonstrate how profoundly the idea of gender is interwoven with that of signification' (9). In her 'Introduction', Boheemen also expresses the hope that 'the study as a whole is... inspired by the vision of a new political project: the analysis and articulation of the many and profound ways in which the connotations of gender are used for the purposes of signification'. 'A Modern feminism', Boheemen argues:

> aware of the dichotomous and ultimately self-defeating effect of an oppositional logic (which leads to separatism rather than inclusion), points to the implication of gender and signification in the hope that the conflation will eventually lose its seemingly natural self-evidence. Since we live and write in a patriarchal culture, the notion of a gender-free or even truly dialogic – rather than oppositional and hierarchical – signifying system is no more than an imaginary ideal at present. Realizing that all writing that makes sense is implicated, even if antagonistically, in the dominant structre of sense making, one can, nevertheless, keep pointing to the implication of gender in signification in the hope and trust that the knot will ultimately disintegrate.
>
> (10)

Hélène Cixous

Cixous wrote her thesis on Joyce. *The Exile of James Joyce* (London: John Calder, 1972) is a translation of her monumental study of Joyce's work which was originally published in French in 1972. *The Exile of James Joyce* rivals Ellmann's *James Joyce* in its scope, but its treatment of Joyce's life provides a different perspective on Joyce's life and work than does Ellmann's much more traditional biographical study. Because of the academic requirements imposed on her, Cixous' first study of Joyce relies on a much more traditional scholarly framework than her subsequent writings, but in the 'Interview with Hélène Cixous' (*Sub Stance*, **13** [1976]) by Christiane Makward, Cixous says that she 'invested very little in the academic type of production'. She found it 'constraining' and had no 'good memories of it' (Cited, Scott: 10). *The Exile of James Joyce* traces Joyce's life and writing in a standard chronological order, but the perspective which it offers on his life and writing manages in part to evade the constraints which Cixous later admitted to disliking. This perspective is reflected in the titles of the five major divisions of the work: 'The Family Cell', 'Private and Public Heroism', 'The Choice of Heresy', 'Exile as Recovery', and 'Joyce's Poetics'. Cixous examines Joyce's life in terms of the psychological states which Joyce experienced and considers his 'exile' not only in terms of his removal from Ireland but also as a psychological and ontological state essential to his writing.

Joyce's Exile

For Cixous, exile is a term which applies to both Joyce's life and his artistic poetics. Exile describes Joyce's life in Europe and the intellectual and psychological condition which was essential to his writing. She examines Joyce's essay 'Portrait of the Artist', written on 7th January 1904, as a document which offers Joyce's 'first signature as an artist' (212), and she finds the language of this essay 'particularly interesting' because it combines 'Joyce's own personal speech' with a hesitance which she believes 'cloaks [Joyce's] fear'. 'Stylistically', she suggests, 'it could pass for an obscure parody of the decadent late nineteenth-century art, but it is the form taken by the twenty-two-year-old Joyce's metaphysical anguish, the product of his frustrations, his inexpressible aspirations, his apprehension at the choice that lay before him, the choice of following the beaten track or of making his own way'. While Cixous sees Joyce's artistic signature in the essay, she believes that Joyce also ended the essay in the way that he did and gave it its title in a 'last attempt to remain where he was, at the crossroads of possibilities, in the sphere of cowardice and ambiguity' (212). While it bears the title 'Portrait of the Artist' it depicts not an artist – 'there is scarcely a trace of the actual artist in it' – but an '"imperson", struggling impersonally to bring into the world that being within it that desires to come into fuller existence' (213). It also represents what Cixous terms 'the curve of an hesitation'. It asks the question '"what shall I be?" but the questioner does not wish for a reply'. The essay does point the way, however, to the exile into which Joyce must go:

> He has now to expel all official history in favour of his own, to retreat without loss. His claims that he can show others the way are simply a last lie he tells himself, to disguise the fact that the choice has already been made. It is not possible to transform the world by beginning with an island, nor to recommend that all work together if one's own practice is an arrogant individualism; one cannot be both inside and outside.
>
> (221)

Cixous believes that '*Dubliners* should be reconsidered in the light of this 1904 *Portrait.*' This reveals it as a 'collection of manifestoes' and a 'denunciation of social paralysis coupled with an exhortation to shake it off'. In part this exhortation is self directed; although '*Dubliners* was to produce *Ulysses*... [it] was still written in a style of critical realism which could have produced quite the opposite' (221). In the June after Joyce wrote the essay, he met Nora Barnacle, and Cixous sees the essay 'speak[ing] of the need for [the] encounter and revelation' which was provided when they did meet. It would be difficult to overemphasise the importance for Joyce's artistic career which Cixous places on this meeting and Nora's subsequent role in his life. In terms of his ability to become an artist, she states that 'Joyce had to meet her, he was at last ready':

> She was sufficiently transparent and simple to appear strange and distant; she could strengthen him and deliver him from fear and hesitation. He was at last able to celebrate that marriage of the self, with no unmanning fear of being in the wrong.
>
> (221)

Joyce's meeting of Nora ended his period of transition; the early essay was 'the last stammerings of an uncertain and contradictory rhetoric'. Cixous contends that it was only after meeting Nora that Joyce 'felt... he really had the right to be an artist and creator', and that this right was also the 'right to welcome and to integrate with the mind his own estranged body'. It was only '[t]hrough Nora the true spouse', Cixous insists, that Joyce 'could at last proclaim himself as autonomous artist, his own husband and father at last' (221).

In the section of her book entitled 'The Fear of Marriage and the Dream of Freedom' Cixous considers how Joyce's changing attitudes towards women, particularly Nora, manifest themselves in his writing. Noting that 1931 was both the year of Joyce's marriage to Nora and of his father's death, she speculates on the reasons behind the Joyces' marriage. She asserts that what she calls the 'regularization' of Joyce's life with Nora 'was carried out for material rather than social reasons: there was no longer any risk of being suspected of conformism, but it was necessary to envisage the eventuality of his death and to think about protecting his children' (49). Certain fears which may have inhibited Joyce earlier are by 1931 no longer significant: 'Joyce no longer risks being transformed by marriage into a successor of his father; he is no longer afraid of Nora, society, the Church, or public opinion'. Joyce is also able to limit the significance of the marriage, and the 'gesture has only the strictly limited value he gives it: that of a "legal fiction"' (49).

Cixous examines Joyce's earlier fears about marriage in the context of Irish views on marriage, arguing that for 'the young Joyce marriage had signified the threat of responsibilities to be borne, or of modifications to be made in the self, in a sense that was anything but pleasing to a young autocrat':

It is normal that the problem should have taken its place in his mind at an early stage, for the home and the tribe are holy places of marriage. But the whole of Ireland is caught in a tormenting, exhausting involvement: the alliance with the Church is unforgiving; marriage and the flesh can only be opposed, but the problems created by puritanism... would only constitute, so to speak, the 'classical' obstacles, stemming in the last analysis from the psychology of the Catholic married couple, if they did not also form part of a complicated local situation that alienates the man.

(52)

Joyce's fears were also reinforced by his awareness of his father's position in respect to marriage and the Irish political system. 'What possessions', Cixous asks, 'could a Joyce own in 1904?' 'Caught between the family with its moral and vital imperatives, and a social and economic dependence in a colonial political system, he becomes the slave of his home, family, and nation.' James Joyce refused the solution offered by a 'career at the Catholic university' because that would have compromised 'his "moral nature"'. Ultimately, Cixous believes, '[h]onour and fear are linked together at the origin of Joyce's refusal to marry' (52).

Joyce imposed upon Nora the sort of relationship he had with her. He stood firmly against her desires to marry, refusing to 'turn[ ] back to what he calls "the system"' (54). Cixous sees Joyce placing the problem on Nora, and 'it is up to Nora, if she can, to change her wishes'. Joyce sees himself as preoccupied in a battle that he would risk losing were he to marry: 'He... is struggling against "incredible difficulties" but heroically "despises them": "I make open war upon the Catholic church by what I write and say and do. I cannot enter the social order except as a vagabond"'. He invents a 'form of love that suits his soul and mind', but after 1905, 'he has to give up the idea of sharing his mind with her because "with one entire side of my nature she has no sympathy"'. Cixous suggests that in all of Joyce's 'idealistic formulations' one 'cannot fail to recognise... a desire for a holy union': 'Joyce to some extent plays the part of God, and wishes to raise Nora to this level.' This creates a problem, for while Joyce longs for a 'holy union', he also 'rejects Christianity' for 'becoming a part of the social order'. A further problem is created by his sense of the sacred. Cixous cites a letter to Nora, written on 29 August, 1904, wherein Joyce 'refers to a holy night which in his language is a kind of marriage':

I consider it as a kind of sacrament and the recollection of it fills me with amazed joy. You will perhaps not understand at once why it is that I honour you so much on account of it as you do not know much of my mind. But it... left in me a final sense of sorrow and degradation – sorrow because I saw in you an extraordinary, melancholy tenderness which had chosen that sacrament as a compromise, and degradation because I understood that in your eyes I was inferior to a convention of our present society.

(*L*: II, 49; Cited, 55)

The problem is that while Joyce 'has transformed' the night 'into an exalting imitation of ritual,... Nora sees in it nothing but a degradation close to parody' (54).

Cixous sees many of the problems which Joyce and Nora experienced resulting from his determination to maintain his heroic exile. Joyce can take a firm stand against the Church and turn his nights with Nora into holy rituals, but Nora sees herself as 'only yielding to Joyce's selfish fancies' (55). The matter is made more complicated by their lack of a shared vocabulary: 'when Jim says "I want more than your caresses", he wants her soul and is prepared to give his own in return. But in the context of Dublin, Jim's periphrases and private language are not easy to grasp.' 'All their misunderstandings', Cixous explains, 'stem from his refusal to use symbolic words and his wish for Nora to understand him by implication, that she should leave unspoken the words (marriage, love, only, fidelity) which he cannot say without derogating from his own moral code.' Fortunately these problems were not severe enough to 'hinder Jim from considering Nora as his wife and living with her through all the problems of a lower-middle-class couple such that it could have served as a model for the similar couple in *Ulysses*' (55).

If the relationship between Jim and Nora serves as a relatively happy model for what Cixous terms the 'comic captivation of Bloom', in other texts it offers a model for relationships that were far from happy. 'The Boarding House', offers a view of marriage in which the man, Bob Doran, is tricked by the complicity between Polly Mooney and her mother. Noting that Joyce dedicated the story to his brother, Stanislaus, Cixous sees the story as a 'parable in which [Joyce] defends his decision to reject marriage' (61). While Joyce 'imagined that he had not been caught by the Polly trick', he 'never hides very far away from his work'. Cixous cites the opening lines which describe Polly:

> Polly was a slim girl of nineteen; she had light soft hair and a small full mouth. Her eyes, which were grey with a shade of green through them, had a habit of glancing upwards when she spoke with anyone, which made her look like a little perverse madonna.
>
> (*D*: 62, cited 61)

'And Nora was a slim girl of nineteen', Cixous states, adding that 'Polly and Nora have too many elements in common, and those precisely the most secret, which no-one would know while Jim and Nora were alive' (61). Nora was also the model for Gretta Conroy, but she provided not only the 'physical model' for Polly Mooney, but her 'life and past' as well as her 'family background': 'the mother had got rid of the alcoholic father with the same Christian fortitude. Polly has the same eyes that troubled Joyce so much.' The question of Polly's rather contrived innocence is a little more problematic. 'Joyce constantly compared Nora to Our Lady, not because [she] was a pure, venerable Marian figure, but because Joyce was still passionately attached to the church whose interdicts he rejected and yet desired.' Cixous believes Joyce's attachment to the church was so powerful that 'he could not have loved a woman without taking for his starting-point the first image of woman impressed upon him from child-hood upwards, that of Our Lady'. Women were a 'replacement' for the Virgin, and this 'dictates all relationships with women in Joyce's life and work' (62).

Joyce himself explained the comparison, 'often tell [ing] Nora that she has "marked his life as strongly as the Virgin previously had oriented it"'. Cixous uncovers the stereotypical image of the virgin/whore in Joyce's attitude towards Nora:

> She exalts, strengthens, tempts and attracts him; he longs to be open and honest before her, shameless and as much, as entirely, himself as possible. But he longs also to be the spouse and ravisher of the Virgin, to feel the terrifying joy of sacrilege and the glorious joy of replacing the Holy Spirit.
> (62)

While Joyce's comparison of Nora and the Virgin is involved in his depiction of Polly as a 'madonna', Cixous does not believe that Nora's own perversity was the model for Polly's:

> Joyce uses Nora to provoke God; she is instrumental if not an accomplice; she loses the possibility of innocence as she becomes gradually initiated into his defiance. In 1904, she had to be a madonna with a gift for perversity; in 1905 she may well have acquired from Jim a certain practical ability. But Polly's perversity has an immediate quality that Nora's never had.
> (62–3)

Cixous notes that Polly is called 'a little hypocritical madonna' in the 'manuscript of the first version', and points out that while neither Nora nor Polly were hypocrites, that is what Polly 'is preparing to be' (62–3).

The attitude towards marriage in the *Dubliners* stories is an important part of the strategies which Joyce developed as he exiled himself from the Church and distanced himself from the moral paralysis of his countrymen. But while the marriages of those stories can be read as a 'comic parody of a typical middle-class marriage' and a shared 'target of Jim's and Stannie's allied sarcasm', for Stephen Dedalus, hero and artist, it becomes what Cixous describes as 'such an obsessive problem that any approach, real or imaginary, to the sacrament or any idea of a future married life will set off aggressive behaviour patterns in the "hero", and later, in the "artist", genuine hallucinations' (66). Marriage is a central issue for Stephen as an 'eventual vocation' and the 'centre of that psychological crisis during which Stephen's choices are made' (67). The struggles and revolts which Stephen experiences are, as Cixous shows, remarkably similar to those which Joyce underwent. In trying to develop and follow the aesthetic principles to sustain him in his chosen role as a creative artist in exile, Joyce developed a moral code that could be as equally demanding and rigid as that which he rejected in the Church. Joyce refused to marry Nora when she discovered that she was pregnant. Cixous notes his explanation of this refusal to Stanislaus: 'the struggle against conventions in which I am at present involved was not entered into by me so much as a protest against the conventions as with the intention of living in conformity with my moral nature' (*L*, II: 99; Cited, 73). 'Such', Cixous explains 'was the declaration in real life which was to become Stephen's fine Satanic formula, "I will not serve that in which I no longer believe, whether it call itself my home, my fatherland, or my church"' (*P*: 247, cited 73). Cixous believes that Stephen's failure to love God may be linked with a weakness in Joyce's love for Nora: 'It may be that Joyce could not succeed in loving Nora as much as himself, either. The refusal of love is both subjective and objective: there is refusal to love and refusal to be loved' (73).

Cixous sees all of Joyce's domestic relationships as being ultimately subordinated by the priority of his role as an artist, and she notes the conflicts which this created when Joyce's son was born during the time when Joyce was trying to get *Dubliners* published: 'the child and *Dubliners* at once became opposed, not because Joyce was not pleased to become a father, but because Nora was taking much more interest in the child than in the written new work'. Joyce 'signified the existence of the conflict by symbolic gestures of refusal: two months after the child's birth, it still had no name' (64). Joyce seems to have been much more protective of his work than of his family: 'Children of flesh and blood were never to be a major concern of his, except when the work would permit of it' (65). In Joyce's mind even Nora became a sort of rival for his attention, and Cixous sees 'Jim both provok [ing] and fear [ing] the inevitable rivalry between Nora and his writing'. This fear and provocation is traceable in *Exiles*, and Cixous thinks that Joyce 'puts himself on trial' in the 'shaming admissions' of the play, 'intending to acquit himself in the end, but meaning first to admit and accept all the wrongs he has done':

> Bertha, alias Nora, the companion of the writer Richard Rowan, has two rivals whom she assimilates together: the one is Beatrice who has inspired Richard from afar and is the pale, cold embodiment of the artist's relationship to his inspiration; and the other is Richard's work itself, which deprives Bertha of the real presence of the man she calls *my* lover, when he sits up all night in the study, giving himself to the work rather than to the woman who longs for him.
>
> (65)

As Joyce continued to write, the situation grew worse, and he seems to have exiled himself from his family and into his work: 'Jim was to succeed so well in destroying the characteristics of marriage that little or nothing remained of the couple's subjection to the function of procreation.' Nora's maternal nature disturbed Joyce so much that 'he was only tempted to leave Nora when she took on the appearance of the mother'. Cixous considers the damaging effect that this must have had on the two children who 'had to be sacrificed to Jim's happiness with Nora':

> Lucia and Georgio had to pay for their parents' decision to be first and foremost Nora and Jim, in order that Jim might freely be James Joyce. This is why Nora's maternal feelings gradually atrophied as she became more and more Jim's companion. Later Joyce would see the double consequences of this wilful deformation of marriage: on the one hand, the children of a couple who live like Adam and Eve in a world unlike Eden are indirectly affected by an overwhelming freedom (when they needed Nora's protection she could only answer that she had but one 'child' – her husband); and on the other, Lucia as she grew up found Nora to be 'father's companion' rather than mother.
>
> (66)

Cixous contends that this produced the 'tragically violent jealousy whose movements can be perceived in *Finnegans Wake*'. Joyce's self-imposed exile in his written work entailed an abdication from the role of father of flesh and blood children. Joyce did later pay more attention to Lucia, but Cixous sees this as the result of Joyce's 'genuine obsession' with Lucia's mental illness rather than as a case of 'normal fatherly care' (65). In the *Wake*, the 'couple Jim and Nora is succeeded by that of Jim and Lucia'; the text is a 'work of fatherhood and incest, whose language echoes that of the daughter' (66).

Joyce's Poetics

Cixous is particularly interested in how Joyce's poetics affected his treatment of reality, and her study is framed by an assessment of the relationships between Joyce's writing and reality. It opens with a brief consideration of the relation between Joyce's realism and symbolism and poses the question: 'How far and to what degree can one speak of "realism" in Joyce's art?' (x); it concludes with an investigation of 'The Language of Reality' and how in Joyce's writing 'Language Replaces Reality' (673–736). Considering Joyce's Irish background and his family, Cixous states: 'The family, the economic and social problems, are... both concrete elements of surrounding reality – an end in itself, but limited – and the means by which the artist's mind is sharpened'. Ultimately, however, 'any realism is at once overtaken and assimilated, to become the surface of a symbolism which is made less and less publicly significant as it is more and more charged with personal meaning, until, with *Finnegans Wake*, it becomes a Joycean form of occultism, initiation to which is achieved by a progress *through* Joyce enabling one to reach reality' (ix–x).

Cixous agrees with J.-J. Mayoux who, in *Joyce* (Gallimard, Paris, 1965), asserts that Joyce had the 'double consciousness of one watching himself live' (44, cited x), and she suggests that Joyce 'already possesses' this 'double consciousness' '[w]hen he writes *A Portrait*'. This enabled Joyce 'to reconstitute by memory a time which is experienced and now past':

> This retrospective glance at his own history reveals both the *image* he has of himself (not himself), and the exterior forces which have caused him to develop in opposition to them; what he sees is the social alienation of his family and of Ireland to which he has responded by withdrawing, by declaring his *difference*, while still, in the tones of the romantic and idealistic *fin-de-siècle* artist, claiming the role of moral reformer within the very society that he rejects.
>
> (x)

Of course, the view of the family and of the economic and social reality that emerges from within Joyce's artistic 'double consciousness' will not be identical with historical 'reality', and Cixous realises that to 'obtain a true picture of the reality of this Ireland... one must take into account the part played by aesthetic transformation and refer to the available biographical documents'. Cixous makes extensive use of Ellmann's biography, Stanislaus Joyce's *My Brother's Keeper* (New York: Faber and Faber, 1958) 'and especially the *Dublin Diary* of 1903–04, which is about the period when James Joyce passed from being aware of his genius to giving it free play' (xi). While she relies on such biographical material, however, Cixous's primary interest is in how the biographical events were transformed as Joyce subjected them to the 'double' vision of his artistic processes.

Cixous believes that much of Joyce's work, including *Ulysses*, is realistic: 'After the moral history of *Dubliners*, after the spiritual gestation of the archetypal artist and the discovery of the subject's own style, after the skilfully demonstrated statement that the Artist creates, starting from his inner exile, a work outside which... he stands, Joyce wrote *Ulysses*, the work which reconciles unity and multiplicity to an end which is both realistic, moral, and universal' (673). Her definition of realism needs to be scrutinised, however, because she thinks that the 'object of realism is not "reality"'. In *Ulysses*, 'the reality of Ireland is only a part of an infinitely larger whole'. Cixous does not see Joyce's text as 'the modern *Odyssey*', because 'the Odyssean symbolism with its network of correspondences leads scarcely further than an ethical statement'. Furthermore, even Homer's epic is 'also part of an infinitely larger whole, taking on meaning from that whole (all Western culture, its historical duration, and its myths) and from its relationship with the concrete reality of the here and now'. Describing Joyce's 'programme' as 'nothing less than a project to write the book of books, to find a... "structural scheme" in which... each component part (art, organ, hour, etc.) should create its own language', Cixous sees *Ulysses* as a 'monstrous epiphany' revealing the 'total manifestation of reality through language' (674).

Like Eco, Cixous finds the medieval concept of the 'summa' essential to understanding Joyce's aims. From this concept 'Joyce takes the concept of totality, while abandoning its content, that order and hierarchy which made the correspondence-system possible'. Joyce's rejection of the idea of 'one unique style, one author's commentary' enabled him to replace it with 'a multiplicity of styles' (674). This multiplicity shifts the emphasis from the writer to reality as the 'form of what is written' (687). While the 'form mimics reality', without any authorial comment or judgement, it is not a 'technique... of identical reproduction'. Joyce uses 'language and all of its... possibilities of expression as *equivalent matter*' and 'juxtapos[es] the work and the world with no intermediary' in order to 'bring out all the hidden meanings in the concrete subjective'. Like Derrida, Cixous finds meaning determined in part by differences: 'all the meanings [of Joyce's writing] are already contained in the discrepancy or differences between absolute reality, reality as read, and reality as written' (688).

While she sees the differences between these realities containing the meanings of the text, Cixous also believes that the 'fluidity of form' to which Joyce's multiplicity of styles contributes, is a result of the 'displacement of reality, or rather [of] the modifications which the notion of reality here begins to undergo'. In *Ulysses*, reality ceases to be a 'common universal objective experience' and becomes a 'particular, subjective, often incommunicable experience':

> If *Ulysses* apparently takes place in Dublin... it is really only a framework and a setting. Dublin exists, but much more as an animate object, a giant body, a corporate character, than as a stage. 'The' consciousness is made up of all individual conscious minds, and the absence of anyone else as an audience means the disappearance of the traditional signposts used in prose writing to facilitate the transition from one person or place to another, such as 'he said', 'he replied', and so on.
>
> (696)

Cixous ultimately considers *Ulysses* as a 'book of consciousness' and contends that '[o]nce one has registered' this 'fact', 'history ceases to exist': 'The reduction of chronological and objective time is expressed as an image by the compression of all time into one single day... all the hours of which are lived through as experience but at different depths and to different rhythms'. Providing the text's 'space of reality', its 'one consciousness' is 'globally and cosmically inclusive', and eliminates the distinctions between the 'events in outer or inner worlds' (700). Along with the lack of the 'traditional signposts' for distinguishing between characters, the lack of any identification of the characters 'by an omniscient author' renders the reader 'unable to distinguish where he is, in whose mind or at what time in that mind'. This produces a duality in language analogous to the double consciousness Mayoux attributes to Joyce:

> In effect, everyone has two languages; the one carries along with it the specific signs of the individual's existence and thought as they are in the present, but marked by the past, in a form that is absolutely personal and recognisable, while the other is the common language of the senses, of permeability to daily life – the colourless language of indifference common to all of the inhabitants of the same city, who are all informed to much the same extent of those facts and circumstances which do not effect their personal lives.
>
> (700)

The two languages which Cixous discovers in Joyce are in part the result of a technique which she sees as essential in Joyce's poetics; the technique of 'interpenetratability'. The Dubliners who play minor roles in the book are 'divided into individuals – but only their names differentiate them, because they are all alike and all like Dublin': 'Their language is superficial, their speeches interchangeable, and the reader has to pay very close attention in order to see how the roles are distributed among these minor characters' (700). The major characters of Stephen, Bloom and Molly also operate to a certain extent in accordance with the technique of interpenetratability: 'in the inner world in which [they] move... images, facts or events may be encountered in exactly the same way by Bloom's mind and by Stephen's mind, as though the universal consciousness were really a continuous space permitting any idea to be thought, without telepathy, by anyone'. Cixous sees this as indicative of the fact that Joyce's 'vision of reality has nothing left in common with the traditional arrangement usual in novels'. She also hypothesises that if the thoughts are no longer owned by 'one particular ego, then the sum of all thoughts is reality, and Bloom, Molly and Stephen are nothing more than objects of cognition floating in a *continuum*' (700).

There is a limit to Joyce's use of interpenetratability, and 'only in the "Circe" episode', Cixous states, 'are the boundaries of the self shattered, as the experience of dissolution is dramatised in a kind of play'. The extensive use of interpenetratability in the 'Circe' episode produces a 'polycentricity' with which Joyce launches an 'attack upon the unity of the theological world with its single centre' (700–1). Cixous sees Joyce 'attempting to set up a vision of his own', which is 'ex-centric as far as the creation is involved' and 'a world which can escape from the Absolute which rules the world God has created'. In this context Joyce's writing operates as a radical attempt at subverting a God who is perceived as a source of restriction:

> Everything which usually constitutes or contributes to the traps and nets in which God holds the world and the mind captive, subjected to his Presence

and Omnipotence, is endangered by Joyce's art – spacial orientation, currents in time, duration and evolution, dialogue which supposes a relationship between two people and hence a space established firmly between two fixed points, and grammar that imprisons words between the rails of reason, obedient to the laws of the divine Logos. All these suffer in Joyce's world.

(701)

In so far as Joyce's writing subverts this theological foundation of phallocentrism it would seem to be in harmony with the aims of female writing which attempts to overcome the restrictions of the phallocentric tradition. Cixous defines phallocentrism in 'The Laugh of the Medusa':

> Nearly the entire history of writing is confounded with the history of reason, of which it is at once the effect, the support, and one of the priviliged alibis. It has been one with the phallocentric tradition. It is indeed that same self-admiring, self-stimulating, self-congratulatory phallocentrism.

(249)

Cixous finds Joyce's attack upon phallocentrism also aimed at the theological and philosophical notions of teleology: his writing 'tries to replace the imagery common to Western thought, with its implications of a beginning and an end, a here and a there, a past and a present, self and an other, by a world without history, a continuous world of osmosis' (701). This has a profound effect on us as readers because 'people and things... appear to us without being subject to our minds' usual process of examination and recognition; races, knowledge, cultures, personal histories, childhood memories, desires all mingle, with no concerns for the normal boundaries of mine and thine, *hic* and *ille*, *tunc* and *nunc*'. This might appear threatening or even chaotic, but Cixous contends that it 'is not chaos, but the polycentricity that has replaced egocentricity or theocentricity'. She believes that Joyce even allows his polycentric writing to expose the limits of the characters that he has created: 'Even Stephen and Bloom only succeed in directing this disorder to a limited extent; their minds interpenetrate, and fantasies move from one to another, without at once being noticed.' The traditional, novelistic convention of separating realism from fantasy no longer applies: 'Life and death communicate in the vertiginous movements of the *danse macabre*' (701). Joyce's polycentrism makes it possible for him to 'dismember history and time, conjugating past and future in the present tense, and even going so far as to attribute to the dead past an imaginary future which contradicts the real past, permitting, for example, the final apparition of Rudy, Bloom's son who died at the age of eleven' (702).

Stephen's desire to awake from the 'nightmare of history' was Joyce's desire to be free from imprisonment by the history of the culture from which he chose to exile himself. Cixous ultimately sees Joyce as a 'learned man of language... prey to despair and a rival of God, whose ambition is to create the ever-elusive – not Mallarmé's "The book", but the Book which, once read, would not contradict its creator..., the Book that would remain alive, everchanging, moving, ageing, never fixed on the page as a given, signed, complete universe' (735). Cixous thinks that Joyce 'well knew' the death which results from the writer who 'murder[s] his own art' by ceasing to write, and she sees *Finnegans Wake* as an example of Joyce's drive to 'seek out and invent a kind of writing that would not stop its evolution and development once the writer had left it, which would continue developing because it contained an infinite supply of meanings'. For Cixous, the *Wake* is 'Joyce's last will and testament'. The final 'the' of the text is an 'admirable but unique contrivance', but it is not the infinity of which Joyce dreamt. Rather, it is 'the suppression of the ending which is instead replaced by the beginning... And after all, the work is still limited, by the very fact of its having a beginning' (735).

Cixous anticipates what later, poststructuralist critics have said about the *Wake* when she states that it is not a finite *book*, but an example of writing that withholds the last word, that is intended to last for ever...' (735). It demands a curious logical contortion to account for the relationship between its first and last pages: '"At the end", it suceeds itself, and since its beginning is its end, it is both mother and murderer of itself, giving both birth and death to itself' (735). It is 'therefore not surprising', Cixous argues, 'that the word chosen to be the last and designated to be the first, should be "the" – the definite article, the word which points out but which by itself means nothing, a dead word, a sign which depends upon what follows it' (736). Cixous compares Joyce with a hero who in 'uselessness, madness, and terror... writes... until he is himself nothing but the effort of his writing'. She also compares what she perceives Joyce as saying with 'what overwhelms Stephen':

> freedom only exists outside the culture in which one is irremediably imprisoned;... one only sleeps out one's life to the accompaniment of history as told by a God who speaks the same language as oneself;... only within this history does one have a place to occupy and a part to play. If God speaks the language of men, He does so because men have invented God speaking their language, and because they claim to justify themselves and to render themselves innocent by attributing to God the Word that gives the signal for the slaughter to begin.
>
> (736)

'Joyce: the (r)use of writing'

Cixous' essay 'Joyce: the (r)use of writing' (*Post-structuralist Joyce* [Cambridge: Cambridge University Press, 1984]) affords the opportunity to experience Cixous' work on Joyce after she moves away from the traditional, academic framework of writing, which, as we have seen, she found 'very constraining'. The subtitle of the essay is 'Discrediting the subject', and Cixous begins with a clear indication of how the essay should be read: 'Here begins a reading of Joyce which will point out by means of certain fragments of *Dubliners*, of *A Portrait*, or of *Ulysses* how Joyce's work has contributed to the discrediting of the subject'. Borrowing an idea from Julia Kristeva's 'Introduction' to *La Poétique de Dostoievski* (Paris: Seuil, 1970), Cixous outlines the context for her reading of the fragments from Joyce's texts: 'how today one can talk about Joyce's modernity by situating him on "that breach of the self" opened up by other writings whose subversive force is now undermining the world of western discourse' (Kristeva: 15, cited 15). The essay does not explicitly offer itself as a feminist reading, but it clearly views Joyce's writing as participating in the sort of subversive strategies which Cixous identifies, in 'The Laugh of the Medusa', as the strategies necessary for breaking up the 'arid millenial ground':

> his writing, which is justly famed for its system of mastering signs, for its control over grammar (including its transgressions and dislocations which cut across a language which is too much a 'mother' tongue, too alienating, a captive language which must be made to stumble), how this writing takes the risk of upsetting the literary institution and the anglo-saxon lexicon: by hesitating over the interpretation of signs, by the vitiation of metaphor, by putting a question mark over the subject and the style of the subject.
>
> (15)

The style of Cixous' essay is richer and much more dense than that of *The Exile of James Joyce*, and the essay reads as if Cixous were incorporating some of the Joycean strategies that she discusses into her own style, as if she were striving to allow her writing to articulate its subject instead of writing about it in the traditional academic style. Consider, for example, how easily she moves from text to text and subject to subject in outlining the progression of Joyce's writing in three progressively-expanding sentences whose subjects include an expanding meditation on the trinity:

> Between Daedalus and Icarus: *Ulysses*. And: 'My will: his will that fronts me. Seas between' (*U*: 217). From father unto son, via the mother, always, begun again. This delayed birth constitutes the movement of a work which playfully undermines gestation, the delay inscribing itself in the various falls, losses, repeated and unexpected exiles, which are all the more astounding in that the goal seems accessible, is named, puts itself forward, fascinates, is not hidden but rather pointed out (I, the Artist, the Word), is not forbidden but rather promised, and in that the subject, held in suspense, pursues it with … the weapons of the self (silence, exile, cunning), marking out its passage with theories, incorporated hypotheses of formalization: one or two ideas from Aristotle, a pinch of St. Thomas; a chapter on poetics and literary history; several chapters on the problems of autobiography; and, in a pre-Freudian context, an implicit theory of the authorial unconscious, and of the textual unconscious, in a blasphemous anology with the Arian

heresy, showing in the Trinity the three-sided, divinely ordered production that allows the Father to see through the Son's eyes, where the Holy Spirit would be like the chain linking the Name of the Father to the Name of the Son, the scriptor to writing: the breath of the unconscious on the text.

(16)

One could follow various chains of signification which Cixous weaves through these three sentences: from the classical, Hellenic narrative of Daedalus to the Judeo-Christian trinity; what happens in *Ulysses* concerning the father, mother and son; Joyce's use of Aristotle and St Thomas and his anticipation of Freud. These topics are not dealt with in the traditional form of subject–predicate sentence patterns but woven together in a way that puts a strain on the traditional paradigms of logic for sentence and paragraph development. The reader can follow the topics along associative chains like those which we saw Eco identify in *Finnegans Wake*. Cixous considers the kind of double pattern which her earlier study associates with Joyce's double consciousness. Here, however, she refers to *Ulysses* as a 'Quest, odyssey, with a double hero' (16).

Cixous analyses the opening paragraph of 'The Sisters' in some detail and states that in this passage, 'we shall grasp the first manifestation of the slide from the one to the plural...' (17). It is in this 'slide' that the discrediting of a singular subject can be experienced as the movement 'from the disquieting plural of One, slipped between the narrator and the I subject, between the one and the other, between master of diction and master of interdiction, between pseudo-father (priest, imitator) and pseudo-son, between true words and bad words (*mots vrais et mauvais mots*)'. The reading of the passage from 'The Sisters' is offered as a marginal reading in at least two senses of the term: Joyce's passage is chosen because of its marginal position 'on the border of the Joycean corpus', and the reading itself attempts to expand the margins of the interpretive process, pushing it towards new margins or limits for engaging with the passage to be examined. This is typical of a poststructuralist commentary, as is Cixous' interest in Joyce's passage as a ' [s]cene of decentering of the subject'. Cixous treats the opening paragraph of 'The Sisters' as:

> the locus of a consciousness which censorship hardly separates from the unconscious which speaks in a dream a little later in the story. Scene of the decentering of the subject, as it immediately strikes the readers *of* the text (*in* the text): since a reading subject is present, and on the level of the text. Thus my reading is always preceded by the reading of the other-scriptor, which is preceded by the reading of the other-subject: and this reading is as (far from) innocent as the text which produces it...
>
> (17)

Not only is Cixous' reading concerned with the double in Joyce's text; it also offers itself as a double text. This is exemplified in the passage 'this reading is as (far from) innocent as the text which produces it'. Cixous' use of parentheses around 'far from' allows us to read the passage either with or without the negative modification of 'far from': we can read her text as one which is 'as innocent' as Joyce's text or as one which is as 'far from innocent' as Joyce's. The two poles of – innocence and + innocence provide the textual space for what Cixous has already identified as the 'slide from the One to the plural', and neither Joyce's text or Cixous' commentary will offer the subject of an unequivocal innocence. As Cixous' commentary entails a very close reading of Joyce, it is helpful to consider the passage from 'The Sisters' in its entirety:

> There was no hope for him this time: it was the third stoke. Night after night I had passed the house (it was vacation time) and studied the lighted square of window: and night after night I had found it lighted in the same way, faintly and evenly. If he was dead, I thought, I would see the reflections of candles on the darkened blind for I knew that two candles must be set at the head of a corpse. He had often said to me: 'I am not long for this world', and I had thought his words idle. Now I knew they were true. Every night as I gazed up at the window I said softly to myself the word paralysis. It had always sounded strangely in my ears, like the word gnomon in the Euclid and the word simony in the Catechism. But now it sounded to me like the name of some maleficent and sinful being. It filled me with fear, and yet I longed to be nearer to it and to look upon its deadly work.
>
> (*D*: 9; Cited, 17)

Cixous begins her analysis with a consideration of what Joyce 'said about his book': 'Letter to C. P. Curran, a friend, 1904: "I call the series *Dubliners* to *betray the soul* of that hemiplegia or *paralysis* which many consider a city" (*Letters*, I. 55)' (17–18). She creates a double text by repeating key words and phrases from Joyce's description: 'I emphasize: "*betray*", "*the soul*", "*paralysis*": to betray, by naming, to write in order to betray, to betray "the soul" of / that paralysis / which many consider a city'; her aim is to emphasise the 'metonymic substitution of "the sickness" for the sick body' and the 'traditional dichotomy of soul (manifest in)/ body'. These operate as a 'substitutive reinforcement, a parodic mechanism, playing between sickness and city'. They also establish two poles that structure the double writing in which Cixous is interested. In the play 'between sickness and city', 'the one [term]' substitutes for 'the other in inverse proportion to the expected order: Dublin is sick – Dublin is its sickness – *The* sickness *is*, Dublin is put in its stead'. At this point, Cixous suggests, the reader 'becomes aware of limits beginning to dissolve in the perversion of signifiers' (18).

Cixous returns to the realism which she considered in her earlier study of Joyce. Citing a letter to the publisher of *Dubliners*, Grant Richards, in which Joyce claimed to have 'taken the first step towards the spiritual liberation' of Ireland, she argues that the representation of Joyce's realism is at least 'modulated' even in his early stories: 'Even if their author

intended *Dubliners* to belong to the world of meaning and expression –
Joyce insisting on what he *meant* to the very word ("in accordance with
[...] the classical tradition of my art") – at least one sees how representation is immediately modulated in so far as the discourse has less bearing
on a concrete outside, on a reproducible real, than on the gaze directed
at the referent (the Dubliners).' Joyce may have thought that he was
writing about the concrete reality of Dublin, but his writing also manifests
the self- or auto-referential aspect which we considered in the chapter on
semiotics. Joyce's writing not only directs its gaze toward Dubliners, but
back to itself, to the 'nature of that gaze, and even on the name, the letter
of that gaze: so initially there is only deferred representation, a perceptible
hesitation on the surface to be inscribed' (18). Cixous believes that '[o]ne
could modify the orders which Joyce gave himself by articulating them
with certain declarations which seem to point towards the idea... of text
as either pathbreaking or as a substitutive formation'. Stephen's declaration 'This race and this country and this life produced me [...] I shall
express myself as I am' (*P*: 211; Cited, 18), 'could equally well be read,'
Cixous argues, as the 'recognition that writing is a mode of production
determined, beyond the biographical, by the socio-cultural system' (18).

Poststructuralist feminism and Freud's notion of the *heimlich* provide
Cixous with a further expansion of the context in which she examines and
situates Joyce's writing. She believes that in Joyce's notion of 'spiritual
liberation' 'there remains, lurking, that theological left-over instituted in
the notion of the "spiritual" which holds the text in front of the mirror'.
This positioning of the text in front of the mirror is Cixous' metaphor for
a confirmation of the text by the text which cuts the role of the reader
out of the reading–writing process. Using the classical 'spiritual' paradigms of traditional theology will confirm the text as spiritual: 'Spiritual
mirror, spiritual chapter'. A more valid 'spiritual liberation' – and here
Cixous' argument echoes her ideas on feminist writings in 'The Laugh of
the Medusa' – is to be achieved by transgressing the borders of the
classical–theological and realist traditions: 'Is not the "spiritual
liberation",' she asks, 'brought about via a liberation of signifiers, fraudu-
lently crossing the "classical" realist border, and that of its solemn double,
symbolism'. Joyce's texts need to be considered in terms of the 'scene of
writing' which, 'when only just set' is 'slipping, turning, and always
decentered' (18). Joyce's confident assertion on 'spiritual liberation' is
only one aspect of his text. In addition to the subject's confident assertion
of what he, or she, knows, there always lurks what the subject ('ego, the
it, the id, the subject') does not know. The '*unheimlich* effect... sets up
a play between the familiar, and the sudden breakdown of the familiar,
between the home (*Heim*) and the hidden (*heimlich*), between my self and
that which escapes me' (18–19). In Joyce's text the Freudian 'fear of
being blinded', which is a result of the *heimlich* revealing itself, is 'an

indispensable axis crossing the Joycean space' (19). This fear is also a 'substitute for the fear of castration: fear which in its turn produces the other
self, that kind of other which is kept handy in case the self should perish'.
'[I]n literature', Cixous argues, this other self,

> becomes 'the double', a stranger to the self, or its indirect manifestations:
> doubling of the self, split self, and all those subversions of the subject, *visibly
> at work* in the excerpt [from 'The Sisters'] quoted: where 'I' (the narrator)
> weigh up my strength, my existence, my grasp on reality, and my abdicating
> by examining the power of words.
>
> (19)

The '(r)use of writing' to which Cixous' title refers is '*(R)used writing,
writing governed by ruse*: which is therefore luxury writing, because in order
to play tricks and to sow seeds, you have to produce wild goose chases,
you have to modify the traditional mode of the narrative which claims
to offer a coherent whole' (19). The reader learns to modify through
commitment to a 'double apprenticeship':

> the necessary one which is reading–writing a text whose plurality explodes
> the painstakingly polished surface: and the one which is, in the very practice
> of a reading not condemned to linearity, an incessant questioning of the
> codes which appear to function normally but which are sometimes suddenly
> rendered invalid, and then the next moment are revalidated, and, in the
> inexhaustible play of codes, there slips in, indecipherable and hallucinatory
> by definition, the delirious code, a lost code, a kind of reserve where
> untamed signifiers prowl, but without the space of that reserve being
> delimited.
>
> (19)

Ulysses provides Cixous with an illustration of this intrusion of a 'de-
lirious' or 'lost' code. In the 'middle of a majestic episode ("Nestor")
which bears the meaning of History, which resounds with the echoes of
battles, with questions concerning a country's past... there slips onto the
scene of representation and into a network of correspondence tightly
worked by the idea of historical causality, a riddle posed by Stephen':

> – This is the riddle, Stephen said:
> *The cock crew,*
> *The sky was blue:*
> *The bells in heaven*
> *Were striking eleven.*
> *'Tis time for this poor soul*
> *To go to heaven.*
> – What is that?
>   – What, sir?
>   – Again, sir. We didn't hear.

Their eyes grew bigger as the lines were repeated. After a silence Cochrane said:
– What is it, sir? We give it up.
Stephen, his throat itching, answered:
– The fox burying his mother under a hollybush.
He stood up and gave a shout of nervous laughter to which their cries echoed dismay.

(*U*: 22; Cited, 20)

Cixous believes that this riddle 'forces the reader into a dumbfounded identification with the pupils'. The 'genre of the riddle, a literary and detective-story genre, which assumes... that there should be a solution somewhere, the one who asks being... the one who possesses the knowledge' – all of these traditional conventions 'combine[ ] to make you "take seriously" the existence of an answer' (20). Joyce's writing subverts these conventions, however, and denies the reader the meaning that she, or he, confidently expects. Stephen's answer to the riddle, Cixous contends, 'reveals not a positive knowledge, but the gap in knowledge, the knowledge of nonknowledge, the author abandoning his rights over language'. This entails what Cixous calls the 'desacralization of reading in the sense that reading is implicitly the rite of passage into culture' (20). The sonorous echoes in the passage provide a 'miming [of] tension', and Cixous lists some of the ways in which the 'preciseness of... terms' and the answer 'ape[ ] scientificity or the absolute', reinforcing the expectation that the logic of the riddle must lead to an answer (19). In the end, however, there 'remains the untamed subject: the fox'. 'That is all,' Cixous declares, adding that Stephen's nervous laughter 'is... the laughter of the perverse text', a laughter that is 'hard to bear, just as it is difficult to accept that frustration is normal in the intellectual sphere'. This frustration is 'experienced as the subterfuge of castration' and the point at which 'you must stop demanding meaning', and at which 'academic discourse is brought to its limit' (21).

Because of the operations of the double in Joyce's writing, the reader is offered two choices in the face of the crisis of meaning which texts such as the riddle precipitate. The first 'course[ ] of action' entails 'trusting to the known facts about Joyce's work, particularly his intensive use of symbols, and his obsessive and often explicit concern to control word order'. This results in a 'prejudging' of the book as 'a full text' that is 'governed by "the hypostasis of the signifier"', a text which conceals itself but which has something to conceal which is findable'. Cixous sees this course of action producing a 'reassuring position' that is almost necessary because academic discourse operates (in either a 'conscious or unconscious fashion') by 'pushing Joyce back into the theological world from which he wanted to escape', by 'squeezing him "through the back door"'. (In support of her argument that academic criticism can operate in this way,

Cixous cites 'versions of Joyce as a Catholic, Medieval Joyce, Irish Joyce, Joyce the Jesuit in reverse and hence the right way around as well, etc.'.) The alternate course for reading Joyce, and the one which Cixous advocates and follows herself, requires the reader to 'imagine a reading which would accept' the sort of 'discouragement' offered by the riddle of the fox, 'not in order to "recuperate" it by taking it as a metaphor for the Joycean occult (which would... be right but would only be taking account of the formal aspect of that effect of privation), but rather by seeing in that trap... the sign of the willed imposture which crosses and double-crosses the *whole* of Joyce's work, making that betrayal the very breath (the breathlessness) of the subject'.

Cixous' intention is to open up within her own work the (at least) double play of signification which she perceives at work within Joyce's text, to allow her reader to experience not an 'academic' discussion *about* the ways in which Joyce's writing operates, but a writing which articulates the same double strategies as Joyce's writing. It is this experience of the double in Joyce's writing (and in writing in general) that is offered when Cixous writes that 'betrayal' is the 'very breath (the breathlessness)' of Joyce's 'subject'. The reader can read the writing in a more or less, conventional, linear fashion, but the operation of 'breathlessness' within the parentheses breaks the linearity of the reading, forcing the reader to go back and consider how 'breathlessness' contradicts and negates, from within the parentheses, the signification of 'breath'. The either/or logic of traditional binary logic (nothing can simultaneously 'breathe' and be 'breathless') is undermined as the bracketed signifier, 'breathlessness', which should offer subordinate support and clarification for 'breath', the signifier outside of the bracket, actually contradicts it and produces a meaning that is at least a double meaning: 'betrayal' is the 'very breath' of Joyce's 'subject' *and* 'betrayal' is the 'breathlessness' of Joyce's 'subject'. It is just such a contradictory double that Cixous finds in the riddle. Stephen does offer an answer to the riddle: 'The fox burying his mother under a hollybush', but this answer does not satisfy us because it disappoints our expectations which are based on the traditional concepts (the genre of the riddle, there should be an answer, the riddler should be able to solve the riddle) which Cixous outlines.

When Cixous finally turns to a close analysis of the passage from 'The Sisters' (her detour through the fox riddle serves at least two purposes: it allows the reader to gain a better understanding of the 'double' modes of signification in Joyce's writing and it enables Cixous to follow a logic other than the academic, linear logic which demands that the subject should be examined in a straightforward, economic, linear fashion), she suggests that the 'farce of breaking-up which interferes directly with the order of *Ulysses*' is 'easy to spot' in that text 'because it is isolated almost as a symptom...' (21). The unattached element (the fox, the answer to the riddle) is 'indirectly granted a transgressive violence... in which a *gratuitousness*... comes to the surface and makes significance quiver as if it were the *nervous laughter of writing*' (21–2). In *Dubliners* and *A Portrait*, however, the 'unattached element' and the 'breaking-up' that interfere with narrative order also operate, although their operations are not as easily detected as they are in *Ulysses*. The symptom which reveals their operations, however, is still the 'laughter' of writing. Cixous looks at 'The Sister's' image of the smiling priest letting his 'tongue lie upon his lower lip' (*D*: 13), and identifies its psychological signification of a 'phallus playing dead' (30, n. 10). She states that the 'vocal outburst' of the laughter of writing in this case 'stands in contrast to the horrible and silent smile of the corpse', and that this 'silent smile' is the 'inscription under the insidious sound "s" ["*s*ilent", "*s*mile"] of unspeakable vice, of sin which is suggested, "murmured" but unfinished, of the perversion of relations between subject and object, between body and soul, life and death, sound and meaning... work and magic...' (22).

Examining the psychological implications of the relationship between the old priest and the young boy, Cixous finds that it revolves around 'relations of reversal and overstepping' (22). The attributes of the priest become those of the boy when the priest gives the boy knowledge that he had hitherto not possessed. The priest teaches the boy about written knowledge: 'he told me that the fathers of the Church had written books as thick as the *Post Office Directory* and as closely printed as the law notices in the newspaper, elucidating all these intricate questions' (*D*: 13). For Cixous, this knowledge, both hidden and revealed, in the story, is inextricably linked with the materiality of writing. When the boy receives knowledge from the priest, 'the attributes of one term slip onto another in the terrifying materialization of the power of the letter' (22). Cixous offers a lengthy and complex introduction to her analysis which is essential to her view of how 'The Sisters' operates:

> if you know that the narrator whose thoughts suggest these opening sentences [of the first paragraph] is the disciple of a queer disappointed priest in whom 'there was something gone wrong', if you know that the priest, initiator, had taught the boy Latin, a tongue which is doubly foreign, dead, theological, magical, and also 'how complex and mysterious were certain institutions of the Church which I had always regarded as the simplest acts' [*D*: 13], that the priest amused himself 'by putting difficult questions to him', then you sense the harrowing intensification of an examination which centres on the highest knowledge, below the decaying garments of the master and behind the mask of 'simplicity': there the master represents an unfathomable authority, and the scene is from the outset the sacred one, profaned by a highly 'incarnate' death: if there is complicity between the subjects such that the curiosity of the one regarding the other seems to announce some morbid identification, if the dead priest's smile parts the disciple's lips, it is because there is at stake between them the access to an object of desire, which in the end is perhaps nothing other than the very

play of inscription in so far as certain signifiers can hollow out an 'other' place in the text, the sexual metaphor for which is given later: the narrator's dream reveals the secret, desirable and fearsome nature of it: shows itself moving, appealing, withdrawing, miming the exile of jouissance, displacing the prohibited place, which is never seen, where the priest's head, the grey *disembodied* face, has *something* secret to tell which is never told.

(22)

Like the answer to the riddle of the fox, the priest's secret is refused for the reader. Like the passage in which the riddle occurs, 'The Sisters' sets up a context which gives the reader the expectation that he, or she, will be given a meaning and then withholds the meaning while allowing the reader to experience the dissolving of the context which created the expectation of meaning for the reader in the first place. The meaning seems to reside in a ' [h] idden recess' on the other side of the 'long velvet curtains' (*D*: 13) of which the boy dreams, but the reader gradually experiences the

[h] idden recess receding in a sinister movement to vanish on the other side of soft curtains... through the veils of perverted confession, summoned by the head, object-subject ('*it* smiled'), 'very far away' to 'some land where the customs were strange – in Persia I thought... But I could not remember the end of the dream'.

(22)

Cixous follows the gradual receding of the meaning which the reader seems to be promised in psychological terms. She sees the boy's inability to remember the end of his dream, 'parodying the excentricity of the subject' in the context of the 'pursuit of *Where id was, there ego shall be*' (22). In the boy's dreams, the priest-as-id 'signals with dead tongue and disembodied head'. Cixous traces the gradual disappearance of meaning along a 'metonymic chain where the other place always has its other' (23):

Far, antique, strange, Persian, perverse, perdition piercing, slipping, transgressing the occidental/oriental line, sending the sacred back to a desecration, continually emptying out speech, shifting the name for strangeness without representing the signified, the fleeing letter offering itself only in order to efface itself, drawing the subject further on... beyond the Church, beyond Persia how far? on the dribbling trace of the other's halting words.

(23)

This cutting off of meaning is something that Cixous believes happens from the very beginning of the story. The title, 'The Sisters', signifies an '"other" place which cuts off meaning, as the head is cut off – the title of the story... excludes the reader from meaning...'.

This cutting off of meaning can be considered in the context of the doubling of the subject, the process which Cixous believes to be so important in Joyce and which, as we have seen, she uses in her own writing. Through the process of doubling, the subject splits and becomes involved in the movement from the '[o]ne to the plural', making it impossible for the reader to grasp a single, unified subject (17). At the beginning of the essay, the bracketing of the 'r' in 'Joyce: the (r)use of writing' allows the title to be read both as the 'ruse' and the 'use' 'of writing'. Cixous writes on the ways in which Joyce's writing is a 'ruse' that produces 'wild-goose chases' like the search for the answer to the fox riddle, a search that fails because the text cuts off meaning; at the same time, she claims that 'in order to play tricks' like this, one has to *use* the 'traditional mode of the narrative which claims to offer a coherent whole' and then 'modify' this 'traditional mode' in order to produce the *ruse*: the *ruse* of subversive writing requires the *use* of a traditional mode of writing in which the traditional mode is modified for subversive ends (19). This is but one example of the 'double' ('use' as 'ruse' and vice versa) writing that Cixous finds produced in Joyce's text.

A further example of double writing is offered in Cixous' use of the sub-title 'Discrediting the subject'. We have already looked at how Cixous sees the subject of Joyce's writing displaced in the 'slide from One' (the 'One' of the stable, unified, capitalised subject) 'to the plural' (17). Her subtitle 'Discrediting the subject' offers an account of the effect of Joyce's writing upon the traditional concept of the subject *at the same time* that it refers back to how '(r)use' 'discredits the subject' of Cixous' own writing in an explosion of the single, unified subject. What is the subject of Cixous' essay (if essay is still an appropriate term to apply to this writing)? The answers (for there is always more than one) include: Joyce's use of traditional narrative; his subversion of this mode in the 'ruse' of riddles and a decentring of the subject; specific citations of different texts ('The Sisters', *Ulysses, A Portrait of the Artist, Finnegans Wake*, letters, etc.) which produce a double, 'use'/'ruse' writing; Cixous' own use of Joyce's subversive techniques; the 'subject' which is 'discredited'; and the subject of the discrediting process itself – the process of the ruse that appears to proffer a subject while actually discrediting it.

To appreciate fully Cixous' analysis of 'The Sisters', it is necessary to examine her close inspection of the opening paragraph from the story. The first several pages of her essay (with their detour through Joyce's relation to various traditions and the fox riddle operating as a kind of delay) seem to be a part of the discrediting signified by the subtitle, but Cixous does eventually return to the opening paragraph of Joyce's story. Her analysis consists of nine short sections, the first of which compares the title's signifier of females and the first sentence's reference to the (male) priest:

'(1) *The Sisters: "There was no hope for him this time: it was the third stroke."*' Cixous describes the title as 'split off from the body of the text' and as a 'floating head(ing)' which reveals that she sees this splitting-off producing a signification of the priest's head as the boy sees it in his dream. The subject of the two sisters who care for the priest is 'usurp [ed]... right up to the end of the story' (23).

'(2) "*There was*"'. Cixous thinks that the 'impersonal (neuter)' of 'there' announces 'impersonal being' as the subject of the story. This is also involved in the double play of a signifying 'chain' which 'personalis [es] subject/animation/death'. 'The effect of the impersonal as subject is double: the consolidation of the personalization of a non-human, and the depreciation of the human'. The priest (signified of 'him') is a 'personal subject... buried as complement to the object ('*for him*'). This results in 'the *waiting* for the subject ('*him*') in as much as he is a person' (23).

At this point Cixous announces her interest in the possibility of a 'relationship between... waiting and repetition and time'.

'(3) "*There was – it was*":' Cixous terms this an 'anaphora', the rhetorical device which entails the repetition of a word or words, and points out that there is a 'sign of repetition from the very first sentence'. The phrases '*this time*' and '*third stroke*' are an '*involution*' which is a 'closing up of repetition in identity... instead of [an] evolution'. As a subject of the story the priest is closed up by the announcement that 'There was no hope for him this time' and by the reference to the third stroke which signifies his death. There will be no direct access to the priest-as-subject, only a mediated access through the other characters which is also a mediation through the past tense. Furthermore, as the priest is paralysed he is referred to in the third person, so that the 'subject ('*him*') does not speak'. The narrator who does speak through the 'I' and pronouncement of the 'it', 'first person singular, third person neuter singular', is involved in a '[b] reach of the subject [that is] hidden in the heart of the text'.

'(4) "*Paralysis*":' While Cixous obviously agrees with the emphasis which Joyce placed on this word (and which has been traditionally accepted without question by all of his critics), she sees the term signifying in a much more radical way than do those critics who read *Dubliners* as representational stories depicting Joyce's view of the spiritual malaise which he felt afflicted his city. She describes the word as 'the signifier which, with its foreign, savage grip, sucks up the text, invests it, immobilizes it in space and time: the whole [of the first paragraph] converges in it and stops the text' (23). The 'enigmatic' 'power' of the term is 'supported by an equally wild set of replacements: "*gnomon*", "*simony*", "*catechism*". Paralysis inscribes impotence in the kind of "slip" in the text... [it] inscribes the whole of the text as analysis–paralysis (relaxing of the muscles, play of opposites, stiffness/fixity/lack of control' (23). A text which should volunteer meaning becomes 'like a text mined by the riddle which produces its involution'. The boy's speech is 'exhausted in its pursuit of meaning', and as he compares the sound of 'paralysis', with that of words like '*gnomon* in the Euclid' and '*simony* in the Catechism' his speech 'comes up against the occlusion of an Elsewhere fixed there by an antique language (g–k–Euklid, KateKhism, Gnomon)' (23).

The rest of Cixous' analysis is devoted to how 'the word *paralysis* functions in the text' (24).

'(6) "No *hope*": waiting, hope, space ahead: exit?' asks Cixous. The answer is this 'No' which in the phrase 'no hope' operates as a 'cancellation before the letter which from then on does violence to the very time of writing'. The boy's phrase 'filled me with fear' expresses a part of the 'hope and fear [which] build up tension in the anticipation of the sacred', but this anticipation leads only as 'far as "filled with fear", where fear fills up the hollow left empty by hope'. Cixous asks if 'there was ever hope?' Her answer describes hope as that 'weighty impersonal which does not make me aware of being pitiable'. As a sign, 'hope' marks the 'uncrossable frontier between the signifier and the signified'. In the phrase 'no hope for him this time' 'hope' is detached from a subject [and] constitutes itself as an insane, empty absolute.'

'(7) "*It was the third stroke*"' signifies an 'absence' which Cixous sees linked with 'repetition'. The repeated ('third') stroke signifies the absence of the first stroke and is also a part of the signifying network that operates around the 'reverberation of time which scores the text uninterruptedly ("*often*", "*every night*", "*night after night*")'. Cixous sees a further textual space, which is related to both absence and hope, produced by the drive of the boy's desire. The 'reverberation of time' is 'reinscribed' through an 'oblique projection of the space' which the boy's drive produces. The drive produces this textual space as 'in its movement towards:... "*I longed*"', a phrase wherein Cixous sees 'time and place... articulated by desire'. This desire creates a tension which makes the text quiver from '*hope*' to '*fear*' (24). The boy was 'filled... with fear' but 'longed to be nearer' to the source of his fear (*D: 9*). Cixous considers the boy's desire as part of 'a homosexuality which is only admitted in the dark folds of a confessional'. The 'stroke' ending the first sentence signifies a 'death blow' that is involved with the 'desire to kill', a desire Cixous finds eclipsing the homosexual desire (24).

At this point Cixous makes a 'tactical regrouping around... privileged signifiers' like 'paralysis', 'sinful', and 'word'. Such signifiers produce 'axes which are literally visible; and audible'. The axis of words creating visible images produces:

> The obvious play of light and shade [which] is put in question by the text's

uncertainty, vacillating, like all the logical pairs which function insubordinately in the grey margin of doubt (life/death, hope/fear, true/empty) ('idle': empty – then vain, without foundation; lacking; lacking an occupation; unoccupied → not working). Doubtful light or shade, which presents the always deferred place of revelation: the trajectory of the question is guided by a system of '*faint*' signs, of reflectors, of filters (the reflection of candles, for there would be two candles at the head: the light seen from outside, returning to the inside...).

(24–5)

The lack of any clear-cut subject (although readers who cling to a representational reading of the story as a 'realist' text which uses 'symbolism' will maintain that there is such a subject) is something that Cixous links to the extensive opaque-quality of the text. The images of 'light and sight work together, first of all to point out that the focusing of the light source has the effect of sending the subject back, at the very moment of its appearance, into the opaque, the colourless, the night time place of its mutations'. This leads Cixous to the eighth section of her analysis:

'(8) " *Night after night I had passed the house (it was vacation time)*"': Cixous considers this passage a part of a 'decomposition of the repetition night after night;' the 'night [is] not perceived as dark but pierced by "and studied the lighted square of the window"' (25). Cixous asks us to note how the subject, the 'I', of the sentence is doubly split, first by the parenthetical 'it was vacation time' and then by the 'and': 'Note the violent splitting of the subject: I had passed (–) and I had studied. Cut by '*and*'; cut by (–)' (25).

The parentheses in the sentence function in very similar fashion to those Cixous uses in her own writing, and her use of them to produce a doubling of the subject could be modelled on the parenthetical operations that she uncovers in Joyce. 'The parenthesis [is] by definition withdrawal', and Cixous observes in the boy's sentence, 'something introduc[ing] itself which you do not want introduced'. This 'something' is the double subject '("*vacation time*" [as] vacant time)', [which is also] *time without work*. There are several possibilities for the appearance of the boy's parenthetical explanation of why he was not at school. It is the:

> Sign of a movement of denial, of excuse, speech suddenly flagging, an indication of the bad conscience which is the source of the text and of... and of silences, and of the ambiguities which constitute the 'bad' side of the priest's discourse. Set apart, this time and this parenthesis which are isolated by the time set apart: '*it*': impersonal; '*was*': state; '*vacation*': empty; '*time*'. Impersonal, empty, state, time (+Name=the true name of the story). Empty time between two times; time without studying after a time of study; dead time; guilty time.

(25)

All of these Cixous extrapolates from the parenthetical statement '(it was vacation time)' as various reasons for the boy's need to make the statement, to explain his position outside of the house where the priest lies dying. The statement also triggers off the 'double time articulated by *after*, *after* – *now*, *now*, and by the dyads – *passed and studied*, *faintly and evenly*...' Yet this movement also produces a paradoxical 'effect of immobility ("and night after night I had found it lit I had found it lighted in the same way"). The phrase 'in the same way' offers another doubling which Cixous describes as "the same and the other in the same"' (25).

Cixous finds Joyce's text intriguing and is interested in the source of the intrigue and the 'fixation with the same which holds and intrigues' her: '(and I, the reader, am thus fastened in the text)' (25). In part, the attraction lies in the text's articulation of a movement that is never questioned: 'the question '*why*' all these toings and froings?' is 'left out'. Cixous raises the possibility that the absence of this question might be symptomatic: 'I might read into this, if I were to stray a little, the symptom of the text's neurosis: he passed and passed again as if he could not get away from it.' Ultimately, the 'design "*fear (-hope) longing*" signifying the 'predominance of the [boy's] desire to draw near which collides with the window' 'master[s]' and 'constrain[s]' both the opening paragraph and, indeed, the 'entire story'. In the darkness of the tale 'something is repressed whose return governs all of the subject's thought processes':

> I cannot see him because he is not dead, because he is going to die. If he were dead I could see him; when he is dead I will see him; I want him to die so that I can see him; I want him to die. That is not said.
>
> (25)

'(9) "*He had often said to me: "I am not long for this world"*".'
This he of course signifies the priest, but the pronoun avoids naming him. 'He' remains:

> the unspecified subject, whose corpse lies across the fictive space, emerges at, or just after, the moment of his death through this citing of a prophecy which is in the process of coming true, only finding the words once they are already lost:
> '*Idle*', '*true*'.
>
> (25–26)

Cixous views the operations of the boy's desire as an articulation of the process that Freud termed the return of the repressed. She sees his '[s]carcely repressed... desire' returning like 'an innocent killer' searching for 'satisfaction in... words which make a cunning detour': 'He has said: I am not long for this world. And I had thought his words *idle*. Now I knew they were *true*. Every night as I gazed up at the window I said softly to myself the word paralysis' (*D*: 9; Cited with Cixous' emphasis, 26).

Together, 'word' and 'paralysis' constitute what Cixous calls a 'dangerous pair once you realize that the signified really invests the signifier' (26). Like Eco, Cixous emphasises the importance of metonymy in Joyce. The 'name of the sickness effectively [is] the sickness, the sickness by metonymy, being the name of Dublin, and the name of the city itself'. These metonymic connections support the 'monstrous metaphor' with which 'the entire text would constitute itself' as the pronouncement: 'saying-Dublin = saying-death'. Along the metonymic track, however, 'parody slips in'. Like Eco, Cixous sees the metonymy working in 'both directions': 'if the sickness *is* Dublin, Dublin is the sickness'. The contiguity of the metonymic signifiers produces 'to infinity the exchange which blurs the direction of causality'. It is no more possible to say that the sickness is caused by Dublin than it is to say that the city is a result of the sickness. The operations of the various signifiers that Cixous has been investigating constitute a play in which 'The Sisters' produces 'its own reflection' and which also results in the 'reiteration of the signifier'. Cixous sees 'the hesitation of the letter' in the text's production of its own reflection, and this hesitation (Dublin = city = sickness = paralysis = word = paralysis = sickness = city = Dublin, etc.) makes it 'impossible to set up a subject and intentionality, in that it is so difficult to extricate language as such from what language says to itself across the words of the subject'.

Cixous believes that the subversive nature of Joyce's writing emerged very early in Joyce's career. Unlike the commentators who see *Finnegans Wake* and parts of *Ulysses* as the scene of Joyce's radical writing, Cixous finds 'The Sisters' as one of the sources of Joyce's subversiveness. In terms of the story's characters, Cixous sees Joyce's writing already producing a kind of '*langwedge*' (*FW*: 73. 01), or language-as-a-wedge, that is foregrounded in the *Wake*. Instead of representing the objective world of culture and linking world and word, the language drives a wedge between character and culture and word and world: 'It is impossible', Cixous argues, 'for the narrator to constitute himself as an imaginery unity by gaining assurance from a language which escapes mastery, especially since the signifiers from a foreign tongue only make his voice echo; they cannot be used, sound objects without signification, even if they do appear in the same semantic field of the culture' (26). Producing her own pun to suggest the extent to which 'The Sisters' initiates Joyce's version of the revolution of the word, she suggests that:

> With the inscription of 'Paralysis', and of what it carries in its *wake* ('gnomon', 'Euclid', etc.), the nascent revolution put into practice by Joyce takes effect, a revolution which shakes the foundations of 'the metaphysical enclosure' dominated both really and metaphorically by the discourse of the master (the master of God's discourse, struck down, dying, aphasic). This exile, in the ephemeral but primordial signifier which aims to 'betray' the

sickness-Dublin, has as a secondary effect the betrayal of the place from which it strikes; *Ulysses*, and its task of demolishing cultural conservatism, starts here, in this text where no-one knows anything except for the text which does not know that it hides.

(26, emphasis added)

The purpose of the signifier in subversive writing is not the same as that of its counterpart in phallocentric writing. In the latter, the signifier works toward the conservation of the proper name (of the city, of the person, of God, above all, of the father). In writing which works to subvert the phallocentric tradition, the proper name is put at risk and eventually ruined. This is an idea explored by Barthes and Derrida and one to which we will return in the chapter on Joyce and poststructuralism. It is also the idea which Cixous uses to conclude her study of 'The Sisters'. Examining the narrator's line 'It sounded to me like the name of some maleficent and sinful being' (*D*: 9; Cited, 27), Cixous contends that '[w]hat is said of "*Paralysis*" goes a long way.... The common noun for the sickness is also the proper name of a maleficent and sinful being: the imagined spectacle of the soon to be dead [priest], letter of the gaze, is repeated in the echo of the word 'paralysis', letter of the letter' (27–8). The operations of the signifier 'paralysis' move it from 'word [the boy's] to being [the priest's, the boy's, the city's], from voice [the boy's] to sin [the unnamed transgression], the disguises of the forbidden (*l'interdit*) are multiplied, stirring up the desire to *see*'. The object of this 'desire to see' is the '*deadly work*' of paralysis as: sickness, transgression, signifier, and source/cause of death. 'Thus it is the name which kills: the empire of the signifier which will be subsequently extended to the point of producing *Finnegans Wake*, infinitely mocking the conscientious control of the scriptor' (28).

Cixous expands her view of 'paralysis' as signifier to include an assessment of its role as a precursor of the 'Word' in *Ulysses* and the *Wake*: 'Word, master of its grammes, inseminating itself by the introduction of the letter L into its body [paraLysis], which gives it the dimensions of the concrete infinite, "word", "world", "work", lapsus at the source of *Ulysses*, comical straying of the signified which [Joyce as] the scriptor from the beginning, in *Dubliners* called from the place of jouissance into the realm of the sacred' (28). Cixous finds much room for a serious and perhaps even uneasy contemplation of the subversive nature of Joyce's writing; in 'The Sisters', his 'game is still impregnated with unease because the enterprise of turning away from the beaten track is a new one, and one does not yet know what mutation of the language will be brought about in the long run by the liberation of the signifier'. Ultimately, however, Cixous recognises the essentially heroic and comic elements of Joyce's writing as it allows the reader to experience a delight even while paying attention to its subversive operations:

how can you not delight in this inaugural audacity which burns its boats, scuttles the theological foundation of the word, reduces the master to silence, inflicts on the name-of-the-father an eclipse behind a miserable curtain, underlining in a blasphemous fashion the lettered character of the spoken word, bursting apart the ceremonial of reading and more generally of culture by rejecting from the outset any hope of a response, by taking back in the very gesture of giving (' *No*'/'*hope*'), affirming nothing except on the level of the voice by means of a repetition which magnifies the spoken, an affirmation which is supported and put at risk by a questioning of the very function of the spoken...

(28).

For Cixous, 'there will be no end to the dream' in Joyce's writing. That which is behind '"The Sisters's" velvet curtains gives on to that which, if there is something, is something which retreats before the name'. This 'something' involves the operations of the all-too-human desire which we all share. The 'distressing' 'saying' of this 'something', this 'it' 'can only be heard through the annihilation of the master who guarded the Referent' (28–9). For Cixous, a large part of Joyce's genius lies in his willingness and ability to subject himself to the splitting of the subject, to discredit himself as subject and become the 'divided scriptor [who] takes it upon himself-as-subject... to return the story from his pen to the reader–postman, to return the signified to the signifier's address, and to do this without "dismay"' (29).

Julia Kristeva

We have already looked at Kristeva's view of Joyce's writing in relation to Menippean satire and the carnivalesque, and we have also considered how she sees his writing functioning according to the 0–2 logic which subverts the 0–1 logic of theological discourse and the discourse of the Western, phallogocentric, epic tradition. Kristeva clearly values the subversive nature of Joyce's writing, and considering *Finnegans Wake* within the political context of the collapse of capitalist society, she argues that the 'equivalent... of the language of *Finnegans Wake*' is the 'one language that grows more and more contemporary' (Kristeva, 1980: 92). We will resume our consideration of Kristeva's use of Joyce's texts as models for her theories of language here by considering her views on femininity and theory and looking at how she uses Joyce's writing in this context. There are two objections which might be raised against a consideration of Kristeva's views of Joyce as feminist views, and the reasons behind such objections are touched on in Scott's *James Joyce*. Because Kristeva offers ' [t] he most widely known feminist appropriation of Lacan', her ideas on Joyce could equally be considered in the chapter on Joyce and psychoanalytic theory. Kristeva also 'has allied herself... with male theory', and her 'position is to accept the existence of a male-centred "symbolic" order, and to work strategically to deconstruct it from the inside' (Scott, 1987: 12). As a result of this there are no doubt many feminists, particularly among separatist feminists, who would object to Kristeva's feminism; nevertheless, Kristeva does work on the role of the feminine in discourse, and her appropriation of Lacan's theory is, as Scott points out, a 'feminist appropriation'.

In Chapter Five of *Desire in Language*, 'From one identity to another', Kristeva posits that 'every language theory is predicated upon a conception of the subject that it explicitly posits, implies, or tries to deny' (124). Kristeva outlines some of the ways in which the subject has been theoretically treated during the history of Western philosophy and writing, including the influential theories of the subject found in the writings of Descartes, Husserl and Freud. Her goal is to arrive at a semiotic theory of the subject which she can relate to her theories of the mother and the maternal in language. Drawing on the Freudian and Lacanian concepts of the subject she arrives at the idea of a 'subject-in-process' which bears some similarity with the continually changing subject identified in Joyce by Cixous (135). Kristeva, however, elaborates a concept of the subject which can support the signifying economy of the 'undecidable character of any so-called natural language'. The support of this economy of the signifier cannot be 'the transcendental ego alone'. While 'there would be a speaking *subject* since the signifying set exists... this subject, in order to tally with its heterogeneity, must be... a questionable *subject-in-process*'. This subject can be apprehended thanks to 'Freud's theory of the unconscious' because 'through the surgery [of this theory] practiced in the operating consciousness of the transcendental ego, Freudian and Lacanian psychoanalysis did allow... for heterogeneity, which, known as the unconscious, shapes the signifying function' (135). 'In the light of these comments', Kristeva offers a 'few remarks on the questionable subject-in-process of poetic language'. These comments reveal her views on the role of the maternal in poetic language and that language's relation to the incest taboo.

Kristeva sees 'semiotic activity' introducing a 'wandering or fuzziness into... poetic language', and, from the sort of 'synchronic view' of language that we have already considered, this activity is a 'mark of the workings of the drives' (136). Like Cixous, who considered the fundamental operations of the drive in 'The Sisters', Kristeva sees the function of the drive revealed in sets of opposites: 'appropriation/rejection, orality/anality, love/hate, life/death'. The diachronic perspective sees the semiotic activity as one which 'stems from the archaisms of the semiotic body'. Before the mirror stage enables the individual to perceive itself as an image that is identical, and 'consequently', Kristeva adds, 'as signifying', the semiotic body 'is dependent vis-à-vis the mother'. The individual is prepared for the future role as speaker and 'for entrance into meaning and signification' by 'semiotic processes' which are simultaneously 'instinctual and maternal'. Once the individual enters the symbolic realm and gains access to 'meaning and signification', however, the instinctual and maternal aspects of the semiotic processes must be repressed: 'Language as symbolic function constitutes itself at the cost of repressing instinctual drive and continuous relation to the mother'.

In contrast to the subject of language as symbolic communication, the 'questionable subject' of poetic language ceases to repress the instinctual and maternal, 'reactivating this repressed instinctual, maternal element'. Kristeva sees the constitution of (non-poetic) 'language-as-symbolic function' dependent on the incest prohibition, a dependency which it shares with the constitution of 'women as exchange objects': the 'prohibition of incest constitutes, at the same time, language as communicative code and women as exchange objects in order for society to exist'. Poetic language, however, is subversive and disruptive of social order, and *would be* for its questionable subject-in-process the *equivalent of incest*'. In this context, Kristeva sees the poetic language of *Finnegans Wake* playing around the incest prohibition, but she considers in biographical terms the HCE–Issy relationship which we saw examined by Benstock in fictional terms. Arguing that the 'passage into and through the forbidden, which constitutes the sign and is correlative to the prohibition of incest, is often explicit as such', she cites as an example, 'Joyce and his daughter at the end of *Finnegans Wake...*' (136).

Kristeva stresses the equivalence between poetic language and incest 'for three reasons'; they are: a) formalist poetics is mistaken in its notion that poetic language can be 'solely interpreted' 'as a preoccupation' with signification 'at the expense of the message'; 'rather it is more deeply indicative of the instinctual drives' activity relative to the first structurations (constitution of the body as self) and identification (with the mother)'; b) 'because it utters incest, poetic lanague is linked with 'evil'; 'literature and evil... should be understood beyond the resonances of Christian ethics, as the social body's self-defense against the discourse of incest as destroyer and generator of any language and sociality'; c) 'one must, in discussing poetic language, consider what [the] presymbolic and trans-symbolic relationship to the mother introduces as aimless wandering within the identity of the speaker and the economy of its very discourse... this relationship of the speaker to the mother is probably one of the most important factors producing interplay within the structure of meaning as well as a questioning process of subject and history' (137).

Kristeva places a great deal of emphasis upon the function of rhythm, and particularly 'sentential rhythms' in poetic language. While she relies on Céline to illustrate her argument, what she says about sentential rhythm's ability to displace the denotated object of the sentence and to produce a meaning that is 'other' to that provided by the constitutive grammar of the sentence has an obvious relevance to Joyce. The sort of movement from the singular subject to the plural which we saw Cixous analyse in Joyce's writing provides an analogue for the ways in which Kristeva sees the 'elided object in the sentence relat[ing] to a hesitation (if not an erasure) of the *real object* for the speaking subject' (141). Cixous pinpointed such a hesitation in 'The Sisters' continual deferral of the feelings between the boy and the priest and of the subject named by the title of the story. Many critics have commented on Joyce's well-known use of 'hesitation' (both as the word by which Parnell was betrayed and as a narrative technique) in the *Wake*. Kristeva insists that we

> must also listen to [and read the texts of] Céline, Artaud, or Joyce... in order to understand that the aim of this practice [of sentential rhythms which elide the object and render the subject questionable], which reaches us as a language, is, through the signification of the nevertheless transmitted message, not only to impose a music, a rhythm – that is, a polyphony – but also to wipe out sense through nonsense and laughter

(142).

Joyce's celebrated declaration that his Wakean language is 'nat language in any sinse of the world' (83. 12) exemplifies Kristeva's point. A message comes across, but the polysemy of the language defies the determination of any univocal, monological meaning. Is the language 'not' language or a 'nigh' language? In any 'sense', any 'sins' or 'since' of the 'word' or 'world'?

In the chapter 'The Father, Love, And Banishment', Kristeva contrasts Joyce with Beckett. She examines Beckett's writing and considers the texts *First Love* and *Not I* as a 'parenthesis... adequately circumscribing' Beckett's 'known novels and plays' (148). This parenthesis works as a sort of bracket in which Kristeva pauses in her investigation of poetic language to consider Beckett's writing as somehow antithetical to the sort of subversive and carnivalesque poetic language that she advocates. She offers as 'the complete opposite of Beckett's universe', a 'Venetian ambience', and one only need pause to consider Venice's association with the carnival in order to grasp Kristeva's implied idea of Beckett. Her Beckettian parenthesis, however, makes the idea explicit as Kristeva links it to a 'microcosmic' account of 'the now carnivalized destiny of a once flourishing Christianity'. Kristeva's two-novel parenthesis of Beckett's *First Love* and *Not I* 'includes everything' that poetic language should subvert:

> a father's death and the arrival of a child (*First Love*), and at the other end, a theme of orality stripped of its ostentation – the mouth of a lonely woman, face to face with God, face to face with nothing (*Not I*). Beckett's *pietà* maintains a sublime appearance, even on her way to the toilet. Even

though the mother is a prostitute, it doesn't matter who the actual father is since the child belongs solely to its mother (*First Love*).

(148)

Kristeva compares 'the babblings of a seventy-year-old-woman' in *Not I* with Molly's speech in *Ulysses'* 'Penelope' episode, describing the former as the 'antonym of a hymn or of Molly's monologue', which are 'no less haloed, in all their nonsense, with a paternal aura' (148–9). The babblings of Beckett's old woman, 'ironically but obstinately rais[e] her toward that third person – God – and fill[ ] her with a strange joy in the face of nothingness'. Kristeva ironically comments that '[r]aised, demystified, and for that very reason more tenacious than ever, the pillars of our imagination are still there. Some of them, at least...' (149).

Kristeva clearly believes that the pursuit of the father, even the dead father – and even if written in an ironic mode, as it is by Beckett – affirms rather than dislodges the importance of the paternal and sustains the monologic discourse of the phallocentric. 'The primary, obsessed man', however, 'never sees his father as dead' (150). The paternal strength remains in the son, and the writer who remains in the position of being in relation to the father (even the dead father) narrates not in a poetic language, but in a monological communicative language that demands an addressee: 'As long as a son pursues meaning in a story or through narratives, even if it eludes him, as long as he persists in his search he narrates in the name of Death for the father's corpses, that is for you, his readers'. Beckett writes 'the myth of the bachelor', of the 'banished lover, with all his calculations... and his nighttime "stewpan" keeping him bedtime company better than a bride... ' (151). He also 'writes against Joyce, too, ascetically rejecting the latter's joyous and insane, incestuous plunge summed up in Molly's jouissance or the paternal baby talk in *Finnegans Wake*'. Kristeva sees 'Beckett's tragic irony' offering an 'impossible subjectivity' that is an 'equally impossible femininity' (154). *Not I* offers a 'sweet relief' from its 'heartrending statement of the loss of identity', but this relief is 'produced by the most minute corruption of meaning in a world unfailingly saturated with it', in a world, in other words, dominated by the non-poetic monologisms of phallogocentric discourse. Kristeva contrasts Beckett's achievement with 'the overflowing Molly and Finnegan's negative awakening': between the two 'stands a jouissance provoked by meaning's deception, which nevertheless inevitably perseveres through and beyond this unavoidable third person' (154).

Kristeva is particularly interested in the history of the 'Religion of the Father', and she sees Joyce's writing producing a revolutionary upheaval in this history. There was an 'attempt... at the beginning of the Renaissance, to save the Religion of the Father by breathing into it, more than before, what is [sic] represses: the joyous serenity of incest with the mother' (156). Such attempts, Kristeva argues, were '[f]ar from feminist,

[and] can be seen as a shrewd admission of what in the feminine and maternal is repressed'. These attempts failed and the 'Renaissance was to revive Man and his perversion beyond the mother thus dealt with and once again rejected'. One of the consequences was that 'Humanism and its sexual explosion, especially its homosexuality, and its bourgeois eagerness to acquire objects (products and money) removed from immediate analysis (but not from the preconscious) the cult of natality and its real symbolic consequences' (157). This, however, was not such a bad thing according to Kristeva who says that the removal was 'So much the better' and argues that 'through such scorn for femininity, a truly analytic solution might... take place at last'. It took shape, at 'the end of the nineteenth century' when 'Joyce, even more than Freud', affirmed 'this repression of motherhood and incest... as risky and unsettling in one's very flesh and sex'. In Joyce's writings:

> by means of a language that 'musicates through letters', [the repressed (motherhood and incest)] resume within discourse the rhythms, intonations, and echolias of the mother–infant symbiosis – intense, pre-Oedipal, predating the father – and in this the third person. Having had a child, could a woman, then, speak of another love? Love as object banished from paternal Death, facsimile of the third person, probably; but also a shattering of the object across and through what is seen and heard within rhythm; a polymorphic, polyphonic, serene, eternal, unchangeable jouissance that has nothing to do with death and its object, banished from love.
>
> (157)

Philippe Sollers

The inclusion of the male French writer, Sollers, under feminist critiques of Joyce would no doubt meet with objections from feminists who hold that males are biologically and culturally incapable of fully comprehending feminism, yet Sollers offers some unique insights into Joyce and women. Sollers is primarily a writer of fiction, but he also expresses an impressive awareness of Joyce's work (an awareness noted by critics of Sollers' own writing). In 'Joyce & Co.' (*In the Wake of the Wake* [Madison: Wisconsin UP, 1978]), he considers Joyce's relations with women and his creation of female characters from the perspective of a French poststructuralist, psychoanalytic writer. He begins by asserting that 'Joyce traces the limits of any maternal, national language' and offers an analysis of this language which counterbalances the ideas we saw offered by Gilbert and Gubar:

> What is a meaning in the language of a mother country? The private property of child speech, which makes groups of adults reprieved children; but also a referential functioning of the subject toward his or her bodily matrix and a barrier erected by the preconscious against the unconscious.
>
> (107)

Sollers is highly psychoanalytic in his comments on Joyce, and he offers an interesting view of Joyce's relations with the women who assisted him. Arguing that '[n]ot enough attention has been given to the fact that throughout his life Joyce wrote with money provided by women', Sollers considers this union of female money and male writing as 'the point at which a romance "novel" knits together, notably between literature and psychoanalysis'. He considers the relations between Joyce and his 'first patroness', in an unusual light:

> Mrs. McCormick... was absolutely bent on having Joyce psychoanalyzed by Jung at her expense. Joyce refused the proposal and Mrs. McCormick stopped her allowance. We begin to see here the exact antithesis of the classical analytic situation, a question of *no longer* paying someone who does *not* want to be psychoanalyzed.
>
> (109)

For Sollers as reader/analyst of Joyce-as-life-and-text this is only the beginning of a narrative: 'Nor is this the end of the story, since Joyce's daughter, Lucia, who early shows signs of serious mental disturbance, will be treated by this same Jung, the Jung who had written a highly critical article on *Ulysses*, accusing Joyce of schizophrenia' (109). Sollers speculates on the psycho-sexual implications of these events:

> A woman gives Joyce financial help so that he can write. But she wants him to have analysis. Joyce refuses. Punishment: no more money. Joyce's daughter is ill. She is treated in place of him. Suppose that Joyce's daughter is one of his *letters*: the letter falls into the hands of Jung, which is to say that it misses Freud.
>
> (109)

What Sollers sketches out here is a poststructuralist version of a textual economy in which value, gender, agreement/refusal, psychoanalysis and father–daughter relationships all play a part.

Like Kristeva, Sollers in part views gender relations in writing in terms of incest. He describes Joyce as writing 'from a hyper-complex system of kinship' and emphasises 'by "generalized incest"' that Joyce 'explores *all* the possible discourse positions between mother–son, father–daughter, father–son, etc' (117). Joyce does not really achieve this until *Finnegans Wake*; in *Ulysses*, 'this is not yet the case':

> The father–son couple (Bloom–Stephen), the question of filiation by spiritual paternity, is brought up against the great final matrix of enunciation, Molly. Paternity is 'depreciated' in relation to the engulfing monologue. Molly's password is 'I am the flesh which always says yes', constructed on the inversion of the Faustian 'I am the spirit which ever denies'.
>
> (117)

Unlike most of the critics whom we have examined so far, Sollers thinks that Joyce transcends the limitations of gender and 'go [es] on to write in non-centered enunciation positions'. What Joyce 'gets beyond', Sollers contends, 'is very precisely the position of female paranoia' (117). Unlike schizophrenia, which 'allows the possibility of leaving sexual difference out of count, paranoia poses sexual difference in all its force'. Sollers thinks that Joyce's movement beyond female paranoia helps to account for the difficulty of his writing: 'if Joyce is a difficulty, it is because his writing comes to edge on this psychotic axis where, in principle, language is marked in the fact of its lacking' (117).

Sollers sees *Finnegans Wake* as a text which 'makes names *germinate*', and the primary 'principle name[ ], veritable compass card of meanings... found in *Finnegans Wake*' is the female ALP:

> First, the feminine position: ALP, Anna Livia Plurabelle. Position one and multiple, but principle of unification. Anna Luna Pulchrabelle. A flux of multiplicities (rivers) but unitary, the one as *she* the same in its variations. Bizarre, isn't it, the *one* which is *there* the *a* which is *the* masculine *one* which is *the* as *she*.
>
> (117)

Sollers describes Joyce as the 'anti-Schreber', and contrasts the male paranoia that Freud and Lacan analysed in Schreber's *Memoirs of My Nervous Illness* with the female paranoia he believes Joyce manages to transcend. Male paranoia is the 'insane attempt for a man to become the woman of all men' (118–19). In Schreber it entails a 'castration he awaits, wants, and fears all at the same time'. This castration 'constitutes a limit in relation to which it can be said that [Schreber] cannot act in the real'. In contrast to this, 'Female paranoia... [is] more radical' and 'gives rise to a different erotomania of writing'. It produces 'texts given in terms of novel, of fiction, but they are very often dictated in a manner close to a more or less automatic writing' (119).

Sollers offers the hypothesis 'that in female paranoia there is a foreclosure of the word, the verb, which signs a kind of absolute impossibility of acceding to the symbolic'. It is from just such a 'radical negation of writing' that Sollers believes Joyce 'writes... and speaks':

> He writes and speaks in that impossible place where there ought not to be anything speaking or writing, and he brings it to a highly worked sublimation. In other words, Joyce gets something to come which in principle ought not to come. Which is undoubtedly the reason for the ferocious *Verneinung* Joyce suffered from his contemporaries and continues to suffer from those who have followed them.
>
> (119)

While he recognises the importance of the notion of 'matricidal writing' in Joyce, Sollers argues that it 'must not... be allowed to conceal the position of incestuous discourse with the mother which emerges with Molly in *Ulysses*. It is in Molly's monologue that Sollers sees Joyce leaving criticism in general 'nonplused' and 'a whole criticism, above all written in English, standing petrified to attention before this monument-attempt upon the mother as language' (119–20).

The traditional view that Joyce's writing was influenced by Dujardin is, for Sollers, a misunderstanding of the '[h]eight of irony' produced by Joyce's 'pretend[ing] to have been influenced... by... Dujardin, and... his totally unimportant book' when he was actually writing from beyond the position of female paranoia. Molly's language is a 'Molly-recrimination-monolanguage' which is 'transformed by the *Wake* into the joyance of languages' (120). Sollers sees the end of the *Wake*, like that of *Ulysses*, 'entrusted to a woman':

> this time it is the daughter flowing and flying and returning into the paternal bosom: Anna Livia... arriving madly now as mother and as daughter on the horizon of the mouth of her son–husband–father, the ocean. And everything will begin again beyond the reunification, the fullness, the completeness, in that other beating rhythm of the one and the multiple which can only be written *anew*.
>
> (120)

Joyce's exploration of a power that can be related to Kristeva's 'female semiotic' produces a major disruption of traditional notions of gender and sexuality which has had a daunting effect on Joyce's readers:

> It is this saturation of the polymorphic, polyphonic, polygraphic, polyglotic varieties of sexuality, this *unsetting* of sexuality, this devastating ironicalization of your most visceral repeated desires which leaves you... troubled when faced with Joyce. Freud, Joyce: another era for manwomankind.
>
> (120)

Christine van Boheemen

The Novel as Family Romance: Language, Gender and Authority from Fielding to Joyce was 'engendered by Continental European theory'. Although it is offered as a 'contribution to Anglo-American scholarship on the English novel', its theoretical perspective derives largely from semiotics, psychoanalysis, feminism and deconstruction, and demonstrates, as we have already noted, a considerable indebtedness to French theorists in these areas (1). Van Boheemen develops a central argument for her study that includes the 'interrelationship of authority and gender', and she offers five questions which outline the focal points of her concerns:

> How can the conceptualization of origin, traditionally personified as masculine, become feminine? What does the change signify with regard to the

history of authority and legitimation, the notion of subjectivity? Has the idea of woman's otherness become the emblem of modernity? Why the necessity for the metaphor of gender? Moreover, what are the implications for women writing and speaking in a Modern epoch?

(2–3)

The 'Circe' episode of *Ulysses* provides an example of the transformation from the masculine to the feminine that is central to the concerns of the study. Addressing a girl, Bloom declares 'Speak, you! Are you struck dumb? You are the link between nations and generations. Speak, woman, sacred lifegiver!' (xv. 4647–49; Cited, 1). Van Boheemen contends that Bloom's words 'project as the be-all and end-all material nature and biological reproduction in the figure of woman; and the desire of both Bloom and *Ulysses* is to make this woman speak, to hear the voice of origin' (2). She believes that in Bloom's words, the 'idea of woman as image of nature and as means of passage of the flesh of masculine identity... [is] changed to take on a transcendental, mythic power, that of giving life'. This idea, she argues, is 'in marked contrast to the orthodox Christian view, which reserved absolute origination and authority to the masculine principle, God the Father' (2).

While a transformation such as this might be considered as an example of the sort of overturning of opposites (male and female) that is advocated by deconstruction, van Boheemen does not see it as such. Although she thinks that *Ulysses* 'flaunts its "feminine" indeterminacy and celebrates flux and open-endedness', she also argues that 'Joyce's Modern foregrounding of language, like his staging of Molly Bloom, should not be seen as overturning the plot of patriarchy' (7). Like Cixous, van Boheemen sees Joyce's writing producing a 'strategy of doubling'. She does not see this as part of a subversion of the phallocentrism, however, but as a strategy 'meant to safeguard patriarchy, however paradoxically, in designating not material reproduction but textual productivity as origin' (8). While it is 'not wrong to think of Joyce as the precursor of *écriture féminine*', he is a precursor only. His style 'flaunts its subversive otherness, coded feminine' (41), but instead of subverting patriarchal dominance it reinforces the subordinate position of the female by appropriating it. Indeed, van Boheemen sees such appropriation as characteristic not only of Joyce, but of Modernism in general: 'Modern thought from Joyce to Derrida rests upon a double dispossession or repression of "femininity" and the appropriation of otherness as style' (8). Like some of the other studies we have examined, *The Novel as Family Romance* sees Joyce using the position of the female but not producing any serious subversion of the feminine's subordinate position within the patriarchal structure.

Fundamental to van Boheemen's feminism and her view of Joyce is the belief that it is not possible to work outside the patriarchal system: 'I have no illusion', she states, 'that it is possible to step outside the sway of the patriarchy' (42). Unlike Kristeva, who sees working with patriarchal myths and patterns as a choice, van Boheemen would seem to believe that female critics have no alternative but to participate in existing patriarchal structures:

> the female critic who wishes to object to the use of gender as metaphor and who desires a change in the contemporary inscription of woman as a primarily sexual creature rather than the *animal rationale*... lacks a point from which to move the world of discourse. Moreover, in writing, she inevitably makes herself the accomplice of the patriarchal project. If she cannot escape participation, however, she can choose her own subject matter and style.
>
> (42)

Van Boheemen sees the subversion of existing phallocentric structures as an ongoing project of writing with an outcome that has yet to be realised: 'All inscriptions and legitimations are human products, and the future need not be like the present. If that future is to come about – however impossible it may be, at present, to *think* it – we must continue to investigate the complex figurations of woman, origin and authority in the discourses of our culture' (43). One of van Boheemen's specific aims is to 'create awareness of the implication of connotations of gender in signification'. To this end, she strives to 'deliberately reemphasize difference, pointing again and again to the moments when the textual (hence patriarchal) requirement of single origin and meaning perverts the logic of noncontradiction' (43).

Van Boheemen examines *Ulysses* as an open-ended text in which the strategy of doubling is an essential narrative operation. She considers this doubling within the context of the evolution of the English novel. Doubling gradually evolves into a part of the strategy of maintaining open-endedness through the avoidance of resolution. The 'doubling of characters... provides a resolution... in *Tom Jones*', but this gradually changes: 'even if we limit ourselves to literature in English, the number of plots that do not resolve their doubling but exploit it is convincingly large':

> Oscar Wilde moralized *The Picture of Dorian Grey*; Stevenson suggested the psychic cohabitation of a Dr. Jekyll and Mr. Hyde, Henry James turned the screw of the alter ego in many of his stories. That the reading public accepted this convention suggests that the modern assumption of division in the human psyche... was no longer an overwhelming threat.
>
> (135–6)

While the notion of doubling entails such variations on the traditional theme of the doppelganger, van Boheemen sees the open-endedness of *Ulysses* resting on a doubling that has more profound implications affecting our notions of representation:

> the open-endedness of *Ulysses* may reveal... underlying assumptions, prob-
> lems of conceptualization and personification relating to representation
> itself. The Joycean text... rests upon the strategy of using the successful
> inscription of the 'other' (in Joyce, women) as legitimation for the new sig-
> nifying practice... [I]f family romance as an epigenetic centre is discarded,
> it is replaced by a different conceptualization of origin and identity which
> in the final analysis proves equally mythic.
>
> (136)

While the Joyce section of *The Novel as Family Romance* is primarily concerned with *Ulysses*, van Boheemen does examine the ways in which the
Wake produces a double writing. Joyce's final work is the culmination of
a development which begins with *Dubliners*. After the collection of short
stories, Joyce's 'strategy will be more and more deliberate ambiguity,
more use of language to undo differences rather than to affirm or create
them' (137). His writing is a 'heretical way of writing which culminates
in the free "chaosmos" of *Finnegans Wake*'. In order to demonstrate the
doubling of this 'heretical' writing, van Boheemen examines Joyce's combining of *twilight* and *toilette* in order to produce 'the resultant single
word, *twalette*'. This term creates a 'blurring of categories' which 'inheres
in a revision of the material part of the sign', and '[i]t is this self-
inscription of the "other" into the graphic symbol... which produces a
double or even plural signification'. The 'advantage of this [double]
strategy of writing', van Boheemen contends, 'is precisely its ambiguity':

> it both affirms and denies identity. It keeps the conventional meanings while
> revising them; it violates the principle of single identity, while not wholly
> destroying it; it erodes the very logic/logos of signification without a total
> deterioration into chaos; it questions the self-evidence of the logos of
> Genesis, while remaining within its domain.
>
> (138)

It is in *Ulysses*, however, that van Boheemen is primarily interested. While
pointing out that '*Finnegans Wake*... shakes more cornerstones of
Western metapysics', she thinks it 'sufficient to remind ourselves that the
language of this capstone to Joyce's oeuvre seems deliberately designed to
reflect a decentering ambivalence towards the central logical axiom of
Western thought' (138).

Van Boheemen believes that 'Joyce's strategy of questioning the logos
show[s] affinity with the insights of Derrida' (171), and in her sixth
chapter, 'The Difference of *Ulysses* and the Tautology of Mimesis', she
details some of these affinities. '[W]hat Joyce attempts through his
writing', she suggests, 'is similar to what Derrida tries to attain in his readings of philosophy – an unsettling of the conventional categories of

thought, of the hierarchising strategy by which we order reality and structure representation, always a decentering that tries to unsettle the logos and not to undo it' (139–40). Joyce's writing uses mimesis not as 'a one-directional operation', but as a 'double process, a simultaneous and mutual confirming constitution of presence' (165). It achieves this through a 'deconstruction of plot' in which '[s]elf and world, language and reality mirror and sustain each other in a single act of mutual polarity'. The narrative of *Ulysses* not only represents what we usually understand by the term *story*, but also produces another double operation: it mirrors the 'shape and presence of "life"' and, '[a]t the same time, the order of the objective world confirms the order of the story' (165).

It is in the seventh chapter, 'The Syntax of Return: "Still an Idea Behind It",' that van Boheemen focuses on this issue of gender and the feminine in Joyce's writing. She sees 'Penelope' as one of the most important episodes in *Ulysses* and argues that it 'should be seen as the *mise en abîme* of the otherness, and difference, of *Ulysses* itself':

> As a *ricorso* it is self-contained, separated from the action. It presents itself as an afterthought, an 'ek-static' supplement to the main body of *Ulysses*. Still, even if 'Penelope' stands outside and apart, the flow of its language, transgressing the boundaries set by syntax and decorum, continues the stylistic practice of the text as a whole.
>
> (173)

Although the 'Penelope' episode is in some ways separate from the rest of the text, it is also a microcosm of the text. It not only 'continues the stylistic practice' of the preceding chapters, but 'presents it in a concentrated and heightened form'. It confirms the otherness of the text: 'by repeating, clarifying, and intensifying the style of writing in the body of the text, ['Penelope'] affirms and signs the alterity of *Ulysses*' (173).

Earlier in her study van Boheemen records the common critical view that the 'most striking quality of Molly's monologue is its absence of traditional punctuation' (173). She returns to this idea in order to suggest that the 'flow of the eight sentences', which are indicated by punctuation, 'is often read, as Joyce said he intended it to be read, as the representation of the "other"': 'as feminine language – alogical, flowing, inconsequential, and in every way the opposite of the masculine logos of predicative meaning' (173–4). Van Boheemen suggests an alternative reading of the episode based, not on the usual practice of reading it as a presentation of Molly's character, but on a reading of its syntactical functions: 'if we forgo a mimetic view of the figure of Molly and try instead to define her syntactic function in the texture of words... Molly's language proves more than the speech of a woman or even the idea of a woman'. The episode does offer insights into Molly's character, but van Boheemen is more interested in the ways that it transgresses traditional forms of logic: 'Undermining the possibility of discrimination, distinction, and denial, "Penelope" suspends the either/or of a logic into a both/and (or neither/nor) as well as or/rather'. Furthermore, while it is 'embodied differently' in 'Penelope' the 'preclusion of distinct meaning and identity... is the characteristic quality of *Ulysses* as a whole':

> 'Penelope' presents the concentrated essence of the style of the text, and in its achievement retrospectively affirms and confirms the otherness of the work as a whole in structure, style, and theme. 'Penelope' presents itself as both the capstone and the cornerstone of *Ulysses*, its arche and its telos.
>
> (174)

Taking a 'closer look at Molly's style' as it is found not in 'Penelope', but 'in the main body of the text', van Boheemen offers an analysis of 'metempsychosis' which contradicts the ideas we saw presented by Gilbert and Gubar. Gilbert and Gubar contend that Molly's 'implicit metamorphosis of it into the babble of "met him pike hoses" exemplif[ies] the parrot-like blankness with which Joyce's women respond to abstract concepts' (1988: 170). Van Boheemen points out that it is 'Molly's husband, Leopold, who... remembers the typical quality of his wife's style', and she believes that he does so 'lovingly' (174). 'Molly... does not desire epiphany', van Boheeman states; 'on the contrary she seeks liberation from the obfuscation of meaning brought about by a logocentric culture'. Molly does 'turn[ ] Greek into the speech of an uneducated Irish housewife', but van Boheemen compares this with 'Joyce turn[ing] the Greek epic into an Anglo-Irish novel'. 'Moreover', she adds,

> these words ['met him pike hoses'] are plain because they redirect the reference to a transcendent signifier, an intangible mystery of the soul, to common, familiar English words already in use in Anglo-Saxon days, referring to the piece of clothing covering the least spiritual part of the body. It is as if Molly's 'voicing' of the written word of the text... echoes it in such a deflatingly revealing way that we seem to overhear the uncanny voice of original otherness, an otherness outside *doxa*, subverting the fixity of conventional meaning in an obliquely sly, knowing way.
>
> (175)

It is perhaps worth noting that the conflicting views of van Boheemen and Gilbert and Gubar can be explained in part by their contrasting theories of language. Gilbert and Gubar view Molly as Joyce's misogynistically condescending 'realist' representation of a woman; van Boheemen thinks that Joyce is producing something 'other' than the language of realist literature and that his writing questions the very concept of mimesis upon which realist writing is premised. Gilbert and Gubar think that Molly's 'met him pike hoses' is a result of Joyce's attempt at depicting a realistic woman with a 'parrot-like blankness'; van Boheemen sees it as a 'rendering of the unconscious of "metempsychosis" and take [s] Molly's voice as that of the "other"... predicating origin not as a transcendent presence but, if at all, as material, physical, organic' (175).

Molly's language is, for van Boheemen, a language of the 'other' which 'speaks of Joyce's notion of "feminine" language' (177). Van Boheemen's analysis of the style of Molly's language leads to three important conclusions: '"Penelope" and the other passages featuring Molly's style characterize her as an emblem of otherness;... the style of this otherness is a figure for the otherness of the text as a whole;... this otherness is never absolute' (177). The condition of the other, to van Boheemen's mind, is dependent on that in relation to which it is other. The 'other' within a dominant discourse is 'always a variant of, and within, the dominant discourse'. This means that 'Molly... can never speak for herself as wholly other' for two reasons: a) 'she is Joyce's creature and the product of a masculine imagination'; b) 'a language of the essentially other, "alias" *écriture féminine*, is a logical impossibility'. This assertion clearly puts van Boheemen in an antithetical position to some of the feminist arguments that we have considered, and her argument is well worth examining:

> The original 'other' (feminine) identity can *qua* identity not express itself in language, for language, after all, is the very instrument and constitution of the logos/logic of difference. Extending this conclusion to the otherness of *Ulysses*, one notes that just as Molly's voicing of Greek polysyllables is a dislocation within the bounds of signification, so *Ulysses* is a rewriting of the epic which, in deconstructing the tradition of narrative, remains within the boundaries of its genre. Just so the otherness of deconstructive readings, including this one, remains within the philosophical tradition of Western metaphysics.
>
> (177)

This explanation of her assertion that *écriture féminine* is a 'logical impossibility' demonstrates van Boheemen's willingness to use traditional logic in support of her view of Joyce and confirms her belief that it is not possible to work outside of the patriarchal structure. This puts her in a different position to critics who, like Cixous, not only believe that patriarchal patterns can be subverted, but who also attempt to write in a subversive mode. At the same time, her argument does attempt a certain self-reflectiveness ('including this one'), and this indicates that van Boheemen is willing to attempt something like the double writing (it refers both to itself and to other texts and arguments) which she values in Joyce.

In the last analysis, van Boheemen believes that Joyce's depiction of women, and particularly of Molly Bloom, is a result of a paradoxical ambivalence. There is 'his struggle to unsettle the logos of difference'

which results, as van Boheemen demonstrates, in Molly's role as the producer of a language and style which is the 'other' of the text; at the same
time this struggle 'paradoxically proves... to be inspired by a desire for
totality and wholeness which, if not dependent on patriarchal repression,
hinges on appropriation and assimilation...' (184). In her conclusion, van
Boheemen argues that 'it would be simplistic to take [*Ulysses*'] apparent
celebration of the feminine sexuality... as expressing the demise of
[patriarchal] logocentrism...' (199–200). Like Henke, who raises the
possibility that Joyce could well have used a female writing in order to
demonstrate his own mastery, van Boheemen considers the possibility
that the 'sheer obsessiveness of the concern with gender and the body
may... be taken as a magic gesture of self-defensive warding off': 'Joyce's
inscription of the "other" as flesh may be such a self-protective gesture,
aimed at laying [to rest] the specter of spiritual annihilation' (200). In
other words, the concern with the feminine may have been no more than
Joyce's attempt to retain a masculine, phallocentric, and because of the
patriarchal privileging of spirit, spiritual dominance: 'In signing women as
flesh, Joyce still implicitly signs himself as spirit or *Geist*' (200). Clearly,
van Boheemen would seem to agree that Joyce was capable of writing a
'gramma's grammar', but she would probably want to qualify her agree-
ment with the possibility that it may have been a writing to celebrate the
victory of *his* creative spirit.

•5• 'TOO JUNG AND EASILY FREUDENED'

Joyce and Psychoanalytic Theory

PSYCHOANALYTIC CRITICISM IS an area which has flourished in Joyce studies over the last twenty years. Biographical critics like Richard Ellmann have been interested in Joyce's acquaintance with Carl C. Jung, who was familiar with Joyce's work and who treated Joyce's daughter, Lucia, for a short time for her mental illness. Jung wrote a preface for Gilbert's book on *Ulysses* which 'made' 'Joyce's book... an example of the schizophrenic mind'. He later 'greatly improved' it and 'published it separately in 1932' (Ellmann: 628–9). We have already noted how Joyce's patroness, Mrs McCormick, withdrew her support from Joyce because of his refusal to undergo analysis with Jung. According to Ellmann, Joyce did not understand the reason for Jung's attitude toward him. He asked Dr Daniel Brody, the owner and manager of the Rhien-Verlag in Zurich, why Jung was rude to him. Brody's famous response was, of course, 'There can only be one explanation. Translate your name into German' (628).

Joyce was a contemporary of Sigmund Freud's, and his knowledge and use of Freud's theories has been the focus of considerable speculation and investigation. A major interest of critics in this area has been the extent of Joyce's familiarity with Freud's theories. Joyce did own copies of some of Freud's works, but he protested against the suggestion that he had been much influenced by psychoanalytic theory. In his complaint to Brody about Jung's rudeness, Joyce is supposed to have said 'I have nothing to do with psychoanalysis' (Ellmann: 628). During his 1936 trip to Copenhagen Joyce made his now well-known statement to the Danish writer Tom Kristensen: 'I don't believe in any science... but my imagination grows when I read Vico as it doesn't when I read Freud or Jung' (693). As we saw in the chapter on structuralism, Margot Norris argues fairly convincingly that *Finnegans Wake* operates according to the processes of 'distortion, displacement, and condensation' which produce the 'ordering and organization of materials' in Freud's model of the dream (Norris, 1974: 99). Until further conclusive evidence is discovered, however, the answer to the question of whether Joyce knew more Freudian theory than he was willing to admit will remain uncertain.

Like the students and disciples of Freud and Jung, psychoanalytic critics of Joyce are divided into two camps depending upon the school of analysis to which they belong. A third analytic perspective (clearly related to the Freudian) has emerged from the theories of Jacques Lacan, the French psychoanalyst who refined Freud's theories and incorporated them into his own. There is something of an analogy in the division between the Freudian/Lacanian theorists and the Jungians and the structuralist theorists and semioticians we considered earlier. Because Freud is so important in poststructuralist theory and Lacan can be considered as a poststructuralist, Freudian and Lacanian critics have survived the shift from structuralism to poststructuralism, while the theories of Jung, like those of the structuralists, seem to have become less important as a means of understanding Joyce's text. Because there are far too many psychoanalytic studies of Joyce to be considered here and many more studies which are not primarily psychoanalytic but which make some use of psychoanalytic theory, the studies we will examine below are offered only as a representative selection.

Elliott Coleman

Jung's theories place great emphasis on the concept of the collective unconscious, the idea of the archetype, and the view that males and females possess qualities of their opposite sex, the male having an (female) *anima*, the female, an (male) *animus*. In 'A Note on Joyce and Jung' (*JJQ*, 1, 1 [Fall], 1963), the Jungian critic Elliott Coleman suggests that Jung's theory of the anima and the animus 'certainly helps the reader to understand better the transformations that take place in Nighttown'. He also offers the possibility that Jung may have found some 'support' for 'his theory of anima-animus' in the 'Circe' episode of *Ulysses* (11). 'It is remarkable', Coleman comments, 'in a summary of the animus how Jung comes to mention the name of Circe herself' (14). Whether or not this is proof that Joyce's writing did influence Jung is uncertain. What is certain is that Jung used Joyce and his daughter as a 'classical example' of his theory. Coleman quotes Jung's letter to Patricia Hutchins:

> If you know anything of my Anima theory, Joyce and his daughter are a classical example of it. She was definitely his 'femme inspiratice', which explains his obstinate reluctance to have her certified. His own Anima, i.e., unconscious psyche, was so solidly identified with her, that to have her certified would have been as much admission that he himself had a latent psychosis. It is therefore understandable that he could not give in. His 'psychological' style is definitely schizophrenic, with the difference, however, that the ordinary patient cannot help himself talking and thinking in such a way, while Joyce willed it and moreover developed it with all his creative forces, which incidentally explains why he himself did not go over the border. But his daughter did, because she was no genius like her father, but merely a victim of her disease. In any other time of the past, Joyce's work would never have reached the printer, but in our blessed XXth century it is a message, though not yet understood.
>
> (Cited: 15)

Rosa Maria Bosinelli (Bollettieri)

A 'contribution to... Joyce's encounter' with Freudian psychoanalysis is offered by Rosa Maria Bosinelli Bollettieri's 'The Importance of Trieste in Joyce's Work With Reference to His Knowledge of Psycho-Analysis' (*JJQ*, 7, 3 [Spring], 1970). This article outlines some of the difficulties which still persist today about Joyce's knowledge of Freud, arguing that 'in spite of the influence of an environment in which Freud's ideas had aroused great curiosity and of the opportunity this environment might have offered him for a study, Joyce had no direct contact with psychoanalysis, remaining, if anything, diffident of it throughout his life' (177). Bosinelli Bollettieri reviews Joyce's comments to Budgen and the material on the subject from Stanislaus Joyce and Ellmann. She cites the letter by Italo Svevo, who, according to Stanislaus, 'tried vainly to convert James to psycho-analysis'; 'I can only make one critical comment... Sigmund Freud's thought did not reach Joyce in time to lead him to the conception of his work... In 1915, when Joyce left us, he knew nothing of psycho-analysis' (181). Bosinelli Bollettieri finds no 'evidence that later, in Zurich and Paris, [Joyce] made a deep study of Freud', and she concludes her study by commenting that Jung's failure to cure Lucia 'further complicated Joyce's love–hate relationship with psycho-analysis' (182).

'Psychoanalytical Criticism and Metapsychology' (*JJQ*, 18, 3 [Spring] 1981) (published under the name Rosa Maria Bosinelli) 'attempts to analyze one or two aspects of psychoanalytic criticism as applied to literary texts, with particular reference to the work of James Joyce' (349). This article offers very useful guidelines to some of the problems involved in using psychoanalytic theory for literary interpretation. Bosinelli begins by outlining 'three principal interrelated features' of 'psychoanalysis as a discipline':

1) It has a therapeutic function which is validated in empirical terms by the disappearance of pathological symptoms and the positive restructuring of the personality.
2) It involves a dynamic interpretation of the development of the personality from birth to the resolution of the adolescent's identity conflict.
3) It has a theoretical side. Psychoanalysis is a 'complex set of constructs and general assumptions on which specific hypotheses are based... a broad framework for the study of human behaviour', allowing for the interpretation of personality structure and its development. It provides a psychological metatheory, a metapyschology which avails itself of various models. The heuristic value of these lies in their ability to account for the greatest possible number of psychological and psychopathalogical phenomena.

(350)

Bosinelli cites Mark Shechner's 'Joyce and Psychoanalysis: Two Additional Perspectives' (*JJQ*, **14**, 4 [Summer] 1977), an article 'illustrating the state of psychoanalytic approaches to literature'. Shechner states that:

we are as yet far from being able to organize these studies into a composite psychoanalytic picture of Joyce's mind, though areas that were once obscure are coming into focus and we can see far more clearly than we could even five years ago the outlines of Joyce's *un*consciousness.

(Shechner: 418; Cited, 350)

Bosinelli states that even if '"a psychoanalytic picture of Joyce's mind" is achievable in the first place, we still have to ask whether it is useful'. She identifies several important questions which arise from Shechner's comments as well other earlier studies:

Are the 'outlines of Joyce's consciousness' illuminating to the critical appreciation of his work? Does an analysis of Stephen as a potential schizophrenic threatened by insanity enhance the aesthetic value of the character? If the answer is yes, then reference to psychoanalysis is more than justifiable, it is welcome.

(350)

As the basis for her evaluation of the usefulness of psychoanalytic theory, Bosinelli uses the principle that 'one of the functions of literary criticism is to elucidate the "value" of the artistic product under scrutiny... by means of enlarging the area of potential fruition it can offer'. While conceding that there are 'highly illuminating' 'studies drawing inspiration from Freudian concepts', she explains that 'if... we show that a fictional character is affected by the oedipus complex (or that the author is, for that matter) we simply contribute to the validation of one of Freud's assumptions... rather than in any way justifying a value judgment on the work' (350–1).

If psychoanalytic theory can 'elucidate the value' of a literary work there are still questions of 'correct methodology and scientific validity' to be answered. 'Once agreed that the theoretical basis for a psychoanalytic approach to the literary text is a general system [or] metapsychology', Bosinelli states, '... we are faced with a series of questions' (351). These are:

1) Which model (or models) is the critic referring to?... The choice of a model should be made explicit beforehand so as to allow one to test the congruity between the adopted system and the obtained results.
2) Is the empirical procedure adopted methodologically consistent with the model, i.e., do the data obtained necessarily result from a correct, empirical application of the model?
3) Is the interpretation of the data consistent with the model?
4) If a preliminary hypothesis has been formulated does the interpretation of the data confirm it?

(351)

Once these questions which 'refer to the description of a correct experimental design' have been answered, the problematics of their 'applicability to literary criticism' should also be considered. Bosinelli discusses two considerations, one of which she relates to Joyce, outlining the difficulties of using scientific models for textual interpretation:

1) First, when we approach a literary text we are not carrying out an experiment, as defined in scientific method, because the researcher is in no position to manipulate variables. In other words, we cannot take 'If Stephen had *not* gone to the library' as an independent variable...
2) Second, the utilization of such models can be made difficult by the fact that they overlap and integrate with one another. Consider, for instance, the interrelation between the topographical model (unconscious, preconscious, and conscious) and the structural model (id, ego, superego), or the interrelation between the dynamic and the economic model.

(351)

These problems can be avoided through 'metapsychological models' which 'can be used in the same logical and chronological order as they were formulated... i.e., as a product of the therapeutic operation and not as a premise that need influence and guide the therapy' (351–2).

Some psychoanalytic critics analyse biographical information about an author in order to psychoanalyse the author as an analyst might deal with a patient in a therapeutic session. Bosinelli points out a problem in the 'analogy with the therapeutic session'. While most critics might 'disclaim... the relevance' of this approach 'on the ground that the author is not there to give us the clues available in the psychiatric session', the analogy between therapy and textual analysis persists. Bosinelli notes its reappearance in Shechner's article, 'Exposing Joyce':

> In practice, the absence of associations is often amply compensated for by rich contexts which are their equivalents and would, in the clinical situation, be put to the same use by any analyst. Joyce is a splendid case in point, for his career is as well-documented as any we have; his journals, letters, *obiter dicta*, drafts and abundant manuscripts, in addition to his published work constitute a texture of associations from which analysis can make its way.
>
> (Shechner, 1976: 274; Cited: 352)

Bosinelli finds arguments like Shechner's 'indefensible'. '[I]f we were to accept the possibility of analogy', she argues, 'it needs to be remembered that the relationship between analyst and patient (author) is founded on language (the written text) as the only means of communication and that this communication occurs only *inside* the psychoanalytic situation'. Bosinelli explains that '[b]iographical elements... have some value only insofar as they arise in the linguistic mediation inside the established relationship' which 'accounts for [the rule that] patient and psychoanalyst cannot meet outside the analytic situation'. This rule helps to 'avoid emotional involvement that escapes control' and 'prevent material that does not belong to the psychotherapeutive relationship from intruding into the specific linguistic mediation of the analysis' (352).

Bosinelli does value psychoanalytic theory as a method of interpretation, but she offers the following caveat:

> A literary critic can examine the text according to the same interpretative techniques available to the analyst in the therapeutic session, but the discovery of mechanisms similar to those that may emerge in a therapeutic session should not lead him to make deductions that have little or nothing to do with the text itself. Thus outside evidence of a biographical nature becomes 'redundant' and absence of it is unimportant.
>
> (353)

In the study of Joyce 'we often do find references to "real" events', but Bosinelli contends that 'the only "reality" we should be concerned with is [Joyce's] literary tale, the linguistic mediation I referred to above' (353).

William Walcott

An example of a fairly early Jungian critique of Joyce's work is provided by the analyst William Walcott's 'Notes By a Jungian Analyst on the Dreams in *Ulysses*' (*JJQ*, 9, 1 [Fall], 1971). Walcott's study is concerned primarily with Joyce's use of synchronicity, a concept which also has considerable importance in structuralist theory. In Jung's psychological theory, synchronicity is 'a complement to the cause-effect principle of causality, namely, the theory of meaningful coincidences: simultaneous occurrences related in time with an astronomical probability of chance' (48, n. 3). The study examines Stephen's Haroun al Raschid dream as a 'foreshadowing' of Stephen's 'confrontation' with Bloom in 'Circe', and Walcott argues that the dream 'can be taken as *genuine psychology* which attests to Joyce's anticipation of Jung's theory of synchronicity' (37). The thesis of 'Notes' is that an 'intensive analysis of the Haroun al Raschid dream, the major link in the chain of foreshadowing coincidences forged by Joyce, brings one to a psychological explanation that ties them all together as well as illuminating the meaning for Stephen of his meeting with Bloom' (37).

In part, Walcott's essay is written as a reply to David L. McCarroll's 'Stephen's Dream – and Bloom's' (*JJQ*, **6**, 2 [Winter], 1969), and Walcott argues that 'failing to work with Stephen's dream as a whole got McCarroll into trouble from the very start', thus introducing the importance of wholeness in Jung's theories as a critical criterion for Jungian studies of Joyce (38). The idea of *participation mystique* which Jung borrowed 'from the anthropologist Lucien Levy-Bruhl', is another Jungian concept which Walcott employs. This is the concept of 'the occurrence of almost identical thoughts, or feelings, or images to two or more people simultaneously' (43). For the most part, Walcott relies on the traditional concepts of plot and character to analyse the dream, pointing out examples of foreshadowing, 'participation' and synchronicity as he discovers them. He treats Joyce's 'stream of consciousness' as Jung's 'collective unconscious' and argues that Joyce 'seemed to understand the possibilities [of Jung's theories] intuitively'. Joyce need not have read any Jung because 'great artists draw upon some deep... reservoir of unconscious knowledge of human psychology' (44). 'Whatever Joyce's conscious intentions', he argues, 'the synchronicities and *participations* connecting Stephen and Bloom... occur to prepare the *protagonists* for the spiritual and psychological union to come, or to show the reader that they are prepared... Perhaps... this was Joyce's conscious intention, if so, what fantastical psychological insight that man possessed' (44).

Mark Shechner

The 1976 issue of the *JJQ* (**13**, 3 [Spring]) offers numerous insights into the development of psychoanalytic studies of Joyce, and the Guest Editor for that issue, Mark Shechner, is also the author of an early major foray into psychoanalysis as a method for interpreting Joyce, *Joyce in Nighttown: A Psychoanalytic Inquiry into 'Ulysses'* (Berkeley: UCLA Press, 1974). The issue also offers Schechner's 'James Joyce and Psychoanalysis: A Selected Checklist' and 'Exposing Joyce'. The former provides references for some twenty-five or so dissertations, articles and books on Joyce and psychoanalysis from the 1950s onwards (it also includes Rebecca West's *The Strange Necessity* published in 1928); the latter encapsulates the Freudian psychoanalytic approach to Joyce and assesses its weaknesses and strengths. Shechner begins by acknowledging what he perceives as the weaknesses of his book: 'If... I would not write the same book I started seven years ago it is because I know more about both Joyce and psychoanalysis than I used to and have acquired scruples about the discipline that I did not possess at the outset' (266). He also expresses the belief that the '"field" of psychoanalytic criticism... [is] a dubious entity'. Expressing a view that is later echoed by Fritz Senn, he explains that 'debates over method and philosophy... appear to outnumber, and certainly outweigh in interest, actual applications to literature' (266). The 'effect' of this 'has been to complicate our view of what constitutes the theory and to render its application more uncertain'. Shechner laments the loss of what he calls 'a certain lurid ferocity: primal scenes, phallic assaults, and fecal gifts are no longer declared to constitute the core meaning of some meek and unsuspecting text' (266).

Shechner (270) offers a list of what he sees as a 'critical core of propositions about the mind from which a satisfactory analysis can be performed'. These propositions are clearly Freudian:

1) *The dynamic unconscious*, the repository of repressed wishes which are incessantly seeking expression and whose access to conscious thought and the means of enactment depends on the efficiency and tactical prowess of what we commonly call the 'defense mechanisms' of the ego.
2) *The system of intrapsychic dynamics*, shared... by all depth psychologies, which constitute a set of rules for transforming motives into statements, fantasies, dreams, symptoms, etc. These unconscious principles of transformation include condensation and displacement, projection and introjection, repression and the return of the repressed, object choice and identification, reversal, splitting, isolation, and symbolization.
3) *The authority of the past*, with its legacy of infantile loves and infantile rages.
4) *Infantile sexuality*, with its complement of symbiotic, oral, anal, and oedipal varieties of love and aggression that persist into adulthood and complicate our lives with their insistent demands.
5) *Psychic determinism*, the principle that no thought, word or act is accidental, that is, lacking a meaningful antecedent in the mind.
6) *Psychic conflict*, the mind's unremitting struggle with itself that finds expression in ambivalence, shame, guilt, and the extraordinary human capacity for self-defeat.

Shechner contends that ' [h]ad we nothing else in psychoanalysis to work with... a rich and detailed applied criticism could be fashioned from these theories alone' (270).

Darcy O'Brien

Several of Shechner's criticisms of psychoanalytic approaches to inter-pretation are echoed in Darcy O'Brien's 'A Critique of Psychoanalytic Criticism, Or What Joyce Did and Did Not Do' (*JJQ*, **13**, 3 [Spring], 1976). O'Brien is particularly scathing in his attack on the 'simpletons' who have not paid enough attention to Freud's development of his the-ories and on the authors of *A Skeleton Key to 'FinnegansWake'*. He criticises the 'absurdity' of the title and places it in a 'class with *Everything You Ever Wanted to Know about Sex*' and argues that it 'should be adapted by some guru of our time with an eye to a fast buck: *A Skeleton Key to Life*' (275–6). The targets of O'Brien's criticism is the systematisation of Freudian theory and two 'chief fallacies of psychoanalysis as a system of of literary interpretation...: the analogy drawn implicitly or explicitly between dreaming and literary creation, and the moral assumptions of psychoanalysis, which are bourgeois'. O'Brien argues that neither fallacy 'has been sufficiently noted... by critics of Joyce, many of whom share Freudian assumptions whether they call themselves Freudian or not' (276).

O'Brien believes that when 'psychoanalytic criticism confronts the "Circe" episode of *Ulysses*... we find the writer–dreamer analogy, and by extension, the characters in the novel are characters in the author's dream; the author puts his dream into verbal form, and the psychoanalyst, that is, the critic, steps in to analyze the dream-work' (281). O'Brien attacks Shechner for attempting 'to give the writer credit as a fabulous artificer' because the resulting interpretation from such an approach 'invariably coincides with psychoanalytic archetypes and patterns, conforming to the pyschoanalytic model of the human personality as a drainage system that springs leaks when it gets plugged up, the phenomenon termed repression' (281). A Freudian interpretation of 'Circe' is not 'wrong', O'Brien argues, 'more than it is often irrelevant and obsessive':

> To read 'Circe' as a symbolic rendering of Joyce's overcoming or resolution of infantile conflicts is to look far beneath the episode, and why should we assume that the truer truth is that which lies beneath? If we are going to consider Joyce's infantile conflicts at all moreover, the writer–dreamer analogy should be dropped and we should be able to see that the writer who completed so mature a work as *A Portrait* had put his infantile conflicts behind him, temporally speaking, whatever conscious use he might make of psycho-sexual extravagance in *Ulysses*.
>
> (283)

O'Brien sees *Ulysses* as 'a work of clarity... translucent'; 'its readers need factual information,' he argues, 'not treasure maps'. He attacks Shechner as a 'psychoanalytic critic' who, in *Joyce in Nighttown* (Shechner: 140–8) 'asks us to believe... that':

> Bloom's fantastical rise and fall in 'Circe' as a Parnell–Messiah figure is best comprehended as a symbolic enactment of Joyce's sexual conflicts, an allegory of the dynamics of ejection, impotence, and castration.
>
> (283)

According to O'Brien, Shechner misses the complexity of the episode and makes it seem more obscure than it is: 'As in all of its incidents', O'Brien says, 'the sexual is interwoven with the political, the religious, and the social, and to say that any one is a screen for the other, to fail... to comprehend all simultaneously... to maintain that an archetypal pattern of truth lies hidden beneath the... surface... is to make oneself a modern Augustine' (283–4). Aiming these criticisms at Shechner, O'Brien states 'Replace Christ with Freud and you get this':

> We *can* say with some certainty in Joyce's case that an oedipal crime is strongly suggested and also that the sense of guilt attaches itself to the anus and anal behaviour. Bloom's fantasies and Joyce's letters bear witness to that.
>
> (Shechner, 1974: 150; Cited: 284)

The problem with Shechner's analysis, according to O'Brien, is that the 'Freudian critic is absolutely certain... that there is an oedipal crime at every bottom, and that if guilt does not attach itself to the anus it will cling to one hole or another.' Such certainty is either naive or dishonest because the critic 'pretend[s] inductive while practicing deductive reasoning' (284).

O'Brien also finds it necessary to attack Shechner's Freudian analysis of Joyce's humour. In *Joyce in Nighttown*, Shechner argues that:

> The exposure of Bloom's guilt in 'Circe' gives rise to at least two affective responses on Joyce's part: a sense of pride and power in having overcome repression and a helpless sense of exposure or shame – the feeling of being watched and judged inadequate. It is for that reason that the confessional seeks the protective cover of a comic saturnalia... The fantasies are real but theatrically overdone, as if in apology for the truths they contain. We may expect in such a circumstance that the comedy will be most hilarious wherever the fantasy is most revealing, and such a formula does seem to describe Bloom's fantasy life in 'Circe'. The deeper we go the funnier it gets.
>
> (Shechner: 150–1; Cited: 284)

This offers only a 'partial truth', O'Brien says, and he finds it 'sad to see' Shechner limited by his 'dependence' on Freud's *Jokes and Their Relation to the Unconscious* as a 'sacred text'. In describing 'Joyce's humour as a protective cover', Shechner 'cling[s] too faithfully to the Freudian theory that laughter indicates that repressed material is escaping in the form of noise'. O'Brien believes that Joyce's comedy is 'not a protective cover' and that while '[s]exual guilt and its confession make up a part of [his] humour... so do [Joyce's] perspectives on all other aspects of life' (284). The problem with confining oneself to one particular theory of comedy as Shechner does, is that it limits one's appreciation of what O'Brien describes as 'Joyce's protean comic spirit' (285).

Jean Kimball

Kimball's 'Freud, Leonardo, and Joyce: The Dimensions of a Childhood Memory' (*JJQ*, 17, 2 [Winter], 1980) offers a case study in Freudian analysis of parts of *A Portrait* and *Ulysses*. In earlier studies, like 'James Joyce and Otto Rank: The Incest Motif in *Ulysses*' (in the 1976 'James Joyce and Modern Psychology' issue of the *JJQ*, 13, 4) and later ones like 'Family Romance and Hero Myth: A Psychoanalytic Context for the Paternity Theme in *Ulysses*' (*JJQ*, 20, 2 [Winter], 1983), Kimball demonstrates the importance of determining the possible psychoanalytic sources Joyce might have used and how works like Otto Rank's *Incest Motif in Poetry and Saga* (Leipzig: Dueticke, 1912) can offer insights into Joyce's knowledge of psychoanalysis and provide a general context for considering the psychoanalytic implications of his work. 'Freud, Leonardo, and Joyce' however, offers a much more detailed Freudian interpretation than either of these other studies. Kimball uses the 'discovery... that as early as 1911 or 1912 Joyce owned Freud's essay on Leonardo' as the basis for her claim that Joyce's acquaintance with psychoanalytic theory 'well before the publication of *Ulysses* and probably even before the completion of *A Portrait* clears the way for a new perspective on Freudian motifs in both novels'. She explains that these 'motifs... have indeed been identified and discussed almost from the beginnings of Joyce criticism, but with almost no attempt to trace these motifs to a specific source in the body of Freud's writings' (165). Her belief in Joyce's ownership and knowledge of Freud's *Eine Kindheitserinnerung des Leonardo da Vinci* (Leipzig and Vienna, 1910) leads her to compare Freud's portrait of Leonardo with Joyce's creation of Bloom. The 'curious affinities' which she uncovers between Freud's 'picture of the historical Leonardo' and the 'fictional surrogate of Joyce's middle years' 'can hardly be accidental', Kimball contends, 'especially as they relate to Freud's emphasis on "Leonardo's double nature as an artist and as a scientific investigator"' (Freud, 1910: 73; Cited: 166).

Kimball outlines qualities shared by Leonardo and Bloom which 'extend beyond [their] shared scientific propensities to "unusual traits and apparent contradictions"':

> In a society characterized, Freud says, by 'energetic aggressiveness towards other people', and in that respect no different from the Dublin milieu in

Ulysses, Leonardo, like the 'prudent member' in Dublin, 'was notable for his quiet peaceableness and his avoidance of all antagonism and controversy' [Freud, 1910: 68]. Seemingly 'indifferent to good and evil', he nevertheless had such feeling for birds that he was said to have made a habit of buying them in the market... to set them free [Freud, 1910: 69], and Bloom cites his feeding of the gulls (*U*: 153) as evidence of 'doing good to others' (*U*: 453) and having a 'good heart' (*U*: 471). Leonardo, Freud relates, 'condemned war and bloodshed', though this 'feminine delicacy of feeling did not deter him from accompanying condemned criminals on their way to execution in order to study their features distorted by fear' and sketch them [Freud, 1910: 69]. And Bloom, who rises to eloquence in his rejection of 'Force, hatred, history, all that in 'Cyclops' (*U*: 333), has earlier in the episode expanded at length, as 'Herr Professor Luitpold Blumenduft', on the 'codology' of the anomalous effect on a hanged man of having his neck broken (*U*: 304–305).

(166–7)

While she thinks these similarities are important, Kimball believes that the '"peculiarity of [their] emotional and sexual life"' 'points most clearly to the kinship between Bloom and Leonardo' (167). After detailing the similarities between Bloom and Freud's Leonardo in this context, Kimball concludes that 'though we can be sure that the Bloom in Joyce was alive when Joyce read Freud, we cannot be sure to what extent his shape was revealed to Joyce or even determined for him by the factual details and interpretations offered by Freud' (167).

Because she believes that the 'kinship' between Freud's Leonardo and Bloom' is 'in any case... extended to Stephen', Kimball contends that the 'childhood memory crafted for [Stephen] reveals remarkable parallels with Freud's interpretation of the childhood memory which he makes the focus of his study of Leonardo'. The central relationship that Freud elaborates in his study of Leonardo's memory is not surprisingly Leonardo's relationship with his mother. Kimball suggests that Joyce 'adapted the features of the memory to conform to autobiographical fact', maintaining the 'Freudian context' as he did so (167). This adaptation produced a 'symbolic construct' that 'prefigures themes which deepen and darken from *A Portrait* to *Ulysses*' (167–8). In the latter work, the 'central importance of the artist's radical ambivalence towards the simultaneously supportive and menacing tie with his mother... is complicated by his need to accept his relationship with his father' (168). Kimball finds the 'combination of appropriation and transformation' in both of Joyce's novels, but sees the 'implications of the Freudian portrait of Leonardo' 'more or less superimposed' on *A Portrait* because Joyce's novel was a 'form already substantially complete'; in *Ulysses*, however, Freud's portrait of Leonardo 'fuses with Joyce's own perspective and becomes an integral part of the symbolic pattern of the novel' (168).

Kimball begins her analysis of *A Portrait* by establishing a Freudian context for Stephen's infant experiences. Examining the opening story of the 'moocow coming down along the road' (*P*: 7), Kimball draws on Freud's theories of the 'sucking period' in infant life in order to examine the opening story as a childhood memory, which, 'like Leonardo's, arises out of the sucking period'. 'We have', she states, 'the cow, and we also have the lemon platt, a "tit-bit", made of lemon-flavoured barley-sugar, which also requires sucking' (169). Unlike Freud's portrait of Leonardo's memory, however, the memory of Joyce's young protagonist 'starts from the father'. Kimball points out that the 'hairy face' and 'glass' of Stephen's father are images that can also be found in Freud's 'Analysis of a Phobia of a Five-Year-Old Boy' and 'his early study of "Little Hans"'. Freud's 'case study of "Little Hans"', she argues, 'could... provide Joyce with a bridge between the exclusive maternal relationship which Freud posits for the child Leonardo and his own more normal family constellation, which in turn defines Stephen's memory':

> His father, who like Hans' father, has a 'hairy face', looks at Stephen 'through a glass', because, unlike Hans' father, Simon Dedalus wears a monocle, which he is shown using at the Christmas dinner and later at the Whitsuntide play [*P*: 29, 77]. And Stephen's memory, through association with Freud's explanation of Hans' phobia, becomes coloured with a repressed hostility and fear toward the father which is connected with excessive affection for the mother, who appears in her proper person (assuming the cow to be a symbol for the boy's earliest relationship with her) only after the father's place in his boyhood has been acknowledged.
>
> (170)

In keeping with the kind of Freudian approach that she takes, Kimball places considerable emphasis on the sexual aspects of Stephen's relationship with his mother. Stephen's mother changes the oilsheet 'after Stephen has wet the bed', and 'Joyce', Kimball says, 'is quite certainly aware of the sexual connotations of this typical happening'. She points out that Joyce purchased 'Jung's essay on the significance of the father... in Trieste... and could have read the casual comment that "from the Freudian standpoint... bedwetting must be regarded as an infantile sexual substitute"'. Joyce's depiction of Mrs Dedalus 'playing the sailor's hornpipe for him to dance', is, for Kimball, a 'subtl[e] continu[ation]' of the 'chain of sexual associations' because '"horn" is one of the battery of phallic synonyms which Joyce uses in his notorious pornographic letters written to Nora in 1909' (170). Freud's discussion of the vulture as an image of the threatening mother provides an expansion of the context in which Kimball analyses Stephen's relationship with his mother. She sees Mrs Dedalus's 'hornpipe' creating an image of the 'phallic mother', and 'Stephen's association of his mother with the "hornpipe" veils the repressed memory of this theoretical construct [the curiosity about maternal genitalia] which is common to most boys' (170, 171).

Kimball contends that the two threats of blindness in *A Portrait* – Dante's threat that an eagle will pull out Stephen's eyes and the breaking of his glasses at Clongowes – should be considered in the context of the story of Oedipus:

> The link between blindness and punishment is, of course, involved in Stephen's first questioning of the authority of the Church, after his unjust punishment at Clongowes, and the punishment of the pandybat echoes throughout *Ulysses* until, in 'Circe', it attaches again to Oedipus... [A]s Stephen adds to the riddle of the Sphinx, solved by Oedipus, a sexual component of his own: 'The beast that has two backs at midnight' (*U*: 560), through which he links Oedipus to Hamlet and to Stephen.
>
> (172)

Freud's 1910 essay 'The Psycho-Analytic View of Psychogenic Disturbances of Vision' is 'not cited in the Leonardo study', but Kimball believes that it is 'extremely relevant to Stephen's memory, since in it Freud introduces the "talion punishment" by the ego when the sexual instinct makes excessive demands on the eyes'. Freud describes this punishment in terms of a 'punishing voice... speaking from within the subject' (Freud: 216–17; Cited: 172). Kimball applies this in her analysis of Dante's threat to Stephen and argues that 'though Dante defines the punishment, it is Stephen himself... who makes a litany of it'. She compares Stephen's ego with Freud's punishing ego: 'Literally, as the small boy repeats the rhyme to himself, the "punishing voice" of Freud's reconstruction is "speaking from within the subject", and the lifelong punishment of the fear of blindness is indeed, in true oedipal fashion, self-inflicted' (172).

Freud highlights 'the darker shadows' of the 'connection between mother love and the problem of homosexuality... in his reconstruction of Leonardo's childhood', and Kimball finds these shadows 'suggested even in the early pages of *A Portrait*' (174). The connection between mother love and homosexuality results from the male child's belief that the mother has the same genitalia as himself: 'The "erotic attraction" of his mother for the very young boy "soon culminates"... in a longing for her genital organ, which he takes to be a penis".' Kimball lists two possible outcomes of this longing: the child's 'later discovery that [the mother has no penis] often turns this longing to disgust, which may lead to permanent homosexuality; or the '"fixation on the object that was once so strongly desired"... may well persist in "fetishistic reverence for a woman's foot and shoe" as a "substitutive symbol" [Freud, 1910: 96]' (174). Kimball uses the context of the foot fetish to explain Stephen's image of his mother's 'jewelly slippers' which are 'so hot' and have 'a lovely warm smell' (*P*: 10), and suggests that the image presents a 'picture whose fetishistic overtones are emphasised by the appeal to the sense of touch and smell' (174).

The 'homosexual connotations of Simon Moonan as "McGlade's suck"' says Kimball, 'are reinforced by the association with the "cocks" of the lavatory at the Wicklow Hotel' (*P*: 11) which follow 'almost immediately' after the image of the slippers. Kimball also sees the 'juxtaposition of the memory of the comforting mother with the dimly grasped implications of the relationship between Simon Moonan and McGlade point-[ing] to the same contradictory mixture in the "queer word" *suck* (*P*: 11) as is found in Leonardo's memory of being suckled at his mother's breast as it combined with the homosexual fantasy of *fellatio*' (174).

For the rest of her study, Kimball moves back and forth from Freud as an influence on Joyce and Freudian theory as a context for interpreting Stephen's attempts to free himself from the power of his mother. She pays particular attention to the 'Circe' episode of *Ulysses* and to Stephen's assertion in the 'Oxen of the Sun' that 'In woman's womb word is made flesh but in the spirit of the maker all flesh that passes becomes the word that shall not pass away. This is the postcreation' (*U*: 391, cited 177). Describing the philosophy of these lines as a 'bridge to eternity', Kimball suggests that in 'Circe' it 'is – verbally at least – guaranteed by the father':

> confronted by the apparition of his dead mother, who reaches for his heart with the crab's claws (*U*: 582), Stephen, denying the power of her memory to paralyze him, smashes the chandelier with his ashplant, which for this purpose he transforms verbally into '*Nothung*!' (*U*: 583), Siegfried's mystical sword handed down from father to son (Thornton, p. 418). In the ensuing darkness – 'ruin of all space' and time's ruin as well – the way is cleared for... the postcreation, and Joyce, through a dreamlike word magic, has affirmed his artist's release from the domination of the maternal fixation which Freud pictures as Leonardo's fate.
>
> (177–8)

In his essay on Leonardo, Freud links the vulture of Leonardo's childhood dreams with an 'association between the vulture and motherhood, originating in Egypt' (170). Kimball sees Joyce's 'replacement of Mut, the vulture-headed goddess... by the bird-headed Egyptian god Thoth' in *A Portrait* and *Ulysses* as 'further signal[ing]' Stephen's 'release... from the power of the mother': 'Though Mut gives birth', she states, 'Thoth creates a world, and the Egyptian connection suggested by Freud is thus used by Joyce to affirm the freedom and the power of the artist as self-created creator' (178).

Sheldon Brivic

Brivic published several articles during the 1970s on Joyce and psychoanalytic theory, and his work in this area culminated in *Joyce Between Jung and Freud* (Port Washington, NY: Kennikat Press, 1980). While his next book, *Joyce the Creator* (Madison: Wisconsin UP, 1985) demonstrates Brivic's continuing interest in psychoanalytic theory, *Joyce Between Freud and Jung* is, as the title suggests, much more orientated towards it. The aim of the book is to 'understand the development of [Joyce's] mind as it went into and came out of [his] works', and the 'main tool' that Brivic employs is 'Freudian psychoanalysis', augmented by some Jungian theory (4). In the 'Introduction: Joyce in Progress', Brivic explains that he:

> will first use Freudian insights to show how Joyce's mind was formed and to explore its unconscious aspect. Then I will show the relation between these influences and Joyce's conscious, mature ideas, which I'll partly explain in Jungian terms.
>
> (5)

Brivic's thoughts on Joyce's knowledge of Freud and his attitudes towards him are also outlined in the introduction:

> Joyce's biography records his ironic and hostile comments on psychoanalysis, but these remarks may have been reactions against exposure, competition and scientific rigour ([Ellmann, 1982]: 393, 538, 642). He often argued that Freud's ideas were better expressed elsewhere as by Vico or the Church ([Ellmann, 1982]: 351, 486, 706), another matter than denying Freud's truth. Stephen favours Aquinas's theory of incest over Freud's, implying that the two economic views of emotion are not dissimilar (*U*: 205). In gathering Joyce's critical remarks, Ellmann may have intended to correct the impression, prevalent during the forties, that Joyce was the most Freudian of novelists.
>
> (9)

Jung, of course, broke away from Freud and came to oppose many of his old teacher's ideas. Brivic sees the contrast between their differing concepts of the unconscious as an important analogy for the difference between Joyce's early and late works. Jung felt that the collective unconscious held authority over the individual. Explaining that in 'giving up Freud's heroic effort to control the mind through reason, Jung gave power to the unconscious mental forces... as beings deserving life', Brivic establishes a central context for his use of both psychoanalysts:

> This grant of authority to the unconscious is a crucial distinction between Freud's thought and Jung's; and also between Joyce's early works, where the prime issue is whether people can control their own lives and the later ones in which they follow their destinies with growing dynamism.
>
> (11)

A central division between Freud and Jung is that Jung's view of archetypes still allows room for religious beliefs while Freud's view of the unconscious does not. In Freud, the 'male and female images... from the unconscious [are] based on exaggerated infantile memories of parents... Jung argues that these parental images are endowed with... power and universality in forms like God, Satan, or the Blessed Virgin... memories of parents are not adequate to explain such gigantic entities...'. In Freud, the 'source of the mind' is 'individual experience'; in Jung, 'each person has to realize his independence upon a permanent collective unconscious'. Freud sees the unconscious responsible for the creation of myths, culture, and even God. Jung's collective unconscious is 'represented in mythology and culture tradition'. 'In effect', Brivic says, 'Jung formulates a universal religion of archetypes based on recurring patterns in the minds (mainly dreams) of his patients and in the spiritual literature of the world' (11).

In his first chapter, 'Stephen Oedipus: The Grave of Boyhood', Brivic analyses the opening chapter of *A Portrait* from a perspective that is very similar to Kimball's, although Brivic offers a much more in-depth discussion than Kimball could in the limited space of an article. Like Kimball, Brivic makes use of Freud's Leonardo essay and examines Stephen's boyhood development in terms of such Freudian concepts as the oedipal complex, the desire for the maternal leading to homosexuality, the phallic mother and the fetish object as substitutes for maternal genitalia. Brivic attempts a more complex analysis than Kimball's as can be seen in his discussion of the scene wherein Stephen meditates on the word 'suck':

> Suck was a queer word... the sound was ugly... in the lavatory... his father pulled the stopper up by the chain after and the dirty water went down through the hole in the basin. And... the hole in the basin had made a sound like that: suck. Only louder.
>
> To remember that and the white look of the lavatory made him feel cold and then hot. There were two cocks that you turned... He felt cold and then a little hot... the names printed on the cocks. That was a very queer thing.
>
> And the air in the corridor chilled him too. It was queer and wettish.
>
> (*P*: 111; Cited: 24)

Like Kimball, Brivic notes the sexual connotations of words such as 'queer', 'suck', and 'cock', but he also notes a great many more sexual symbols. He sees maternal genitals 'represented quite vividly by the swirling hole', and interprets 'hot and cold', as *Ulysses* does, 'to describe Bloom as bisexual' (*U*: 535), in terms of an ambivalent sexual orientation. In this passage, he argues, 'alternating cold and hot suggests ambivalence in Stephen's reaction to the scene' (11). Brivic also believes that the image of the father pulling the stopper 'may be a screen for the primal scene, the earliest vision of intercourse'. Furthermore, 'through the dream technique of distortion by reversal', he explains, 'pulling the plunger may stand for pushing it, but it also represents injury of mother by father'.

Brivic sees what he describes as the 'bathroom vision of anxious mystery' as evidence of Joyce's 'consciousness of Stephen's unconscious' (11).

Brivic uncovers many more symbols in *A Portrait*'s first chapter which he analyses in a Freudian, sexual context. He sees the bath as a symbol of the female for the young Stephen, and he links Stephen's fear of his punishment by Father Dolan with the fear of castration. He also interprets Stephen's 'indignation' over the punishment with a frustration at the 'sensuality of the beating [being] nipped in the bud' (34). Stephen 'at first thought [Father Dolan] was going to shake hands with him because the fingers were soft and firm' (*P*: 52; Cited: 34). Brivic sees Stephen's mistaken belief as 'an erotic, probably masturbatory fantasy from Stephen's unconscious', and he interprets the visit to the rector as 'Stephen's assumption to manhood', an assumption that is 'accompanied by images of his entering a female':

> '... he would be in the low dark narrow corridor... entered the low dark narrow corridor... passed along the narrow dark corridor...' (*P*: 54–55). After the triple emphasis indicates the special significance of the hall, Stephen passes through a pair of doors to be hailed by the rector as 'my little man' (*P*: 54–55).
>
> (35)

Unlike Kimball, Brivic does not trace Stephen's development as a necessary separation from the mother, but as a gradual sublimation of primal feelings into intellectual concepts: 'In later chapters' the 'desire for the mother... and the paternal threat' 'grow more and more sublimated and disguised... so that by the end of the book the issues become intellectual, the desires, aesthetic, the threat a principle'. The 'fundamental model' for all of this and, indeed 'with modification, for *Ulysses*', is 'established' in 'the first chapter' of *A Portrait* (35).

Unlike Ruth Bauerle who sees Bertha as a prototype of Leopold Bloom, Brivic, in his chapter '*Exiles*: Living Wounding Doubt', compares Robert with Bloom, Beatrice with Stephen's mother, and Bertha with Molly: 'If Richard corresponds to Stephen, Robert to Bloom, and Bertha to Molly, then Beatrice must correspond to the ghost of Stephen's mother... Robert is a livelier figure, and even resembles Bloom, with none of Bloom's goodness' (118). As a context for the sexual aspect of the play, Brivic cites a letter which Freud wrote to William Fleiss in 1899: '... I am accustoming myself to regarding every sexual act as an event between four individuals' (Cited: 119). Freud's 'statement', he suggests, 'coincides resonantly with *Exiles*, which actually presents a sex act between four individuals'. Jung's theory of the anima and animus also provide Brivic with a perspective on the play:

> In Jung's terms, Beatrice is that part of Richard's major archetype, the *anima*, which is not projected on Bertha, while Robert is that part of

Bertha's *animus* which Richard does not satisfy. Jung would grant that the unsatisfied archetypal margin tends to resemble the difference between one's mate and one's parent of opposite sex, for he describes *anima* and *animus* as parental images. Jung, in fact, spoke of every complete marriage as a four-part structure called the 'marriage quaternio'.

(119)

In terms of Jung's universal archetypes, Brivic sees the play dealing 'with problems that are universal: the difficulty of desiring what one supposedly already has, of getting outside one's own limits and finding new life in another' (120). The play also offers what was to become a 'key point of Joyce's thinking': the 'acting out of neurotic needs'. Brivic discusses this neurosis in the context of the play's 'manifestly compulsive quality which alienates audiences', suggesting that it may be a part of the play's relative unpopularity as a dramatic work (120).

From a Freudian perspective, Brivic sees *Exiles* as a play about 'oedipal exile from Eden', its 'dynamic... dictated by neurosis even while it represents real spiritual powers which rational explanations of self-interest can't explain' (120). Richard's 'unfitted' (*E*: 125) personality makes him 'unsuited for seduction [but] makes him capable of love, capable of the need that holds Bertha'. Their 'neurotic needs for threat and order bind them within an enclosure of mutual self-knowledge' (120). Returning to the sexual implications of the play, Brivic contends that '[w]ether or not such obsession is inseparable from love, it may well be linked to what is most intense and lasting in sexual relations' (121). Freud stated that neurosis uses the 'creation of uncertainties' as one of the 'methods... for drawing the patient away from reality and isolating him from the world' (Cited 121). Brivic sees this as an analogy for Richard's condition at the end of the play when 'he tells Bertha he doesn't care what she says'. Like Freud's neurotic, '[h]e shifts concern from the outside world to his doubts within'. 'In fact', states Brivic, 'Richard can indulge his doubt of Bertha because he holds her by his wound, and withdrawal into self is one of the means by which lovers regenerate themselves through contact with their deepest feelings' (121).

In terms of its position among Joyce's other works, Brivic sees the play demonstrating a necessary uncertainty. Citing Freud's idea that uncertainty grows with the compulsive neurotic 'tendency... to move... "ever more closely to satisfaction",' Brivic explains that:

> As Joyce's works grow more positive about the possibility of pleasure, an ever more elaborate network of formal, intellectual and mythic defenses must be engaged, and uncertainty is at the center of this network. Freud says that as compulsives move toward increasing satisfaction, they may be in danger of paralysis of the will because they will see every decision as balanced.

(121)

Brivic points out that '[p]aralysis of the will' was Joyce's 'main subject' as a novice fiction writer, and that while Joyce 'condemned it in *Dubliners*', he found 'himself stuck with it in the decade of writing *A Portrait*' even though he 'tried to free himself from it...' With *Exiles*, Brivic believes, Joyce struck a balance in his view of paralysis: 'His works from *Exiles* on both glorify paralysis insofar as it is self-imposed and grieve for it because it really is not' (121).

Kimball suggested that in *Ulysses*, Stephen's release from the mother is essential to his freedom as an artist. In contrast to this comparatively simple view of the mother–son relationship, Brivic finds a complex set of interrelationships at work. Where Kimball focuses on the escape from the mother figure in the 'Circe' episode, Brivic points out that 'Stephen's most intense and terrifying vision of mutilated mother *and menacing father* occurs... during the climaxes of "Circe"' (131, emphasis added). He also notes that Simon Dedalus is involved in the attempt to subject Stephen to maternal subjugation that in 'the midst of Stephen's attempt to soar, his father appears and says "Think of your mother's people!" (*U*: 579)' (131). Like Kimball, however, Brivic thinks it important to note the function of Stephen's mother as a *phallic* mother. He cites the passage in which she appears:

> *Stephen's mother, emaciated, rises stark through the floor in leper grey with a wreath of faded orange blossom and a torn bridal veil, her face worn and noseless, green with grave mould. Her hair is scant and lank. She fixes her bluecircled hollow eyesockets on Stephen and opens her toothless mouth uttering a silent word (U: 579).*
>
> (132)

Brivic notes 'five images of castration' in this passage: 'torn veil, hair, eyes, nose, and teeth', and points out that the mother's threat is a 'phallic threat: "Beware! God's hand!" (*U*: 582)'. Where Kimball sees Stephen's use of his ashplant/magical sword as an attack which contributes to his freedom from the mother, Brivic sees Stephen's attack with his ashplant as an 'attempt at patricide', which 'doesn't change anything', because 'Stephen inevitably undoes it directly afterward by waving his "green rag" (*U*: 592) at the soldiers and inviting them to knock him down' (132).

Brivic views the events of 'Circe' in the context of Stephen's thoughts and feelings throughout the day: 'The entire sequence of events late in "Circe" – injured mother, patricide, reversal and male threat – is only an expansion of the combination operating in Stephen's mind all day – a severe version, altered by death, of the complex of maternal haven and paternal threat in *Portrait*' (132). Rather than seeing the mother figure in 'Circe' as a threat to Stephen's existence as an artist, as Kimball does, Brivic considers her as a variation of the virgin–whore stereotype identified by many of Joyce's feminist critics: 'The virgin–whore duality has now [in 'Circe'] become biased toward the whore side'. This idea of the stereotype is linked by Brivic with the theme of incest: 'Stephen's pre-occupation with the image of mother as whore is accompanied by an explicit concern with the idea of incest between mother and son'. Brivic uses the Freudian theory of fetishism in the same context as Kimball does (the slipper fetish, for example), but he also employs it to analyse Stephen's version of Shakespeare in 'Scylla and Charybdis'. Stephen's 'Shakespeare', he suggests, 'is essentially a bard of fetishism. Stephen has shown fetishism since the first chapter of *A Portrait*, but it is acute at this point because the cutting off of his mother's life has aggravated his anxiety' (133).

Where Kimball sees the threat of the mother as a result of her power to prevent Stephen from becoming an artist, Brivic sees it as a result of a transference that Stephen has made himself. 'In "Scylla and Charybdis"', he says, 'Stephen transfers power from the father to the mother so that its threat is felt to originate with her' (133). This maternal-ising of the threat of the father renders it less threatening and 'alleviates it, for sexual submission to the mother is not as abhorrent as to the father'. Brivic sees this transference of power as a result, in part, of Stephen's masochism, a masochism which is 'played down in *Ulysses*', but nevertheless makes Stephen 'continue[ ] to think of himself almost incessantly as being attacked or threatened' (133). Freud 'found that the common desire of masochists to be beaten by women, when examined in depth, turned out to be based on fantasies of sexual assault by the father, who is disguised as an aggressive woman... The disguise of a paternal threat as maternal is a common practice of compulsive masochists...'. Brivic sees Stephen acting in 'accordance with this strategy' as he 'reverses the prevailing image of the primal scene in his lecture [on Shakespeare] from father injuring mother to mother injuring father: "You are the dispossessed son: I am the murdered father: your mother is the guilty queen" (*U*: 189)'.

While Freud's theories enable Brivic to uncover the complex psycho-sexual networks of Stephen's character, he finds that they do not allow him to understand the 'Joycean system' in 'its own terms' (140). Brivic describes his Freudian analysis of Joyce's work as 'simply explaining it causally'. In order to try and explain Joyce in his own terms Brivic turns to Jung, because he believes that there are 'extensive links between Joyce's thinking and Jung's': 'both Joyce and Jung built their systems on traditional religious categories and patterns. One of the most basic of these is the distinction between spirit and matter, and this division separ-ates Stephen from Bloom' (141). This difference between spirit and matter is manifest, according to Brivic, in the characters of Stephen and Bloom. 'Joyce's structural diagram' of *Ulysses* provides an 'indication of how carefully the body–spirit duality is designed into the book'. The diagram:

> assigns an organ for every episode except the first three. These three epis-
> odes, the 'Telemachia', deal with Stephen, and the only other episode
> which Stephen clearly dominates is 'Scylla and Charybdis', the organ of
> which is the brain. Bloom's episodes, however, focus on many organs and
> organ systems. Joyce may be suggesting by this arrangement that Bloom has
> most of his organs except for a brain while Stephen is a disembodied mind.
>
> (141)

These associations are sustained by the dietary habits and bodily functions
of the two characters, and Brivic points out that 'after rejecting room and
board at the Martello tower in the first episode', Stephen 'does not eat
in *Ulysses*, while considerable emphasis is placed on [Bloom's] eating
and... bodily functions' (141).

Brivic believes that what he calls the 'matter–spirit polarity' also structures the 'attitudes... towards sex' held by Stephen and Bloom. While
'Stephen loathes and denigrates women... Bloom adores and deifies
them'. The ways in which Stephen and Bloom think and feel about
women are 'analogous to their attitudes toward the world'. Brivic finds
it significant that the 'major convention of European Literature' upon
which the Stephen/Bloom polarity is based – the Petrarchan equation of
'man's relation to woman [and] his relation to the world' – coincides
with 'Jung's theory of the anima'. For Jung, 'the major component of a
man's unconscious will be a female archetype which he will project to
make up his environment' (141).

The respective attitudes which Stephen and Bloom hold towards
women (and the world) are an important part of their personalities, and
Brivic sees Joyce's protagonists personifying the paired opposites of
Jungian personality types with their respective introverted and extroverted
characteristics. The type personified by Stephen is spiritual and stable, and
easily disturbed by changes in identity, while the one personified by
Bloom is physical and mutable, more pliant and accepting of change.
Brivic demonstrates how each character serves all four of the functions
which Jung attributes to each type, concluding his discussion with a
summary of the contrasting attitudes towards identity held by Stephen
and Bloom:

> The 'self-disunity' and 'lack of credibility' of this type are central problems
> for Bloom: his identity is not consistent. Whereas Stephen is disturbed,
> especially in 'Proteus', to feel himself shifting roles constantly, Bloom
> moves from one feeling to another with such facility that he may be said to
> enjoy it; it is his equivalent of Odysseus's adaptability.
>
> (152)

Freudian theory enables Brivic to deal with the complexities of the characters' psychosexual makeup; Jungian theory enables him to deal with their

contrasting personalities. In terms of their personalities, the 'division between the two characters is not so pronounced from a Freudian point of view'. 'Jung's distinctions', Brivic suggests, may 'operate on a more conscious level, a level closer to the surface than Freud's, and therefore may be overstepped more easily by the intelligence'. 'After all', he concludes, 'the kinds of distinctions Jung makes have been explicit for thousands of years...; whereas Freud's discoveries, though implicit in Sophocles, Shakespeare, and others, were shockingly new' (152).

According to Brivic's Jungian reading of *Ulysses*, the opposition between the personalities of Stephen and Bloom makes it possible for them to share what he terms 'a fertile interface' (179). Where Freud's unconscious is a complex network of competing and conflicting sexual and emotional impulses, Jung's collective unconscious provides 'the unknown or unconscious space' in which Bloom and Stephen 'can confront each other without competing or projecting', an area 'in which creative perception can occur' (179). 'If Bloom is extraverted and Stephen, introverted', Brivic explains, 'then Stephen is Bloom's unconscious and Bloom, Stephen's'. Furthermore, the 'relation of the male pair' of Stephen and Bloom, 'is parallel to that of man, whose major unconscious element is *anima*, [and]... woman, whose major element is *animus*'. In this way Molly is also involved as an integral part of the relationship, and 'Stephen, Bloom and Molly will gain spiritual power, potential to change towards wholeness, as a result of the disorientation connected with their encounters with each other and with the others' needs'. The conflicts which alienate the characters from each other exist on one level; at another level there exists the possibility of the characters overcoming the alienation which results from these conflicts:

> The world Joyce depicts combines the reality of alienation with the possibility of communion because he realized that the hang-ups that limit our freedom to behave rationally are the very features that promote the energy of the irrational and the possibility of change... [I]t is possible without looking beyond the end of *Ulysses* to see Joyce's characters gaining spiritual potential by being drawn beyond themselves.
>
> (181)

Brivic does not see *Ulysses* as a perfect Jungian model, and he describes the 'consummation of Simon and Leopold illustrat[ing] a key psychological problem': the book's 'intention... to illustrate love and parenthood is compromised because Bloom, who occupies the paternal position in the novel's structure, is not psychologically a father at all, but a son – and a perverse son' (194). This split between Bloom's structural function and his psychological role creates another problem:

> If Stephen and Bloom are both sons, the theme of paternity in the novel loses its authority and the heterosexuality the book glorifies seems like sub-

terfuge. If Stephen, Bloom and Molly were to unite, they would soon find themselves in need (and in danger) of a third man who would act as father to them.

(194)

A further problem results from 'Joyce's attempt to differentiate' Stephen and Bloom 'so that each can relate to the other as [a] meaningful complement'. Brivic thinks that this attempt 'founders on the fact' that Stephen and Bloom 'have essentially identical complexes':

> Both men are obsessed with the idea of father taking away mother from them and violating her (God taking May Dedalus, Blazes taking Molly). Both regard mother as having betrayed them, view sex as a violent activity... and tend to associate with mothers and feel tempted by fathers. Both incline toward fetishism and other strategies of perversion.
>
> (194)

The one major difference that Brivic finds between the two characters 'on this level' is that 'Stephen takes a rebellious attitude toward the situation they are in, while Bloom has submitted'. In Jungian terms, however, these two attitudes are merely the opposite sides of the same coin: 'both are in the same neurotic situation, aspects of the same man fixed in this situation by his mind' (194).

Brivic finds Freudian models of interpretation more suitable for Joyce's earlier works and Jung's models more appropriate for later works like *Ulysses* and *Finnegans Wake*. He sees the *Wake* completing 'the process begun in *Ulysses* of seeing every feeling of love as love for a fantasy even while recognizing that people not only interact, but give and take all of life across these dreams'. The *Wake* 'is Joyce's most Jungian book', but it incorporates many elements which are suitable for Freudian analysis: 'Joyce does not forget the physical roots and connections of spiritual impulses. His root language is also rude, and his awareness of psychosexual mysteries and morsels is most extended and penetrating in his last, most shameless work' (203). In his analysis of Joyce's last work, Brivic spends a considerable amount of time using Freud to support a primarily Jungian analysis of the sexual basis of the familial relations between the children Shem, Shaun and Issy and their parents HCE and ALP.

From Brivic's perspective, 'The Mime of Mick, Nick and the Maggies', in the *Wake*'s ninth chapter, shows Joyce 'prob[ing] the childhood roots of neurosis and art' (203). 'Here', Brivic says, 'HCE's sons, Shem and Shaun, are seen playing with sister Iseult and her girl friends'. The central significance of the riddle which 'the girls ask Shem' is, according to Brivic, its sexual connotations:

> Among the various meanings of heliotrope [the answer to the riddle]... are the color of her panties, her vagina... and intercourse: 'the monthage stick in the melmelode jawr... Up tighty in the front, down again on the

loose, drim and drumming on her back and a pop from her whistle. What is that, O holytroopers? Isot givin yoe? (*FW*: 223)

(203)

To Brivic's mind, 'Joyce believes that women incessantly confront men with this question and that the pattern of a man's reaction is formed in childhood'. Brivic distinguishes between Shem-Glugg, as an 'artistic, autobiographical' personality who is 'unable to answer correctly', and Shaun-Chuff who, according to the *Wake*, 'is really the rapier of the two though thother brother can hold his own...' (*FW* 224. 33; Cited: 203). He describes Shem-Glugg as a suitable candidate for Freudian analysis: 'Shem-Glugg is a masturbator and incontinent pervert, as well as being a pacifist with no respect for social status'. The 'reasons for Glugg's inhibition from active genital life and competition center around guilt over his mother and fear of his father and of some terrible injury sustained by his mother' (203). Brivic draws this information from the following passage:

> This poor Glugg! It was so said of him about of his old fontmouther... O dire! And all the freightfullness whom he inhebited after his colline born janitor. Sometime towerable! With that hehry antlets on him... So that Glugg... in that limbopool which was his subnesciousness he could scares of all knotknow whither his morrder had bourst a blabber... (*FW*: 224)

(203)

Fear of the maternal 'makes Shem regress from forward movement into a backward movement which is typical of him and linked to incontinence' (204). Brivic sees the 'key sexual difference between the brothers' as the difference between perversion and repression. Perverse Shem 'expresses forbidden desires'; repressed Shaun 'denies them' publicly, 'thereby allowing himself to secretly satisfy them'. In terms of the differences between private and social spheres of action, Brivic sees Shaun 'demonstrat[ing] by his popularity and success how society favours repression over self-consciousness' (204). Drawing on Alison Armstrong's 'Shem the Penman as Glugg as the Wolf Man', Brivic considers the possibility that 'images' of Shem-Glugg's 'angskt' may be based in part on material from Freud's 'From the History of an Infantile Neurosis', the essay which presents 'Freud's famous account of the obsessed "Wolf-Man"'. Armstrong quotes the phrase 'Warewolff! Olff! Toboo!' (*FW*: 225. 8; Cited: 204), but Brivic does not accept this as definitive proof that Joyce did use Freud's study. He does, however, see Glugg-Shem demonstrating 'obsessive characteristics' like those of Freud's subject: 'Having failed with girls', Brivic explains, Glugg 'sits on his toilet reading Aquinas autoerotically: 'With his tumescinquinance in the thight of his tumstull... Experssly at hand counterhand" (*FW*: 240.8)' (204).

For Brivic, one of the central purposes of Shem-Glugg's creativity produces suitable material for psychoanalysis. The character at first reacts violently to his sexual frustration, 'but he then turns his aggression inward to divide himself into an artist and chase himself into exile: "He would split" (*FW*: 228. 5)' (204). The artist is caught in the same complex of desires and drives that both Kimball and Brivic see as a driving force for Stephen Dedalus, and the 'main purpose of his art is to expose to the world the genitals and primal sin of his parents'. This takes place in a passage of 'ambiguous images of castration':

> He would bare to untired world... how wholefallows, his guffer,... he too had a great big oh in the megafundum of his tomashunders and how her Lettyshape, his gummer... she has never cessed at waking malters... since the cluft that meataxe [his tomahawk] delt her made her microchasm as gap as down low... He would jused sit it all write down... (*FW*: 229)
>
> (204)

Brivic summarises what he sees as the essential psychoanalytic implications of this passage and relates them to the overall aims of Joyce's work:

> He [Shem] sees his mother's chasm or gap as a product of his father's brutality and insists that the flawed father 'too' has a hole, emasculating him to the level of filial passivity. This is an accurate account of the purpose of Joyce's work. And it includes an element of maturity, for the realization that your father has the same weakness you have leads to the possibility of fatherhood through the realization that your children will see you as a behemoth even though you are still a boy inside. Fatherhood and manhood are illusions, 'founded on the void' (*U*: 207) of infantile ignorance which glorifies the father... A man who fully believes he has the independence to fill the traditional role of manhood is fooling himself from the point of view of Joyce's century.
>
> (205)

Like Norris, Brivic sees the *Wake*'s language operating according to the mechanism which Freud discovered in his analysis of the dreamwork, and he believes that Joyce took these techniques from Freud: 'The dream techniques of isolation, undoing and displacement of feelings onto small details, which the *Wake* evidently derives from Freud, characterize the waking life of the obsessive' (212). Psychoanalytic theory leads to the conclusion that 'Joyce was playing games with himself in the *Wake*'. Brivic would seem to find Joyce's sublimation of the sexual drive as an important factor in the game playing of his creation of the book, and he also offers a light-hearted assessment of its importance for Joyce's readers: 'The "ideal reader suffering from an ideal insomnia" (*FW*: 120. 13) to whom Joyce addresses himself obviously does not have enough sexual intercourse – but who does?' (212). He justifies what might well be taken as a flippant comment with his assessment of the *Wake* as 'both the least repressed and most repressed of Joyce's work' and as 'his most serious and least serious'. *Finnegans Wake* represents the culmination of 'Joyce's tendency to be increasingly unrestrained in dealing with sex throughout his career':

> it wallows in incest, particularly the latest permutation of Joyce's attachment to his mother, an unhealthy, polarized love of father for daughter. The book also indulges itself outrageously in patricide, scatology, homosexuality and other taboos. And yet, grotesquely bemired with scandal as [it] is at times, the book is more careful than anything else Joyce wrote except the imitative *Chamber Music* in avoiding real conflict or threat.
>
> (212)

The key to Joyce's avoidance of threat is, according to Brivic, his successful use of psychological mechanisms to transform violence 'into a puppet show or comedy routine, seen from a distance, recounted by a scholar, isolated from feeling or associated with mythic rebirth'. The *Wake* informs HCE as Mr Finn: 'Phall if you will, but rise you must' (*FW*: 4. 14), and Brivic cites this passage as evidence that 'No one really gets hurt and the painful aspect of sex is also censored, as the benign harmlessness of father HCE indicates' (212).

Daniel Ferrer

Daniel Ferrer is a French Joycean, who, along with Derek Attridge, edited *Post-structuralist Joyce: Essays from the French* (Cambridge: Cambridge University Press, 1984), the collection of essays, including one by Ferrer, which introduced a collection of French, poststructuralist readings of Joyce to his English-speaking readers. Ferrer's essays on Joyce include 'Circe, regret, and regression' (in *Post-structuralist Joyce*); 'The Freudful Couchmare of Λd: Joyce's notes on Freud and the Composition of Chapter XVI of *Finnegans Wake*' (*JJQ*, **22**, 4 [Summer], 1985); and '*Archéologie du regard dans les avant-textes de* 〈〈Circé〉〉' (in *James Joyce 1: "Scribble" 1 genèse des textes* [Paris: Lettres Modernes Minard, 1988]). Ferrer's work could also be considered in the chapter on Joyce and post-structuralist theory, but 'Circe, regret and regression', uses Freud's notions of repression and of the *Unheimliche* and attempts to move 'beyond the Oedipus complex' (137) in a psychoanalytic reading of Circe. 'The Freudful Couchmare of Λd' presents Ferrer's discoveries concerning Joyce's knowledge and use of Freud, and these discoveries are of a major importance for psychoanalytic studies of Joyce.

Ferrer uses the following passage from Freud's *Totem and Taboo* as one of the epigraphs for 'Circe, regret and regression':

> Moreover, if the name of the dead man happens to be the same as that of an animal or common object, some tribes think it necessary to give these

animals or objects new names, so that the use of the former names shall not recall the dead man to memory. This usage leads to a perpetual change of vocabulary, which causes much difficulty to the missionaries...

(Cited: 127)

This passage assists in the creation of the context of the 'uncanny' which Ferrer establishes at the outset of his essay. The recall of the dead in Freud's passage signifies the return of someone, or something, that would be familiar but also, at the same time, strange, in an eerie way. It is in such terms that Ferrer describes a reading of 'Circe': 'What are we entering as we enter Circe, the fifteenth chapter of *Ulysses*? We are entering, or rather re-entering, a world which is strange and yet familiar' (127). This simultaneous strangeness and familiarity brings Freud's '*Unheimliche*' ('uncanny') 'to mind', Ferrer suggests, and this 'uncanny' is what sets 'Circe' off from the other episodes of *Ulysses*:

it is not quite sufficient to account for everything that is at stake in this chapter, for all the things which set it apart from all the other chapters while it remains part of the book. Our recognition that the uncanny lies at the heart of Circe, and that Circe is acted out at the heart of the uncanny, can only be a first step. But it is precisely the first step which is a problem here: can any step in Circe ever be a *first* step?

(127)

Ferrer suggests the metaphor of a mirror for a reading of 'Circe', a metaphor which he takes initially from the mirror in which the faces of Stephen, Bloom and Shakespeare appear:

the reader of *Ulysses* has, without realizing it, been in Circe for a long time when he reaches Chapter 15. The setting, the characters, the situations, even the vocabulary, are already familiar to him, and he cannot resist an inexorable sense of *déjà vu*... it is important that he should *not* resist. For, just as the only way of going deeper into a mirror (or rather, of seeing one's reflection going deeper) is to back away from it, the only way of advancing into Circe is by constantly retracing one's steps.

(128)

As 'Circe' is not only Joyce's chapter, but also a woman, Ferrer adopts the metaphor of 'exploring' a woman as a second metaphor for reading. He also invokes the notion of the uncanny in this meeting: 'Exploring Circe (and any other woman) is always a homecoming to familiar territory. But, inevitably, the homecoming seems uncanny'. The uncanny occurs as we 'meet familiar objects and characters, phrases and scenes', but 'at the same time... notice that they all undergo very strange metamorphoses'. Ferrer's example of this change is Bloom becoming first 'lovelorn, longlost, lugubru Booloohoom' and then 'Jollypoldy, the rixdix doldy (428/433–4)' (128). The metaphor of the mirror is thus refined to that of a distorting mirror, and the distortion helps sustain the sense of the uncanny: 'The strangeness will persist' (129).

Ferrer casts some of the major events which are 'mirrored' (in more than one sense) in the episode in the terms of the structures of sexual desire, displacement and the fear of castration:

> Bloom, as a cuckold, replaced in his wife's bed by a more manly man, symbolically castrated and soon, perhaps, syphilitic, sees himself as Shakespeare...; Stephen, in so far as he resembles Shakespeare (i.e. his father), sees himself as cuckolded, castrated and syphilitic. Bloom is consoling himself by identification with a great man... Stephen, on the contrary, is attacking his own image, and simultaneously, his father with whom he has identified.
>
> (130)

There are many possible readings of this mirroring and ' [e]ach reader must continue to unfold for himself the picture of Shakespeare with the horns'. Ferrer alters his metaphor momentarily in order to describe the chapter as a 'magic lantern, producing phantasies whose function is to consolidate the self' and which operates, at the same time, as 'an infernal machine which destroys identities and shatters reality' (130).

In keeping with the poststructuralist perspective of his essay, Ferrer's psychoanalytic concern with the chapter is combined with an interest in the effects which Joyce's writing has on the idea of mimesis or representation. After testing his mirror 'hypothesis' by applying it to the appearance of the ghost of Stephen's mother, Ferrer emphasises the importance of 'Circe's' 'literary technique' of hallucination. It is important to recognise, according to Ferrer, that Joyce is not depicting or representing hallucination but using it as a means of expression. This is a difficult concept to grasp, and, as Ferrer states: 'It takes a time to accustom ourselves to the idea that the hallucination is not being represented: it is a mode of representation' (133). Like other poststructuralists (Derrida, for example, as we shall see later), Ferrer does not use the linguistic paradigm which considers language as a means of representation which presents, or re-presents, a meaning or content. Understanding the hallucination of 'Circe' is 'not a question of content, but of writing – and of reading' (133).

Ferrer is concerned with the nature of hallucination and makes use of Freud's *The Interpretation of Dreams* in order to define it. Hallucination is a 'perception which comes not from the external world, but the internal world' (140). For Freud, 'hallucinations, like dreams, produce perception of a "regressive" character':

> The cathexes from the Ucs (Unconscious) proceed backwards to the sensory end of the psychic apparatus. This *topical* regression (the transition from a

system of the psychic apparatus to an anterior system) results in a predominance of visual images (see the theatrical form of Circe), which correspond to the 'ideas of things' characteristic of the Ucs system which is the source of the hallucinatory cathexis.

(140–1)

Such an unconscious cathexis can also 'reactivate' '"verbal ideas"'... stored in the Pcs system (Preconscious)'. These ideas can 'reach the conscious perception, but to do so they must go through the Ucs system by means of a topical regression and conform to the rules of the Ucs system'. Ferrer explains this as a '*formal* regression' which the ideas 'must undergo'. The ideas are treated as 'ideas of things' (rather than purely abstract ideas) and are 'subjected to the primary processes' of the Unconscious-perceptive system. Ferrer describes this process in 'Circe' as the way in which 'each sentence is the consequence of other sentences which occurred earlier in the novel, and which are subjected to the mechanisms of condensation and displacement, to such an extent that the reader sometimes finds it difficult to recognize the originals'. This process also produces 'many of the numerous tableaux, vignettes and incongruous situations' of 'Circe', and these are 'nothing more than the materialization of verbal clichés from previous chapters, made absurdly concrete' (141).

In the chapter on Anglo-American feminists we examined Scott's use of Ferrer's theory about the female in 'Circe'. Scott is particularly interested in Ferrer's idea of the 'multitudinous mother', a mother figure which Scott treats as an archaic figure prefiguring the patriarchal dominance of Western thought by the figure of the father. Ferrer distinguishes between 'at least two levels of interpretation, which are related to the two contrasting aspects of Circe...' (136). As the 'archetype of woman' Circe is a 'mother-figure' with a dual aspect: 'now a figure of fun like a music-hall clown – Bloom's mother; now a terrifying bogey ("Rawhead and bloody bones") – Stephen's mother' (137). In terms of the oedipal system, the mother is masculinised (as noted by Brivic) and becomes 'the intruder in the father and son relationship which the heroes are trying to build up. She is responsible for the prohibition which hangs over incest between the father and son, a taboo whose exceptional force Stephen recalls in tones of regret' (137). In this context she operates as a phallic figure:

The persecuting ghost of the mother stands between the union of father and son, taking over the function of prohibiting incest which normally belongs to the father. But the ghost also represents the father, whose forbidden love hides itself as persecution, just as Stephen's love hides itself as hate. This could explain all the sexual ambiguities we have noticed, as well as the phallic nature of the spectre, which 'rises stark' like an erect penis, which is a ghost like the Holy Ghost – who, we are reminded several times, got the Virgin pregnant – and which is like that other 'ghost' which appears a few pages further on as a violent emission of semen: '*He gives up the ghost. A violent erection of the hanged sends gouts of sperm spouting through his death clothes on to the cobblestones*' (523/549).

(137)

Other aspects of the female include 'cannibalism, [and] double function as container and contents'. In order to 'cover... these aspects', Ferrer says, 'we must go further, beyond the Oedipus complex... and look at highly archaic images, such as that of the "combined parent-figure" or, more precisely, the mother as universal receptacle of good and bad objects' (137).

Ferrer thinks that the appearance of the ghost is 'related to much more than just the recent death of Stephen's mother' (138). It is also the 'return of [a] distant past' which is connected to the psychological return of repressed psychic phenomena. Ferrer contends that the 'theatre of Circe is all about' 'the work of mourning', and that this work 'brings us back to a very early phase of the individual's development': 'The actual loss of the beloved is never more than a repetition of a loss already suffered'. To explore the role of the mother figure in this repetition, Ferrer uses the work of Melanie Klein who, in 'Mourning and its Relation to Manic-Depressive States' (*Contributions to Psycho-Analysis 1921–1945* [London: Hogarth Press/Institute of Psychoanalysis, 1950]), shows that 'the child goes through states of mind comparable to the mourning of the adult, or rather... this early mourning is revived whenever grief is experienced in later life' (311; Cited: 138). In the process of mourning 'the adult normally reacts by setting to work the same defence mechanism which he has already used':

> While it is true that the characteristic feature of normal mourning is the individual's setting up the lost object inside himself, he is not doing so for the first time but, through the work of mourning, is reinstating that object as well as all his loved *internal* objects which he feels he has lost. He is therefore *recovering* what he had already attained in childhood.
>
> (Klein: 330; Cited: 138)

Stephen's mourning is an example of this mourning which 'is always re-gret, leading to regression', and it 'reactivates what... Klein calls the "manic-depressive position", with its images of the mother as a complete but ambivalent object, concentrating the good and bad elements of partial objects, and carrying its weight of anxieties linked to the damage inflicted on this object by the sadism of the subject' (138).

Ferrer finds this 'in keeping with the changing nature of the ghost [of

Stephen's mother]'. The ghost is 'sometimes protective':

> Who saved you the night you jumped into the train at Dalkey with Paddy
> Lee? Who had pity for you when you were sad among strangers?... I pray
> for you in my other world. Get Dilly to make you that boiled rice every
> night after your brain work. Years and years I loved you, O my son, my
> firstborn, when you lay in my womb (516/581).
>
> (138)

At other times the ghost is 'sometimes threatening: "Repent! O, the fire
of hell... Beware! God's hand!"' The 'manic-depressive position' is also
'consonant with [the ghost's] mutilated appearance' (138).

   This view of the ghost offers a further insight into the nature of the hallucination, which '[a]t this level... may be explained as an attempt to
expel into the outer world the persecutor who is threatening the subject
from inside' (138). Stephen's encounter with the ghost of his mother is
an encounter with a repressed part of his own psyche which appears to
threaten him. This reveals a 'fresh difference between the hallucinatory
staging of the mother in Circe and the dreamed-narrated apparition which
we met in the first chapter' (139). In the first chapter the 'image of the
dead mother' is 'neutralized' by the narrative which 'enshrin[es] her in
a well-wrought dream', and tries to heal her by the use of words, of stylistic devices... of increasing perfection at each re-appearance'. The aim of
the ghost in 'Circe, by contrast... is no longer perfection but destruction'
(139). Ferrer sees the ghost in 'Circe' operating 'beyond the mirror stage'
which initiates the identity of a unified subject. It produces a 'return to
the original state of fragmentation' or in 'Kleinian terms' a 'regression
beyond the depressive position to the paranoid position, in which the
subject, whose Self is scarcely integrated at all, is constantly being over-
whelmed by his anxiety...'. This is the 'archaic phase' from which, Ferrer
states '[o]ur ghost comes directly'. The ghost is 'far more than a phantasy
from the past... it is the central core of the general regression which makes
up Circe':

> The mother, as fundamental object, returns in an emphatic manner, but she
> returns as a corpse, and, worse still, in a state of decomposition. This unen-
> durable return sets off the decomposition of the entire universe: '*Time's livid
> final flame leaps and, in the following darkness, ruin of all space, shattered glass and
> toppling masonry*' (517/583).
>
> (139)

The functions of the ghost go beyond the limitations of the phallic
mother figure to the function of the mother as an archaic, primeval force
as '[a]ll things revert to primeval chaos, that is, back to the womb, considered this time as the receptacle for all partial objects, a field in which
drives, and more particularly destructive drives, are freely released' (139).
   Ferrer's 'The Freudful Couchmare of ∧d: Joyce's Notes on Freud and

the Composition of Chapter XVI of *Finnegans Wake*' offers a much different approach to Joyce than 'Circe, regret and regression'. It provides an account of Ferrer's investigation into Joyce's notebook that 'is now catalogued under the number Vl. B. 19' (367). In late 1925, Joyce 'used this notebook extensively for the composition of chapter XVI of *Finnegans Wake*', and Ferrer uncovers what he describes as 'a fairly large number of seemingly unrelated words and phrases' in the notebook 'which in fact come from the third volume of Freud's *Collected Papers*' (367–8). 'This volume', Ferrer explains, 'had just been published by Leonard and Virginia Woolf at the Hogarth Press, 52 Tavistock Square, London, W.C. and the Institute of Psychoanalysis, MCMXXV,' and 'contains Freud's five celebrated case studies in a translation by Alix and James Strachey'. The five case studies are 'Little Hans', 'The Rat Man', 'President Schreber', 'The Wolf Man', and 'Dora'. Ferrer explains that he was 'able to identify references to only' 'Little Hans' and 'The Wolf Man' (368) although 'Dora... is nevertheless present in *Finnegans Wake* ("dora-phobian" – *FW*: 478.32)', and 'her name appears in a passage rich in Freudian references' (378).

Ferrer's discovery reveals that Joyce used Freud more extensively than he seems to have been willing to admit. Of course, it cannot cast any light on why Joyce should have been so anxious about admitting to Freud's influence on him, but it offers substantial evidence for psychoanalytic critics, who, like some of those whose work we have considered, believe that Joyce did make considerable use of Freud. Ferrer believes that we 'need to know precisely what caught Joyce's attention', and that this 'is not always what we could have expected'. He offers a 'list of the note-book entries and the corresponding sources from the *Collected Papers III*'. The first group of references are to 'Analysis of a Phobia in a Five-Year-Old-Boy', 'an account of the treatment of a young boy ("Little Hans") suffering from several phobias (notably a fear of horses) which Freud relates to his repressed sexual curiosity and to his Oedipus complex'. Ferrer discovers references to this study on pp. 17–19 and 35–38 of the notebook. 'After this', he explains, 'come thirty pages' with no references to Freud (373). He believes that 'Joyce apparently skipped "The Rat Man" and "President Schreber" and resumed with "The Wolf Man"'. 'The most striking feature of this "case of infantile neurosis"' states Ferrer, 'is a dream of several white wolves sitting in a tree, staring at the dreamer through his bedroom window' (373). Ferrer finds further references to Freud on pp. 68–70, 76–78, 84, 90–91, 94 and 100–101 of the Notebook.

While listing all of the references uncovered by Ferrer would be supererogatory, some of Ferrer's comments on the references are well worth noting. Joyce's reference to Freud's statement on '"the timeless-ness of the unconscious" [Freud, 1925: 477]' leads Ferrer to note that 'like *Finnegans Wake*, the Freudian unconscious is outside of the realm of time' (373). Ferrer establishes the following reference:

P. 70
-vice   'If in my patient's case the wolf was merely a
father surrogate   father surrogate, the question arises
(vice father   whether the hidden content in the fairy
crossed out)   tales of the wolf that ate up the little goats
                         and of "Little Red Riding-Hood" may not
                         simply be infantile fear of the father.'
                         [Freud, 1925: 502]

(374)

Although Joyce's reference (on the left-hand side) appears slight, Ferrer points out that the reference is 'the basis of an important aspect of a passage from Chapter Fifteen [which is] full of references to psychoanalysis and swarming with multitudes of wolves... The words themselves appear in the sentence "A child's dread for a dragon vice-father" *FW*: 480. 25–26'. Ferrer also uses this reference as 'an example of Joyce's working method with his notebooks':

> He notes down a phrase ('father surrogate'), then he adds (immediately or later) something that modifies and enriches it ('vice' has obviously been inserted above 'father', with a pun, of course, on the two meanings of *vice*). In *Finnegans Wake*, 'surrogate' was altogether eliminated, making the reference quite undetectable, but the original psychoanalytic context is retained and proliferates.
>
> (374)

Ferrer expresses surprise that Joyce 'skipped' the other three case studies 'because they contain many things that one might suppose to have been of special interest to him' (378). He suggests that the omission of the studies 'could imply a deliberate avoidance or a deliberate choice':

> Was Joyce refusing to dwell on a female case (Dora) or on the question of psychosis (Schreber) because at that time he was suppressing his doubts about Lucia's mental health? Was he disturbed by the similarity between the Rat Man's case and his own fantasies (rat phobia, anal eroticism)? Or did he study 'Little Hans' and 'The Wolf Man' with a specific purpose? Was he attracted by the fact that they both were dealing extensively with infantile sexuality...?
>
> (378)

Whatever the reasons for Joyce's selections and rejections, the material that he did use was treated like that of any other author: 'Joyce treated the Freudian text in the same way he treated his other sources, that is as a quarry for unusual or foreign words and phrases which he sometimes used later and sometimes left forgotten in his notebook' (379).

In a letter to Miss Weaver which Ferrer cites, Joyce explained that

Chapter Sixteen 'ought to be about roads, all about dawn and roads...' (*L*, I: 232; Cited: 379). Ferrer suggests that 'as we now have it... if we were to describe the chapter these would not be the first elements we would mention'. The 'drastic evolution' from a chapter about 'dawn and roads' to one about 'a coitus between a father and a mother, and the nightmare of one of their children', Ferrer believes, 'can be explained by the contact with Freud' (379–80):

> Joyce realized... that voyeurism (an essential characteristic of HCE) derives from infantile sexual curiosity, curiosity about the parents' genitals ('Little Hans'), and about the true meaning of the 'primal scene' ('The Wolf Man'). He felt that in this *ricorso* chapter he had to stage the trauma that was going to make of Shem and Shaun new HCEs in this respect. Moreover, the inclusion of Freud's primal scene was an opportunity of adding one more item to the list of founding myths that constitute *Finnegans Wake*.
> (380)

Julia Kristeva

Nearly all of Kristeva's work could be said to be concerned with psychoanalysis, but as we have already seen, her work is also closely involved with semiotics and the female in language. Kristeva has written on particular passages in Joyce's work (the *Wake*'s story of the 'Ondt and the Gracehoper', for example), but she refers to Joyce's writing primarily as a model for her semiotic and psychoanalytic theories of language. In *Powers of Horror: An Essay on Abjection* (New York: Columbia UP, 1982), Kristeva draws on Freud and Lacan (among others) as well as on her experience with '"borderline" patients' speeches and behaviour' (7) in order to develop a theory of abjection, and she uses Molly's monologue from *Ulysses* as an example of writing which 'causes [the abject] to break out in what [Joyce] sees as prototype of literary utterance' (22).

Kristeva's concept of the abject is difficult to grasp because it rests on philosophical as well as psychoanalytic notions: 'within abjection', 'looms... one of those violent, dark revolts of being, directed against a threat that seems to emanate from an exorbitant outside or inside, ejected beyond the scope of the possible, the tolerable, the thinkable' (1). Yet this state of 'being' is also involved with the operations of desire: 'It beseeches, worries, and fascinates desire, which, nevertheless, does not let itself be seduced' (1). The abject is also experienced by the self as a psychological entity: 'The abjection of the self would be the culminating form of that experience of the subject to which it is revealed that all its objects are based merely on the inaugural *loss* that laid the foundations of its own being' (5). Kristeva considers abjection in relation to Freud's theory of the unconscious and the operations of repression and denial and concludes that Freud's notions may be insufficient for an analysis of the abject. 'Facing the ab-ject and more specifically phobia and the splitting of the ego', Kristeva suggests, 'one might ask if those articulations of negativity germane to the unconscious (inherited by Freud from philosophy and psychology) have not become inoperative' (7).

Kristeva describes the subject who experiences abjection as 'an exile who asks, "where?"', which may suggest why she sees abjection breaking out in the work of Joyce. Joyce's political and geographical exile, along with his culminating, voluntary self-exile into a language of his own making, is perhaps echoed in Kristeva's description of the 'one by whom the abject exists'. He is:

> thus a *deject* who places (himself), *separates* (himself), situates (himself), and therefore *strays* instead of getting his bearings, desiring, belonging, or refusing. Situationist in a sense, and not without laughter – since laughing is a way of placing or displacing abjection.
>
> (8)

The importance of Joyce's writing as laughter has been explored by Philippe Sollers, who, in 'Joyce & Co.' offers the hypothesis 'that *Finnegans Wake* is a word, one immense word but in a state of skidding, of lapsus' (Sollers: 112). Sollers sees the *Wake*-as-word functioning 'on a simple nucleus where to give *one* word (or rather an "effect of word") there is a coming together of at least three words, plus a coefficient of annulation'. Sollers offers the example of Joyce's 'sinse', which is simultaneously '*since, sense,* and *sin*' and describes the '"syllogistic" development of this condensation... as follows: ever since (time), there is sin and sense. All in a flash in SINSE'. The condensation produces laughter because in this one word, 'as in a thousand, you have a thesis on language and one man's fall from paradise; and, simultaneously, it is funny' (113).

Sollers supports his argument about the humour of Joyce's writing with a French reading of the *Wake*'s opening 'riverrun' as '*rire-vers-l'un*', or laughter-towards-the-one (113). This laughter towards the one results from Joyce's ability to live in a state of 'triadicity'. Noting that 'riverrun' 'has not so far been interpreted in such a way', Sollers goes on to argue that:

> When it is noted... that the *last* word [of the *Wake*] is THE, followed by a blank, with no punctuation mark, and that this terminal THE is calculated so as to turn round to the beginning, then nothing prevents, from end to beginning, the reading THE RIVERRUN, which is obviously the course of the river but in which can also be heard and seen THREE VER UN, three toward one. No surprise that Joyce ceaselessly meditated (and played) on the trinity – and were you yourselves living in a state of triadicity, *plus one*, nothing would appear more normal to you than such things. Basically, it is all very simple. The most astonishing thing is that it seems to be difficult,

in other words that those who are the maddest declare to be mad those who are like that.

(113–14)

Joyce's ability to write in this state of triadicity within a language that he describes as a 'trifid tongue' suggests the condition of the deject who is 'engrossed', in Kristeva's terms, by a 'space that engrosses the deject, the excluded'. This 'space... is never *one*, nor *homogeneous*, nor *totalizable*, but essentially divisible, foldable, and catastrophic' (Kristeva, 1982: 8).

The view of Joyce as a writer in whose writing the abject breaks out is supported by Kristeva's view of abjection's connection with the perverse and the artistic. Several of the psychoanalytic readings of Joyce that we have examined emphasise the importance of Joyce's use of prohibitions like the incest taboo, and Ferrer sees 'Circe' allowing for the return of repressed material at a level that goes beyond the Oedipal complex where Freud situates the prohibitions against incest. In other words, Joyce could seem in certain parts of his writing to articulate the abject which is 'perverse because it neither gives up nor assumes a prohibition, a rule, or a law... but turns them aside... uses them, takes advantage of them...' (15). Joyce's operations on language, particularly the English language, in *Finnegans Wake*, could be explored as an artistic exploration of the abject, and Joyce considered as a writer, who, 'fascinated by the abject, imagines its logic, projects himself into it, introjects it, and as a consequence perverts language – style and content' (16).

It is in Molly's monologue that Kristeva sees abjection. She describes the 'rhetoric of Joycean language' as 'dazzling, unending, eternal – and so weak, so insignificant, so sickly' (22). Molly's monologue is 'what [Joyce] sees as prototype of literary utterance'. 'If that monologue spreads out the abject', says Kristeva, 'it is not because there is a woman speaking':

> But because, *from afar*, the writer approaches the hysterical body so that it might speak... using it as a springboard, of what eludes speech and turns out to be the hand to hand struggle of one woman with another, her mother of course, the absolute because of the primeval seat of the impossible – of the excluded, the outside-of-meaning, the abject. Atopia.
>
> (22)

Kristeva cites the following passage from the monologue:

> the woman hides it not to give all the trouble they do yes he came somewhere Im sure by his appetite anyway love its not or hed be off his feed thinking of her so either it was one of those night women if it was down there he was really and the hotel story he made up a pack of lies to hide it planning it Hynes kept me who did I meet ah yes I met do you remember Menton and who else who let me see that big babbyface I saw him and he not long married flirting with a young girl at Pooles Myriorama and turned

my back on him when he slinked out looking quite conscious what harm
but he had the impudence to make up to me one time well done to him
mouth almighty and his boiled eyes of all the big stupoes I ever met and
thats called a solicitor only for I hate having a long wrangle in bed or else
if its not that its some little bitch or other he got in with somewhere or
picked up on the sly if they only knew him as well as I do yes because the
day before yesterday he was scribbling something a letter when I came into
the front room for the matches to show him Dignam's death

(U: 738–739; Cited: 22)

Kristeva locates the abject in this passage 'not... in the thematic of masculine sexuality as Molly might see it', nor 'even in the fascinated horror
that the other women, sketched out in the back of the men, imbue the
speaker with'. 'The abject lies', says Kristeva, 'beyond the themes, and for
Joyce generally, in the way one speaks' (23). Abjection:

> is verbal communication, it is the Word that discloses the abject. But at the
> same time, the Word alone purifies from the abject, and that is what Joyce
> seems to say when he gives back to the masterly rhetoric that his *Work
> in progress* constitutes full powers against abjection. A single catharsis: the
> rhetoric of the pure signifier, of music in letters – *Finnegans Wake*.
>
> (23)

John Bishop

Joyce's Book of the Dark: '*Finnegans Wake*' (Madison: Wisconsin UP,
1986), offers a reading of the *Wake* from the vantage point of Bishop's
somewhat eclectic theoretical point of view. In the introduction to his
study Bishop presents an assessment of the attitudes towards Freud shared
by many of Joyce's critics. 'Mere mention of Freud', he says 'will raise
hackles on one side of the room and banners on the other' (15). Bishop
himself has no reservations about using Freudian theory to make sense of
Joyce's 'UNGUMPTIOUS', and realises that this 'ungumptious' 'is both
distinct from and yet related to the "Unconscious" in its more orthodox
forms'. For Bishop, the appearance of the unconscious in the text and
the arguments of 'many Joyceans' are evidence that 'there can be no
question... psychoanalysis had an impact, a deep one, on *Finnegans
Wake*'. Noting the text's description of itself as 'an intrepidation of our
dreams' (338. 29) as well as its pun on 'libidinous unconscious' in
'LIPPUDENIES OF THE UNGUMPTIOUS' (308. R2), Bishop argues
that these terms, ' [l]ike all the many psychoanalytic tags drifting through
Finnegans Wake... suggest similarities and differences, both of which are
important to weigh'. Bishop's book is, in part, an attempt to weigh these
differences. What Bishop describes as 'Joyce's vexed relation to Freud' is
'complex' enough that it cannot 'be solved by oppositional diatribe, doc-
trinaire advocacy, or... simple disregard' (18). Citing Adaline Glasheen's

comment that the 'relation of *Ulysses* and *Finnegans Wake* to [Freud's *The Interpretation of Dreams*] ... deserves the fullest, deepest study', Bishop sets out to offer a 'Joycean reading of Freud, and not a Freudian reading of Joyce' (18).

Bishop thinks it 'impossible for any reader seriously interested in coming to terms with *Finnegans Wake* to ignore *The Interpretation of Dreams*, and he believes that Freud's work 'broke the ground that Joyce would reconstruct... and, arguably, made *Finnegans Wake* possible':

> it was in the cultural air that any early twentieth-century European would have breathed, and it is everywhere implicit in Joyce's 'nonday diary'. Its first chapter, not least, provides an excellent summary of the nineteenth-century literature on sleep and dreams, and those that follow have not been surpassed in exploring what dreams mean and how they work. No subsequent treatment of the subject fails to show its influence. The book is important to *Finnegans Wake*, however, not simply because it treats so elaborately of *Dreams*, but because it is equally about *Interpretation*, which is any reader's only business; and it is about the interpretation of a kind that unyieldingly brings the simple and central question 'What does it mean?' to a species of peculiarly nonsensical, obscure and garbled literary text – 'the text of the dream' ([*The Interpretation of Dreams*]: 552), the puzzling and troubling 'mumurrandoms' (*FW*: 358. 3) that any dreamer 'remumble[s] from the night before'... Particularly because the only real evidence of 'dreaming' comes in the dark language of these 'murmurable' 'murmoirs' (294. 7, 387. 34...), some interpretive technique *distinct* from those brought to bear on consciously constructed narratives will be essential to a reading of what Joyce called his 'imitation of the dream-state'.
>
> (16)

Bishop balances his view that Freud's study is 'an indispensable text to bring to *Finnegans Wake*' with a consideration of Joyce's 'well-known derogations of Freud and "the new Viennese school" (*U*: 205)'. It 'would be foolish to disregard' these derogations, states Bishop (16–17). 'They suggest that, perhaps, what should be obvious: that both as a "competent" thinker and man – a "competitor" and not a follower – and especially as an artist whose work consistently explored "the inner life", Joyce was of necessity in competition with psychoanalysis, and all the more particularly because of its claims to authority' (17). Bishop believes Joyce's competitive attitude towards psychoanalysis is 'implicit' in a remark that Joyce made to Mary Colum upon discovering that Colum was 'attending a series of lectures by Pierre Janet: "You could learn as much about psychology from yourself as from those fellows"', Joyce is reported as saying (Cited: 17). Bishop sees this as a fair comment. 'And why not?' he asks, explaining that while a 'great deal has been said about the heroism of Freud's self analysis... relatively little' has been said 'about Joyce's, in the writing of *Ulysses*, which [Joyce] regarded as "essentially the product of his whole life"'. Discussing what Joyce may have learned about himself psychologically while writing *Ulysses*, Bishop argues that 'it would be difficult to conceive of anyone spending seven years on a text that heavily autobiographical, reworking on a daily basis the personal and literary past, without emerging from the experience radically changed' (17).

Describing *Ulysses* as a 'work thematically absorbed with the issues of fathering and self-fathering', Bishop suggests that one way of interpreting the text is to:

> see it as the process whereby an arrogant little man, a young Joyce who in fact had published under the name 'Stephen Dedalus', rewrote himself so entirely as to emerge from the experience not simply with the humane capabilities of a Leopold Bloom, and not simply even with the expansive good humour and affability that every reader of the biography will know, but as one of the twentieth century's great men of letters.
>
> (17)

Perhaps echoing Stephen's desire to awaken from the nightmare of history, Bishop describes Joyce's production of *Ulysses* as a successful attempt at changing the past: 'The book, through its microscopic examination of the inner life, altered the past in every possible way' (17).

It is, however, with the *Wake* and not with *Ulysses*, that *Joyce's Book of the Dark* is concerned, and, returning to his interest in Joyce's relation to Freud, Bishop expresses his belief that it would 'do Joyce insufficient credit... to read *Finnegans Wake* as a "creative" reworking of understandings that might be had much more straightforwardly through a reading of Freud' (17). To read Joyce in this way, one would have to ignore that 'Joyce clearly went about reconstructing the night in his own idiosyncratic way'. Using Freud's text to interpret Joyce would be unsatisfactory because 'if most of the night is void of recollectible dreams, a work aspiring to their interpretations would be only of partial relevance'. Ultimately, Bishop believes that Joyce did enough of his own dream work to justify reading his literary work on its own terms: 'Joyce thought about psychic interiors throughout his literary career and about "nightlife" daily for almost twenty years (150. 33, 407. 20). It was his work'. Relying only on Freud's theories to interpret Joyce one would have to overlook Joyce's dislike of authority and theory, the self-sufficiency of his writing, and his preference for Vico over Freud:

> As an author who distrusted authority in all its forms, [Joyce] preferred to all theory nagging, living, concrete immersion in the material under his scrutiny ('I hate generalities' [*JJ*, 565]). If, as he said, '*Ulysses* is related to this book as the day is to the night', we should expect *Finnegans Wake* to behave with all the uncapturable richness of *Ulysses*, exploring its dark subject thoroughly, systematically, but not systemically. Finally, too, as Joyce's comparative remarks on Freud and Vico suggest, his real authority

in the study of the unconscious was Vico, and even here he distanced himself carefully ('I would not pay overmuch attention to these theories, beyond using them for all they are worth' [*L*, 1: 241]).

(17–18)

Bishop believes that many of the so-called Freudian elements that critics have discovered in Joyce are actually Viconian, and he argues that Vico developed many ideas which were similar to Freud's but expressed them in simpler terms. In discussing the 'mind that Joyce sought to recon-struct' in the *Wake*, for example, Bishop contends that in 'a direct and substantial way', this mind 'was equivalent to the aboriginal mind that Vico sought to comprehend in Book II of *The New Science*'. Citing a passage in which Vico discusses 'poetic wisdom' and 'ignorance' (*The New Science*, 340, 375), Bishop argues that Vico is actually discussing what Freud later called 'the dreamwork' and the 'unconscious', and was simply 'lacking [in] psychoanalytic terminology...' (182). In a similar vein, Bishop compares the aims of twentieth-century psychoanalysis with Vico's view of man's rationality:

> Twentieth century psychoanalysis proposes to isolate and cure the irration-ally disturbed components of personality by analyzing the fears and fixations inherited from parents in an impressionable, irrational infantile past. Vico's axiomatic observation that rationality is a man-made structure historically evolved out of animal unreason will suggest why Joyce would have regarded Freudian theory as a diminution of Vico's insights.
>
> (183–4)

Vico's 'poetic wisdom' is the result of his attempt at 'rationally' trying 'to reconstruct the minds of those irrational first men whose animal instincts began to determine the subsequent evolution of history and human con-sciousness' (185). Bishop believes that Vico's work in this area 'encom-passes the psychoanalytic work that Freud achieved in reconstructing the infantile mind whose fears and pleasure determine the shape of personal history'. 'Here, too', Bishop argues, 'Joyce learned much more from *The New Science* than a principle of eternal recurrence.' Vico provides Joyce with insights into the human mind that were later to be reformulated by Freud, but it was from Vico, and not Freud that Joyce gained his under-standing: 'Vico... anticipates Freud, and ultimately contributes to *Ulysses* and the *Wake* by drawing a rich fund of insight from the observation and the memory of human infancy' (185).

There is apparently very little information about the unconscious and dream work that Joyce could not have either discovered in Vico or learned for himself. Bishop believes that Vico anticipated most, if not all, of Freud's insights but lacked the vocabulary to develop and refine them: 'Just as the limits of his culture's vocabulary cause Vico to adopt the term "ignorance" to denote "unconsciousness", so he uses the term "poetic wisdom" to denote the manifold forms of unconscious thinking that Freud would study more specialistically in his work on infantile sexuality'. Poetic language, however, does allow Vico to develop some refinement in his theories, and '[t]reating of "metaphor", "synechdoche", "metonymy", "allegory", and "myth", rather than of "condensation", "displacement", and "indirect representation", Vico's "Poetic Wisdom" is a form of Freudian dreamwork' (190). Vico even 'anticipates the account of infantile sexuality given in Freud's theories of genitality'. To Bishop's mind, Joyce would have preferred Vico to Freud because he shared Vico's more expansive vision of human development:

> But Joyce, who described the secret pressures of the stomach on rational thinking in the 'Lestrygonians' episode of *Ulysses*, the patterns of economic management imposed on consciousness by the evacuatory organs in 'Calypso', and the evolved forms of human enterprise made possible by the biological endowment of lungs on mankind in 'Aeolus', probably preferred to Freud's theories of genital organization Vico's broader account of how 'gentile' human nature rolled up into the head not simply out of the loins but out of the entire body of his aboriginal infant giants.
>
> (193)

Even if Freud's theories do help to explain some of the ways in which the *Wake* is structured and produces meaning, then, according to Bishop, they can really do little more than translate Vico's ideas into Freudian terminology in order to comprehend ideas and principles that Joyce either developed himself or derived from Vico. Bishop does show how Freud's theories can cast light on things like the 'infantile regression' which the 'old man who sleeps at the *Wake*' (317) undergoes, but his study emphasises that these theories are simply 'freudened' versions of Vico and of Joyce's own insights into the mind and the night.

•6• 'HIS MARX AND THEIR GROUPS':

Joyce and Marxist Criticism

CRITICS INTERESTED IN the issue of Joyce and politics can be divided into three general groups: biographical critics interested in Joyce's personal political beliefs; historical critics concerned with the relations between Joyce's work and Irish politics; and Marxist critics. While the latter share many of the concerns of biographical and historical critics, their primary interest lies in investigating Joyce's writing from the theoretical perspective afforded by Marxism, and it is on these critics that this chapter will concentrate. Joyce's own political allegiances are well documented in such biographical studies as Herbert Gorman's *James Joyce* (New York: Rinehart and Co., 1948), Richard Ellmann's biography, and Hélène Cixous' *The Exile of James Joyce*. Together, these studies reveal that Joyce held no serious political beliefs, in the conventional sense of the phrase, except for the 'socialist creed which he vociferously proclaimed between 1903 and 1906' (Cixous: 182). What Cixous calls Joyce's 'socialist pose' was

> [y]et another form of individualism... a conception of himself which took an original form and did not last long; its contents were scarcely political at all, containing for example no trace of Marxism. If he had any political opinion, it was rather a sceptical realism, which throughout his life caused 'healthy' reactions to international problems and situations; he generally resolved them by absence and abstention. If Marx did fascinate him, it was because Marx was Jewish and because through Marx he already perceived something of Bloom.
>
> (198)

Bernard Benstock's *Joyce-Again's Wake: An Analysis of 'Finnegans Wake'* (Seattle: University of Washington Press, 1965) details Joyce's use of socialism, Russian history and Marxist politics, but cautions that Joyce's 'preoccupation with Russia in the *Wake* is historical rather than ideological...' (51). Benstock also points out that Joyce's 'dabbling in [socialist] jargon' 'hardly commits' him to the cause of socialism. He cites Gorman's assessment of Joyce's socialism – an assessment agreeing with Cixous' view – as:

> thin and unsteady and ill-informed and [Joyce] knew it to be so. Indeed, it was more of a sympathy than a conviction, a feeling that the perfect freedom in life with the absolute minimum of restraining laws was an ideal devoutly to be desired.
>
> (Gorman: 183; Cited, Benstock: 51)

Joyce's use of Vico's cycles may have allowed him to arrive 'at his own dialectics', but Benstock warns of the difficulties in trying to shape the particulars of Joyce's work 'to fit a preconceived political doctrine' (52). It may be helpful to keep this warning in mind as we look at some examples of Marxist criticisms of Joyce's work.

From Russia with Dzhois

The winter 1968 issue of the *JJQ* affords us the opportunity of seeing how Joyce was viewed from the officially-approved Marxist perspectives of the USSR and that part of Germany once known as the German Democratic Republic. William B. Edgerton's 'Dzhoising with the Soviet Encyclopedias' (*JJQ*, 5, 2, 1968) outlines the reception of Joyce in the Soviet Union and offers a translation of three encyclopedia articles on Joyce and his work. Edgerton begins by outlining the Soviet history of Joyce's work up until 1968:

> James Joyce has never quite made the grade in the Soviet Union. Fragments of his *Ulysses* were published in Russian translation as early as 1925 in Moscow, and an abridged Russian version of *Dubliners* came out two years later in Leningrad. There was another flurry of activity between 1935 and 1937, when a new edition of *Dubliners* was reprinted, some of Joyce's poetry was published in an anthology, and eleven issues of the periodical *Internatsional'naia literatura* carried Russian translations of chapters from *Ulysses*. During the past thirty years, however, it appears that nothing whatever from the pen of Joyce has been printed in the Soviet Union.
>
> (125)

The articles which Edgerton translates represent views from 'three widely different periods in Soviet history':

1930, before the relative artistic freedom of the 1920's had succumbed to Socialist Realism; 1952, during the final wave of Stalinist terror...; and 1964, just before the end of the Kruschev era.

(125)

Ivan Kashkin's article in the *Literaturnuia èntsiklopediia*, III (Moscow, 1930) describes 'Dzhems Dzhois' as a 'psychoanalyzer' and a 'master of international (especially American) modernism' (125). It traces the development of Joyce's work from *Dubliners* through to *Ulysses*, explaining that Joyce 'writes slowly, scorns tradition, and does not allow publishers to soften the sharpness of his attacks' (126). Kashkin values Joyce's work for its contribution to Marxist historical development in giving an 'extraordinarily acute portrayal of [an 'old multinational' culture's] hypertrophy and disintegration in the consciousness of the decadent bourgeoisie and bohemians' and 'clearing the way for the literature of the future', but condemns Joyce for his lack of any vision of an alternative to the culture which he attacks (128). 'What looks like the growth of conflict in D.'s [Joyce's] work', argues Kashkin, 'is in reality movement "from nowhere into nothing"' (126). While *Dubliners* is admired for a 'naturalistic and traditional form' that 'strikes at the petty Philistinism' of Dublin, Joyce is attacked for holding views similar to those of Stephen Dedalus:

A déclassé product of the impoverished freethinking bourgeoisie, a labouring intellectual, an ideological expellee from Jesuit dogma, blasphemously reviling traditions but floundering in the tenets of his scholastic religious attitude, a poet close to radical bohemianism, Stephen reflects to a significant degree the views of D. himself.

(126)

Joyce's lack of a Marxist vision means that *Dubliners*' 'muffled protest' and *A Portrait*'s 'tormented searchings' can lead nowhere but to the 'static state of extreme spiritual bankruptcy and futility' of *Ulysses*, and Joyce is roundly criticised for the latter work:

In *Ulysses*, in which a by no means remarkable day in the life of the most mediocre people is described in 1000 pages, the world has stopped for D. in tense expections of a crash. A rebel and an innovator in form, D. is still a prisoner of the old scholastic and ascetic psycho-ideology (Aristotle and Thomas Aquinas). This tragic dualism in D. and the futility born of it lead him into passivity and analysis, but here too the dry and merciless revelation of self and surroundings is replaced by a romantic heroicization of the figure of Stephen...

(126–7)

Kashkin sees Joyce's style corresponding to his 'passéism and passivity'. It has a 'secondariness in artistic expression' which manifests itself in

Ulysses' 'parodying of old forms', its 'hundreds of quotations', and its 'following the patterns of the Odyssey...' (127). Assessing Joyce from a 'strictly artistic point of view', Kashkin argues that:

> perhaps the most flawless of all Dzhois's works are certain of his short stories in the tradition of Flaubert, with their sober and capacious plasticity. But as soon as D. abandons the classical shell and throws off the burden of the past, the inner disorder shows through, the form disintegrates as a result of its hysterical eccentricities and is dissipated in parody, and the creative visage of Dzhois is distorted by a sickly grimace.
>
> (127)

In a criticism that may sound odd in an era of perestroika and glasnost, Kashkin concludes with his view of Joyce as 'having lost his way in formal refinements... perishing as an artist along with the class stratum that he portrays' (128).

The *Bol'shaia sovetskaia èntsiklopediia*, or Large Soviet Encyclopedia, of 1952 offers an unattributed summary of Joyce's work, the brevity of which Edgerton attributes to the 'final wave of Stalinist terror' (125). More acerbic than Kashkin's criticism of Joyce, the 1952 article offers no positive consideration of Joyce at all. It describes Joyce as a 'representative of the reactionary school that is characterized by the subjectivist depiction of the "stream of consciousness"' and argues that 'he is played up as a leader of European and American Decadence' (128). *Ulysses* is criticised as a 'portrayal of the perverted psyche of a vulgar Philistine' and a 'rummaging about among his dirty sensations' which is 'devoted to the reactionary purpose of showing man as antisocial and immoral' (129).

A little more sympathetic than the 1952 article is E. V. Kornilova's entry in the *Kratkaia literaturnaia èntsiklopediia*, Short Literary Encyclopedia, II (Moscow, 1964). Kornilova's article views Joyce as a victim of 'the oppression to which Ireland was subjected by the English and Irish capitalists', but also sees him as lacking belief in both 'the effectiveness of the struggle for national liberation' and the 'ideals of the movement for cultural liberation' (129). *Dubliners* is described as 'a picture of the dreary life of Dublin city dwellers', and there is a trace of admiration in Kornilova's suggestion that Joyce's stories 'criticized the English rulers of Ireland and their Irish collaborators'. *A Portrait* is considered as 'more or less autobiographical', and the same sort of ambivalence that characterises Kashkin's criticism of Joyce can be detected in Kornilova's description of Stephen Dedalus as a character who,

> in his struggle against moral oppression breaks with his family and his Philistine environment and rejects religion, in the dogmas of which he had been brought up. Along with this he refuses to take part in the struggle for the liberation of his people, and shutting himself up within his creative work,

which he considers to be the only self-contained value, he voluntarily leaves Ireland, even though the break with it is a tragic experience for him.

(129)

Kornilova is equally ambivalent in assessing *Ulysses* as a 'merciless condemnation of the bourgeois world' whose 'author underwent the ruinous influence of this world'. As a result of this experience, Joyce's 'nihilism, a sensation of doom and futility, and a lack of positive social ideals give the picture he created an atmosphere of hopelessness' (129–30). *Ulysses* is also 'characterized by a very complex symbolic structure, which lends itself to various and even mutually contradictory interpretations…'. Elements of Joyce's style such as his 'fusion of various stylistic manners', his 'parodic use of ancient and Biblical motifs', and his 'highly refined word creation' are considered as 'contrivances' which 'lead to the disintegration of the literary form of the novel'. Kornilova argues that this disintegration is 'graphically demonstrated' in the *Wake* and summarises Joyce's last work as a 'fantasmagorical combination of reality and dreams that bears witness to the decline of D.'s literary talents' (130).

In 1976 a change in the Soviet attitude to Joyce was signalled when *A Portrait* appeared in a Soviet journal. As Emily Tall states in 'James Joyce Returns to the Soviet Union' (*JJQ*, 17, 4, 1980), the novel was published in the journal, *Inostrannaia literatura* (*Foreign Literature*), which is 'one of the most widely-read in the country', and its publication 'marked the high point… in a struggle to rescue Joyce from the oblivion to which he had long been consigned by official policy' (341). This was by no means a sudden change, and Tall cites three Soviet 'scholars of English literature', 'Valentina Ivasheva, Nina Mikhalskaia, and Diliara Zhantieva', as those who, in the late 1960s, 'elaborated the new orthodoxy, separating the acceptable from the unacceptable in Joyce': 'They rated *Dubliners* highest for its "realistic" exposure of the "spiritual paralysis" and "atmosphere of oppression" in Ireland and for Joyce's "masterful psychological analysis"' (341–2). These three scholars disagreed over *A Portrait* 'with two of them condemning the book for the individualism of the hero and his break with society' much as the earlier critics had done (342). The third scholar, however, called the book '"an outstanding work of art" with "great lyricism and human warmth"' (Cited, Tall: 342). *Ulysses*, in Tall's words, 'fared worst': 'Although some areas of acceptability were carved out– the earlier, more "realistic" chapters, plus some aspects of Joyce's social criticism and techniques of psychological analysis – these were held to be vitiated by Joyce's "universal pessimism" as well as the traditional sins of formalism, naturalism, nihilism, and Freudianism'. Like Kornilova in the 1950s, the 'Soviet critics of the sixties' saw *Ulysses* as 'still the prime example of how "modernism destroyed a great artist"' (342).

While Ivasheva, Mikhalskaia, and Zhantieva 'worked out in criticism' what Tall describes as the 'orthodox position' on Joyce, some of Joyce's work was being translated elsewhere in the Soviet Union. In Lithuania 'the well known Lithuanian poet and translator, Tomas Venclova (b. 1937), was asked to translate portions of *Ulysses*', with the result that 'Telemachus', 'Proteus', and 'Calypso', were published in 1968, 'the first time that *Ulysses* had appeared in print in the Soviet Union since 1936', (342). In Georgia, the task of translating *Ulysses* was undertaken by Nico Kiasashvili, the Shakespearean scholar to whom Richard Ellmann sent a copy of *Giacomo Joyce*. In 1969, Kiasashvili 'published Georgian and Russian translations' of *Giacomo Joyce*. As Tall relates, this translation was '[unlike] Kiasashvili's earlier forays into Joyce territory, which had only local readership', and it 'came out in *Literaturnaia Gruziia*, a Russian-language literary monthly published in Georgia' (343). At the same time that Kiasashvili was working on his translation of *Ulysses*, 'other efforts at a reappraisal of Joyce were being made in Moscow' (343–4). Tall identifies Yekaterina Genieva as a major figure in one of these reappraisals. In 1970, Genieva 'successfully defended' the 'first... ever' dissertation on Joyce 'in the Soviet Union', and '[c]hallenging the reigning dogma, she asserted that Joyce was a humanist, not a pessimist, that he continued the tradition of the realistic novel, and was, indeed, "one of the greatest writers in the history of world literature"' (344). This was a major event for Soviet studies of Joyce, and Tall reports that the Genieva's defence 'was attended by many of the foremost Soviet specialists in Western literature'.

Along with Genieva's defence and the appearance of Kiasashvili's Georgian translation of the first three chapters of *Ulysses*, Tall considers a 'third event of 1970' as the 'most fascinating of all': Victor Khinkis, 'one of the Soviet Union's best translators of English and American Literature' 'began work on a Russian translation of *Ulysses*' (346). Tall concludes her overview of these developments by pointing out that whatever the problems which Joyce's Soviet translators experience, '[o]fficial Soviet Policy calls for translating the great works of literature; even those critics who don't care for Joyce particularly have said that *Ulysses*... [is] "already a possession of our century" and "without it you can't understand many things"' (346).

Some English-Speaking Marxists in Joyce's 'Groups'

Alick West

In 1936, Alick West's *Crisis and Criticism* (London: Lawrence and Wishart, 1936) offered a Marxist analysis of *Ulysses*, and this analysis affords the opportunity of understanding how Marxist theory produced a view of Joyce in the English-speaking world similar to that which it produced in the Soviet Marxists we have considered. West begins by emphasising the importance of a social context for aesthetics in Marxist criticism:

> Marxism does not neglect aesthetics. It transforms the aesthetic experience. Aesthetic activity, like every other, changes as a society changes. The charge against Marxism of ignoring aesthetics ignores this fact, and continues to think and feel in the aesthetic terms of the past. The present trend in criticism towards relating literature to some greater reality is part of a process that began with romanticism; and the critical work we have referred to retains and accentuates the idealistic and religious aspects of romantic aesthetics. Marxism is only concerned critically with this aesthetic activity. Hence the accusation from those held by the past that Marxism neglects their aesthetics.
>
> (20)

While 'literary judgement is a proper study for Marxist criticism', such judgement cannot be based on an aesthetic value divorced from a social context: 'A work of literature... embodies a particular social attitude; in certain social conditions this attitude can be advantageously advanced by certain social classes, and the work is then said to have value' (100). The social context for literature is the 'social organism to which literature has to be related... humanity in its advance to socialism', and the 'function of criticism is to judge literature, both content and form, as a part of this movement'. Criticism 'can only fulfill this function if it takes part in this movement itself on the side of the workers of the world' (103).

West uses *Ulysses* '[t]o illustrate' his Marxist method of interpreting literature. He chooses Joyce's text because it 'reveals in the creation of literature the same kind of conflict' that West sees in literary criticism concerning the function of interpretation and the role of aesthetics (104). Like those critics who neglect humanity's advance towards socialism as the proper context for the operation of literary aesthetics, Joyce offers no 'aim' for which the 'social energy' that he depicts can 'work' (127). West arrives at this conclusion by looking at the 'two lines' which sustain a 'particular tension' in the plot:

> Bloom discovers that his wife is going to have a visit from her lover in the afternoon, meets him several times before the rendezvous, wonders whether he will go home and stop it, but decides to do nothing. Stephen guesses that the man with whom he lives in a disused Martello Tower is scheming to get the key from him and lock him out, and in the small hours he finds himself homeless. Both series of incidents are, however, thin and fragmentary, in the sense that one moment is separated by scores of pages from the next. They also do not hold the book together.
>
> (105)

Concerned with discovering what does provide unity for the book, West argues that a more 'traditional style would have given a continuous presentation' of the characters (118). Joyce, however, 'shows the individual action [of each of the characters] within the totality of relations existing at the moment'. The effect of this technique is that 'traditional unity is broken; in its place is the unity of Dublin'. What is ignored in replacing a unity of the characters' actions with a unity of place is precisely the 'social organism' of 'humanity in its advance towards socialism'.

Although West believes that Joyce ultimately fails to produce an aim for social advancement which would be acceptable in terms of the Marxist demand for satisfactory social realism, he also sees Joyce's creation of a unity of place offering a vision of social organisation that could have been developed in acceptable Marxist terms. Joyce's technique of developing a unity of place 'comes from a new vision of society growing out of its new social basis' (118). The Marxist theory of the relationship between the individual and society is that:

> Reality is not what is perceived as such by members of the bourgeois class because of its direct effort on their financial and emotional affairs. Reality, as expressed through this technique (the statement will have to be considerably modified), is the sum of all relations, whether directly connected or not. This technique is an expression of those forces to which Marx gave formulation when he said that society is the totality of relations.
>
> (118)

In *Ulysses*, there is 'not only a continual jumping from one line of action to another; there is also a change in the conception of the individuals performing these actions' (119). Stephen and Bloom are interdependent and 'conceived in terms of relation, not of distinct demarcated consciousness... Bloom is not himself without Stephen, nor Stephen without Bloom'. To a certain extent, West believes, 'Bourgeois individualism is abandoned for a new social vision' and 'Joyce hastens the advance to socialism to the extent to which he hastens this change of outlook' (119). What prevents Joyce from fully developing this social vision is a flaw which Joyce shares with other members of the bourgeois class – an inability to decide on a particular course of action:

> Joyce... exemplifies the typical difficulties of intelligent, sensitive members of the bourgeois class. He has the sense of change, he wishes to take part in it; but he is unable to decide for any particular activity.
>
> (118)

Like the Soviet critic Kashkin, West sees Stephen's situation reflecting Joyce's. While Joyce and Stephen both reject the Catholic Church neither of them move beyond this initial stage of rejection:

The refusal to serve the Catholic Church, the body which holds the keys of heaven and hell, had become service of the Catholic Church, the ally of British capitalism on earth; for it provided the justification of reaction. But as long as Joyce continued to write through Stephen, he had to go on repeating the proud defiance of the Church, for that was Stephen's only reality. He could not develop this defiance of hell into a defiance of capitalism, because he believed in the Church and God by negation.

(116)

The rejection of the Catholic Church operates as a negative force which prevents Joyce from accepting socialism: 'Joyce was prevented from accepting directly and openly the ideas of socialism by his individualistic denial of, and his negative belief in, catholicism' (117). While Joyce comprehends the division between socialist and capitalist social structures and has a sensitivity to both socialist development and the contradiction it engenders between itself and capitalism, he also wishes to work within an old literary tradition:

Though Joyce rejected [socialism] when the issue was put to him in terms of action, he felt the movement very strongly, and took active part in it when it did not bear the name of the movement to socialism. Joyce has been profoundly sensitive to the development of the basis of socialism and the contradiction between that basis and the old capitalist relations; and he has realised and hastened the corresponding change in our attitude, intellectual and emotional. His work is an attempt to find an expression for that change, while remaining within the old tradition.

(117)

West believes that the 'strength of Joyce's technique' in *Ulysses* lies in Joyce's ability to express the book's content 'through bodily movement' (126). He sees the ship which Stephen sees entering Dublin Bay at the beginning of *Ulysses* involved in such a movement. 'What [Stephen] sees':

is an objective reality, described with objective exactness ('her sails brailed up on the crosstrees'); but through the associations of 'crosstrees' with cross and so with the Catholic Church, and through 'homing' – for Stephen is in search of a father – the objective world is transformed into Stephen's world. This silent movement of the ship is like a musical chord, which continues to sound through the book (it was already mentioned how Mrs Bloom throws a penny to a sailor from this ship), and at the end it is resolved, when Bloom and Stephen having met they listen to the Odyssey of this same sailor in the cabmen's shelter.

(126)

West argues, however, that while such techniques produce a 'slow charging of the atmosphere... with the expectancy of change', *Ulysses* ultimately 'brings no satisfaction to that sense of change'. 'We are stimulated', he states, 'and then nothing comes but barren mysticism, insincerity and coldness'. Joyce, West contends, lacks a certain commitment:

> Joyce does not throw his whole heart into anything: not into Stephen,
> because he knows this lonely challenger of God is miles behind the fight;
> not into Bloom, because he is partly a rest from Stephen and a parody of
> him. He plays off one against the other, and does not fully believe in either.
> Neither singly nor in conjunction, do they represent anything which the
> social energy Joyce arouses can identify itself with.
>
> (126)

While the book embodies 'the two styles of change and stability', Joyce 'seems to play with' them much as 'he plays with his two chief characters' (127). Similarly, Joyce creates contradictions, but plays with them and 'does not resolve them'. He 'only shifts from one foot to the other, while he sinks deeper into the sandflats':

> Joyce cannot identify himself with any particular phase of social movement.
> The book is partly an act of vengeance on the social forces, as a part of which
> he could find no satisfying activity – on catholicism and capitalism, on his
> own ideals, on the new form of organisation whose development he sensed.
> Everything is annihilated in universal meaninglessness: he sat on his low-
> backed car and looked after their low-backed car. But at the same time all
> these forces are also used to develop an activity – this particular way of
> writing – which will be satisfying to the weary man-child. Resentment and
> weariness seem to me the fundamental mood of *Ulysses*.
>
> (127)

Terry Eagleton

In *Exiles and Émigrés: Studies in Modern Literature* (London: Chatto and Windus, 1970) Eagleton examines Joyce in the context of modern writers for whom exile or émigré status was a major factor in their work. Eagleton's study is in part an attempt to answer the question 'Why... should it be that, at the heart of this felt disintegration [of English society], the great art of English literature should have been the work of foreigners and émigrés?' (15). The viewpoint from which Eagleton investigates the work of the 'foreigners and émigrés', Eliot, Lawrence, Pound, Yeats and Joyce, is that of social class. Expressing his awareness of the 'severe penalties which contemporary criticism has in store for anyone rash enough to venture the suggestion that "literature" and "class" can be significantly related', Eagleton qualifies his view of the relationship between class and literature:

> What I am concerned with is not some crude reduction of imaginative liter-
> ature to a kind of 'class-determinism': that is to say, with the method often,

and wrongly, thought to be Marxist. I am concerned to see the ways in which the social attitudes adopted by particular twentieth-century writers shape or limit their power to achieve that sense of interrelation between concrete living and the shape of a complete culture which the greatest nineteenth-century authors displayed.

(11–12)

In contrast to twentieth-century writers, nineteenth-century authors like Blake, Wordsworth, Dickens and George Eliot were 'able to fuse the profoundest inwardness with the specific life of their own times with a capacity to generalise that life into the form of a complete vision' (10).

This unified vision was no longer possible in the twentieth century, Eagleton explains, because of the 'inability of indigenous English writing, caught within its partial and one-sided attachments, to "totalise" the significant movements of its own culture' (15). The years of the First World War constitute a period when 'English civilization itself was called into radical question', and '[a]fter this period... exhaustion, futility and disintegration strike at the heart of conventional English society'. The work of English writers like Waugh and Huxley 'responded to the crisis of its society... with an external cynicism [and] with a sense of disgusted futility which was itself a symptom, rather than a creative interpretation, of disturbance' (15). In contrast to this situation, Joyce and the other modernists whose works Eagleton investigates 'had immediate access to alternative cultures and traditions: broader frameworks against which, in a highly creative tension, the erosion of contemporary order could be situated and understood' (15). Joyce 'rejected that native lineage' upon which Yeats drew and 'moved to Europe; but he was able to use some of its tools to create an aesthetic and a mythology within which the determining contemporary experience could be grasped'. He 'rejected' the 'specific contents' of both the Catholicism and Nationalism which he inherited, 'yet he remained enduringly indebted to its totalising forms, within which art and religion, history and politics, could still be seen in organic interconnection' (16). Eagleton believes that Joyce maintained an '*ambivalent* stance towards his culture' which is related to the 'tension' and the 'pattern of attraction and repulsion' informing his work. Like Yeats, Joyce 'reveal[s] a complex relation to [his] own societ[y] which was not, on the whole, reproduced in England' (16).

The problems which Eagleton identifies in English novelists are problems which he sees as being 'hinged on the common difficulty of discovering, in a social condition felt as fragmentary and flawed, a vantage point from which a coherent moral and artistic statement could be made' (138). For writers like Joyce, Eliot and Yeats, however, the 'mode of myth' enabled them to achieve a certain coherence: 'myth has again and again been offered as fulfilling the purposes which, in the work of [English novelists], could not be attained by a significant organisation of ordinary experience' (139). Unlike West, Eagleton does not see Joyce as failing to resolve the contradictions that his work creates, but as using myth to unite them in a coherent whole. Eagleton's more sophisticated view of the relationship between literature, its aesthetics and its social context is also much more expansive than West's and is able comfortably to accommodate myth as an integral part of the dialectical processes between the writer and society and literature and its social context.

Eagleton cites Eliot's admiration of *Ulysses*' 'deployment of myth as a way of lending cohesion to the "vast panorama of anarchy and futility that is contemporary civilisation"' but suggests that what Eliot really 'appreciated in the novel... was primarily the parallel it offered to his own *Waste Land*' (171). He thinks it important to understand the 'paradoxical sense in which Joyce is most different from Eliot where he seems most alike':

> in the flagrantly imposed quality of the mythic structure itself. The outrageousness of *Ulysses* is that the myth by which the experience of Dublin is welded into synthetic unity has no inward and necessary conjunction with that experience at all: one could imagine Joyce having put a quite different myth to the same purpose, with the same exhaustive ingenuity. And this, indeed, is part of the novel's point: the relation between myth and experience is so patently gratuitous that their interpenetration can only be aesthetically, rather than 'realistically', convincing... [I]t is hardly possible to doubt that it *is*, self-consciously, artificial, in a way that Eliot's does not at points *appear* to be.
>
> (171)

To Eagleton, Eliot's seemingly 'neutral' use of myth is actually part of a 'rigging of local detail to confirm a tendentious private view which is then offered as neutral – as a product of the European mind' (172). In contrast to this, Joyce's highly contrived and self-consciously artificial use of myth paradoxically achieves an 'autonomous' 'naturalistic reality':

> what is striking about *Ulysses* – what is, in fact, part of its overall irony – is that its level of naturalistic reality, rigidly controlled as it is, in every quarter, by the exigencies of myth, remains densely and specifically autonomous. The myth is, as it were, so intimately moulded to Dublin life, so persistently and pervasively present, that to all intents and purposes it disappears. It is so intricately in command of the whole creation that its presence is at no particular point obtrusive. The contrast with Eliot is thus significant: for Eliot's use of myth to communicate a personal attitude can be felt, on occasions, in precisely that kind of unwarranted local intervention.
>
> (172)

In Chapter One we examined structuralist views of myth and touched on the possibility that Joyce's use of myth could be considered as the sort of process to which the anthropologist Lévi-Strauss applies the term *bricolage*. Eagleton thinks that *Finnegans Wake* is 'best understood in the light of those modes of explaining myth developed by the structuralist school of anthropology' (173), and that what 'is operative' in the text is 'a kind of poetic rationality akin to what Lévi-Strauss has named *bricolage*':

> a ceaseless combination and permutation of the fragments of a multiple number of myths into a kind of meta-myth, a total structure with a number of interpenetrating levels, any one of which can be 'read off' in terms of any number of others.
>
> (173)

Combining Lévi-Strauss's concept of *bricolage* with Marxist dialectic, Eagleton views the *Wake* as a novel which

> stacks myths behind myths behind myths, combining dissolving and integrating them in a number of simultaneous perspectives, such that an examination of the dialectical logic at work throughout the book would strictly require the sort of three-dimensional model which structural anthropologists have in fact constructed to grasp the endlessly complex workings of primitive mythologies.
>
> (173)

From his Marxist perspective, Eagleton sees Lévi-Strauss's analysis of primitive myths uncovering a sort of dialectical process which requires a process of decoding that can uncover the ways in which meaning moves from one structure to another:

> Lévi-Strauss points out that there is at work, in these primitive mythologies, a kind of dialectics by which the fragments which compose a particular mythical totality can be simultaneously 'decoded' on a number of other models, so that the whole system is in constant interaction; there is... a mechanism inherent in the system which allows meaning to be constantly transferred from one level or structure to another.
>
> (173)

This process of decoding is very similar to that which we saw Umberto Eco follow as he used terms from the *Wake* in order to show how the text operates to produce the very terms with which it defines itself. Like Eco, Eagleton sees the *Wake*'s puns and other 'auditory allusions' as the text's basic structural units, but while he shares Eco's view of the sort of associations that the reader must follow in decoding the *Wake*, Eagleton also perceives a dialectic process at work in the relations between the text's phonetic units:

> In *Finnegans Wake*, that dialectic is present as auditory allusion: each unit of sound has a multiple set of implications which permits it to be endlessly combined with other, similarly allusive units, to form structures which can in turn be broken down and reconstituted into larger or subsidiary myths. The function of *bricolage* is served here, essentially, by the pun. In the same way, a character in *Finnegans Wake* can exist simultaneously on four or five

levels of mythic meaning: characters, like words, behave as symbols through which different levels of myth can be reciprocally mediated to one another.

(173)

Although he sees Joyce's uses of myth in *Ulysses* and the *Wake* as very different from each other, Eagleton believes that they ultimately serve the same purpose: in the *Wake*, '[a]s in Ulysses, the whole of this mythical structure may be said to project certain of Joyce's own attitudes: a particular view of history, and of the nature of historical change, can no doubt be distilled from its complexities' (173).

Eagleton's Marxist view of Joyce is much clearer in *Criticism and Ideology: A Study in Marxist Literary Theory* (London: Verso, 1978) than in *Exiles and Émigrés*. While the latter is concerned primarily with Joyce's exile and the relationship between that exile and the ways in which Joyce used myth to produce a coherent vision, the former elaborates a complex Marxist theory and uses Joyce's writing in order to illustrate that theory. One of Eagleton's primary concerns in *Criticisms and Ideology* is with the relationships which exist between political ideology and literary form, and one of the tasks which Eagleton sets for himself is to dispel the idea of a 'direct, spontaneous relation between text and history' (70). According to Eagleton this is an idea that belongs to a 'naïve empiricism which is to be discarded'. A text 'may speak of real history, of Napoleon or Chartism', he argues, 'but even if it maintains empirical historical accuracy this is always a *fictive* treatment – an operation of historical data according to the laws of textual production' (70). In historical literary works the 'particular history' which the work presents 'is being fictionalized', which means that it is 'construed in terms of an *ideological* production of its agents' modes of ideological insertion into it...' (70, emphasis added). Construing the history of a literary work in this manner means that it is 'rendered as *ideology to the second power*' (70).

The way in which history 'enters' a text is 'precisely *as ideology* as a presence determined and distorted by its measurable absences' (72). The reader can have no direct experience of history in a text, only an experience of it 'in the form of a double absence':

> The text takes as its object, not the real, but certain significations by which the real lives itself – significations which are themselves the product of its partial abolition. Within the text itself... ideology becomes a dominant structure, determining the character and disposition of certain 'pseudo-real' constituents. This inversion, as it were, of the real historical process, whereby in the text itself ideology seems to determine the historically real rather than *vice versa*, is itself naturally determined in the last instance by history itself. History, one might say, is the *ultimate* signifier of literature, as it is the ultimate signified.
>
> (72)

Like the semioticians whose studies we examined in Chapter Two, Eagleton views literary texts as a signifying practice, and it is in this context that he introduces the emphasis that Marxism places on historical, social and material formations: 'For what else in the end', he asks, 'could be the source and object of any signifying process but the real social formation which provides its material matrix?' (72).

While Eagleton suggests that the 'real social formation' is the 'source' and 'object' of the literary text's signification, he also thinks it necessary to define that text's 'signified' in order to 'resolve a possible ambiguity as to what precisely constitutes' its signified (80). Distinguishing between the text's 'pseudo-real' constituents and the 'historically real', he explains that the 'signified *within the text* is... its "pseudo-real" – the imaginary situations which the text is "about". But this pseudo-real is not to be directly correlated with the historically real; it is, rather, an effect or aspect of the text's whole process of signification.' The signified of the 'whole process' of the text's signification 'is ideology, which is itself a signification of history'. Eagleton offers a diagram (Fig. 8) (which is similar to the one by Barthes which we looked at in Chapter Two) in order to clarify these relations.

The relations between ideology and the text are complex, and Eagleton finds it necessary 'to be more precise both about the ideology which the text works, and the process of that working' (80). The text 'does not simply "take" ideological materials which are extrinsic to it', because ideology 'pre-exists the text'. But 'the *ideology of the text* defines, operates, and constitutes that ideology in ways unpremeditated, so to speak, by ideology itself'. The 'ideology of the text', however, 'has no pre-existence: it is identical with the text itself'. There is thus a 'double relation... between text and ideology': the 'objectively determinable relation' between them, and 'that relation as "subjectively" flaunted, concealed, imitated, or mystified by the text itself' (80–1).

The relations between a text and the pre-existing ideology can be perceived in the text's reproduction of the 'common discourse of its society',

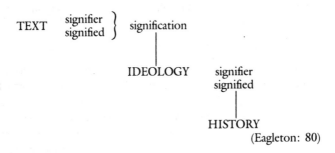

Figure 8

and with the exception of 'works whose "relation" to ordinary language is one of direct negation [Eagleton cites the example of texts 'written in the language of an imperial ruling class'], every text bears some relation' to this discourse (82). There are two ways in which a text can operate with the discourse of its society: it can offer an imitation of that discourse which 'seems to reproduce it' or it can employ 'devices' which 'radically transmute such speech'. Eagleton cites *Finnegans Wake* as a text which operates according to the second of these methods. Its 'linguistic devices... signal a set of mutations of ideological "discourses" in a wider sense – perceptions, assumptions, symbolisations'. Through the 'workings of aesthetic ideology', Joyce's text 'achieves' a 'production of already-produced categories'. The *Wake* provides an example of a text which, 'through its formal devices, establishes a transformative relation between itself and ideology which allows us to perceive the usually concealed contours of the ideology from which it emerges' (82).

As we have already seen, Eagleton sees much of the power of Joyce's work resulting from Joyce's position in exile. He also compares Joyce's relationship to his own Irish society with the 'fraught, problematic relation to society [which] is, so to speak, confiscated [from "native" English writers] by the *émigré* writers – James and Conrad... Eliot and Pound' (126). This confiscation is made possible in England as the 'petty-bourgeois realist tradition declines towards the end of the century into naturalism (Gissing, Wells, Bennet)', and Eagleton sees a 'similarly ambiguous relationship occurring in twentieth-century Irish society, to produce the major art of Yeats and Joyce' (126). In focusing specifically on the case of Joyce, Eagleton makes the comparison more clear:

> There is a sense in which James Joyce's relation to W. B. Yeats is analogous to Henry James' relation to Joseph Conrad. Both Joyce and James displace into the devotional realm of art itself the unity which the two other writers still struggle to locate in a social tradition. Born into the Catholic petty bourgeoisie, Joyce rejected the Romantic Anglo-Irish tradition as bankrupt (he thought Yeats 'a tiresome idiot... quite out of touch with the Irish people'), and its mystificatory aesthetic of inspirational spontaneity; art instead was a productive *labour*, a massive, life-consuming substitute for the social identity denied by a stagnant, clericist, culturally parochial Ireland.
>
> (154)

While Joyce's social class was different to Yeats', he was 'as ambiguously related to Irish nationalism as Yeats'. Citing Joyce's support of Sinn Fein as well as his 'deluded' comparison of 'the socialism of its leader Arthur Griffiths to Labriola's Marxism', Eagleton describes Joyce's 'abandonment of Ireland' as 'in part a protest against the bourgeois limitations of nationalism', and 'a decisive rupture with its sentimental patriotism, superstitious religiosity and cultural philistinism'. Yeats isolated himself from Irish nationalism by identifying with what Eagleton describes as 'Ascendency reaction'; Joyce did so through an 'opposing commitment':

> Writing to his brother from Trieste... he insists that a 'deferment to the emancipation of the proleteriat, a reaction to clericism or aristocracy or bourgeoisism would mean a revulsion to tyrannies of all kinds'. In the determinate absence of such emancipation in Ireland, Joyce's painful self-liberation from clericism and imperialism had to be achieved, materially and spiritually, through his art.
>
> (154–5)

Eagleton's view of the contradictions in Joyce's work is much more complex than that provided by West, who saw Joyce's work in terms of a fairly simple set of contradictions that Joyce failed to resolve. For Eagleton, Joyce's art 'is not to be seen as the "expression" of the contradictions of Joyce's own "class situation",' but as 'internal contradictions' which are a '*production*, not a reflection, of the ideological formation into which Joyce as historical subject was ambivalently inserted' (155). By 'putting that ideology to work', Joyce's text 'exposes its framing limits'. The aesthetic ideology of Joyce's work is not a 'simple "reflection" of the ideological formation as a whole', but the production of a more complex formation:

> Joyce was born into an ideological sub-ensemble which formed a contradictory unit with the dominant ideology. That relation was then over-determined by his expatriatism, which reproduced that initial contradictory unity in quite different terms. The complexity of this formation is 'produced' at the level of Joyce's aesthetic ideology.
>
> (155)

The naturalistic strand in Joyce's work reflects the 'double relation' which we have seen Eagleton define as characteristic of the text-ideology. In 'one sense', Joyce's 'literary naturalism is... a fidelity to the "realities" of petty-bourgeois Dublin'; at the same time, 'it is also a commitment to a cosmopolitan perspective within which those "realities" could be critically distanced'. Unlike the English writers caught within the crisis of their society, Joyce could use this cosmopolitan perspective which his exile afforded in order to produce a unified vision sustained by the contradictions of naturalism and classical realism:

> Naturalism for Joyce signifies petty-bourgeois paralysis, but is also contradictorily unified with the serene realism of classical epic and the 'realist' scholasticism of the hegemonic Irish order. In *Ulysses*, accordingly, a pedantically 'scholastic' and 'materialist' mythology is used to situate materially-bound society. Conversely, Joyce's commitment to a transcendence and recuperation of Irish society through art links him with certain Romantic and aesthetic aspects of the hegemonic aesthetic ideology...
>
> (155)

Joyce's links with these latter elements of aesthetic ideology are at work in *Stephen Hero*'s use of the 'idealist notion of the "Romantic artist"... as a characteristically *petty-bourgeois* ideology of artistic production' (155).

Eagleton also sees Joyce's work as much more complex than West does, and he states that the 'complex transactions' between naturalism and realism and text and ideology 'overdetermine the crisis of literary discourse to which Joyce belongs' (155). He sees this crisis in *Dubliners*' production of 'frustrated desires, fading memories and impotent dreams' all of which 'play listlessly within a drably naturalistic context, to encapsulate the spiritual inertia of contemporary Ireland'. Like Cixous, Eagleton emphasises the importance of the blanks and absences in the style of the short stories. He describes this style as 'resolutely uncommitted, blankly self-effacing' and 'resonant with absences [which] embody themselves in the calculatedly meagre, inconclusive quality of the narratives themselves' (156). The style 'undercuts' the stories' detailed naturalistic 'content' and its implications of an 'intimacy with Dublin life' (155). Like *Ulysses*, Eagleton contends, *Dubliners* 'defiantly' withholds 'organic closure' (156).

In contrast to West's earlier assessment that Joyce failed to resolve the contradiction symbolised in *Ulysses* by Bloom and Stephen, Eagleton argues that they are resolved. Where West sees Bloom and Stephen representing the material and the ideal respectively, Eagleton sees them as 'material existence' and '"alienated" artistic consciousness', and he argues that the text '"resolves" the contradiction between' them 'in its *formal* tressing of naturalist and mythological codes, just as Joyce himself surmounts this duality in his "author-as-producer" aesthetic' (156). In his ambivalent relation to the Romantic aesthetic ideology, Joyce 'rejects the Romantic subjectivism of Stephen, while preserving (unlike Bloom) the essentially Romantic creed of total self-dedication to art'. This 'formal interpenetration' also serves another purpose:

> [It] is an immense, self-flaunting structural irony, so elaborately and exhaustively achieved that it draws attention to its flagrantly synthetic basis in Homeric myth. Indeed the factitiousness of that formal 'resolution' is satirically revealed in the novel's *content* – in the unepiphanic non-event of the meeting of Stephen and Bloom, the central absence around which the text's complexities knot. The unity of material life and self-exiled artistic consciousness which Joyce seeks is achieved not *in* the work but *by* it...
>
> (156)

Like Eco, who draws on Jakobson's idea that the aesthetic text is characterised by self-reflectiveness, Eagleton sees Joyce producing a text which is in certain ways a text written about itself: '*Ulysses* is a novel about the conditions of its own production, subsisting in its ironic identity with and dissonance from the Homeric myth which provides its "raw materials".' In a view of *Ulysses* which shares several similarities with Eco's view of the *Wake*, Eagleton explains that *Ulysses*' 'seamless, organic composition of those materials [from the Homeric myth] is a phenomenon of the text as autonomous *product*, by which the very completeness of its closure invites the reader to deconstruct the text into the contradictions of its process of production' (156).

Like his view of *Ulysses*, Eagleton's thoughts on the *Wake* also show some similarities to Eco's ideas about Joyce's text. Eco sees the *Wake* as an open text, and while Eagleton thinks that it is 'a work which is at once "closed" and "open"', his view of its 'open' status is similar to Eco's theories on its open, universal and codified/codifying status: 'by attempting to absorb the whole of reality into itself, [it] becomes coterminous with the universe, and so an "open" play of codes, differences, transformations' (157). On the other hand, as a 'closed' text, the *Wake* is 'an elaborate, self-sealing system, powered by the "totalising" drive which Joyce inherited from the scholasticism to which he declared himself in everything but the premises'. The elements which make the text at once open and closed are combined with Joyce's view of 'reality itself' as 'one immense organic artefact, a sealed, interpenetrative system powered by its own laws, ceaselessly in flux yet fundamentally stable' (157). The result of this combining is that the 'organic literary work thereby becomes a "scientific" model of the world itself, enacting in the laws of its structure the dynamic stasis of the cosmos itself'. Joyce incorporates the human element of the world into his vision as 'specific sectors of [the] cosmic process, determined by its unalterable laws, moving inexorably through their Viconian cycles to provide the spectatorial artist with his classical vision of "security and satisfaction and patience"'. Joyce is linked with Yeats through an aesthetic ideology, which, 'like that of the mature Yeats marks a retreat from a history of crisis'. But in contrast to 'Yeats, Eliot, and Lawrence', Eagleton concludes, 'Joyce remains a progressive, prototypically urban producer, exploiting difference, disconnection, splitting, permutation and simultaneity as the very forms of his art' (157).

Fredric Jameson

Like Eagleton, Jameson is a Marxist critic who has both written on Joyce and used Joyce's work in order to illustrate Marxist theory. In *Marxism and Form: Twentieth-Century Dialectical Theories of Literature* (Princeton: Princeton UP, 1972), Jameson uses *Ulysses* as part of his analogy to explain the dialectical development of music which resulted in Schoenberg's twelve-tone system. In very crude terms, dialectical development follows the pattern of thesis, antithesis and synthesis in which a thesis is opposed by an antithesis with which it is sublated in the production of a synthesis that will, in turn, function as a thesis with which the dialectical progress will continue. In his investigation of T. W. Adorno's theoretical perspective on Schoenberg, Jameson discusses the breakdown of the opposition between the 'momentary intersection of [polyphonic] voices in movement' and the 'massive intertwining of harmonic levels in a chord structure' (30). In what Jameson describes as the 'seething texture of Schoenberg's mature works', this antithetical opposition 'is abolished, and the [tone] row, which may at first have resembled an intricate, lengthy, highly articulated theme or melody, also serves... as the building block for the vertical dimension of the score'. The row serves two functions which had previously been assigned to the antithetical melodic and harmonic axes, and it may be crudely considered as a dialectical synthesis of these two previously opposed elements of musical composition. The 'twelve tone system serves as a kind of unified field theory for music, in which the data of harmony and that of counterpoint can now be translated back and forth' (30).

Establishing an analogy with the development of the novel, Jameson explains that:

> In the form of the novel this evolution follows a rigorous and exemplary internal logic: the earliest realistic novels justify their contingent elements – descriptions, historical background, choice of a particular subject such as the life of a soap manufacturer or a doctor – on the purely empirical grounds that such phenomena already exist in the world around us, and that they therefore need no justification.
>
> (30–1)

In the writing of Zola a major development occurs, and 'this empirical motivation is joined by a second one', which exists in a sort of antithetical relation to the motivation of earlier realistic writing (31). The second motivation 'rises oddly behind [the first] like the symptom-formulation of a repressed impulse: this is the tendency to turn such facts, which seem to have no intrinsic self-justifying meaning in themselves, into symbols or grossly materialized pictures of meanings'. In *Ulysses*, these two motivations are synthesised within the novel's structure:

> Finally, with Joyce's *Ulysses*, which seemed at the time so naturalistic and conclusive a slice of life, this impulse has become a conscious intention, and the literary materials lead a double life on two separate levels, that of empirical existence and that of a total relational scheme not unlike the twelve-tone system itself, where each empirical fact is integrated into the whole, each chapter dominated by some basic symbolic complex, the motifs of the work related to each other by complicated charts and cross references, and so forth.
>
> (31)

This is the first of three dialectical patterns of development that Jameson finds at work in Joyce. The second is provided by Joyce's writing style, which offers an 'exemplary progress from a derivative personal style... through the multiple pastiches of *Ulysses*, toward something which transcends both style and pastiche altogether and which, like the twelve-tone system in the musical realm, may stand as a distant representation of some future linguistic organization of a postindividualistic character' (34). A third dialectical pattern operates in the relationship between 'matter' and 'spirit' and produces 'the synthesis of Joyce, in which matter once again seems momentarily reconciled with spirit, all the objects and detritus of the city luminous and as though informed by subjectivity' (42). This synthesis, however, is marked by a 'precariousness', and its 'seams show': 'there is something willful and arbitrary about the relationship of the individual chapters to each other, and the new reconciliation is paid for as dearly as that of Schoenberg in music' (42).

Elaborating his theory of the dialectical development of literature, Jameson explains that the 'dialectical model allows a given phenomenon to be perceived as a moment or single interlocking section in a single articulated process' (312). There is, however, an 'initial problem which a dialectical theory of literature has to face': 'the unity of the literary work itself'. A literary work's 'existence as a complete thing... an autonomous whole... resists assimilation to the totality of the historical here and now... just as stubbornly as it refuses dissolution in some supraindividual history of forms' (313). This problem is exemplified by *Ulysses*, for if one considers the 'real' historical period of 1922, one must ask 'in what sense' Joyce's book 'can... be said to be a part of the events which took place in [that year]?' 'It is clear', Jameson concludes:

> that even the self-sufficiency of the work of art varies, depending on whether it deliberately invites comparison with the whole of what already exists in the form, as with the Renaissance sonnet or the Japanese haiku, or, like *Ulysses* and *The Divine Comedy*, aims at replacing all of culture by summing it up in a single book of the world, where, however, the idea of the Book remains itself a fact of culture and element in the generic background against which the work is perceived.
>
> (313)

The problematic relationship between *Ulysses* and history upon which Jameson touches in *Marxism and Form* is dealt with in much more detail in '*Ulysses* and History', Jameson's contribution to *James Joyce and Modern Literature* (London: Routledge and Kegan Paul, 1982). In *The Political Unconscious: Narrative as a Socially Symbolic Act* (Ithaca: Cornell UP, 1981), Jameson argues for 'the priority of the political interpretation of literary texts' on the grounds that such interpretation:

> conceives of the political perspective not as some supplementary method, not as an optional auxillary to other interpretive methods current today –

the psychoanalytic or the myth-critical, the stylistic, the ethical, the structural – but rather as the absolute horizon of all reading and all interpretation.

(17)

It is from this position that Jameson begins '*Ulysses* in History' by considering earlier interpretations of Joyce's text which he describes as 'boring': 'those we can really make an effort to do without... in a social and global situation so radically different from that in which the canonical readings of this text were invented' (173).

Jameson is concerned with 'traditional interpretations' which 'have become so sedimented into our text... that it is hard to see it afresh and impossible to read it as though those interpretations had never existed' (174). The interpretations he has in mind are included in the sort which are specified in his above argument for the priority of political interpretation. In '*Ulysses* in History', Jameson focuses on the 'threefold' group of 'mythical... psychoanalytic, and... ethical readings':

> These are, in other words, the readings of *Ulysses*, first in terms of the Odyssey parallel; second, in terms of the father–son relationship; and third, in terms of some possible happy end according to which this day, Bloomsday, will have changed everything, and will in particular have modified Mr. Bloom's position in the home and relationship to his wife.
>
> (174)

Taking 'this last reading first', Jameson wonders why we try to transform Molly's monologue into something that it is not: 'why we are so attached to the project of making something decisive happen during this representative day, transforming it... into an Event'. More importantly, Jameson asks 'why we should be so committed to this particular kind of event, in which Mr. Bloom is seen as reasserting his authority in what can therefore presumably once again become a vital family unit'. Reminding us that Bloom 'has asked Molly to bring him breakfast in bed the next day', Jameson raises a question which is relevant to some of the feminist studies of Joyce that we considered:

> In this day and age, in which the whole thrust of militant feminism has been against the nuclear and the patriarchal family, is it really appropriate to recast *Ulysses* along the lines of marriage counselling and anxiously to interrogate its characters and their destinies with a view towards saving this marriage and restoring this family? Has our whole experience of Mr. Bloom's Dublin reduced itself to this, the quest for a 'happy ending' in which the hapless protagonist is to virilise himself and become a more successful realisation of the dominant, patriarchal, authoritarian male?
>
> (174)

Anticipating the objection that this sort of reading 'is part of the more general attempt to fit *Ulysses* back into the Odyssey parallel', Jameson suggests that such myth criticism fails to comprehend that the 'bankruptcy of the ideology of the mythic is... one feature of the bankruptcy of the ideology of modernism in general' (174–5). Furthermore, establishing the Odyssey parallels for *Ulysses* is 'scarcely a matter of interpretation – that is, no fresh meaning is conferred either on the classical Homeric text, nor on the practices of contemporary birth control, by matching these two things' (175). Because 'we can scarcely hope to read *Ulysses* as though it were called something else', Jameson suggests 'that we displace the act or operation of interpretation itself'. The parallels provided by Homer's text 'can... be seen as one of the organisational frameworks of the narrative text: but it is not itself the interpretation of that narrative, as the ideologues of myth have thought' (175).

For Jameson, '[g]enuine interpretation is something other than' the establishment of mythic parallels, and it 'involves the radical historisation of the form itself: what is to be interpreted is then the historical necessity for this very peculiar and complex textual structure or reading operation in the first place'. Jameson is 'anxious to rescue Joyce from the exceedingly doubtful merit of being called a symbolic writer', and to this end, he emphasises the importance of realising that the 'symbolic in literature' is 'bankrupt' (176–7). Drawing on 'Barthes' opposition between what exists and what means', Jameson asserts that 'the practice of symbolism... involves the *illicit* transformation of existing things into so many visible or tangible meanings' (176, emphasis added). Jameson contends that 'any art which practices symbolism is already discredited and worthless before the fact', because it ignores the dissociation of being and meaning which is so important to the crisis of modernism. It is not possible to begin interpreting *Ulysses*, or indeed any other modernist text, without first comprehending that the historical reasons for the 'modernist crisis' of the 'dissociation of the existent and the meaningful, that intense experience of contingency' is a development in human consciousness (177). The modernist 'discovery of the absurd and of the radical contingency and meaninglessness of our objective world is simply the result of the increasing lucidity and self-consciousness of human beings in a post-religious, secular, scientific age' (177).

Jameson asserts that 'we can make a beginning on' the 'radical historisation of the [literary] form' – the process of historisation which 'genuine interpretation' requires – 'by evoking the philosophical concept, but also the existential experience, called "contingency"' (175–6). This 'experience of contingency' 'confronts us' with the historical paradox that the city is meaningless (177). Situating this paradox in the historical context of modernism, Jameson explains that 'in previous [pre-modernist] societies':

> it was Nature that was meaningless or anti-human. What is paradoxical

about the historical experience of modernism is that it designates very precisely that period in which Nature – or the in- or anti-human – is everywhere in the process of being displaced or destroyed, expunged, eliminated, by the achievements of human praxis and human production.

(177)

Ulysses is a part of the 'great modernist literature', and, along with the work of writers such as Baudelaire and Flaubert, it is a 'city literature: its object is therefore the anti-natural, the humanised, par excellence, a landscape which is everywhere the result of human labour'. '[E]verything', Jameson explains, '– including the formerly natural, grass, trees, our own bodies – is finally produced by human beings'. Approaching the contingency produced by the modernist dissociation of meaning and existence from another perspective, Jameson asks: 'How can human production be felt to be absurd or contingent, when in another sense one would think it was only human labour which created genuine meaning in the first place?' The 'missing step' to explain this apparent contradiction is 'the gap between the fact of the human production of reality in modern times and the experience of the results or products of that production as meaningless'. This 'step' is also the 'essential mediation', that is 'surely to be located in the work process itself, whose organization does not allow the producers to grasp their relationship to the final product' (177).

Jameson discusses this work process as an example of reification at some length. He explains that 'one of the basic forms taken by reification as a process... can be called the analytical fragmentation of older organic... traditional processes' (178). This process of fragmentation 'can be seen on any number of levels':

> that of the labour process first of all, where the older unities of handicraft production are broken up... into the meaningless yet efficient segments of mass industrial production;... that of the psyche of psychological subject now broken up into a host of radically different mental functions, some of which – those of measurement and rational calculation – are privileged and others – the perceptual senses and aesthetics generally – are marginalized;... that of time, experience, and storytelling, all of which are inexorably atomised and broken down into their most minimal unities, into that well-known 'heap of fragments where the sun beats'...
>
> (178).

In terms of the three kinds of criticism that Jameson thinks 'we can really make an effort to do without', reification 'accounts... for the inadequacy of that third conventional interpretation of *Ulysses*... namely the fetishisation of the text in terms of "archetypal" patterns of father–son relationships, the quest for the ideal father or for the lost son, and so forth'. Jameson sees the concern with such interpretive approaches to the text as an 'obsession' with the relationships rather than a genuine concern with the interpretation of the text, and he argues that the 'privileging of such impoverished interpersonal schemas drawn from the nuclear family itself are to be read as break-down products and as defense mechanisms against the loss of the knowable community'. Instead of seeing the Bloom–Stephen relationship in terms of quest for a father (or son) as so many critics do, Jameson argues that:

> The father–son relationships in *Ulysses* are all miserable failures; above all the mythical ultimate 'meeting' between Bloom and Stephen; and if more is wanted on this particular theme, one might read into the record here the diatribes against the very notion of an Oedipus complex developed in Deleuze and Guattari's *Anti-Oedipus*, which I do not necessarily endorse but which should surely be enough to put an end to this particular interpretive temptation.
>
> (178)

Jameson sees the reifying, 'psychoanalytic or Oedipal interpretation' as no more than a 'subset of the *Odyssey* or mythical temptation', and neither approach can produce anything more than a 'matching up' of elements from Joyce's text with their 'mythic parallels' (179). He is interested in a 'rather different form of reading which resists [the mythic reading] in all sorts of ways, and ends up subverting it' (179). This reading 'interrupts the other, consecutive kind, and moves forwards and backwards across the text in a culminative search for the previous mention or the reference to come':

> as Kenner and others have pointed out, it is a type of reading, a mental operation, peculiarly inconceivable before printing, before numbered pages, and more particularly, before the institutionalisation of those unusual objects called dictionaries or encyclopedias.
>
> (179)

Warning against the temptation to 'assimilate the kind of reading to the more customary thematic or thematising kind, were we to compile lists of recurrent motifs, such as imagery, obsessive words or terms...', Jameson argues that such approaches cannot cover 'what happens in *Ulysses*, where the object of the cross-referencing activity is always an event' (179). These events include 'taking old Mrs. Riordan for a walk,... or the assassination in Phoenix Park twenty-two years before' (179–80). Such 'seemingly thematic motifs are here always referential; for they designate content beyond the text, beyond indeed the capacity of any given textual variant to express or exhaust them'. It is in the process of 'cross-referencing... that the referent itself is produced, as something which transcends every conceivable textualisation of it' (180).

The 'different form of reading' for which Jameson argues should also be able to deal with the 'recurrence of events and characters' in the text as 'a process whereby the text itself is unsettled and undermined, a process

whereby the universal tendency of its terms, narrative tokens, representations, to solidify into an achieved and codified symbolic order as well
as a massive narrative surface, is perpetually suspended'. Jameson calls this
process 'dereification', which indicates another reason why he sees the
interpretive strategies accounted for by reification as unsuitable strategies
for interpreting *Ulysses*. He describes the process of dereification in 'terms
of the city itself', not a city as a conglomerate of products (halls,
churches, houses, shops, streets, vehicles, etc.) but as a space for human
experience:

> the classical city is defined essentially by the nodal points at which all those
> pathways and trajectories meet, or which they traverse: points of totaliza-
> tion... which make shared experience possible...
>
> (180).

This 'spatially' defined city is mediated linguistically through a 'kind of
speech which is neither uniquely private nor forbiddingly standardised in
an impersonal public form, a type of discourse in which the same, in
which repetition, is transmitted again and again through a host of eventful
repetitions, each of which has its own value... gossip' (180–1). This,
Jameson believes, is the dereification that *Ulysses* achieves: Dublin as a city
manifest in the humanised 'ur-form' of a village which provides the spaces
for a 'shared experience' among its inhabitants:

> [I]n that great village which is Joyce's Dublin, Parnell is still an anecdote
> about a hat knocked off, picked up and returned, not yet a television image
> nor even a name in a newspaper; and by the same token, as in the peasant
> village itself, the ostensibly private or personal – Molly's infidelities, or Mr.
> Bloom's urge to discover how far the Greek sculptors went in portraying the
> female anatomy – all these things are public too, and the material for endless
> gossip and anecdotal transmission.
>
> (181)

Jameson considers the political implications of *Ulysses* as a dereification
of the city into a space where experience can be shared and mediated
through gossip by comparing Joyce's gossip with Heidegger's '*das gerede*'
– gossip as 'idle chatter', or the 'very language of inauthenticity...' (181).
'For certain conservative thought, and for that heroic fascism of the
1920s', he explains, 'the so-called "masses" and their standardised city life
had become the very symbol of everything degraded about modern
life...', and 'gossip... is stigmatised as... that empty and stereotypical
talking *pour rien dire* to which these ideologues oppose the supremely
private and individual speech of the death anxiety or the heroic choice'.
Although Joyce was 'a radical neither in the left-wing nor the reactionary
sense... [he] was at least a populist and a plebian'. In support of this
position, Jameson cites Joyce's complaint '"I don't know why the com-
munists don't like me... I've never written about anything but common

people"' (181). 'In class terms', says Jameson, 'Joyce's characters are all resolutely petty-bourgeois'. But this 'apparent limitation' is given a 'representative value' and 'strength' by Ireland's 'colonial situation' (182). 'Whatever his hostility to Irish cultural nationalism', Jameson contends, 'Joyce's is the epic of the metropolis under imperialism, in which the development of bourgeoisie and prolateriat alike is stunted to the benefit of a national petty-bourgeoisie':

> indeed, precisely these rigid constraints imposed by imperialism on the development of human energies account for the symbolic displacement and flowering of the latter in eloquence, rhetoric and oratorical language of all kinds; symbolic practices not particularly essential either to businessmen or to working classes, but highly prized in precapitalist societies and preserved, as in a time capsule, in *Ulysses* itself.
>
> (182)

The reason that *Ulysses* is 'also for us the classical, the supreme representation of something like the Platonic idea of city life', says Jameson, is 'partly due to the fact that Dublin is not exactly the full-blown capitalist metropolis, but... still regressive, still distantly akin to the village, still un- or underdeveloped enough to be representable, thanks to the domination of its foreign masters' (182).

The role of gossip in the operations of dereification is to act as the 'element in which reference... or the referent itself... expands and contracts, ceaselessly transformed from a mere token, a notation, a short-hand object, back into a full-dress narrative'. Pointing out that the 'process is... more tangible and more dramatic when we see it at work on physical things', Jameson cites examples of the process at work on:

> the statues, the commodities in the shopwindows, the clanking trolleylines that link Dublin to its suburbs (which dissolve, by way of Mr. Deasy's anxieties about foot-and-mouth disease, into Mr. Bloom's fantasy projects for tramlines to move cattle to the docks); or the three-master whose silent grace and respectability as an image is at length dissolved into the disreputable reality of its garrulous and yarn-spinning crewmen...
>
> (182).

As a 'final example', Jameson cites the 'file of sandwichmen whose letters troop unevenly through the text'. Bloom's fantasy about the boards carried by these men strikes Jameson as an 'ultimate visual reification... virtually in analogue to Mallarmé's "livre"':

> Of some one sole unique advertisement to cause passers to stop in wonder, a poster novelty, with all extraneous accretions excluded, reduced to its simplest and most efficient terms not exceeding the span of casual vision and congruous with the velocity of modern life.
>
> (*U*: 592; Cited: 183)

The letters on the sandwich boards provide Jameson with an analogy of the 'visual, the spatially visible, the image [that] is... the final form of the commodity itself, the ultimate terminus of reification' (183). But while the 'ambulatory letters of the sandwichmen are also the very emblem of textuality itself', they, too, can be 'effortlessly dereified and dissolved [as] when, on his way to the cabman's shelter, Stephen hears a down-and-out friend observe: "I'd carry a sandwichboard only the girl in the office told me they're full up for the next three weeks, man. God, you've to book ahead"' (183). The effect of this dereification is a further reification as the 'exotic picture-postcard vision of a tourist Dublin is transformed back into the dreary familiar reality of jobs and contracts and the next meal'. Yet, even this reification does not cease at this mundane financial level, and the transformation is 'not necessarily a dreary prospect': 'it opens up a perspective in which, at some ideal outside limit, everything seemingly solid and material in Dublin itself can presumably be dissolved back into the underlying reality of human relations and human praxis' (183).

There is, however, what Jameson calls a 'price [that] *Ulysses* must pay for the seemingly limitless power of its play of reification and dereification', and, in order to understand this price, it is necessary 'to come to terms with Joyce's modernism', with what we have seen Jameson describe as the 'contingency' and 'dissociation between meaning and existence' of modernism (183). This price is the 'radical depersonalisation' of writing, 'or in other words, Joyce's completion of Flaubert's programme of removing the author from the text – a programme which also removes the reader, and finally that unifying and organising mirage or aftermirage of both author and reader which is the "character", or better still, "point of view"':

> such essentially idealistic (or ideal, or imaginary) categories formerly served as the supports for the unity of the work or the unity of the process. Now that they have been withdrawn, only a form of material unity is left, namely the printed book itself, and its material unity as a bound set of pages within which the cross-references... are contained. One of the classical definitions of modernism is... the increasing sense of the materiality of the medium itself, the emergent foregrounding of the medium in its materiality.
>
> (183)

While Jameson realises that it is 'paradoxical... to evoke the materiality of language...', he argues that 'none the less, the role of the book itself is functionally analogous, in Joyce, to the materialist dynamics of the other arts' (183–4).

Jameson sees the materialist textuality of *Ulysses* sustaining a 'fluid relationship between the visually reified and the historically eventful' in which these categories 'pass ceaselessly back and forth into one another' (184). This relationship develops toward a climax that Jameson locates in what he calls the 'reading play' of 'Nighttown'. This section of the text is marked by 'seeming eruptions and intrusions of a properly theatrical space in that very different space... of narrative or novelistic represent-ation'. As Jameson is reaching the end of his examination of *Ulysses* at this point, he contents himself with suggesting that 'had we more time... I think we would have been able to show that this new space, with its ostensibly theatrical form (scenic indications, character attributions, printed speeches, notations of expression), has nothing to do with the closure of traditional theatrical representation; far more to do... with that space of hallucination in terms of which Flaubert often described his own creative process...'. The equivalent of the hallucination on the printed page is the process by which the 'ground, the anticipatory-retrospective texture, of narrative... is ruptured' (185). The 'discontinuous images' which result from this ruptured narrative, like many of those in the 'Nighttown' episode, are bound together by the 'typographic and material mechanisms of theatrical and scenic directions'. Like Hawkes, whose view of the 'Aeolus' episode's typography we considered in Chapter Two, Jameson sees the typography of the text as an 'event within the text like others'. Because the typography 'solicits' the 'reified sense of the visual... this sense will now begin to function as it were in the void, taking as its object the material signifiers, the printed words themselves, and no longer the latter's signifieds or representations or meanings' (185).

This 'peculiar climax' of the 'Nighttown' episode in which typograph-ical operations provide a material binding of the hallucinatory, 'discon-tinuous images', produces the 'unmediated experience' of the text as a 'printed book' which only 'seems' to be the 'immediacy of a theatrical representation' (184). According to Jameson, this climax can also 'help us to understand two kinds of things: the peculiarly anticlimatic nature of the chapters that follow it... and the ground on which the depersonalised textualisation of the narrative of *Ulysses* takes place'. Jameson is 'tempted to call' this depersonalised textualisation a 'kind of "autistic textualisa-tion"', and he describes it as the 'production of sentences in a void, moments in which the book begins to elaborate its own text, under its own momentum, with no further needs of characters, point of view, author or perhaps even reader'. Jameson cites the following passages as examples of this textual elaboration:

Mr. Bloom reached Essex bridge. Yes, Mr. Bloom crossed bridge of Yessex. Love loves to love love. Nurse loves the new chemist. Constable 14A loves Mary Kelly. Gerty MacDowell loves the boy that has the bicycle. M.B. loves a fair gentleman. Li Chi Han lovey up kissy Cha Pu Chow. Jumbo, the elephant, loves Alice, the elephant. Old Mr. Verschoyle with the ear trumpet loves old Mrs. Verschoyle with the turnedin eye... You love a certain person. And this person loves that other person because everybody loves something but God loves everybody.

(*U*: 215, 273; Cited: 185)

Passages such as these 'are everywhere in *Ulysses*', says Jameson, and '"point of view" theory does not take on them, nor any conceivable notion of the Implied Author, unless the I.A. is an imbecile or a schizophrenic'. The words are not spoken or thought by any one: 'they are simply... printed sentences' (185).

Jameson concludes '*Ulysses* in History' with a brief consideration of 'Eumaeus' and 'Ithaca' 'These two final Bloom chapters', he suggests, 'pose uncomfortable problems, and not least about narrative itself':

> the subjective or point-of-view chapter, 'Eumaeus', asks us why we should be interested in stories about private individuals any longer, given the extraordinary relativisation of all individual experience, and the transformation of its contents into so many purely psychological reactions. Meanwhile, the objective chapter, 'Ithaca', completes an infinite subdivision of the objective contents of narrative, breaking 'events' into their smallest material components and asking whether, in that form, they still have any interest whatsoever.
>
> (187)

Jameson describes these chapters as 'boring' in the sense that they 'force us to work through in detail everything that is intolerable about [the] opposition' and 'increasing separation', or 'reification' of 'the subject and the object' (186–7). But what Jameson calls boredom 'is not Joyce's failure... but rather his success, and... the signal whereby we ourselves as organisms register a situation but also forms that are finally stifling for us' (187).

The 'situation' of 'Ithaca' is: 'Two men have a discussion over cocoa.' While 'that may be interesting at a pinch', Jameson says, 'what about the act of putting the kettle on to boil – that is part of the same event, but is it still interesting?' (187). Jameson lists 'three senses of the word' which are applicable to the 'elaborate anatomy of the process of boiling water':

> 1) it is essentially non-narrative; 2) it is inauthentic, in the sense in which these mass-produced material instruments (unlike Homer's spears and shields) cannot be said to be organic parts of their user's destinies; finally 3) these objects are contingent and meaningless in their instrumental form, they are recuperable for literature only at the price of being transformed into symbols.
>
> (187)

For Jameson these passages like the discussion over cocoa and the boiling of the water 'ask three questions':

> 1. Why do we need narrative anyway? What are stories and what is our existential relation to them? Is a non-narrative relationship to the world and to Being possible?
> 2. What kind of lives are we leading and what kind of world are we living

them in, if the objects that surround us are all somehow external, extrinsic, alienated?...

3. ... How can the products of human labour have come to be felt as meaningless or contingent?

(187–8)

Jameson believes that Joyce's form has 'a kind of answer' to the third of these questions and that this answer is provided in the 'great movement of dereification... in which the whole dead grid of greater Dublin is, in the catechism chapter, finally disalienated and by the most subterranean of detours traced back... to the transformation of Nature by human and collective practice deconcealed'. Because it provides an answer to his last question, Jameson prefers 'to the vitalist ideology of Molly's better-known affirmation', that of the following passage:

What did Bloom do at the range?
He removed the saucepan to the left hob, rose and carried the iron kettle to the sink in order to tap the current by turning the faucet to let it flow.
Did it flow?
Yes. From Roundwood reservoir in country [sic] Wicklow of a cubic capacity of 2,400 [sic] million gallons, percolating through a subterranean aqueduct of filter mains of single and double pipage constructed at an initial plant cost of £5 per linear yard...

(*U*: 548; Cited: 188)

Remarks on a Marxist

As a sort of coda to Jameson's Marxist view of the relationship between *Ulysses* and history, it may be worth noting the sort of response that Jameson's view of history has prompted from the Joycean, Derek Attridge. Attridge is not a Marxist, but his 'Joyce, Jameson, and the Text of History' (*James Joyce 1: "Scribble" 1 genèse des textes* [Paris: Lettres Modernes, Minard, 1988]) affords us the opportunity of considering the sort of objections that a more conventional reader of Joyce has to Jameson's Marxist view of history. Attridge begins by juxtaposing Jameson's view of history with Stephen Dedalus' assertion that history is '*a nightmare from which I am trying to awake*'. In *The Political Unconscious*, which Attridge describes as 'a text that has to be taken into account by anyone working on the relation between "literature" and "history"', Jameson uses the epigram 'History Is What Hurts' and argues: '*This is indeed the ultimate sense in which History as ground and untranscendable horizon needs no particular theoretical justification: we may be sure that its alienating necessities will not forget us, however much we might prefer to ignore them*' (Jameson, 1981: 102; Cited: 183). At the heart of his response to Jameson's view of history is Attridge's perception of a disagreement between Joyce (represented in the introductory comparison by the view of Stephen Dedalus) and Jameson. According to Attridge, 'Jameson would prefer to believe that a day will dawn, and must dawn, when dreams and nightmares are all dissolved'. In Joyce, however, 'one does not find that sense... dawn at the end of *Finnegans Wake*, for instance, brings no daylight clarity or lucid and lasting truth' (185).

Attridge sees the disagreement between Jameson and Joyce as 'spring-[ing] from a substantial difference in their understanding of the relation between two senses of history' (185). From Attridge's perspective, Jameson's 'History' requires an 'acknowledgement both of the real contradictions that constitute History (or Necessity) and of the constitutive function of the texts in which those contradictions are represented' (185). In contrast to this, Attridge sees 'Joyce's texts... [as texts which] seem to imply that *all* versions of history are made in language and are, by virtue of that fact, ideological constructions, weavings and re-weavings of old stories, fusions of stock character types, blendings of different national languages, dialects and registers' (186). Setting aside the factual historical distinction between Joyce's fictive creations and the referents of the historical realities that he wove together with these creations, Attridge argues that the 'concrete evocation of a Dublin day in June 1904 in *Ulysses* is... a textual achievement in which Leopold Bloom is alive as George Russell, and the burying of Paddy Dignam in Glasnevin Cemetery as historical an event as the running of the Gold Cup' (186). While Attridge sees these distinctions between Joyce and Jameson, he also states that 'Joyce could be said to dramatize and amplify Jameson's argument that although history is not a text, it is "*inaccessible to us except in textual form, and that our approach to it and to the Real itself necessarily passes through its prior textualization*" [Jameson, 1981: 35]' (187).

Offering an interesting reversal of reading strategies, Attridge suggests that '[i]nstead of reading Joyce in the light of Jameson... it might be fruitful to read Jameson in the light of Joyce' (187). 'Can we', he asks, 'regard Jameson's texts as a web of stories, archetypes, verbal strategies, rhetorical ploys, in which the skilful [sic] handling of history as a mode of discourse produces an impression of privileged access to truth or the Real?' This might make it possible to 'regard' the part of Jameson's narrative with which Attridge concerns himself as 'itself an ideological construction, designed to preserve intact a comfortable but threatened position – a position which succeeds in retaining *both* the reassurances of an ultimately knowable ground outside all textual operations (guaranteed for Jameson by the insights of Marx) *and* the invigorating potential of a powerful creative constitutive textuality' (188). This might be a view of Jameson's position which Jameson himself shares, and Attridge points out that 'Jameson, does not, it is true, disguise the logical impossibility of his position in relation to the two alternatives: he calls it a "*paradox*" and refers to its two dimensions as *"inseparable yet incommensurate"* ([Jameson, 1981] 81–2)' (188). Attridge thinks it 'naive', however, 'to think that ideology could be exorcised merely by the invocation of the term *paradox*'. 'This was, after all', he cautions, 'a favourite device of New Criticism, whose ideological stance is now unmistakeable' (188).

Attridge summarises his own view of Jameson as suggesting 'in effect,... that Jameson's text is subject to his own favourite manoeuvre, and that it can be subsumed into the wider notions of textuality, ideology and history that we find represented by Joyce' (190). 'In particular', Attridge contends:

> Joyce's writing (and those features of the literary which it exploits) enables us to challenge the separation of the two senses of 'history' implied in Jameson's argument and Stephen's reflections. It does this by questioning the division of the world into signs and referents, language and existents; it reminds us that signs are referents and existences too, and history as text or ideology is as real as the unfathomable history that hurts or gives us a back kick. In so far as texts – Joyce's or Jameson's – have *effects* on their readers... they are part of the Real.
>
> (190)

Attridge detects what he thinks is a 'false premise' in 'Jameson's version of the Scylla and Charybdis tale': 'that before we can act politically (and all action is to some degree political) we have to find a narrative which "convinces" us as true and all-subsuming'. He responds by contending 'in the spirit, I believe, of Joyce's writing, that we can, and must, continue to find ways of re-writing ourselves, our history, our future, one another, in a constantly reworded engagement with the nontextual Real and with a constant alertness to the effects we are producing by our textual activity' (191). Ultimately, Attridge sees Marxism as a 'rich tradition' with an 'important part to play in that engagement', and he concludes by praising Jameson's *The Political Unconscious* as:

> a superb example of the rewriting of that tradition for a particular time and place – a rewriting which, in its acknowledgement of the textuality of history, is testimony to the historical effectiveness of Joyce's own rewriting of history.
>
> (191)

•7• 'WITH A WHOLE FAMILY OF JAMES, JACQUES...':

Poststructuralist Joyce

POST-STRUCTURALIST JOYCE IS, as we have seen, the title of a collection of studies subtitled *Essays from the French*. According to Derek Attridge and Daniel Ferrer, the editors of the collection, these essays were 'brought together with two kinds of readers in mind... those with an interest in Joyce, and those with an interest in literary theory' (ix). The 'combination of these two concerns', say Attridge and Ferrer, 'is not something fabricated' for their book, 'but a matter of history... which the essays themselves exemplify':

> between the late 1960s and the early 1980s Joyce's writing was a stimulus, a focus, and a proving-ground for new modes of theoretical and critical activity in France, whose widespread impact has been one of the most striking features of the intellectual climate of recent years.
>
> (ix)

In the 'Introduction' to the collection, Attridge and Ferrer offer an explanation for Joyce's importance to writers engaged in these 'new modes' of criticism. 'The point is not that Joyce is the most perfect illustration' of the 'theory of the Text and the Subject... elaborated in Paris'. The theory of the text and the subject denies the possibility of an '*application* of a theory to a text', and affirms theory as a two-way exchange in which 'the text reads the theory at the same time as it is read by it' (10).

Attridge and Ferrer think that this two-way textual operation between theory and text is 'particularly true of Joyce: any reader cannot help but feel that the text constantly overreaches the landmarks established by the best critical constructions'. They describe some of the ways in which they see Joyce's writing performing this 'overreaching' and outline some of the poststructuralist reading strategies with which Joyce's readers can engage his writing:

> It is impossible to exert any mastery over it, its *shifts* are such that you can never pin it down in any definite place – it always turns up again, laughing, behind your back. In fact, the aim is not to produce a *reading* of this intract-able text, to make it more familiar and exorcise its strangeness, but on the contrary to confront its unreadability; not to produce an indefinite accumulation of its meanings... but to look at the mechanisms of its infinite productivity; not to explore the psychological depths of the author or characters, but to record the perpetual flight of the Subject and its ultimate disappearance; not to reconstruct the world presented by the text, but to follow up within it the strategies that attempt a deconstruction of represen-tation.
>
> (10)

These are just some of the strategies that the various essayists in *Post-structuralist Joyce* follow as they engage Joyce's texts. In addition to the studies by Cixous and Ferrer that we have already examined, Stephen Heath, Jacques Aubert, Jean-Michel Rabaté and André Topia all con-tribute to the different views of Joyce from the poststructuralist perspec-tives that are offered in this collection. We will give a brief consideration of their readings of Joyce before moving on to consider some of the intriguing relations which exist between Joyce's writing and the work of poststructuralism's leading theorist, Jacques Derrida.

Stephen Heath

Heath's 'Ambiviolences: Notes for reading Joyce' first appeared in *Tel Quel* (**50** [Summer], 1972). Its appearance in *Post-structuralist Joyce* carries a note from Heath stating that the 'piece is entirely past' and that he could no longer write the article 'in the same way' (31). Heath begins his 'Notes for reading Joyce' by outlining his view of the problem which Joyce's writing in *Finnegans Wake* creates for criticism. This writing produces 'two rigorously complementary poles of critical reaction'. One reaction is to reject Joyce's writing as an 'aberration' when 'faced with the specific practice of writing in Joyce's text' and the resulting 'impossibility of converting that text into a critical object'. The other reaction 'seek[s] to preserve Joyce's text for criticism', and 'finds itself obliged to that end to "reduce" its writing to the simple carrier of a message (a meaning) that it will be the critic's task to "extract from its enigmatic envelope"'. Heath sees neither reaction as satisfactory. The first would leave Joyce's writing unread, which is a choice that many academics make when faced with the difficulties of Joyce's work. The second reaction fails to understand that Joyce's writing in the *Wake* 'resists any homogenization' and 'disturb[s] the categories that claim to define and represent literary practice, leaving the latter in ruins, and criticism too' (32).

Discussing the *Wake*'s relationship to *Ulysses*, Heath states that '[w]hat is in question in the distinction between the two books, the day and the night, is not some quantifiable amount of darkness and daylight (is it really possible still to read Joyce in this way?) but specific practices of writing' (50). *Ulysses* is the 'definitive end of the realist novel' and following its appearance 'it will no longer be possible to write "innocently"... only to repeat in the assumption of a precise ideological position'. Contrasting the writings of the two books, Heath says that *Ulysses*:

> is the negation of the daylight world of the natural attitude; in its urge for totality, in its perpetual process of fragmentation and hesitation of the multiplicity of fictions it assembles, *Ulysses* begins to unlimit that world, replacing it in the intertext of the fictions of its construction. *Finnegans Wake* opens onto a further level, fixing a totality not through an encyclopaedism (which breaks the totality into a multiplicity of fictions) but through an attention to the production of meaning (which breaks the totality into the ceaseless moment of the engendering of fiction in the wake that forges the horizon against which the night and day are grasped in their difference). Its work is on the fiction of language, its procedure that of, in Mallarmé's words, 'le langage se réfléchissant'.
>
> (50)

In foregrounding the *Wake*'s attention to its own production of meaning and its reflections upon the operations of its language, Heath emphasises what the semioticians we have examined call the aesthetic character of the text. Texts like *Finnegans Wake* are not aesthetic in the traditional sense of having, or referring to, beauty or charm (though they may also do this), but in the much more radical sense of perceiving themselves in the self-reflective mode with which Eco characterises the *Wake* as an 'open' text.

The traditional concept of narrative as the linguistic expression of something other than the narrative itself, as a vehicle for the expression of a meaning or content, is questioned in such self-reflective writing. Writing which reflects its own production in the very movement of that production is part of what Heath calls 'a work on and in language' (51–2). Heath also compares this work with 'what Barthes calls its "theatralization"', adding that 'Joyce's writing, following "language... in its incomparable wisdom", opposes a science of writing, a constant attention to language in which the limits of communication are undone in the spreading out of a play of the signifier in the passage through the ceaseless productions of which may be grasped [in Sollers' words] "the drive of meaning"' (52).

In linguistics, in philosophical logic, in grammars and in theories of narrative (literary and non-literary) the concept of the subject (as content, topic, idea, etc.) governs the production of meaning, providing the answer to the question 'what is?' (the meaning, the subject, the answer, etc.). Jacques Derrida's work aims in part at revealing how writing defeats the production of single, monologic, unified subjects that can be summarised as the 'meaning' of writing. Fusing together the words 'differ' and 'defer', Derrida produces the neologism '*différance*' in order to signify the ways in which language is structured by differences which defer and delay meaning. Language is not possible without the differences in sound and inscription that allow language to function. We met with this concept when discussing linguistics' attention to the structural differences that allow similar-sounding words ('kin' and 'bin', for example) to be perceived as different, and we will return to Derrida's theory of *différance* below. Heath uses Derrida's *différance* in order to characterise Joyce's writing in the *Wake*:

> The focus of the writing of *Finnegans Wake* between night and day is given in the 'wake' of the title: between the wake of death and the wake of life (the wideawake language), the wake of the perpetual tracing of forms, as one speaks of the 'wake' of a ship, the disturbance, division, difference traced over the surface of a sea. This wake is that described by Derrida as *différance*, 'the movement by which language or any other code, any system of reference in general becomes "historically" constituted as a fabric of differences'.
>
> (52)

Heath emphasises the temporal aspect of the operations of *différance* in relation to the concept of origin: 'There is no simple origin, no simple source, no immediate presence' (52). He cites Derrida's essay, 'Différance' in *Speech and Phenomena, and Other Essays on Husserl's Theory of Signs* (Evanston: Northwestern University Press, 1973), explaining that the 'movement of *différance* is the horizon of the production of any so-defined presence':

> Each element that is said to be 'present', appearing on the stage of presence, is related to something other than itself but retains the mark of a past element.... This trace relates no less to what is called the future than to what is called the past, and it constitutes what is called the present by this very relation to what it is not.
>
> (Derrida: 141–2; Cited: 52)

Heath states that 'Joyce defines this movement precisely' and that 'the time of *Finnegans Wake* will be the "pressant" (*FW*: 221. 17)', 'not a simple present but a present pressing on, always already hollowed by the mark of the future; the time of the inscription of traces in the infinite movement from the ones to the others, "at no spatial time processly" (*FW*: 358. 5–6)'. Heath explains that:

> The 'world' can be conceived only from the horizon of writing as space of inscription of differences (has it been sufficiently noted to what extent the writing of *Finnegans Wake* is a continual transformation of elements into terms of language and writing?) and the possibility of 'origin' lies only in the wake of the writing, in the perpetual turning of sense into form, of signified into signifier: 'The untireties of livesliving being the one substance of a streamsbecoming. Totalled in toldteld and teldtold in tittletell tattle. Why? Because, graced be Gad and all giddy gadgets, in whose words were the beginnings, there are two signs to turn to, the yest and the ist, the wright side and the wronged side, feeling aslip and wauking up, so an, so farth'.
> (*FW*: 597.7–12) (52–3)

Heath sees the *Wake*'s 'theatricalization' 'illimiting' language, and 'breaking the accepted categories of communication'. Criticism trying to establish a meaning of the text in the terms of 'semantic description' must fail when confronted by the *Wake* because such a description, 'based on the distinction "statement" – "presupposition" – "implication" – "entailment", is deprived of all possible validity by *Finnegans Wake*, which gives no context on which it could be supported' (57). The text's language as 'nat language at any sinse of the world' (*FW*: 83. 12) produces what Heath calls an 'anti-language, a negation of language' (57), and this negation is 'the breaking of the compromise and the accession to language as productivity; its anti-language is not an absence of language but a dramatic presence of language, *mis en scène* on that [textual space of] "scribenery"' (58). Heath uses what he calls an 'optical listen' to illustrate one of the ways in which Joyce theatricalises language. This 'optical listen' operates in the phrase 'for inkstands' (*FW*: 173. 34) a phrase which combines 'inkstand' and 'instance'. Heath disagrees with the widespread belief that the *Wake* is 'a book to be heard rather than read' and points out that 'no reading aloud... can pass "for instance" and "for inkstands" together: the reading must choose'. The choice of one possible reading over the other 'creates a context', but the text offers at least two possible meanings which waver back and forth. Heath argues that in the 'wavering of this back and forward movement the context falls derisively apart' (58).

The *Wake* not only creates difficulties for traditional contextual criticism, but also affects the forms in which such criticism is usually presented. Criticism deals with the meaning of literature as its subject and reproduces this meaning as its own critical subject. Heath explains that Nietzsche's 'subject as multiplicity' is the 'very hypothesis of the writing of *Finnegans Wake* in its dispersion of the subject' (60). The single, unified 'Cartesian subject is a fraud ("cog it out, here goes a sum" (*FW*: 304. 31), a shem, caught up in that interfolding of forms which leaves no return on the self but in that (mis)appropriation of the other'. Similarly, the traditional introduction – body – conclusion form of the critical work is made difficult by the fact that there is 'no conclusion to be reached in a reading of Joyce's text other than an ambiviolent extension of the text in a new practice of writing, arabesquing the page' (61). While he states that '[s]uch an extension is beyond the scope of [his]... simple introduction to Joyce's writing', Heath puts into practice the poststructuralist theory that writing is a recitation and ends (but does not conclude) his contribution to *Post-structuralist Joyce* by citing a 'little-known text by Joyce' which 'may be read as a coda... resuming... in relation to origin and language and subject, the clouding of the "Cartesian spring"':

> A white mist is falling in slow flakes. The path leads me down to an obscure pool. Something is moving in the pool; it is an arctic beast with a rough yellow coat. I thrust in my stick and as he rises out of the water I see that his back slopes towards the croup and that he is very sluggish. I am not afraid but, thrusting at him often with my stick drive him before me. He moves his paws heavily and mutters words of some language which I do not understand.
>
> (*Epiphanies*, 7 (no. VII; Cited: 61–2))

Jacques Aubert

Aubert's 'riverrun' offers a 'reading of the opening lines of *Finnegans Wake*, or, to be more precise, of the opening word' (69). Aubert begins by citing the warning of André du Bouchet that the unreadability of Joyce's text is its 'distinctive characteristic'. Aubert does not associate this warning with a 'blunt refusal, with the suspended activity represented by an abandoned reading' but 'with an initial state of suspense'. 'From the very first word', suggests Aubert, '*Finnegans Wake* sets out to be impenetrable'. After his initial consideration of 'riverrun' Aubert concludes that 'if [it] remains unreadable, it is because it remains *undifferentiated*. Reading is obstructed by a lack of difference... [that] would consist of: either a + (the article, or the subject, or the mark which would transform "r" into "R"), or a – (a silence), or indeed a + ("R") followed by a – (the separation of "river" and "run") followed by a + (a comma)' (69–70). These would restore the opening "riverrun" to a more traditional grammatical form by capitalising it and rendering it as a noun and a verb (i.e. The, or A, river run, or River run). Aubert suggests reading 'the sentence [in which 'riverrun' occurs] quickly... without stopping':

> riverrun, past Eve and Adam's, from swerve of shore to bend of bay, brings us by a commodius vicus of recirculation back to Howth Castle and Environs.
>
> (*FW*: 358.3; Cited: 70)

Reading the term in this context leads Aubert to conclude that the 'motor has started to run', which is his metaphor for the manifestation of 'something resembling a system':

> 'riverrun' figures as the subject of 'brings', it functions as a *noun*, more specifically as *subject*. This places a more familiar system before us, a grammatical one, whose rules may be provisionally accepted.
>
> (70)

This leads to the conclusion that an 'article' as 'the means of the articulation of the noun' is 'missing' and to the question of which sort of article (definite or indefinite, for example) the article might be.

Aubert is interested in the ways in the '*mechanism*' of the articulation 'allows' 'what comes "after"... to define what went "before"' (70). The term 'brings' allows 'riverrun' to be read as a noun. If this initial 'reversibility mechanism' offers one state, a 'final state' is provided by the closing words of the text: 'A way a lone a last a loved a long the'. Aubert sees the 'first task' as discovering 'a possible connection between the two states' (71). This he does by noting 'a degree of complementarity: an article was missing, and the book ends with an article. And there is more', Aubert suggests:

> this closing fragment provides us not only with a definite article and several indefinite articles, but also reveals how indefinite articulation comes about and what motivates its connection with definite articulation.
>
> (70)

After analysing both the definite articles and the indefinite articles, Aubert offers the argument that 'in order to be rigorous and comprehensive, our reading has had to work in both directions, moving both with and against the flow of words'. When we read in this two-way fashion 'we are witnesses to the *actualization of a noun* as it emerges from an echo, by means of the dismemberment and differential analysis of a set of adverbs and of a preposition'. Aubert states:

> It is all the more remarkable to note that in the case of Joyce, the article and the shade of the noun emerge from adverbs and prepositions, and so stand as particular instances of the well attested phenomenon of second-degree formalization (occurring often in the Indo-European languages), by virtue of which 'values originally *assigned* to a word through inflexion becomes values *designated* by a separate word'. To sum up, we could say that the two-way process described above reveals the true *genealogy of the noun*.
>
> (72)

After analysing the possible functions of terms like 'a lone', 'last', and 'loved' Aubert concludes that the initial reading of 'riverrun' 'was not only erroneous, it was also incomplete' (75). It is also necessary to consider the sound of the word: 'For if the printed word was unreadable, being voice-borne it is not altogether impossible for the ear to hear it; it awakens echoes which must... be discussed'. Considering the echoes '*riveraine*' and 'river ran' (first noted by Fritz Senn), Aubert turns to 'examine the space which sustains these echoes, the volume in which they are born, subsist, insist, since it is evidently because of a closure, a wall (the one built by Tim Finnegan the mason?) that they become manifest' (75-6). While he sees that 'river ran' echoes the line from Coleridge's *Kubla Khan*: 'Where Alph, the sacred river, ran', Aubert thinks 'it would be too easy to fall back... on the space of culture' because 'to do so would be to see this reminiscence merely as decorative effect, if not as audible wink' (76). 'In the first place', Aubert explains, 'Joyce has joined together the essential and the primordial':

> Alpha first of all, then the Article, and Articulation, and finally the Sacred; and in such a way that Coleridge's line can also no doubt initiate other series: the mountain (Alp) as source of every river, and nightmare (German *Alp*), the source of... To put it briefly, Joyce here includes, but in a tracing, all possible mythical dimensions: he leaves us with the echo of the mythical, and not the Mythical itself.
>
> (76)

Aubert makes the 'second point' that 'what concerns us here is a true *echo*, and not what is too often understood by the term, that is a reverberation, a reflection, or a simple association'. The function of 'riverrun['s]' echo of 'river ran' is to 'signal[ ] both a precise *text* and its *absence*, its total non-presence'. 'It is not possible', Aubert says, 'to reconstitute the original expression [in this case, 'river ran'] directly and irrefutably from the echo'. This is because 'identification remains fundamentally problematic', even though 'a sound perceived as an echo never fails to recall some expression to mind' (76).

In turning to the 'second echo', '*riveraine*', Aubert argues that it is 'quite complex' 'despite its apparent simplicity'. Its primary frame of reference is the French language (in which it signifies 'dweller on the river bank' (77 n. 71), 'but it has the auditive mark of a French word pronounced by an English speaker'. This 'marks' the 'tension' of 'the gap between two series, English and French, and the connections between them (cf. Napoleon–Wellington in *Finnegans Wake*). A 'third characteristic' of the term 'is related to the text itself: as I. 8, "Anna Livia Plurabelle",... informs us, the "*riveraines*"... are the washerwomen positioned on the banks of the river, a symmetrical pair of witnesses and commentators... on the *flow* of events' (76). While 'riverrun['s]' echo of this function may not register on a first reading, 'by the second one this fact is known and is automatically registered in the mechanism, thus causing a further calling into question of each of the various series' (76).

Aubert shares Heath's belief that the reader cannot reach a conclusion in a reading of Joyce: 'We can come to no conclusion', he declares. The purpose of his contribution to *Post-structuralist Joyce* is 'to show how *Finnegans Wake* is read, how it can be read, and to point out the theoretical problems which, from the outset, the act of reading implies'. Like other poststructuralists, Aubert sees Joyce's text as one that 'constantly calls representation into question'. It does this:

> not only by playing with perspective but also by inverting categories, which runs counter to the mechanisms of language and of myth while also obtaining from them a prodigiously high output, we still must define as rigorously as possible the interconnections between the various systems it uses, linguistic, mechanical, cybernetic and so on, and the modes of articulation of one with another.
>
> (77)

Jean-Michel Rabaté

Rabaté has written a considerable amount on Joyce from a poststructuralist perspective. In addition to 'Lapsus ex machina' his study of the *Wake* in *Post-structuralist Joyce*, Rabaté has also written on parts of the *Wake*'s textual genesis in 'Pour une cryptogénétique de l'idiolecte Joycien' (*Genèse de Babel: Joyce et la création* [Paris: Louis Hay Éditions Du Centre National De La Recherche Scientifique, 1985]). His work also includes the essay (in *James Joyce 1* 〈〈*Scribble 1*〉〉: *genèse des textes*), 'Le Noeud Gordien De 〈〈Pénélope〉〉' which offers, among other things, insights into 'Penelope Bloom's' name as textual signature and 'bloom' as an active, intransitive verb which also signs both Molly's 'Yes' and her name. 'Lapsus ex machina' investigates the *Wake* as a 'system which can be described as a word machine, or a complex machination of meanings... [a] perverse semic machine [that] has the ability to distort the classical semiological relation between "production" and "information", by disarticulating the sequence of encoding and decoding' (79).

Distinguishing between origin and beginning, Rabaté begins 'Lapsus ex machina' by reading the 'Finnegans' of the *Wake*'s title as *fin negans*. The text, he declares, 'begets only beginnings but invalidates all origins'. The following passage is offered as an example of Joyce's 'disarticulat[ion] [of] the sequence of encoding and decoding':

> The prouts who will invent a writing there ultimately is the poeta, still more learned, who discovered the raiding there originally. That's the point of eschatology our book of kills reaches for now in soandso many counterpoint words. What can't be coded can be decoded if an ear aye sieze what no eye ere grieved for. Now, the doctrine obtains, we have occasioning cause causing effects and affects occasionally recausing altereffects.
>
> (*FW*: 482. 31–483. 01) (79)

'The text is not just "coded"', according to Rabaté, 'since the writing of the 'prouts' – combining Proust and Father Francis Mahony disguised as 'Father Prout', in short the professionals and forgers of literature – receives meaning from the readings discovered by a *poeta*, an agent of creative *poiesis* whose gender is ambiguous' (79). Discussing the semiotic processes of encoding and decoding, Rabaté explains that:

> If it [meaning] is not coded, it can be decoded, de-corded, unwoven, line by line, across the polyphonic obliques which intersect in 'counterpoint words'; thus the feedback of 'altereffects' already scrambles the metonymic chain of cause and effects, since a reading – writing of affects, on the alert, supposes the beginning and the begetting of an 'eareye', constantly lured by the text into believing it has only to *beg* the question of sense. Thus, too, can the quest of sense go on: the fact that the hearing glance implied by this paradoxical reading functions as a lapsus gives a hint and points to the way one could attempt to fill the blank space of desire left hollow by – or in – the machine.
>
> (79)

Rabaté's purpose is to answer the question of what the text performs or 'what does it really cause... when the lapse recurs'. In order to try and answer this question he investigates the codes of Joyce's writing 'machine' and 'their relation to the seriality of the chains [of lapsus]' and then 'tri[es] to analyse the site where the lapsus occurs' (79).

Rabaté's metaphor of the machine is one which he borrows from Joyce, who, in a letter to Harriet Shaw Weaver, wrote:

> I am glad you liked my punctuality as an engine driver. I have taken this up because I am really one of the greatest engineers, if not the greatest, in the world besides being a musicmaker, philosophist, and heaps of other things. All the engines I know are wrong. Simplicity. I am making an engine with only one wheel. No spokes of course. The wheel is a perfect square.
>
> (*L*, I: 251; Cited: 80)

Rabaté thinks it important to 'preserve' Joyce's 'triple profession' of 'musician, philosopher, and engineer', and suggests that the 'combinator, the co-ordinator (engineer) caps the other two'. Invoking the self-reflectiveness of the writing, he suggests that Joyce's machine 'has no other aim than that which it accomplishes itself in running'. Joyce's paradoxical description of his text as a 'square' 'wheel' needs no resolution: 'his machine is a circle and a square; he does not reduce either figure to the other, their incompatibility is a driving motor in the progress of the text' (80). Rabaté uses the metaphor of the machine to describe 'not only the book's theoretical functioning, but also the labour with which it was constructed' (81). He also compares this labour with the 'Lévi-Straussian concept of *bricolage*' which we examined in the context of Hart's study of Joyce.

Using *Finnegans Wake*'s concept of itself as a 'wholemole millwheeling vicociclometer' (614.27), Rabaté compares the internal operations of the text with those of a combustion engine: 'This "vicociclometer" is an internal combustion engine which uses the decompositions and recombinations of elements of the past: everything returns and leaves in the anastomosis (systole and diastole) of a notched wheel which distributes male and female roles: to man, catastrophes, and to women, the transmission of the tradition'. 'The letters, ("letter from litter")', Rabaté says, 'always ultimately reveal "the sameold gamebold adomic structure of our Finnius the old One, as highly charged with electrons as hophazards can effective it" (615. 06–08)' (81).

At one point in the text, ALP's letter (which is itself a substitute for the entire text) is punctured with four holes by the fork of the professor as he eats breakfast. Rabaté compares these four holes with the 'four "homely codes" (614. 32), the codes of the family': 'These codes are like the four holes left by the professor's fork on Anna Livia's letter' (81). As 'Beckett identified Viconian structure and rhythm (beat)', so Rabaté compares the production of the four holes with a 'punctuation of history' which 'emerges' in the text 'more or less clearly from one moment to another: "the [...] quadrifoil jab was more recurrent wherever the script was clear and the term terse" (124. 21-2)' (81). Because there is 'recurrence and invariants', Rabaté sees the text drawing its reader 'towards a "structuralist" point of view', and in this context, he compares Joyce with Lévi-Strauss: 'Just as Lévi-Strauss superposes his myths in order to disengage a structure from them, so Joyce superposes his different stories on this atomic structure, this simple schema of oppositions, tensions, desires within the family' (81). Ultimately, however, this atomic structure is not a solid, stable pattern, but a changing network of colliding textual positions. The *Wake* describes itself as a 'collideorscape' (143. 28), and Rabaté feels that 'the verb "collide"... implies the collision, violence and war of contraries and of tongues':

> One feels the effect of this violent accident, of the contingency which makes electrons jump all over the place: the anti-etymological movement leads to the 'abnihilisation of the etym' (353. 22). No return to an Adamic or a natural origin; the fiction of the nuclear Family permits only the nuclear fission of the text.
>
> (81–2)

Rabaté sees the text producing a 'tension' which the reader 'always risks neutralizing' (82). In order to avoid such a neutralisation, he suggests, one should read the text's tension as 'a tension between *structural* and *serial*', the tension, that is, of Joyce's own 'squaring of the circle', which the reader can continue in 'founding a serial practice of language on a structural theory of universal history as the history of the Family'. To this end, Rabaté uses Lévi-Strauss's distinction between serial and structural thought to help him 'define *Finnegans Wake*'. In the 'Overture of *The Raw and the Cooked*', he explains, 'Lévi-Strauss opposes the two systems of thought':

> His fundamental reproach is that 'abstract' painting, like serial music, forgets the first (natural) level of articulation of language. He criticizes contemporary painting, which he compares to Chinese calligraphy, in these terms: 'the forms used by the artist have no prior existence on a different level with their own systematic organization. It is therefore impossible to identify them as elementary forms: they can be more accurately described as creations of whim, fictitious units, which are put together in parodic combinations'.
>
> (82)

Lévi-Strauss provides the terms for the seriality of Joyce's writing as a 'play with creations of whim, through which one give oneself up to a parodic combination – or a combinatory parody – with units which are not units' (82).

Umberto Eco provides Rabaté with useful theses 'opposing the theory of structural communication to that of "serial thought"' (82). Summarising some of the propositions which we examined in our consideration of Joyce and semiotics, Rabaté explains the 'three fundamental points' 'recognized' by structuralism:

> every message can be decoded thanks to a pre-established code, common to the interlocutors; there is an axis of selection and an axis of combination; every code relies on more elementary codes.

In contrast to these points, serial thought contends that

> every message tends to call into question the code, that the 'notion of polyvalence undermines the foundations of the Cartesian axes' of selection and combination, and... that what is essential is to characterize the historicity of the codes, 'to open them up to debate, so as to generate new modalities of communication'.
>
> (82)

'In other words', says Rabaté, 'whereas structural thought aims to discover, serial thought aims to produce'. In *Finnegans Wake*, Joyce employs 'the schemas of communication and code several times... to challenge them'. This occurs in a 'whole part of the book' which is offered as 'a listening in to "communicators", voices or minds like those which inspired Yeats's *A Vision*' (82–3). In the passage, 'Hallo, Commudicate! How's the buttes? Everscepistic! He does not believe in our psychous of the Real Absence' (536. 04–06), Rabaté thinks, '"scepticism" short-circuits "communicator"'. The *Wake* uses various theories of codes but eventually 'crosses' them, and 'shakes them up in order to return us to the here and now of reading – listening: "Now gode, Let us leave theories there and return to here's here. Now hear. 'Tis gode again" (76. 10–11)' (83).

The *Wake* does use structures like triangles, squares, and circles – patterns like those uncovered by Hart – but it also uses 'numerical multiplication' in the productive processes of ' [n] umerical multiplication on the one hand; unfolding, translation, addition of point or line on the other'. The numerous stories that the text relates 'finally compose a figure, a geometrical schema; but whereas the latter is only the place of intersection of a number of series, the former continue mutually to generate' (83). Rabaté traces the proliferation of the series of figures generated by the 'story of Burrous and Caseous'. 'This story may well lead to the triangle A–B–C (167),' he states, 'but it is hastily brought in to "cut a figure", and put an end to the story, and above all, it fails to tie up all the loose ends of the story: it will give way to the direct enunciation "No!" (167. 18)' (83–4). The Burrous and Caseous story generates the following series:

> From the beginning of I. 6... one hears a series of foods (butter and cheese) interweave with a series of names from Roman history (Brutus and Cassius), which seems to imply a series of 'theoretical' or metaphysical oppositions (Time/Space, Sight/Hearing...). The simple fact that food is mentioned entails further references to all the possible foods which summon all the members of the Family (161. 25 31). The rival twins draw all the rivals of history and literature towards food: 'like shakespill and eggs' (161. 31) covers, with 'bacon and eggs', the Lord Bacon who was claimed to be the author of Shakespeare's plays.
>
> (84)

This approach is essentially no different from the one that Eco uses to analyse associative chains, or even from Hart's approach to motifs, and Rabaté realises that in 'order to analyze' the text's seriality, 'analysis of recurrence is not enough, as it would be in the case of motifs'. Like Eco, Rabaté uncovers the reversibility of the series: 'Two allusions trigger off a series, and its reading is necessarily reversible: as Dunne, the inventor of the concept of the "serial universe" puts it, the first term is still outside the series, which comes into effect only with the second term, which implies a regressive analysis'.

Rabaté thinks that how the 'hierarchies of the stories within stories make the circle of language roll, accomplishing this closure/opening of the book... but also dislodge, dislocate, force all the triangles, must be clearly understood' (84). *Finnegans Wake*, he explains, 'is not content infinitely to permutate coupled terms which can only make their triangle rotate; it simultaneously affirms the necessity of the triangle and its impossibility'. The example he uses to illustrate this double operation is Joyce's gloss 'on religious dogma in the story of the Mookse and the Gripes (I. 6)': 'when he gets A and B onto his lap, C slips off and when he has C and A he loses hold of B"' (*L*, III: 285; Cited: 84). The impossibility of all three of the terms, A, B, and C, being held at the same time is 'the impossibility of there being figures of resolution'. There are structural patterns of organisation provided by such things as the 'Rabelaisian list [which is] frequent in *Finnegans Wake*', but these only 'furnish[] a matrix of undeveloped narratives...' (85). Within the text 'each list engenders or summarizes stories' which, in turn, 'constitute the basis of the "infernal machinery"' of Joyce's word machine. Rabaté sees the stories sustaining tradition as 'the passage from story to story'. The historical events narrated by the stories 'can be distributed in this matrix of series in which the functioning of language is unveiled':

> (Hi)story fabricates, and fabricates itself, as an echo-chamber, reflection of past echolias. The echo-economy of *Finnegans Wake*, its amalgamative alchemy, and the permutations of the letters of the alphabet (cf. 284. 11–14), are at once combinatory, and principles of dispersion and enunciation: 'Economy of movement, axe why *said*' (i.e. 'x', 'y', 'z') (432. 35; cf. 167.7).
>
> (85–6)

Rabaté devotes considerable space to suggesting 'a parallel between Chomsky's grammatical theory and Austin's illocutionary theory' in order to 'show how the *Wake*' 'functions as performance, defined by acceptability/non-acceptability... and the performative, defined by success and failure...' (91; cf. 88–91). What is more important to a consideration of his poststructuralist perspective, however, is his use of Derrida's 'dissemination' and '*différance*', Barthes' concept of the 'writable' text, and Lacan's approach to women. In discussing the method by which the 'four old Irish annalists narrate a fixed (Hi)story while spreading... Family gossip with their endless chatter', Rabaté uses the term '*disséminant*' to describe the annalists' spreading of this gossip. In disseminating the gossip they sow seed-terms from which many series will grow (85). The texts of modern writing 'would tend to make not a consumer but a producer of text, of the text conceived as being "writable", not just "readable"' (97). The *Wake* 'would be the "writable" text par excellence', says Rabaté, a text 'constituted by the reader in his reading/listening to the book, the circularity of which moves between the whole and the hole. "His producers are they not his consumers? Your exagmination round his factification for incamination of a warping process" (497. 1–3)' (97). The terms 'whole' and 'all' are condensed in 'WALLHOLE', the term by which Joyce 'makes the hole (HOLE) arise from the whole' (93). In a reading of the *Wake* the 'reader is always between the hole of reading, between two references which disperse meanings and times... and the whole of the whole book taken as a closed system – which is however opened again onto intertexuality and universal history' (93).

Woman is 'the place of the lapsus' which Rabaté finds generated by the *Wake*-as-machine, and ALP's name is the 'inverted signifier' of the lapsus (LAPsus) (95). 'The *hole*', Rabaté explains, 'is the sex of woman' (in Lacan's sense of woman as being 'not whole', '*pas toutes*', 'which is only mentioned in order to bury her in it' (94, 101, n. 44). '*Lapsus* holds the key to the dream just as woman holds the key to the Book in her letter' (94). The 'series overlap', producing 'moments of convergence' where 'all the recurrences explode', and the lapsus 'are the key to [these] moments'. Rabaté thinks that 'There's many a slip 'twixt the cup and the lip' is '[o]ne of the most illuminating proverbs' in Joyce's book, because 'it is one of the links between enunciation (lip), lapsus (slip), and sleep, making possible the great dream of the book' (94–95). It is within these lapsus that 'meaning is made, at least for the affect of the reader/listener' (94). The sleep in which the dream occurs is itself a 'gigantic lapsus: the etymology of *sleep* is from *slaepan*, that is "labi", to slip: as in *Finnegans Wake*: "O foetal sleep! Ah, fatal slip!" (563. 10)' (94). The sleep ('slip') producing the book's dream, is, finally, the site of the many lapsus generated out of (ex) Joyce's word machine:

> Sleep is a *lapsus linguae* and a *lapsus calami* which reappears in the nightmare (*Alp*, in German) of the flow of the story: *Lapse* of time, flow (laps) of the river, bearing off all the heresies, lapses, and relapses. One slips on the reading: 'To be slipped on, to be slept by, to be conned to, to be kept up. And when you're done push the chain' (275, n. 5)
>
> (94).

This 'lavatory chain joins the chain of generations' that produce the *Wake*'s series. The chain of series produce the lapsus as they overlap, and, like the toilet chain, they work in two directions: 'let no more be said about it, but it's already beginning again', Rabaté declares, 'one is drawn along at the other end of the chain' (94).

André Topia

Topia's 'The Matrix and the Echo: Intertextuality in *Ulysses*' (in *Post-structuralist Joyce*) is concerned with a distinction that illustrates a major difference between poststructuralism and other, more traditional, forms of criticism: the distinction between, on the one hand, the function of allusion and reference in writing, and on the other, the function of the text as an intertext. This distinction is one which we have already examined in looking at Kristeva's theory of the intertext, and it is one which Topia brings to bear in his investigation of *Ulysses* as an intertext. More traditional criticism deals with the appearance of parts of one text within another in terms of one writer borrowing, referring or alluding to the work of another writer. Poststructuralism deals with the relationship as an intertext in which the borrowed or re-cited textual passage is, in Derrida's term, 'grafted' on to the new text, into its scene of writing (*Dissemination* [Chicago: Chicago UP, 1981], 355; cf. 355–8). According to Topia, the more traditional view sees quotation, or what Topia calls 'classical quotation', as a 'whole system... [which] rests on two prohibitions: the prohibition against modifying the borrowed fragment and the prohibition against reversing the hierarchy which puts the borrowed text in an auxiliary status (aesthetic, didactic, moral) to the bracket text' (104). In contrast to 'classical quotation', Joyce's approach to quotation – an approach to which Topia sees Flaubert making a major contribution – makes the hierarchical distinction between quoted and quoting text problematic. In quoting other texts, Flaubert 'seems to take responsibility for all the discourse foreign to the text, while actually not doing so, and leaves a margin of hesitation as to its origin'. This is the technique which Topia sees Joyce using 'extensively' in *Ulysses*: 'in the interior monologue, the text splits and disintegrates, becoming vulnerable to a multitude of other texts which it receives without entirely maintaining control over them' (104).

Topia defines two consequences to this approach to quotations: 'first, the possibility of manipulation of the borrowed text', and second, 'a return effect from the new version to the original version which it contaminates and puts in perspective' (104). This second consequence is one which Derrida outlines in *Dissemination* when he says that ' [e]ach grafted text continues to radiate back toward the site of its removal, transforming that, too, as it effects the new territory' (355). Together, the two consequences outlined by Topia produce 'an increasing instability in the notion of origin: discourse weaves through the text in such a way that one cannot really distinguish the original from its more or less distorted version' (104). Topia sees this instability allowing the 'element of parody [to be] injected into the texture of writing in such a manner that the reader is confronted with variations which he is tempted to take for the norm, which in its turn is inevitably subverted by that hesitation between origins'. The final outcome of the process is that the 'text – which one then hesitates to call original, parody or quotation – becomes a place where the author pits discourses against one another, always distorting them slightly' (104).

The intertextual processes range 'from simple copying to rewriting, and pass[ ] through the different degrees of parody and reactivation'. They produce what Topia describes as a 'radical departure from the classical conception of parody, which maintains a scrupulous parallel between the primary text and the secondary text, and where the analogy with the original matrix is preserved to the smallest detail, according to a scale of rigid correspondences and conversion laws demanding perfect mastery of the genre'. There are important distinctions between the process of classical citation and that of the intertext. In the former, the 'relation between the primary text and the secondary text' is a 'dichotomy/transposition between two components differently arranged, according to fixed rhetorical and thematic rules'. The latter 'implies a devaluation of the very structures of writing' (104) and produces a 'system of distortion and contamination by which the parody subverts the text from within' (105).

Before moving on to analyse the intertextual processes as he sees them at work in *Ulysses*, Topia draws on Derrida's analysis of Plato's *Phaedrus* (in *Dissemination*) and compares his view of intertextuality with Derrida's 'idea of writing as loss'. 'Just as writing opens the way to an infinite series of inferior duplicates', he explains, 're-writing by distortion opens a breach in the integrity of the "original" work, exposing it to a series of imperfect copies' (105). Topia defines the 'whole problem' in terms of the 'relation between the original and the series of copies':

> Either the original is radically removed from the copies, ontologically sep-
> arate from them (and then a one-way motion occurs: the original engenders
> the series of copies, but is never threatened by them), or the copies become
> substitutes for the original and pass for it. In this second case the hierarchy
> is reversed.
>
> (105)

The 'main question' about what happens between the original 'pre-text' and the secondary text that quotes from it is the question 'of the gap, of the supplement', and 'this question arises as well in the intertextual conflict as in writing in general'. Topia uses Derrida's concept of the *supplément* to show 'the danger involved' in the quotation as a supplementary text: 'As soon as the supplementary outside is opened, its structure implies that the supplement itself can be "typed", replaced by its double, and that a supplement to the supplement, a surrogate for the surrogate, is possible and necessary' (Derrida: 109; Cited: 105). The 'devaluation' of the text produced by the 'double' (the quoted passage) 'works in both directions', and neither the supplementary, second text, nor the so-called original retains its value. Topia sees this as the 'problem... at the center of what we would call the "vertical" analysis of the intertextual network: the essential movement is in fact when the borrowed text, extracted from its original content, begins to deny its origin and filiation' (105).

There are 'three elements' involved in the intertextual process: 'the borrowing text (or bracket text), the borrowed text, and the original corpus from which the borrowed text is extracted' (105). Once these elements 'are postulated', says Topia, 'the intertextual problem can be envisaged in two ways'. In the first way, '[o]ne might examine the relationship between the original corpus of the borrowed text and version of the borrowed text as it appears, remodelled, in the heart of its new context'. The alternative method of considering the problem produced by inter-textuality might 'stress the relationship between the bracket text and the re-utilized fragment in the midst of the new aggregate formed by their co-existence...'. This second method entails 'working from the hypothesis that [the] co-existence [between bracket text and cited fragment] is more than mere juxtaposition and that the encounter of two texts inevitably engenders a new textual configuration qualitatively different from the simple sum of two units'. Topia draws on the figure of the 'graft' (which, as we have seen, Derrida also uses) in order to describe the quotation 'tak[ing] root in its new environment and weav[ing] organic connections within it'. The fundamental contextual distinction for considering the two views of intertextuality are summarised by Topia as follows:

> From the encyclopedic corpus of examples one passes to an organic corpus with links to both the original network and the final network. The quoted fragment preserves its ties with its original space, but is not inserted into a new environment with impunity, that is, without significant alterations taking place within both the fragment and the new environment.
>
> (105)

Suggesting that 'we place ourselves at the crossroads of the horizontal and vertical networks', Topia sets these distinctions to work in analysing 'first intertextual polyphony ("Lotus-Eaters" chapter) and then the conflict between levels of discourse ("Cyclops" chapter) in *Ulysses*' (106).

Topia describes Bloom's interior monologue in terms of its production of a 'montage' of units, each of which can be read as the 'actualization of a paradigm, the projection onto the space of the page of one or several codes exterior to the text' (107). This 'Joycean intertext is founded on [the] dual relationship' between a 'vertical circulation' of 'recalls, pseudo-quotations, [and] reactivations' and a 'horizontal circulation', or, 'mon-tage' (108). 'Each word' in Bloom's discourse 'maintains a relationship of tension with both the network from which it draws its origin (implicit corpus of existing texts or rhetorical matrices) and the network in which it is included without being altogether integrated (the actual typograph-ical block of the page in *Ulysses*)'. As an example of this twofold relation-ship Topia examines the way in which Bloom's 'long reverie' is 'stirred up by an advertisement for a brand of tea near the start of the "Lotus-Eaters" chapter (73/71–2)'. Topia isolates the words 'choice blend, made of the finest Ceylon brands' for critical analysis and explains that while a 'first reading [of the words] does not differentiate itself from the rest of Bloom's disconnected thoughts', the words are 'in fact the fragmentary reprise of an advertising message read from a box of tea packets glimpsed a few moments earlier'. No quotation marks indicate the source of the words, and Topia sees the 'disappearance of quotation marks [as] crucial:

it eliminates all typographical indicators permitting the distinction of different levels of discourse' (108).

Topia sees Bloom's discourse allowing us to 'witness [ ] the disappearance of the psychological subject of Bloom' as that discourse reflects its own status as quotation (107). In the words from the tea advertisement, this occurs because:

> Nothing permits us to know *a priori* if the sentence 'belongs' to Bloom or not. With no responsible origin of utterance assigned to these words, we integrate them into Bloom's discourse – until we remember that they are the reprise of a quotation, this time presented clearly as quotation, in the preceding paragraph. This hesitation, this faint vibration of the text to which no clear and immediate paternity is attributed, is often found in the Bloomian monologue. Bloom takes over and reactivates discourses formed outside him, for which he takes responsibility – up to a point... the Bloomian utterances, even when they are of his own 'creation', take on an aspect of collective crystallization, of cliché. The properly Bloomian discourses and the exterior discourses are finally all equivalent in a sort of unstable equilibrium... The most personal utterance may take on an aspect of cliché, and the most shopworn stereotype often finds itself promoted to the rank of an original formulation.
>
> (108)

Topia analyses the 'next sentences: "The far east. Lovely spot it must be: the garden of the world, big lazy leaves to float about on, cactuses, flowery meads, snaky lianas they call them"' and points out the 'same problem of attribution' that he uncovered in the first sentence (109). Of the 'five expressions used', he states, 'only one ("cactuses") is not a cliché'. It would be a mistake to read the sentences as Bloom's own 'imaginary description', because their 'very structure... shows that we are at no point dealing with a *mise en scène*, an imaginary discourse, a topography, but that on the contrary the composition of place never goes beyond a series of more or less activated clichés'. Topia sees the sentences offering nothing more than a *topic* which has little to do with 'realistic elaboration' because it is no more than an 'exploratory probing and sampling'. The sentences offer a 'clear designation of the theme... "Far East"' which 'plays... the role of a kind of title... which automatically summons, elicits, and reels off the whole series of generic expressions which fit in and belong to its "compartment".' The words 'Far East' are 'in the end nothing more than a cybernetic key regrouping the whole series of expressions/indices/examples accumulated in Bloom's mind under this heading'. The sort of series that Topia sees developed here is not unlike the series which Rabaté explored in *Finnegans Wake*, and Topia sees them as an important unit in the 'architecture' of *Ulysses* (110). In 'Ithaca', for example, the 'serial order' is 'systematically used' in the catechism's question and answers as a 'development of the compartmentalization peculiar to the topic'.

While Topia does not think that Bloom 'is merely a machine' which carries out textual operations, he does admit that the 'Bloomian text may sometimes appear as a vast tautology' (110). He views Bloom's discourse as a series of clichés and other quoted fragments from a variety of sources which 'seems to be no more than a succession of examples brought from elsewhere'. *Ulysses* is a text 'poles apart from literature whose aim is to bring the real into existence'. Together with his idea that 'we are constantly witnessing the disappearance of... Bloom' as a 'psychological subject' (107), this view of *Ulysses* supports Topia's hypothesis that the 'Joycean text is not "viable"' or 'transformable into the real' (110). Such a transformation is so 'self-evident' in 'works of realist literature' 'that it is obliterated' (110–11). In *Ulysses*, however, 'the matrix' of the codes for the generation of individual expressions is 'set apart from its various imperfect products' (111). To Topia, the 'text appears encumbered with the debris of its own imperfect productions, a little like a machine that leaves in its wake a series of aborted products all bearing the stamp of their origin and designating it, but unable to form a coherent whole'. This 'dissociation' of textual codes and textual expression 'radically interferes with any realist reading of *Ulysses*, preventing the real and the discourse from folding over on each other'.

Topia devotes at least as much attention to his analysis of 'Cyclops' as he does to his investigation of the opening of 'Lotus-Eaters'. In examining 'Cyclops', however, he is more concerned with that chapter's expansion of 'the intertextual mechanisms already noted in 'Lotus-Eaters': dissociation into heterogeneous and antagonistic levels of discourse'. In very general terms, the focus of Topia's analysis of 'Cyclops' is the insertion of fragments from three main classes of writing – 'Journalistic discourse', 'Forms of specific discourses' (including, among others, 'legal jargon', 'medical jargon', 'wall graffiti', 'children's literature', 'religious discourse'), and 'Literary discourses' – into the narrative in a way that creates 'the impression of watching a film into which someone has spliced, at regular intervals, fragments of reels belonging to other films, or a collage where the description of a figurative scene is juxtaposed with fragments of newspapers or posters' (118–19, 117). A major effect of these insertions from Topia's perspective is the '"reification of the topic" in which Roland Barthes saw the decline of classical rhetoric'. The insertions assist in a 'degradation' which 'is all the more striking because of':

> the alternation of strictly journalistic insertions and insertions in epic, oratory or poetic style... The devices circulate from one text to the other (in this sense they are literally 'commonplace'). This indifferentiation, this levelling, is the mark of a radical degradation of rhetorical discourse.
>
> (123)

Topia sees what he calls Joyce's degradation of rhetoric as an important part of Joyce's movement away from so-called 'realism':

> in juxtaposing two types of treatment of facts Joyce does more than simply induce a tension: he dissolves all possibility of a unified real underlying the fiction... The insertions can only transmit a real already infected by conventions. Everything has become stereotype.
>
> (124)

Ultimately, Topia sees the techniques he examines in the two chapters from *Ulysses* articulating the same sort of alienation which we saw investigated by Cixous in her analysis of 'The Sisters'. The distance between 'narration and insertion' produces an 'irreducible faultline' that 'is the symbol of the two discourses which pull Dublin apart':

> on the one hand the speech which repeats, on the other the matrix which reproduces and contaminates: here the infinite series of echoes, there the unrestrained production of the media's rhetorical machine. The whole Dublin paralysis is in this co-existence of the past of the spoken word and the present of the printed word – both transmitting nothing but alienation.
>
> (124)

Jacques Derrida

Derrida's work has provided the theories for many more poststructuralist readings of Joyce than the French studies which we have considered in this chapter. Since Margot Norris's seminal study of *Finnegans Wake* as a decentred (and decentring) work, many readers of Joyce have begun to think that Derrida's textual strategies might provide not only a context for reading Joyce, but also insights both into the ways in which Joyce's writing works and into Joyce's position as a literary writer whose work has had a major effect in areas outside of literature. Drawing on Derrida's essay, 'Structure, Sign and Play in the Discourse of the Human Sciences' (*Writing and Difference* [Chicago: Chicago UP, 1978]), for example, Norris argues that what she describes as the 'literary heterodoxy' of the *Wake* 'is the result of Joyce's attack on the traditional concept of structure itself' (Norris: 121). Joyce's attack, however, 'was not isolated, but belonged to a philosophical and psychoanalytic "event" or "rupture" in the history of the concept of structure, which, according to... Jacques Derrida, took place in the history of thought sometime in the late nineteenth and early twentieth centuries'. If Norris is correct and Joyce's attack on structure is a part of the revolution in thinking about structure which Derrida discusses in his essay, then Joyce should be considered not only as a major writer of fiction but also as 'one of those authors in whose discourse' the practice of 'decentering' and the 'thinking [of] the structurality of structure' have 'kept most closely to its most radical formulation' (Derrida: 280). This would allow us to consider his work in the same context as Nietzsche's 'critique of metaphysics', Freud's 'critique [s] of self-presence... [and] consciousness', and Heidegger's 'destruction of metaphysics'.

Of course, not all of Joyce's readers would agree that this is the context in which Joyce should be studied. In spite of all of the developments towards interdisciplinary exchanges which have taken place in the humanities over the last twenty years, many students and teachers of literature remain committed to the idea that literature should remain a discipline in its own right. This is particularly true of conservative English departments in which there may still be teachers and lecturers committed to the Leavisite idea of the 'Great Tradition' of English Literature and the rather curious notion that a national language and literature can in and of themselves provide a 'discipline of thought'. Leavis, of course, felt that Joyce did not belong in the 'great tradition', because Ulysses lacked 'organic form', and even though he based his opinion, in part, on a work which he had not read (*Finnegans Wake*), his views influenced the treatment which Joyce received in English departments for a considerable time. Of course, readers who hold an ideological commitment to English literature as a moral force would probably not look favourably upon either the *Wake*'s deconstruction of the English language, its treatment of 'great' English writers like 'greet scoot, duckings, and thuggery' (177. 35) or its play on 'literature' as 'litterish' or 'litteringture' (66. 25, 570. 18). What such readers would make of a French philosopher who has the 'gall' to ask '*what is literature?*' need hardly be spelled out (Derrida, *Dissemination*, Chicago UP, 1981: 177).

The relationship between Joyce and Derrida is a relationship between two writers that is also an intriguing encounter between literature and philosophy. Until Derrida's 'more or less extemporary talk... at the Centre Georges Pompidou' (Derrida, 1984: 158 n.1), readers interested in the relationship between Joyce and Derrida had little more than a series of tantalising, but often marginal, oblique comments in Derrida's writings with which to consider the relationship. These include: the comparison between Husserl's ideal, phenomenological theory of history and Stephen Dedalus's view of history as a 'nightmare' in *Introduction to Edmund Husserl's 'The Origin of Geometry'*; a footnote suggesting that 'Plato's Pharmacy' could be taken as a reading of *Finnegans Wake (Dissemination)*; a quotation from *Ulysses* and a cryptic description of Joyce as 'perhaps the most Hegelian of modern novelists' in 'Violence and Metaphysics: An Essay on the Thought of Emmanuel Levinas' (in *Writing and Difference*); references to *Scribbledehobble: The Ur-Workbook for Finnegans Wake* in 'Scribble (writing-power)' (*Yale French Studies*, 58, 1979); and a series of enigmatic comments on Joyce, *Giacomo Joyce*, and *Finnegans Wake* in *The Post Card: From Socrates to Freud and Beyond*. In 'Two Words for Joyce'

Derrida adds to the list by suggesting that *Glas* 'is also a sort of a *Wake*'. Since the appearance of 'Two Words' Derrida has addressed one of the International James Joyce Symposiums, and 'Ulysse Gramophone: L'oui-dire de Joyce' offers what is perhaps the most direct of Derrida's readings of Joyce.

It is in 'Two Words for Joyce' (*Post-structuralist Joyce: Essays from the French*, Cambridge: Cambridge University Press), that Derrida for the first time offered an extensive account of the importance of Joyce in his work: 'every time I write, and even in the most academic pieces of work, Joyce's ghost is always coming on board' (149). The same piece reveals that Derrida has been reading Joyce for a considerable length of time:

> With this admiring resentment, you can stay on the edge of reading Joyce – for me this has been going on for twenty-five or thirty years – and the endless plunge throws you back onto the river-bank, on the brink of another possible immersion…. In any case, I have the feeling that I haven't yet begun to read Joyce, and this 'not having begun to read' is sometimes the most singular and active relationship I have with this work.
>
> (148)

Derrida states that this 'not having begun to read' is the reason that he had 'never dared to write *on* Joyce', but as Derrida's writing often approaches its numerous subjects from a variety of oblique angles and marginal positions, his declaration of not having the nerve to write '*on* Joyce' should be interpreted very carefully. It almost certainly does not mean that Joyce is not important in Derrida's work. Consider, for example, Derrida's gradual amplification of how he has engaged Joyce's writing:

> At most I've tried to mark… in what I wrote of Joyce's scores [*portées*], Joyce's *reaches* [*portées*]. Beyond the musical measure that can be recognized in this word *portée*, which speaks too of the proliferating generous multitude of the animal [*portée* as 'litter'], you can also hear this in it: such and such a text *carries* [*porte*] in truth the signature of Joyce, it *carries* Joyce and lets itself be carried by him, or even carried off [*déporter*] in advance.
>
> (148)

For Derrida the practice of 'marking' (as in the above phrase 'At most I've tried to mark…') is a fundamental process of writing. From a more conventional view of the relationship between writing and the subject of that writing, few readers would disagree with the assertion that Derrida has written *on* Plato, Heidegger or Nietzsche. Consider, however, how Derrida himself articulates this process, at least as his articulation is translated into the English edition of *Positions* (London: The Athlone Press, 1987):

> You know, in fact, that it is above all necessary to read and reread those in

whose wake I write, the 'books' in whose margins and between whose lines I *mark* out and read a text simultaneously almost identical and entirely other, that I would even hesitate, for obvious reasons, to call fragmentary...

(4, emphasis added)

Derrida's description of his work as a 'mark[ing] out and read[ing]' of a text which is different from the text 'in whose margins and between whose lines' he marks and reads reflects his concern with the processes of writing as a subject. His engagement of other texts rarely, if ever, produces a writing *on* what a more conventional critic would identify as the subject of that text. His interests and concerns lie elsewhere.

In the above comments on his 'marking' of Joyce's 'reaches', Derrida exploits the various senses of '*portée*', and the puns between '*portée*', '*porte*', and '*déporter*'. Such playful polysemy and paronomasia are, of course, trademarks of Joyce's *Wake*, and Derrida uses such techniques frequently, even in his 'serious' and 'most academic pieces of work'. This is not to suggest that Joyce has influenced Derrida's work (although he obviously has), but simply to remark on Derrida's obvious comfort and familiarity with Joyce's literary techniques. Derrida himself discusses his relation to Joyce with the metaphor of the machine, but unlike the other French poststructuralists who favour this metaphor, Derrida uses a more up-to-date machine:

Paradoxical logic of this relationship between two texts, two programmes or two literary 'softwares': whatever the difference between them, even if, as in the present case, it is immense and even incommensurable, the 'second' text, the one which, fatally, refers to the other, quotes it, exploits it, parasites it and deciphers it, is no doubt the minute parcel *detached* from the other, the metonymic dwarf, the jester of the great anterior text which would have declared war on it in languages; and yet it is also another set, quite other, bigger, and more powerful than the all-powerful which it drags off and reinscribes elsewhere in order to defy its ascendancy. Each writing is at once the detached fragment of a software and a software more powerful than the other, a part larger than the whole of which it is a part.

(148)

Derrida's account of the relationship between Joyce and himself expresses something of his ambivalent 'admiring resentment' of Joyce. From the initial declaration of not having the 'nerve to write *on* Joyce' which precedes his use of the computer metaphor, Derrida moves on to discuss the extents to which Joyce's writing 'reaches' before changing tack and punning on Joyce's writing as animal 'litter' (a pun which perhaps finds support in the *Wake*'s account of Shem producing ink from piss and shit and Biddy the Hen's discovery of the text in a midden heap). In using the metaphor of the computer to describe the relationship between Joyce's writing and his own – the relationship clearly signified by the phrase 'as in the present case' – Derrida describes two sets of relations:

the first is the ambivalent set between two 'softwares' in which one software is 'minute' and a 'metonymic dwarf' which is nevertheless '*detached
from*' and able to 'exploit [ ]' the other; the second is the equivalent set
of relations between two writing-softwares in which both writings are a
'detached fragment of a software' and, simultaneously, 'a software more
powerful than the other' and a 'part larger than the whole of which it is
a part' (148).

The 'two words' to which Derrida's title refers are '*He war*' from
Finnegans Wake (258.12), and Derrida's discussion is, in part, a meditative
commentary on these words:

> I spell them out: H E W A R, and sketch a first translation: HE WARS –
> he wages war... which can also be pronounced by babelizing a bit (it is in
> a particularly Babelian scene of the book that these words rise up), by
> Germanizing, then, in Anglo-Saxon, He war: he was – he who was ('I am
> he who is or who am', says YAHWE). Where it was, he was, declaring war,
> and it is *true*. Pushing things a bit, taking the time to draw on the vowel
> and to lend an ear, it will have been true, *wahr*, that's what can be kept
> [*garder*] or looked at [*regarder*] in truth.
>
> (145)

Derrida repeats certain key terms from his commentary in order to establish a link between Joyce, writing, the male 'I', the creator YAHWE, and
warfare:

> He, is 'He', the 'him', the one who says I in the masculine, 'He', war
> declared, he who was at war declared, declaring war... and he who was true,
> the truth, he who by declaring war verified the truth that he was...
>
> (145).

Derrida uses these associative terms to support a link between Joyce's
writing and Babel, (a link already clearly established in the *Wake* itself):

> he declared war in language and on language and by language, which gave
> languages, that's the truth of Babel when YAHWE pronounced its vocable,
> difficult to say if it was a name...
>
> (146).

One of Derrida's primary interests in the *Wake*'s violent, Babelian
writing is in the relationship between the text's written language and the
way in which that language sounds when it is spoken. After citing a very
lengthy passage from the *Wake* (258. 11–259. 10) in which the 'rhythm
of the Bible is mimed...' (152), Derrida suggests that we 'limit ourselves,
if one can say this, to all that passes through the voice and the phenomenon, the phenomenon as phoneme' (153). He isolates at the centre of
the 'sequence' from the *Wake* the appearance of the term 'phonemanon':

> For the Clearer of the Air from on high has spoken in tumbuldum tambaldam to his tembledim tombaldoom worrild and, moguphonoised by that *phonemanon*, the unhappitents of the earth have terrerumbled from fimament unto fundament and from tweedledeedumms down to twiddledeedees.
>
> (*FW*: 258. 20–24, emphasis added; Cited: 152–3)

Derrida is interested in 'phonemanon' as a fusion of 'phoneme' and 'phenomenon': the phenomenon of sound and the sound of the phenomenon. This fusion, for Derrida, 'reflects, in a state of extreme concentration, the whole Babelian adventure of the book, or rather its Babelian underside: "And shall not babel be with Lebab" [258. 11–12]'. 'This palindrome', explains Derrida, '... overturns the tower of Babel [and] also speaks the book, and Philippe Lavergne recalls the two Irish words *leaba*, the bed, and *leabhar*, the book' (153).

After considering a 'few examples among others', in which the *Wake* sustains these associations between 'writing', 'war', 'truth', 'sound' and 'book', Derrida suggests that '[i]n the landscape immediately surrounding this "he war", we are, if such a present is possible, and this place, at Babel: at the moment when YAHWEH declares war, HE WAR' (153–4). An 'exchange of the final R [for Y] and [effacing] the central H [of YAHWEH] in the anagram's throat' enables Derrida to 'read' HE WAR as YAHWEH. 'And the Lord, the Most High', states Derrida, '... declares war on them by interrupting the construction of the tower, he deconstructs by speaking the vocable of his choice, the name of confusion, which in the hearing, could be confused with a word indeed signifying "confusion"' (154).

Derrida offers many more insightful comments for a possible reading and translation of 'HE WAR', but we already have more than enough material to produce a preliminary sketch of the overlap between the effects of Joyce's writing and the concerns of Derrida's deconstructive project to enable us to catch a fleeting glimpse of 'Joyce's ghost' as it 'comes on board' Derrida's work. The relationship between Joyce's writing and the sound of that writing is one which we saw Heath consider with his theory of the 'optical listen'. This relationship between spoken and written language, or speech and writing, is a major area of investigation in Derrida's work. Speech and writing function as one of the paired binary opposites which are so important in the structuralist theories that we examined in the first chapter. For Derrida, however, these binary opposites do not exist in the equivalent-but-antithetical relationship which they share in structuralism. Indeed, this is an important distinction between structuralist and poststructuralist theory. In structuralism, binary opposition produces a more or less stable structure supported by opposite but equivalent terms like those operating along the diachronic and synchronic linguistic axes which we considered in structuralist theory or those which Lévi-Strauss defined in the avunculate kinship structure. In the former, the meaning of any particular word is a combination of its diachronic and synchronic function, and there is no particular hierarchical relationship between the two functions. Similarly, Lévi-Straus's avunculate system operates not according to the hierarchical relationship between father and son, but according to the oppositional relationship between the pairs father/son vs. uncle (mother's brother)/nephew(son).

For Derrida, however, binary opposition produces fundamental terms which help to structure Western philosophical thought (phallogocentrism) and determine its values. These terms (male/female, good/bad, light/dark, speech/writing, true/false, etc.) do not exist in a relationship of equal opposition, because one of the terms is always preferred over the other: in what Derrida calls 'classical philosophical opposition', which is precisely the relationship between the terms in the above series, 'we are not dealing with the peaceful coexistence of a *vis-à-vis*, but rather with a violent hierarchy. One of the terms governs the other (axiologically, logically, etc.), or has the upper hand' (*Positions*, 1987: 41). Derrida explains the process of deconstruction as an operation which is performed upon the terms of binary opposition and the network, or 'chain' of terms associated with each of the units in the binary pair. Deconstruction requires a 'double' operation, or a double reading–writing of the text to be deconstructed in which the hierarchical relationship between the binary terms is 'overturned': 'To deconstruct the opposition, first of all, is to overturn the hierarchy at a given moment' (41).

The double strategy of deconstruction begins with a reading in which the text is traversed and the structuring, hierarchical relationships of the binary terms 'marked'. 'The necessity of this phase' of the process 'is structural', because 'the hierarchy of dual oppositions always reestablishes itself' after it has been deconstructed (42). Deconstruction, then, requires an 'interminable analysis'. After the first phase of deconstruction has been accomplished and the binary hierarchies have been marked, the double strategy is completed as 'we... mark the interval between inversion [of the binary terms], which brings low what was high, and the irruptive emergence of a new "concept", a concept that can no longer be, and never could be, included in the previous regime'. Derrida uses the binary terms of speech and writing to elucidate the process:

> this biface or biphase, can be inscribed only in a bifurcated writing (and this holds first of all for a new concept of writing, that *simultaneously* provokes the overturning of the hierarchy speech/writing, and the entire system attached to it, *and* releases the dissonance of a writing within speech...
> (42)

Philosophy traditionally considers speech as superior to writing. As Derrida's writing on Plato (in *Dissemination* and elsewhere) has shown, this preference of speech over writing is a result of the Platonic idea that speech is a superior form of language because it requires presence (of the speaker and listener) and can offer a greater guarantee of truth (the listener can question the speaker as to the truth of his utterance). Writing, on the other hand, implies absence (the writer need not be in the immediate presence of the reader) and offers no guarantee of truth. (In *Dissemination*, Derrida investigates Plato's use of the Egyptian myth of Thoth [the God of writing with whom Joyce will later identify himself and some of his personae] and shows how writing is denigrated as a 'pharmakon' which can poison as well as cure; [cf. 'Plato's Pharmacy', 61–171]).

The possibility of reading/listening to *Finnegans Wake* as a writing which produces 'the dissonance of a writing within speech' would seem to be supported by Derrida's interest in Joyce's paranonmasian fusion of 'phoneme' and 'phenomenon' in the term 'phonemanon'. For here, in writing, the phenomenon of sound, of the phoneme, is articulated in a fusion that sounds dissonant in relation to the two phonemes (and their respective semantic values) which it combines. Although Heath ('Ambiviolences: Notes for reading Joyce', in *Post-structuralist Joyce: Essays from the French*, Cambridge: Cambridge University Press [1984]) contends that 'nothing could be further from the truth' than the idea that the *Wake* is 'a book to be heard rather than read', his technique of the 'optical listen' demonstrates that the book should be heard as well as read: without a hearing of the book, the 'listen' part of Heath's 'optical listen' simply would not make sense. Heath argues 'that no reading aloud can pass "for inkstands" and "for instance" together: the reading must choose; in other words, it creates a context' (58), and this argument clearly suggests that the context for reading aloud cannot encompass all of the contexts which a silent reading can realise. In other words, the *Wake*'s paronomasia – a linguistic device which depends on phonetic similarity – is articulated in a writing which needs to be heard so that its puns can be appreciated. At the same time, the phonetic realisation of the writing in speech would, according to Heath's 'optical listen', be unable to reproduce all of the semantic values in any given pun. In its relation to the contexts produced by the writing, the phonetic realisation of the pun could never be anything more than a dissonant echo of all of the range of possible phonetic readings offered by the writing.

Of course, Joyce was not trying to produce a writing which would deconstruct the traditional, historical and philosophical preference for speech over writing, but as he made sure that everyone knew, he was trying to produce a writing that was grounded on the phonetic relationships between the sounds of the words that he used. As he told Frank Budgen, 'The Holy Roman Apostolic Church was built on a pun. It ought to be good enough for me' (Ellmann, 1982: 546). The phonetic basis of paronomasia was the tool with which Joyce could allow semantic values to proliferate in a polyphonic writing. When it was suggested that the lowly pun could result in 'trivialty', he replied 'Yes, some of the means I use are trivial – and some are quadrivial' (Ellmann, 1982: 546). One of the products of Joyce's 'trivial' and 'quadrivial' means is a 'sound-conducting' (183. 09) writing, a 'sounddance' (378. 29) in which the 'soundest sense' (96. 32) needs a 'soundhearing' (237. 17), a writing that demands to be heard in speech.

One of the central questions posed in Derrida's writing concerns the concept of the structure of a book as a unity: 'In what you call my books, what is first of all put in question is the unity of the book, and the unity "book" considered as a perfect totality, with all of the implications of such a concept' (*Positions*, 1987: 3). This concern with the structure of the book is one of the reasons why Derrida performs what amounts to an interrogation of Hegel's disqualification of the preface in the 'Preface' of *Phenomenology of Spirit* (New York and Oxford: Oxford UP, 1977). Hegel qualifies his preface with the following comments:

> It is customary to preface a work [*Schrift*] with an explanation of the author's aim, why he wrote the book, and the relationship in which he believes it to stand to earlier or contemporary treatises on the same subject. In the case of a philosophical work, however, such an explanation seems not only superfluous but, in view of the nature of the subject-matter, even inappropriate and misleading... . For whatever might appropriately be said about philosophy in a preface... none of this can be accepted as the way in which to expound philosophical truth.
>
> (Hegel: 1; Cited, Derrida, 1981: 10)

Derrida's 'preface' to *Dissemination* puts Hegel's theoretical disqualification into practice by denying its own status as a preface. Derrida plays with alternative 'titles' for his 'non-preface' – '*HORS LIVRE*: OUTWORK EXTRATEXT FOREPLAY BOOKEND FACING * PREFACING' – all of which play with the idea of the preface of the book as a part of the unity 'introduction-body/middle-conclusion'. The 'book' status of *Dissemination* is brought into question with the opening sentence, which announces 'This (therefore) will not have been a book' (3).

Derrida's concern with the concept of the book as a unified totality is also apparent in *Of Grammatology*'s famous pronounement that 'The Outside Ҝ the Inside' (Derrida, 1974: 44) and in his writing on 'The End of the Book and the Beginning of Writing' (6–26). Derrida contends that deconstructive writing begins with its refusal of the oppressive totality of the classical philosophical concept of the book as a unified, organic form. The end of the phallogocentric domination of writing begins with the end of 'linear writing', or what we have seen Kristeva call monologic writing, and Derrida states that the 'end of linear writing is indeed the end of the book, even if, even today, it is within the form of a book that new writings – literary or theological – allow themselves to be, for better or worse, encased' (86). The philosopher who perhaps best articulates the relationship between the end of the book and the beginning of writing is, for Derrida, Hegel, the philosopher whom Derrida calls 'the last philosopher of the book and the first thinker of writing' (26).

As we have already noted, in his essay 'Violence and Metaphysics: An Essay on the thought of Emmanuel Levinas', Derrida offers the cryptic comment that Joyce is 'perhaps the most Hegalian of modern novelists' (Derrida, 1978: 153). As a way of ending (but not concluding) this study of Joyce and critical theory, let us give a brief and necessarily simple consideration to the structure of Joyce's last 'book' which may suggest a further context in which that book can be studied in the future. The traditional 'logic' of the idea of the book dictates that in addition to a beginning, a middle, and an end, the book should obey a certain linguistic paradigm: The book is greater than its chapters, which are greater than their paragraphs, which are greater than their sentences, which are greater than their individual words. This obvious logic of the book is the one which the opening and closing words of Joyce's 'book of Doublends Jined' (*FW*: 20. 15–16) subverts: 'A way a lone a last a loved a long the [| the outside of the book |] riverun, past Eve and Adam's, from swerve of shore to bend of bay, brings us by a commodius vicus of recirculation back to Howth Castle and Environs' (*FW*: 628. 15–16, 3. 1–3). If these words do constitute one sentence as critics like Aubert accept, then one sentence can be greater than two chapters and this sentence belongs to both the first (I.1) and final (IV.1) chapters of the *Wake*. Another possible reading is that the *Wake* subverts the traditional logic of the book by obeying it: if a sentence cannot be greater than a chapter, then the sentence 'A way a lone... Howth Castle and Environs' belongs to one chapter, and the number of chapters in the *Wake* is not seventeen but sixteen, the number of books not four but three. Of course, no reader need accept either of these arguments, but the possibility remains that along with the square and circle which Rabaté investigates, Joyce has also given us a book whose acknowledged 'double' structure can be thought mathematically through the impossible formulae, $3 = 4$ and $17 = 16$. In the context of such formulae, Joyce's writing could be seen subversively evading the restrictions of the very book in which it is contained.

Works Cited

Armstrong, Alison (1973) 'Shem the Penman as Glugg as the Wolf-Man', *A Wake Newslitter*, **10** (August), 51–57.

Attridge, Derek (1988) 'Joyce, Jameson, and the text of history', in Ed. Claude Jacquet, *James Joyce*, 1: '*Scribble*' *1 genèse des textes*, Paris: Lettres Modernes, Minard, 1988.

Aubert, Jacques (1984) 'riverrun', trans. Patrick O'Donovan, in Eds. Derek Attridge and Daniel Ferrer, *Post-structuralist Joyce: Essays from the French*, Cambridge: Cambridge University Press.

Barthes, Roland (1980) *Elements of Semiology*, trans. Annette Lavers and Colin Smith, New York: Hill and Wang.

Barthes, Roland (1972) *Mythologies*, trans. Annette Lavers and Colin Smith, London: Jonathan Cape.

Barthes, Roland (1975) *The Pleasure of the Text*, trans. Richard Miller, New York: Hill and Wang.

Barthes, Roland (1974) *S/Z*, trans. Richard Miller, New York: Hill and Wang.

Bateson, Gregory (1972) *Steps to an Ecology of Mind*, New York: Ballantine.

Bauerle, Ruth, (1982) 'Bertha's role in *Exiles*', in Eds. Suzette Henke and Elaine Unkeless, *Women in Joyce*, 108–131.

Beckett, Samuel, *et al.* (1962) *Our Exagimination Round His Factification for Incamination of Work in Progress*, New York: New Direction Books.

Benstock, Bernard (1965) *Joyce-Again's Wake: An Analysis of 'Finnegans Wake'*, Seattle: Washington UP.

Benstock, Bernard (1985) Ed., *Critical Essays on Joyce*, Boston: G. K. Hall & Co.

Benstock, Shari (1985) 'Nightletters: Women's Writing in the *Wake*', in Ed. Bernard Benstock, *Critical Essays on Joyce*, 221–233.

Benstock, Shari (1982), 'The Genuine Christine: Psychodynamics of Issy', in Eds. Suzette Henke and Elaine Unkeless, *Women in Joyce.* 169–196.

Bishop, John (1986) *Joyce's Book of the Dark: 'Finnegans Wake'*, Madison: Wisconsin UP.

Bosinelli (Bollettieri), Rosa Maria (1970) 'The Importance of Trieste in Joyce's Work with Reference to his Knowledge of Psycho-analysis', *JJQ*, **7**, (3), 177–184.

Bosinelli (Bollettieri), Rosa Maria (1981) 'Psychoanalytical Criticism and Metapyschology' *JJQ*, **18**, (3), 349–355.

Brivic, Sheldon (1980) *Joyce Between Jung and Freud*, Port Washington, NY: Kennikat Press.

Brivic, Sheldon (1985) *Joyce the Creator*, Madison: Wisconsin UP.

Campbell, Joseph, and Henry Morton Robinson (1947) *A Skeleton Key to 'Finnegans Wake'*, London: Faber and Faber.

Chatman, Seymour (1978) *Story and Discourse: Narrative Structure in Fiction and Film*, Ithaca: Cornell UP.

Cixous, Hélène (1976) *The Exile of James Joyce*, London: John Calder.

Cixous, Hélène (1981) 'The Laugh of the Medusa', trans. Keith Cohen and Paula Cohen, in Eds. Elaine Marks and Isabelle de Courtivron, *New French Feminisms: An Anthology*, New York: Schocken Books.

Cixous, Hélène (1984) 'Joyce: the (r)use of writing', trans. Judith Still, in Eds. Derek Attridge and Danile Ferrer, *Post-structuralist Joyce: Essays from the French*, Cambridge: Cambridge University Press.

Cohn, Dorrit (1966) 'Narrated Monologue: Definition of a Fictional Style', *Comparative Literature*, **18**.

Coleman, Elliott (1963) 'A Note on Joyce and Jung', *JJQ*, **1**, (1), 11–19.

Colum, Mary (1922) 'The Confessions of James Joyce', *Freeman*, **5**, (123), (19 July), 450–452.

Culler, Jonathan (1975) *Structuralist Poetics*, London: Routledge & Kegan Paul.

de Beauvoir, Simone (1961) *The Second Sex*, trans. and Ed. H. M. Parshley, New York: Bantam.

Derrida, Jacques (1973) 'Difference', *Speech and Phenomena, and Other Essays on Husserl's Theory of Signs*, trans. David B. Allison, Evanston: Northwestern UP.

Derrida, Jacques (1981) *Dissemination*, trans. Barbara Johnson, Chicago: Chicago UP.

Derrida, Jacques (1986) *Glas*, trans. John P. Leavy Jr and Richard Rand, Lincoln and London: Nebraska UP.

Derrida, Jacques (1978) *Introduction to Edmund Husserl's 'The Origin of Geometry'*, trans. Edward Leavey, Hassocks: Harvester.

Derrida, Jacques (1974) *Of Grammatology*, trans. Gayatri Chakravorty Spivak, Chicago: Chicago UP.

Derrida, Jacques (1987) *Positions*, trans. Alan Bass, London: The Athlone Press.

Derrida, Jacques (1979) 'Scribble (writing power)', *Yale French Studies*, 58, 1979.

Derrida, Jacques (1978) 'Structure, Sign and Play in the Discourse of the Human Sciences', in *Writing and Difference*, trans. Alan Bass, Chicago: Chicago UP.

Derrida, Jacques (1987) *The Post Card: From Socrates to Freud and Beyond*, trans. Alan Bass, Chicago: Chicago UP.

Derrida, Jacques (1984) 'Two Words for Joyce', trans. Geoff Bennington in Eds Derek Attridge and Daniel Ferrer, *Post-Structuralist Joyce: Essays from the French*, Cambridge: Cambridge University Press.

Derrida, Jacques (1985) 'Ulysse gramophone: L'oui-dire de Joyce', in Ed. Claude Jacquet, *Genèse de Babel: Joyce et la création*, Paris: Louis Hay.

Derrida, Jacques (1978) 'Violence and metaphysics: An essay on the thought of Emmanuel Levinas', *Writing and Difference*, trans. Alan Bass, Chicago: Chicago UP.

Eagleton, Terry (1970) *Exiles and Émigrés: Studies in Modern Literature*, London: Chatto and Windus.

Eagleton, Terry (1978) *Criticism and Ideology: A Study in Marxist Literary Theory*, London: Verso.

Eco, Umberto (1979) *A Theory of Semiotics*, Bloomington: Indiana UP.

Eco, Umberto (1989) *Foucault's Pendulum*, trans. William Weaver, London: Secker and Warburg.

Eco, Umberto (1962) *Opera Aperta*, Milano: Bompiani.

Eco, Umberto (1982) *The Aesthetics of Chaosmos: The Middle Ages of James Joyce*, trans. Ellen Esrock, Tulsa: Tulsa UP.

Eco, Umberto (1979) *The Role of the Reader: Explorations in the Semiotics of Texts*, Bloomington: Indiana UP.

Edgerton, William B. (1968) 'Dzhoising with the Soviet Encyclopedias', *JJQ*, 5, (2), 125–131.

Ellmann, Mary (1968) *Thinking About Women*, New York: Harcourt Brace Jovanovich.

Ellmann, Richard (1982) *James Joyce*, Oxford: OUP.

Empson, William (1956) 'The Theme of *Ulysses*', *The Kenyon Review*, 18, Winter.

Ferrer, Daniel (1988) '*Archéologie du regard dans les avant-textes de* ⟨⟨*Circé*⟩⟩,' in Ed. Claude Jacquet, *James Joyce 1: 'Scribble' 1 genèse des textes*, Paris: Lettres Modernes Minard.

Ferrer, Daniel (1984) 'Circe, regret and regression', trans. Gilly Lehmann, in Eds. Derek Attridge and Daniel Ferrer, *Post-structuralist Joyce: Essays from the French*, Cambridge: Cambridge University Press.

Ferrer, Daniel (1985) 'The Freudful Couchmare of Λd: Joyce's notes on Freud and the Composition of Chapter XVI of *Finnegans Wake*', *JJQ*, **22**, (4), 367–382.

Ferrer, Daniel and Derek Attridge (1984) *Post-structuralist Joyce: Essays from the French*, Cambridge: Cambridge University Press.

French, Marilyn (1976) *The Book as World: James Joyce's 'Ulysses'*, Cambridge, MA: Harvard UP.

Freud, Sigmund (1925) *Collected Papers*, trans. Alix Strachey and James Strachey, London: The Hogarth Press/The Institute of Psychoanalysis.

Freud, Sigmund (1910) *Eine Kindheitserinnerung des Leonardo da Vinci*, Leipzig and Vienna, Trans. as 'Leonardo da Vinci and a Memory of His Childhood', trans. Alan Tyson, *The Standard Edition of the Complete Psychological Works of Sigmund Freud*, trans. and Ed. James Strachey in collaboration with Anna Freud *et al.*, London: The Hogarth Press and The Institute of Psychoanalysis, 1953–76, vol. **XI**, 63–137.

Freud, Sigmund (1910) 'The Psycho-Analytic View of Psychogenic Disturbances of Vision', *The Standard Edition*, **XI**, 314–321.

Genette, Gérard (1966) *Figures 1*, Paris: Seuil.

Genette, Gérard (1980) *Narrative Discourse*, Ithaca: Cornell UP.

Gilbert, Sandra and Susan Gubar (1989) *No Man's Land: The Place of the Woman Writer in the Twentieth Century*, New Haven: Yale UP, 2 vols., vol. 1, *The War of the Words*, 1988, vol. 2, *Sexchanges*, 1989.

Gilbert, Sandra and Susan Gubar (1985) 'Sexual linguistics: gender, language, sexuality', *New Literary History*, **16**, 3, 515–543.

Gilbert, Sandra and Susan Gubar (1979) *The Madwoman in the Attic: The Woman Writer and the Nineteenth-Century Literary Imagination*, New Haven: Yale UP.

Gilbert, Stuart (1952) *James Joyce's 'Ulysses'*, New York: Vintage-Knopf.

Glashine, Adaline (1954) '*Finnegans Wake* and the Girls from Boston, Mass', *Hudson Review*, 7, Spring.

Goldberg, S. L. (1961) *The Classical Temper*, New York: Barnes and Noble.

Gorman, Herbert (1948) *James Joyce*, New York: Rinehart and Co.

Greimas, A. J. (ed.) (1970) *Sign, Language, Culture*, The Hague: Mouton.

Hart, Clive (1962) *Structure and Motif in Finnegans Wake*, London: Faber and Faber.

Hawkes, Terence (1977) *Structuralism and Semiotics*, Berkeley: UCLA Press.

Hayman, David (1963) *A First Draft Version of 'Finnegans Wake'*, Austin: Texas UP.

Hayman, David (1978–79) 'Nodality and the infra-structure of *Finnegans Wake*', *JJQ*, **16**, (1–2), 135–150.

Hayman, David (1970) 'The empirical Molly', in Eds. Thomas F. Staley and Bernard Benstock, *Approaches to 'Ulysses': Ten Essays*, Pittsburgh: Pittsburgh UP.

Heath, Stephen (1984) 'Ambiviolences: Notes for reading Joyce', trans. Isabelle Mahieu, in Eds. Derek Attridge and Daniel Ferrer, *Post-structuralist Joyce: Essays from the French*, Cambridge: Cambridge University Press.

Hegel, G. W. F. (1977) 'Preface', *Phenomenology of Spirit*, trans. A. V. Miller, New York and Oxford: OUP.

Henke, Suzette (1982) 'Stephen Dedalus and Women: A Portrait of the Artist as a Young Misogynist', in Eds. Suzette Henke and Elaine Unkeless, *Women in Joyce*, pp. 82–107.

Henke, Suzette and Elaine Unkeless (1982) *Women in Joyce*, Brighton: The Harvester Press.

Hjelmslev, L. (1959) *Essais Linguistiques*, Travaux du Cercle Linguistique de Copenhagen, vol. XIII, Copenhagen: Nordisk Sprog-og Kulturforlag.

Holly, Marcia (1975) 'Consciousness and Authenticity: Toward a Feminist Aesthetic', in Ed. Josephine Donovan, *Feminist Literary Criticism*, Lexington: Kentucky UP.

Howe, Florence (1972) 'Feminism and Literature', in Ed. Susan Koppleman Cornillon, *Images of Women in Fiction: Feminist Perspectives*, Bowling Green, Ohio: Bowling Green University Popular Press.

Irigaray, Luce (1981) 'This Sex Which is Not One', in Eds. Elaine Marks and Isabelle de Courtivron, *New French Feminisms: An Anthology*, New York: Schocken Books.

Jakobson, Roman (1962) *Selected Writings*, 4 vols., The Hague: Mouton.

Jakobson, Roman and Morris Halle (1956) *Fundamentals of Language*, The Hague: Mouton.

Jameson, Fredric (1972) *Marxism and Form: Twentieth-century Dialectical Theories of Literature*, Princeton: Princeton UP.

Jameson, Fredric (1981) *The Political Unconscious: Narrative as a Socially Symbolic Act*, Ithaca: Cornell UP.

Jameson, Fredric (1982) '*Ulysses* and History', *James Joyce and Modern Literature*, London: Routledge and Kegan Paul.

Joyce, Stanislaus (1958) *My Brother's Keeper*, Ed. Richard Ellmann, London: Faber and Faber.

Kashkin, Ivan (1968) 'Dzhois, Dzhems', *Literaturnaia éntsiklopediia*, III Moscow: 1930, cols. 248–251, trans. William B. Edgerton, 'Dzhoising with the Soviet Encyclopedias', *JJQ*, 5, (2), 125–131.

Kenner, Hugh (1978) *Joyce's Voices*, Berkeley: UCLA Press.

Kestner, Joseph (1978–79) 'Virtual text/virtual reader; The structural signature within, behind, beyond, and above', *JJQ*, 16, (1–2), 27–42.

Kimball, Jean (1983) 'Family Romance and Hero Myth: A Psychoanalytic Context for the Paternity Theme in *Ulysses*, *JJQ*, **20**, (2), 161–173.

Kimball, Jean (1980) 'Freud, Leonardo, and Joyce: The dimensions of a childhood memory', *JJQ*, **17**, (2), 165–182.

Kimball, Jean (1976) 'James Joyce and Otto Rank: The incest motif in *Ulysses*', *JJQ*, **13**, (4), 366–382.

Klein, Melanie (1950) 'Mourning and its relation to manic-depressive states', *Contributions to Psycho-Analysis*, London: Hogarth Press/ Institute of Psychoanalysis.

Kornilova E. V. (1968) 'Dzhois (Joyce), Dzheims', *Kratkaia literaturnaia éntsiklopediia*, Moscow: 1964, cols. 654–655, trans. William B. Ederton, 'Dzhoising with the Soviet Encyclopedias', *JJQ*, **5** (2), 125–131.

Kristeva, Julia (1970) *La Poétique de Dostoievski*, Paris: Seuil.

Kristeva, Julia (1980) *Desire and Language: A Semiotic Approach to Literature and Art*, trans. Leon S. Roudiez, New York: Columbia UP.

Kristeva, Julia (1982) *Powers of Horror: An Essay on Abjection*, trans. Leon S. Roudiez, New York: Columbia UP.

Kristeva, Julia (1973) 'The System and the Speaking Subject', *The Times Literary Supplement*, 12 October, p. 1249.

Leavis, F. R. (1962) *The Great Tradition: George Eliot, Henry James, Joseph Conrad*, Harmondsworth: Penguin.

Lévi-Strauss, Claude (1964) *Le cru et le cuit*, Paris: Plon.

Lévi-Strauss, Claude (1972) *Structural Anthropology*, trans. Claire Jacobson and Brooke Grundfest Schoepf, London: Penguin.

Lyons, J. B. (1973) *James Joyce and Medicine*, Dublin: Dolmen Press.

Makward, Christiane (1976) 'Interview with Hélène Cixous', trans. Ann Liddle and Beatrice Cameron, *Sub Stance*, **13**.

Mayoux, J.-J, (1965) *Joyce*, Paris: Gallimard.

McCarroll, David L. (1969) 'Stephen's Dream – and Bloom's', *JJQ*, **6**, (2), 174–176.

McHugh, Roland (1980) *Annotations to Finnegans Wake*, Baltimore: Johns Hopkins UP.

McHugh, Roland (1976) *The Sigla of Finnegans Wake*, London: Edward Arnold.

McHugh, Roland (1968) 'A Structural Theory of *Finnegans Wake*', *A Wake Newslitter*, **V**, 6.

Millet, Kate (1970) *Sexual Politics*, Garden City, NY: Doubleday & Co.

Norris, Margot (1982) 'Anna Livia Plurabelle: The dream woman', in Eds. Suzette Henke and Elaine Unkeless, *Women in Joyce*, 197–214.

Norris, Margot (1974) *The Decentered Universe of Finnegans Wake: A Structuralist Analysis*, Baltimore: Johns Hopkins UP.

O'Brien, Darcy (1976) 'A Critique of Psychoanalytic Criticism, or What Joyce Did and Did Not Do', *JJQ*, **13**, (3), 275–292.

O'Brien, Darcy (1968) *The Conscience of James Joyce*, Princeton: Princeton UP.

Ong, Walter, J. (1981) *Fighting for Life*, Ithaca: Cornell UP.

Peirce, Charles Sanders (1931) *Collected Papers* (8 vols.) Eds. Charles Hartshorne, Paul Weiss and Arthur W. Burks. Cambridge, Mass: Harvard UP.

Piaget, Jean (1971) *Structuralism*, trans. Chaninah Maschler, London: Routledge and Kegan Paul.

Prince, Morton (1969) *The Dissociation of a Personality: A Biographical Study in Abnormal Psychology*, New York: Greenwood Press.

Propp, Vladimir (1958) *Morphology of the Folktale*, Bloomington: Indiana Research Center in Anthropology.

Rabaté, Jean-Michel (1984) 'Lapsus ex machina', trans. Elizabeth Guild, *Post-structuralist Joyce: Essays from the French*, Cambridge: Cambridge University Press.

Rabaté, Jean-Michel (1985) 'Pour une cryptogénétique de l'idiolecte Joycien', in Ed. Claude Jacquet, *Genèse de Babel: Joyce et la création*, Paris: Éditions du Centre National de la Recherche Scientifique.

Rabaté, Jean-Michel (1988) 'Le Noeud Gordien De ⟨⟨Pénélope⟩⟩', in Ed. Claude Jacquet, *James Joyce 1 ⟨⟨Scribble⟩⟩ 1: genèse des textes*, Paris: Minard.

Rank, Otto (1912) *Das Inzest-Motiv in Dichtung und Sage: Grudzüge einer Psychologie des dichterischen Schaffens*, Leipzig: Dueticke.

Saussure, Ferdinand de (1974) *Cours de Linguistique Géneral*, trans. Wade Baskins, London: Fontana.

Scholes, Robert (1982) *Semiotics and Interpretation*, New Haven: Yale UP.

Scholes, Robert (1974) *Structuralism in Literature: An Introduction*, New Haven, Yale UP.

Scholes, Robert (1972) '*Ulysses*: A Structuralist Perspective', *JJQ*, **10**, (1).

Scott, Bonnie Kime (1987) *James Joyce*, Brighton: The Harvester Press.

Scott, Bonnie Kime (1984) *Joyce and Feminism*, Brighton: The Harvester Press.

Shechner, Mark (1976) 'Exposing Joyce', *JJQ*, **13**, (3), 266–274.

Shechner, Mark (1976) 'James Joyce and Psychoanalysis: A Selected Checklist', *JJQ*, **13**, (3), 383–384.

Shechner, Mark (1977) 'Joyce and Psychoanalysis: Two Additional Perspectives', *JJQ*, **14**, (4), 416–419.

Shechner, Mark (1974) *Joyce in Nighttown: A Psychoanalytic Inquiry into 'Ulysses'*, Berkeley: UCLA Press.

Slater, Philip B. (1971) *The Glory of Hera*, Boston: Beacon Press.

Sollers, Philippe (1978) 'Joyce & Co.', *In the Wake of the Wake*, trans. Stephen Heath and Elliott Anderson, Madison: Wisconsin UP.

Solomon, Margaret C. (1969) *Eternal Geomater: The Sexual Universe of Finnegans Wake*, Carbondale: Southern Illinois UP.

Suleiman, Susan Rubin (1985) 'Writing and Motherhood', in Eds. Shirley Nelson Garner, Claire Kahane, and Madelon Sprengnether, *The (M)other Tongue: Essays in Feminist Psychoanalytic Interpretation*, Ithaca: Cornell UP, 352–377.

Sultan, Stanley (1964) *The Argument of 'Ulysses'*, Columbus: Ohio State UP.

Tall, Emily (1980) 'James Joyce Returns to the Soviet Union', *JJQ*, 17, (4), 341–347.

Thornton, Weldon (1968) *Allusions in 'Ulysses'; An Annotated List*, Chapel Hill: North Carolina UP.

Tindall, William York (1959) *A Reader's Guide to James Joyce*, New York: Farrar, Straus and Giroux.

Todorov, Tzvetan (1966) 'Perspectives Semiologiques', *Communications*, 7, 139–145.

Topia, André (1984) 'The Matrix and the Echo: Intertextuality in *Ulysses*' trans. Elizabeth Bell and André Topia, in Eds. Derek Attridge and Daniel Ferrer, *Post-structuralist Joyce: Essays from the French*, Camrbidge: Cambridge University Press.

Unkeless, Elaine (1982) 'The Conventional Molly Bloom', in Eds. Suzette Henke and Elaine Unkeless, *Women in Joyce*, 150–168.

Van Boheemen, Christine (1987) *The Novel as Family Romance: Language, Gender and Authority From Fielding to Joyce*, Ithaca: Cornell UP.

Van Dyck Card, James (1973) '"Contradicting": The word for Penelope', *JJQ*, 10, (4), 439–454.

Vico, Giambattista (1968) *The New Science*, Eds. T. Goddard Bergin and M. H. Fisch, Ithaca: Cornell UP.

von Phul, Ruth (1959) 'Joyce and the Strabismal Apologia', *A James Joyce Miscellany*, 2nd. ser., Ed. Marvin Magalaner, Carbondale: Southern Illionois UP.

Walcott, William (1971) 'Notes by a Jungian Analyst on the Dreams in *Ulysses*', *JJQ*, 9, (1), 37–48.

Walzl, Florence L. (1982) '*Dubliners*: Women in Irish Society', in Eds. Suzette Henke and Elaine Unkeless, *Women in Joyce*, 31–56.

West, Alick (1936) *Crisis and Criticism*, London: Lawrence and Wishart, rpt, 1975.

Wight, Doris T. (1986) 'Vladmir Propp and *Dubliners*', *JJQ*, 23, (4), 415–433.

Wilson, Edmund (1969) *Axel's Castle*, New York: Charles Scribner & Sons.

Yonge, Charlotte M. (1966) *History of Christian Names*, Detroit: Gale Research Co.

Index